Creative Suffering and the Wounded Healer

Analytical Psychology and Orthodox Christian Theology

Byron J. Gaist

ORTHODOX RESEARCH INSTITUTE

Rollinsford, New Hampshire

Published by Orthodox Research Institute
20 Silver Lane
Rollinsford, NH 03869
www.orthodoxresearchinstitute.org

Library of Congress Control Number: 2010926140

ISBN 978-1-933275-40-6

Creative Suffering and the Wounded Healer

Other books published by the Orthodox Research Institute include:

Saint Cyril of Alexandria. *Against Those Who Are Unwilling to Confess that the Holy Virgin Is Theotokos.* Introduction, Greek Text and English Translation by Protopresbyter George Dion. Dragas

Rev. Dr. Steven Bigham. *Early Christian Attitudes toward Images*

David G. Bissias. *The Mystery of Healing: Oil, Anointing, and the Unity of the Local Church*

Panagiotes K. Chrestou. *Greek Orthodox Patrology: An Introduction to the Study of the Church Fathers.* Edited and translated by Protopresbyter George Dion. Dragas

Protopresbyter George Dion. Dragas. *Ecclesiasticus I: Introducing Eastern Orthodoxy*

Protopresbyter George Dion. Dragas. *Ecclesiasticus II: Orthodox Icons, Saints, Feasts and Prayer*

Protopresbyter George Dion. Dragas. *The Lord's Prayer according to Saint Makarios of Corinth*

Protopresbyter George Dion. Dragas. *On the Priesthood and the Holy Eucharist: According to St. Symeon of Thessalonica, Patriarch Kallinikos of Constantinople and St. Mark Eugenikos of Ephesus*

Protopresbyter George Dion. Dragas. *Saint Athanasius of Alexandria: Original Research and New Perspectives*

Protopresbyter George Dion. Dragas. *St. Cyril of Alexandria's Teaching on the Priesthood*

Alphonse and Rachel Goettmann. *The Spiritual Wisdom and Practices of Early Christianity*

Archimandrite Kyprian Kern. *Orthodox Pastoral Service.* Edited by Fr. William C. Mills

Matthew the Poor. *The Titles of Christ*

But He was wounded for our transgressions,
He was bruised for our iniquities;
The chastisement for our peace *was* upon Him,
And by His stripes we are healed. (Isaiah 53:5)

For in that He Himself has suffered, being tempted,
He is able to aid those who are tempted. (Hebrews 2:18)

Table of Contents

Foreword

It is frequently acknowledged that, despite Jung's disclaimers concerning the mutually exclusive boundaries between empirical science and metaphysics, analytical psychology does have important theological ramifications. Similarly, Christian theology has been a historical antecedent to modern psychology, and can arguably continue to be of relevance in this field through the scholarly exploration of its anthropological teachings in a contemporary academic and pastoral context. The primary purpose of this study is therefore, to outline a metatheoretical approach to discussion of the interface between analytical psychology and Christian theology. As a secondary theme, it also attempts to formulate, investigate and explore a theoretical rationale for adopting a depth-psychological approach to working with countertransference dynamics in both psychotherapy and spiritual direction, by including and valuing the spiritual dimension of experience. The concept of 'creative suffering' (De Beausobre, 1940; 1999) is utilized as a way of describing the process through which personal suffering, when experienced creatively, becomes more than the isolated pathological source of the therapist's private emotional wounds, being transformed to provide the main psychological background through which deep healing of the client's own trauma may occur on a personal and transpersonal level. It is, therefore, argued that creative use of the countertransference implies ongoing, active reflection by the therapist on the meaning and purpose of personal suffering, as occurs in some spiritual disciplines. This practice is adumbrated through a framework of conceptualisation derived from Orthodox Christian spirituality, employing the Jungian archetype of the 'Wounded Healer' in parallel to theological claims concerning the suffering of Jesus Christ, and the broader significance of suffering and evil in Christian theology. Parallels, similarities and differences between religious and psychological imagery and concepts are suggested throughout, which may prompt further exploration of areas of convergence and divergence between analytical psychology and Christian theology in particular, and between psychology and religion in general.

PART ONE

Philosophical Rationale, Epistemological and Methodological Assumptions

Introduction

This study is largely theoretical in its range and scope, based on bibliographical discussion of sources, and on the formulation of novel concepts derived from this discussion. It seems important to emphasize from the outset, however, that no claims are made towards presenting a complete theoretical formulation or practical method here. Rather, stimulus is being offered to future attempts by researchers, to elicit the practical potential of a way of working based on a particular metatheoretical[1] rationale — especially, but not exclusively, in contexts where psychospiritual work with others may be appropriate, contexts which may, or may not, include the Christian ministry, pastoral counselling, or dynamic psychotherapy with clients from Christian or other religious backgrounds.

This approach to understanding therapeutic work with clients[2] may be considered philosophically integrative, since to some extent it nec-

---

[1] Papadopoulos (1991) explains: "Theoretical studies investigate the internal consistency of a particular theory i.e. how certain parts relate to others *within* the same framework. *Metatheoretical* approaches discuss the theory from a viewpoint which does not incorporate the basic premises of that theory." (in Papadopoulos & Saayman, 1991; p.54)

[2] Throughout the text, the terms 'therapist,' 'counsellor,' 'spiritual director,' 'psychoanalyst,' 'analyst' 'psychotherapist,' 'psychologist,' 'psychiatrist,' 'minister' etc. may be used, since the text is directed at all such professionals. Bearing always in mind the distinct professional boundaries delimited by these sectors, if a specific profession is intentionally alluded to in a passage, this will be explicitly indicated, or made clear by the context. 'Therapist' or 'counsellor' will be used generically, as *any person working in a capacity which involves establishing and maintaining heal-*

essarily involves what may constitute a theoretical synthesis between the empirical[3] and scientific discipline of Jungian analytical psychology on the one hand, and the spiritual cosmology and anthropology of Christianity, found in a wide diversity of theological works, on the other—in particular, the theology of the Eastern Orthodox tradition[4] in its broadest and most inclusive definition, which *per se* does

ing relationships with others in a professional context—secular or otherwise—and 'client,' 'patient' or even 'analysand,' as any person receiving psychological or spiritual help in this way. For the sake of brevity here, a Christian pastor may regard the term 'client' as referring also potentially to parishioners and spiritual children, though of course this application of the term is inappropriate in pastoral practice, and out of the specific context and comparative purposes of this study.

[3] Jung was especially keen to assign this adjective to the scientific discipline of analytical psychology, as Shamdasani (2003) points out in a recent book significantly titled "*Jung and the Making of Modern Psychology: The Dream of a Science*." An attempt will be made here to respect Jung's philosophical ideal and scientific integrity ("Research in the natural sciences, yes, that I could imagine as the content of a new life," Jung, quoted in Ulanov & Dueck, 2008, p. 31). Hence when comparing and contrasting his psychology with a field of thought he would have considered 'metaphysical' (and therefore not scientific), academic caution will be exercised, while acknowledging that the author cannot, for epistemological reasons which will become apparent throughout, entirely share in Jung's dualistic neo-Kantian separation of 'science' from 'metaphysics.'

[4] It should be prominently borne in mind that the author cannot speak for the entire Orthodox Church; what is presented is one set of possible, reasonably legitimate views. Eastern Orthodox theology will be the primary focus when concepts and ideas from Christianity are introduced, as the theology most familiar to the author, who is a practising Orthodox Christian. It should nonetheless be pointed out, as Gillet (1996) suggests, that "The fundamental principles of Christian spirituality are the same in the East and in the West; the methods are very often alike; the differences do not bear on the chief points. On the whole, there is *one* Christian spirituality with, here and there, some variations of stress and emphasis" (p. x). Church polemics can become quite acrimonious even over what appear to be minor issues, but may be of lesser relevance where a broad theoretical scope is the aim. Also, it is worth noting that, while neither analytical psychology nor Christian theology may legitimately be viewed as homogeneous, monolithic disciplines lacking internal controversies and areas of disagreement, there are arguably nevertheless important shared fundamental concepts in each field of study, which permit meaningful discussion and exploration of their relation as internally consistent theoretical entities.

not exclude a range of writings and insights shared in common with Western churches and other denominations.

This metatheoretical approach to therapeutic conceptualisation does not necessarily assume the presence of active religious faith, observance or denominational adherence on behalf of the psychotherapist who chooses to adopt it; nor does it impose — perhaps even more importantly — any belief systems on clients themselves, since it is intended for using, and designed to be compatible in working with, people of all faiths or none, who are counselling others or receiving counsel in both secular and spiritual settings. One initial underlying philosophical assumption therefore, is that one does not have to *be* religious in order to benefit through learning *from* and *about* religion and spirituality.

Several antique, pre-modern, but also modern 'grand-narrative' (Lyotard, 1984) philosophies of the human person — classical Jungian theory and, of course, Christian theology, not least among them,[5] present a conceptual difficulty to contemporary research, due to tendencies towards essentialism and reification; yet essentialism in grand narratives, despite its thorny political implications, frequently forms the basis of a coherent philosophical framework providing order, personal significance, and useful heuristic concepts, applicable to the practical daily life of real people. On the other hand, the postmodern 'deconstructionist' paradigm of philosophical and academic thought, characteristic of much contemporary Western research in the humanities, offers a pluralism (Cooper & McLeod, 2007) which at its best can be astute, scholarly, critical and respectful towards difference — yet equally often this 'post-paradigm paradigm' may be said to lead to nihilistic, relativistic and/or disorienting conclusions (cf. Rose, 1994).

Therefore, although the virtue of philosophical openness, integration and conceptual harmony between theoretical systems will be

[5] It is, however, important to also acknowledge that neither Orthodox Christianity, nor Jungian psychology actually view themselves — for their own very different reasons — as 'philosophies' or belief-systems. The word 'philosophies' is being used here in its lay sense, very loosely to describe different bodies of theory.

nurtured wherever possible, attention will also be devoted to avoiding the epistemological pitfalls of eclectic philosophical syncretism, and, more generally speaking, the various vicissitudes of premature speculation — especially great care being taken, when introducing concepts and ideas from a specifically religious context into the psychotherapeutic arena, or vice-versa. Although the gnoseological and epistemological foundations of philosophy and religion will be accorded equal respect with those of science, the inherent incompatibilities between religious and secular points of view will not be minimized or denied, nor will the numerous areas of what is sometimes remarkably — but perhaps significantly — acrimonious conflict between these apparent ideological 'opposites' of the modern era, be smoothed over or brushed aside. Indeed, from a Jungian perspective the formulation and development of an integrative theoretical statement may actually be *facilitated* by 'holding' the inevitable metatheoretical tensions which result from the conflicting epistemological and ontological bases of the diverse disciplines and Foucaultian 'discourses' (Horrocks & Jevtic, 1997) drawn upon.

Despite these acknowledged inherent epistemological tensions and the stated risks associated with crossing disciplinary boundaries therefore, this research will attempt to compare and contrast many of the findings of Jungian psychology with the insights of Christian theology, albeit a circumscribed and necessarily partial lay presentation of the theology of the Eastern Orthodox Church, as expressed through the writings of certain selected, mostly contemporary, authors. The emergence of an understanding which constitutes a synthesis, or in Jungian terms, a 'third'[6] way of conceptualising the interpersonal processes taking place in both psychotherapy and spiritual

[6] Cf. comments about the value of this 'in between' stance by Ulanov in Ulanov & Dueck (2008), p.32. Knowledge of the standard usage of Jungian terminology, such as 'third,' 'transcendent function,' 'opposites,' 'Self,' etc. will be assumed throughout, relevant discussion taking place only when appropriate. There are at least two excellent dictionaries of Jungian psychology available, the seminal work by Samuels, Shorter and Plaut (1986) and the quotation-rich primer by Sharp (1991).

direction will be sought, so that the adoption of this holistic, integrative methodology may prove useful to the conscious growth and development of therapists and clients using this research, through paying careful scholarly attention to the implications of creative suffering in the context of everyday life and in the unique somatopsychic and spiritual experience of doing clinical work.

CHAPTER ONE

The Contemporary Spiritual *Zeitgeist*

1 What is Spirituality? Jungian Psychology and the New Age as a Social Phenomenon. A relatively liberal use of the word 'spiritual' is in wide circulation today. Many people readily claim to have 'spiritual,' but not necessarily religious, feelings and experiences. There are even new schools of spirituality being proposed, which eliminate the assumption that a person needs to believe in God, or some form of deity, to practise spirituality. An attempt is made in this book, to suggest that this psycho-spiritual climate is potentially misleading and dangerous, but also fertile with possibilities for sincere seekers and spiritual practitioners. Throughout, clarification of the issues involved will be attempted through the comparison and contrast of the spirituality emerging from two millennia of Orthodox Christian theology, with the historically more recent approaches to spirituality suggested by the philosophical and clinical implications of Analytical Psychology, the system of thought emerging from the writings and clinical practice of C. G. Jung (1875–1961).

In what follows, it may become apparent that a major point of controversy in any discussion between Christianity and the current popular spiritual *zeitgeist*, lies along the epistemological boundary between what is essentially a Gnostic and occult worldview on the one hand, often dressed in the language of science, and a Trinitarian theistic spirituality on the other; this controversy is exemplified by the emergence of the New Age movement, but also perhaps implicitly underlies many current theories of human nature which have been elaborated within a scientific milieu, such as psychoanalysis. It may indeed be, as we shall see, that the same gnoseological impulse which underlies the modern science of psychology, namely the impulse to 'lift the veil of the temple' and peer into the mysteries of the human psyche, can also be found in the many popular expressions of individualistic spirituality which typify the formulation of what may perhaps be described as modern religious sentiments.

A general increase in the popular use of teachings from religion and spiritual disciplines for self-help, is evidenced by texts which are now considered 'classics' in the field, such as M. Scott Peck's *The Road Less Travelled* (Scott Peck, 1990) and Thomas Moore's *Care of the Soul* (Moore, 1992).[1] In fact, it is interesting and probably not just coincidental, that in the U.S. alone the sale of books in the 'New Age' section of bookstores[2] nearly doubled in the three years since the publi-

[1] With particular regard to the seminal work by Thomas Moore mentioned above, it seems significant also to consider that Moore not only presents a way of enriching everyday life experience (in a manner which is consciously different from most 'self-help' literature) but he also contributes to a larger enterprise of reenchantment of the entire psychotherapeutic enterprise, along the lines of his mentor, James Hillman, co-author of a book which goes by the telling title *We've had a Hundred Years of Psychotherapy—and the World's Getting Worse* (1993). In *Care of the Soul,* Moore offers nothing less than a kind of new, post-Jungian manifesto for psychotherapy and for living, by demythologising, or, more accurately perhaps, by making explicit the myths by which traditional psychotherapy has unconsciously operated—namely, that psychopathological symptoms are the unwanted consequences of childhood trauma experienced in a dysfunctional family, and that psychotherapy can offer a salvationist 'cure' for these symptoms by putting things right again. Moore advocates instead the Jungian and post-Jungian position, that it is precisely in paying careful attention to our symptoms, in honouring them as the very voice of the soul in fact, that the soul can be discovered and nurtured. The 'goal' of psychotherapy, according to Moore, is thus not cure, but a kind of cherishing of our individual uniqueness, and a consequent addition of depth to everyday life through the discovery of its numinosity and sacredness. While Moore's writing is as engaging and interesting as his own life experience (he was a Roman Catholic monk for 12 years prior to becoming a Jungian analyst), his project for reenchantment may nonetheless suffer from the very fact that it is based on Hillman's demythologising, anti-essentialist theory.

[2] The 'New Age' section of bookstores is frequently located near 'Self-Help,' 'Psy-

cation of *Care of the Soul* between 1992 and 1995, going from 5.6 to 9.7 million copies (Whelton, 2002, p. 15).

This burgeoning popularity indicates perhaps, that the movement of the collective spiritual *zeitgeist* in western civilisation since the birth of analytical psychology in 1913 (Kirsch, 2000), has been in a direction favourable to the 'transcendental' aspects of personal growth as described in the classical Jungian process of individuation,[3] and to the direct engagement with psychological aspects and dimensions of what in earlier historical periods would most certainly have been conceptualised primarily as being religious experience. While psychologising religion however, these cultural phenomena may also enantiodromically invite and call for the exploration of the spiritual and religious dimensions of the psychological experience.

It may be argued therefore, that in the search for a clearer understanding and definition of modern 'spirituality,' the loosely-termed 'spiritual movement' currently known as the 'New Age' carries many of the prime characteristics of the contemporary pluralistic cultural *zeitgeist.* As an important spiritual movement of the latter half of the 20th century in the West, and a significant point of reference from which to begin consideration of the theological, philosophical and psychological issues which this book addresses, the 'New Age' may therefore be worthy of brief investigation. Indeed, brief analysis of this much-derided—yet also more influential than is generally acknowledged—spiritual movement, will hopefully offer some clarification of the particular psychospiritual background found also at the heart of those contemporary existential and philosophical concerns which underlie a diversity of problems and difficulties presented to

chology,' and 'Religion,' and is increasingly being called the 'Mind-Body-Spirit' section of the bookstore. It is also interesting to note that this section is often considerably larger than the less commercially viable academic sections nearby.

[3] In describing the 'transcendent function' of the psyche, Jung meant "an aspect of the self-regulation of the psyche. It typically manifests symbolically and is experienced as a new attitude towards oneself and life" (Sharp, 1991, p. 136). Significantly, Jung did not in fact affirm the possibility of any knowledge truly transcendent to the psyche.

contemporary psychotherapists by their clients, as well as to spiritual directors by their spiritual children. It is being argued, in other words, that the growth of the ideologically diverse 'New Age' movement may represent a kind of living theological and philosophical collective identity crisis, one undergone existentially by many modern people; and, therefore, a brief examination of its history and characteristics helps to further outline some of those religious concerns which are, as Jungian psychology itself correctly posits, at the very root of contemporary neuroses.

Yet despite the fact that analytical psychology offers itself as a *Heilsweg* (Jacobi, 1973, p. 60) for many of these modern concerns, it must be stated that another reason for considering the 'New Age' movement in greater detail as modern spirituality *par excellence*, is that Jung himself is often cited as being one of its early forefathers. Despite articulate and often justified Jungian clarifications of what constitutes the correct use, and the misappropriation, of Jung's teachings (e.g. Tacey, 2001), it will become clear from what follows that Jung's contribution to the New Age movement is indeed both considerable and of seminal importance, as recognised both by academics in the field, and practising New Agers themselves. Nevertheless, although Jung's prophetic ushering in of the Age of Aquarius (see below) cannot be denied, it is important in this context to point out that, in Jung's own words, "one does not become enlightened by imagining figures of light, but by making the darkness conscious" (CW 13:335). In practice therefore, Jung's more sober teachings regarding the whole *opus* of the process and dynamics of psychospiritual growth, often do contrast starkly with the pollyannish optimism of much New Age thought.

There have been many differing interpretations of the historically recent sociospiritual phenomena coming under the umbrella of the New Age movement (Bloom, 1991; Carr, 1991; Heelas, 1996; Tacey, 2001; Whelton, 2002; Haule, 1999). These phenomena have their most recent and historically visible roots in the social euphoria of the 1960's countercultural 'hippie' movement, but it will be seen that their historical antecedents go back further, to the spiritual crisis of the Romantic era in the 19th century, and before that perhaps to much earlier historical eras. In fact, the New Age movement, in its characteristic mix of occult philosophy and speculation regarding human potential, can be seen as being very much 'old wine in new skins,' nothing less than a modern variation on ancient Gnosticism.

It goes outside the scope of this book to provide any thorough taxonomy or exhaustive description and assessment of the rich diversity of current New Age phenomena, which include such diverse and seemingly disparate fields of endeavour as alternative healing practices (e.g. acupuncture, shiatsu, reflexology, biofeedback), corporate business training (e.g. est, Lifespring, Insight Seminars), astrology and divination techniques, alternative ecology and politics (e.g. Gaia, some branches of feminist thought, and ecopolitics), and of course much of the Human Potential Movement (e.g. rebirthing, past-life therapy, psychosynthesis, primal scream). Particularly in the context of Western postmodern society however, the occurrence of these phenomena may indicate that the current rationalistic approach to psychology and psychotherapy is in fact, failing to respond to those deeper human needs which spirituality and religion have until recently addressed in the more traditional Eastern societies; in the postmodern Western world these needs for profound meaning and connection are perhaps most frequently expressed in New Age terms.[4] Contemporary psychotherapeutic practice is arguably failing

[4] It should be pointed out, however, that the empathic failure in (post)modern society to respond to our deeper human needs, which is perhaps instantiated by the crisis in psychotherapy implied above, may by now have crossed the familiar East/West cultural divide. Would it in fact, be too bold to suggest that *most* forms of traditional spirituality may be rapidly decreasing, even disappearing, in the postmodern information age of the 'global village,' to a *de facto* victory of the western technological and technocratic way of life, and hence to a consequent cultural turn towards western models of self-understanding and self-management? Ironically, as occidental popular culture since WWII has grown more attuned to the profound necessity of engaging with the spiritual dimension of life, the East seems to be in the midst of a cultural and spiritual

to respond to society's deeper needs, since despite its support in academic circles and its congenial adaptation to the contemporary climate of 'professionalism,' 'accountability' and—importantly—economic viability, a large proportion of the population which is turning to New Age practices requires something more, which cannot be offered by structured, directive, interventionist, brief, goal-oriented, behavioural and evidence-based practices which rely on an ultimately scientistic and pragmatic rationale (Smith, 1984).

It can be argued that historically, changes in civilisation accompany transformations in our own self-understanding, as well as our whole picture of what man is, his chief motives and his defining mental characteristics (Foucault, 1990). Western civilisation has its roots in Greek and Roman classical antiquity, which in the West ended historically with the division and fall of the Roman Empire to the 'barbarian' Germanic tribes.[5] The rise of Christianity, which the Roman Empire came to embrace as its official religion in the 4th century, led to a situation of some cultural homogeneity, and this remained relatively constant throughout those times which later (Western) historians have termed the 'Dark' and Middle Ages, a period spanning almost a millennium. The subsequent influx of Byzantine intellectuals like Manuel Chrysoloras and George Gemistos Plethon into Italy throughout the period from the second crusade

crisis itself, as witnessed either in the rigid reassertion of religious traditions through the brittle (and often brutal) enforcement of fundamentalist dogmas, or in the wholesale rejection of tradition and its institutions through political ideology. Further still, when viewed in a more positive perspective, Eastern societies may be rediscovering themselves by reinterpreting their ancient traditions and discovering creative new ways of adapting them to the exigencies of postmodern life. Hence the need to search for a deeper, more fundamental, and simultaneously richer dimension of meaning to human experience—as suggested perhaps by some of the teachings of Jung's analytical psychology regarding the 'religious function' of the psyche—would appear, to this author at least, to currently be an issue of global concern.

[5] A precise and well-documented historical account is beyond the scope of this chapter; the reader is referred to the existing wealth of popular and academic histories of Western Civilisation.

to the fall of Constantinople in the 13th–16th centuries resulted in the Renaissance. Carriers of the classical Greek learning which survived in the Eastern Christian empire, developing organically within and alongside Eastern Christianity[6] brought a revival of lost antique knowledge (the works of Plato and Aristotle, for example, which were also independently salvaged via Islamic philosophy in Moorish Spain) and a rejuvenation of the arts and letters, which then directly prompted and influenced the Reformation in the 16th century following on from the Renaissance. Indeed, the birth-pangs of modern science itself can perhaps be felt astir in the reformist ideas of Protestantism, with its emphasis on the individual's experience of God, and the free interpretation of scripture, over against Church tradition (Thomas, 1971).

It can be further controversially argued (cf. Sherrard, 1978), that the repercussions of Renaissance humanism and the Reformation in turn, signalled the division and decline of the Christian church in the West, which paved the way for the rational philosophy of the Enlightenment era. Until the Age of Reason in the 18th century, the Christian religion had provided the main framework for the spiritual and moral development of the majority of Europeans, but it became increasingly anemic and disembodied through internal conflict. The new, rational world outlook, placed a great emphasis on human discursive reason and individualism, in contrast to the arguably more balanced perspective of the medieval marriage of knowledge with wisdom, and thought with feeling—thereby casting further doubt on the authority of tradition and collective belief. This was the age of scientific revolution, which began with the publication of Coperni-

[6] Byzantine medicine, for example, passed on the teachings of ancient Greek philosophers and significantly improved on them throughout the duration of the Byzantine empire, stimulating the growth of Islamic medicine also in its wake. Contrary to some historical accounts, Christianity had a key role in this development, many of the Byzantine hospitals—the first such institutions in world history—being operated by Christian bishops. The therapeutic character of Eastern Christianity may once again be instanced in this historical precedent.

cus' *De revolutionibus orbium coelestium* in 1543, and was expressed philosophically in the Cartesian *cogito.*

Therefore, as a direct reaction, or in Jungian terms, a compensatory enantiodromic movement, to this meteoric rise of the materialistic scientific *weltanschauung* from the 16th to the 19th century, Western society has perhaps gradually moved on from its relatively recent spiritual premises grounded in a Judeo-Christian past to a new post-Christian cultural epoch, a neo-pagan New Age which has, as already suggested, its immediate historical roots in the Romantic movement, itself paradoxically both a revolutionary forerunner of late modernity and simultaneously nostalgic of a chivalrous, reimagined medieval past. Whelton (2002) writes:

> "Beginning with Jean Jacques Rousseau's sermons on the religion of the heart, the Romantic movement challenged the Enlightenment's claim that only science and rational analytical investigation paved the road to truth, and therefore all reality can be encompassed by the human mind. English Romantic poets such as Lord Byron, Percy Bysshe Shelley, John Keats, William Blake and William Wordsworth contended that our inner experience of emotions and intuition also opened us to a world of truth where science and rational inquiry hold no relevance or authority. [...] To escape this arid desert [of postmodern materialism] and make life bearable, many people today, like the Romantics of the eighteenth century when faced with the naked materialism of the Industrial Revolution, seek refuge in irrational spirituality—enter the New Age movement" (pp. 36–7; p. 11, words in brackets mine).

Where the Age of Reason led to a dissociation of emotion, the Romantic age which followed led to a dissociation of reason—yet both represented a break from the *ancien regime*; indeed, in the five hundred years following the Reformation the head and the heart seemed to have become cultural enemies. Whelton (*ibid.*) directly traces the roots of the New Age movement to the Romantics, describing the lightweight but popular writings of trendy authors such as Shirley MacLaine and James Redfield as "new Romantics" (p. 38). Today, ideas which can be loosely brought together under the umbrella-term 'New Age,' can be seen to coexist more or less uncomfortably alongside the older, traditional forms of spirituality.

The Anglican Dean of Bristol, Wesley Carr, looking at the New Age phenomenon, writes that :

> "There is … no 'new age.' Sometimes the phrase is used as if it stood for a single phenomenon, possibly even an embryonic new religious organisation. But that assumption is erroneous. We are dealing with something less defined or ordered. It is consequently difficult to consider. On the one hand, if we are too specific, we assign the New Age a status which its adherents do not acknowledge and thus misinterpret it; on the other hand, if we are too general we are in danger of underestimating its potential and influence on people" (1991, pp. 14–15).

At a first glance, it would seem something of a theological 'red herring' for mainstream Christianity to consider any interfaith dialogue with as vague and unspecified a *mélange* of ideas as the ones coming under the general heading of the 'New Age'—the very term sometimes provokes reactions ranging from mild amusement to ridicule among many serious-minded theologians, but also among other academics and members of the general public. From an Eastern Orthodox perspective, Ovsiannikov (1995) writes that:

> "The first thing that strikes anyone trying to fathom what New Age really is, is the range of the phenomenon: it is ready to absorb anything. So, theosophical and anthroposophical traditions are included in the New Age, channelling (contacts with any other world, whether in the after-life or with a UFO), shamanism, polytheism and pantheism, neo-paganism and elements from

> Christianity, Hinduism, Buddhism, Islam and Zoroastrianism. 'Non-mainstream spirituality,' as it has been called, lies outside the boundaries of the fundamental West European tradition and dismisses conventional, traditional religions" (1995, p. 14).

There are, however, significant historical reasons for this inveterate eclecticism. In the 1970's, the 'hippie' movement, leading back through the Beat Generation and the Lost Generation to the American Transcendentalists, and thus ultimately to the Romantic movement, was greatly influenced by three famous books: Aldous Huxley's *Doors of Perception* (1954) ; Jack Kerouac's *On the Road* (1955); and Robert Pirsig's *Zen and the Art of Motorcycle Maintenance* (1974). In these three books can be found perhaps the essential ingredients of a post-WWII spiritual and cultural sensibility: experimentation with drugs, eclectic mysticism and altered states of consciousness (ASCs; cf. Tart, 1990), a flirtation with Buddhism and Oriental religions, and a neo-romantic, counter-cultural search for an "alternative" and radical lifestyle, sceptical towards traditional spirituality. It might be suggested, without undue exaggeration, that Hitler's[7] concentration camps had exterminated not only millions of innocents, but also some of the underlying fundamental tenets and premises of Western civilisation—both in its scientific, materialist Enlightenment guise, and in its *ancien régime* Christian foundations. The shocked world after WWII seemed—and still seems today to some extent—a time of spiritual hunger and unrest in which previous conceptions of morality, sanity and reason *had* to be questioned by the young and idealistic, if not by everyone else too.[8]

[7] The Romantic-occult roots of the National Socialist movement are also pertinent to the issues discussed here, cf. Goodrick-Clarke (1985)

[8] Nevertheless, this period was also undeniably a time of great celebration and cultural regeneration; in the poetic words of Jack Kerouac, many people at the time "...danced down the streets like dingledodies, and I shambled after as I've been doing all my life after people who interest me, because the only people for me are the mad ones, the ones who are mad to live, mad to talk, mad to be saved, desirous of everything at the same time, the ones who never yawn or say

The New Age is probably justly perceived as being 'way out'—at best charmingly eccentric, and at worst foolish, let alone morally suspect. Even its enthusiasts, as Dean Carr suggests, would be reluctant to describe the New Age as a specific 'faith,' and are likely to reject use of the label 'religion' altogether—although as we will see, this apparent vagueness in self-definition may be regarded as one of the movement's essential defining (and sustaining) characteristics, since its proponents tend to adhere to a mostly subjectivist concept of truth.

In fact, 'truth' in New Age doctrine, is frequently not truth in any absolute sense, but only solipsistically—many would say narcissistically (Whelton, 2002): truth is seen as being what we subjectively perceive it to be. In the words of actress Shirley MacLaine, a famous proponent of the New Age,

> "If I created my own reality, then—on some level and dimension I didn't understand—I had created everything I saw, heard, touched, smelled, tasted; everything I loved, hated, revered, abhorred; everything I responded to or that responded to me. Then, I created everything I knew, I was therefore responsible for all there was in my reality. If that was true, then I was everything, as the ancient texts had taught. I was my own universe. Did that also mean I had created God and I had created life and death? Was that why I was all there was?" (1987, p. 192).[9]

---

a commonplace thing, but burn, burn, burn, burn like fabulous yellow roman candles exploding like spiders across the stars and in the middle you see the blue centerlight pop and everybody goes 'Awww!' ..." (1991, p. 8). The influence of Romantic philosophy can be discerned clearly in such passages.

[9] MacLaine, Shirley (1987) *It's All in the Playing*, Bantam Books, New York. Compare with Jung's famous passage from his autobiography: "I [...] had been looking about without hope for a myth of our own. Now I knew what it was, and knew even more: that man is indispensable for the completion of creation; that, in fact, he himself is the second creator of the world, who alone has given to the world its objective existence—without which, unheard, unseen, silently eating, giving birth, dying, heads nodding through hundreds of millions of years, it would have gone on in the profoundest night of non-being down to its unknown end. Human consciousness created objective existence and meaning,

Comparison of the New Age mindset with any traditional Christian dogma is indeed difficult, if not impossible, since as the above paragraph suggests, a radically different spiritual *phronema* to the Judeo-Christian one, is involved. 'Truth,' according to this view, is not to be found in the incarnate Christ, but in ourselves—quite literally. As Whelton (*ibid.*), responding to the New Age from an Eastern Orthodox perspective, caustically but astutely asserts concerning the premises held by New Agers:

> "Their claim that there is no objective truth is pure nonsense. For the immediate response to such an absolute statement asserting the nonexistence of truth would be to ask if that was true" (pp. 32–33).

Despite this, even serious-minded modern people who would find 'New Agers' somewhat risible in their claims, may nonetheless show surprising concordance with many New Age beliefs in their lifestyles. The very person, for example, who laughs at the idea of a 'New Age' being ushered in as a momentous historic aeon, may have an equally sceptical attitude towards Christianity's apocalyptic teachings, and to the Church, especially in its institutional forms; yet this same person may nonetheless emotionally sense a profound spiritual significance in man's communion with Nature and with other species, and believe firmly in the interconnectedness of all life on earth as expressed in depth ecology, and they may even believe in the psychosocial importance of rediscovering pagan 'nature' spirituality, and the worship

---

and man found his indispensable place in the great process of being" (1995, p. 285). Although Jung appears to be saying something similar to MacLaine at a superficial reading, on closer inspection he is not arguing that man has 'created' God, life and death *per se*, but that human consciousness gives meaning to these facts by casting its light of awareness upon them. Unlike the inflated position ascribed to him by so many New Age teachings, man is not necessarily perceived as *the* Creator by Jung, but as a co-creator, or 'second creator' through his function of consciousness, a notion perhaps not entirely incompatible with the Orthodox concept of man as *mikrotheos*, or a 'small god'.

of feminine deities associated with it.[10] On a practical level, tired of the limitations of conventional Western medicine, they may at some time have visited an aromatherapist, a homeopath, a reflexologist or an acupuncture clinic; they may have even explored techniques for expanding consciousness and human potential, such as meditation or popular variations of depth psychotherapy, even past-life therapy or rebirthing. Perhaps at some time such persons will even have consulted an astrologer, a palmist, a medium, or had their Tarot cards read, even if they have done so only in a mood of sceptical curiosity. Lastly, this hypothetical 'critic' of New Age spirituality may even believe in the existence of 'angels' as cosmic conduits of intelligence, but without endorsing the Judeo-Christian traditions from which these enigmatic spiritual beings spring, due to what they perceive as an ethical 'dualism' in which these traditions are based.

The above description is, of course, a slightly satirical caricature of the nonetheless very real sense in which New Age ideas have infiltrated the collective consciousness, beginning in the second half of the 20th century. In Britain today for example, communities such as Findhorn in Scotland, the UK's most famous New Age centre, actively promote the alternative lifestyles and beliefs associated with the New Age movement. These ideas have proved quite tenacious, and hence do underline the need for a serious Christian theological response, and for further academic study from other perspectives. As Donebauer (1991) explains:

> "In my view, the New Age is neither a movement nor a religion set apart from others. It is not something one can choose or not to join. It is essentially a view of the time we live in and the

[10] The worship of feminine deities has been a key interest of countercultural movements, since J. J. Bachofen's 19th century writings on the antiquity of matriarchy (cf. 1967). Jung, who together with other intellectuals such as Otto Gross participated in such alternative proto-New Age communities as the one at *Monte Verita* in Ascona, gave further impetus to the importance of 'the feminine principle' in Jungian psychology (cf. Neumann, E., *The Great Mother*, 1963).

world we are creating. It is therefore for everyone" (in Bloom, 1991, p. xiii).

Kerouac's 1950s 'Beat Generation' were the immediate predecessors of the hippies, and their spirituality was unsurprisingly cosmic and pantheistic, very loosely associated with and based on Buddhism. It is in this optimistically apocalyptic post-Romantic atmosphere of social revolution that the contemporary New Age phenomenon could ultimately take root, although the term 'New Age' itself went back to the very beginnings of late modernity in the 19th century, with the founding of the Theosophical Society and the eponymous London-based review *The New Age*, originally a Christian Socialist periodical,[11] but later edited by the theosophist and Gurdjieffian A. R. Orage from 1907. The review took contributions from such luminaries as "... G. B. Shaw, Arnold Bennett, H. G. Wells, F. S. Flint, Ezra Pound, T. E. Hulme, Wyndham Lewis, Katherine Mansfield,[12] Marinetti, and other important radical or new writers" (Bradbury, 1988, p. 578). As such, it can be seen how theosophical and occult ideas were already regarded seriously

[11] Hence also the term 'new age' or 'new aeon' was originally a prophetic reference to the coming of the Kingdom of God in scripture (e.g. Luke 18:29–30). Early socialism, like Tolstoy's and Saint-Simon's, shared many aspirations with Christianity, but focused on purely human means for bringing these about. It is no accident therefore that the political fervour of socialism has much in common with Christian spirituality, and is even perhaps a form of displaced religious zeal, so that a number of the founders of the 'alternative' spiritual movements at the heart of the New Age (such as Annie Besant) can be seen to have had socialist political roots. Similarly, the occult roots of national socialism may vex sincere left-wing idealists wishing to dissociate fascism from liberal socialism, but the appellation of Hitler's National Socialist German Worker's Party cannot go unnoticed; fascist and socialist ideas both trace their origins to the dialectic of liberal atheist revolution.

[12] The paradox of the search for total freedom on the one hand, and blind devotion to a guru on the other, which is sometimes suggested by New Age ideas and cult groups, has at times led to disastrous results. The writer Katherine Mansfield's obedience to her guru Gurdjieff, controversially led to her death through negligence and irresponsible advice on Gurdjieff's behalf while she was staying at his Institute for the Harmonious Development of Man in France.

by many respected intellectuals even before the cultural crisis ensuing WWII. Some of the seminal figures who acted as influential prophets of the New Age thus included: Helena Blavatsky (1831–1891), the simultaneously celebrated and much-maligned founder of Theosophy; G.I. Gurdjieff (1866–1949) the equally controversial Greek-Armenian guru who introduced Sufi ideas and his own philosophy known as 'The Work' to Victorian Europe; but also, as mentioned above, C.G. Jung (1885–1961) himself, who in contrast to Freud was simplistically perceived to view religion and spirituality as being at the crown, rather than the feet, of human achievement.[13] On the Christian side of New Age inspiration (for New Age thought *does* also have Christian roots) can be found the controversial work of Catholic theologian-paleontologist Pierre Teilhard de Chardin (1881–1955) and, more recently, the Catholic monk Thomas Merton (1915–1968).[14]

It can be no historical coincidence, that all these thinkers were for the most part contemporaries, and it probably wouldn't be unreasonable to argue that the philosophical issues they were confronting, despite the diverse and discrepant answers each thinker arrived at in his own right, were similar ones in the period following the Industrial Revolution, the rise of Darwinism, and the politics of the British Empire and its colonial heritage. Similarities in their thought are perhaps inevitable, since they offered spiritual alternatives to the prevailing

[13] Since the work of Jung, much New Age thought has also been influenced by contemporary psychology and psychotherapy via the ideas of Abraham Maslow (1908–70) and the Human Potential Movement, resulting in the 'fourth force' movement of Transpersonal Psychology, which itself can be seen to overlap with the New Age, although it is conceived according to its own remit, as being an academic field of study rather than a spiritual movement.

[14] It should be pointed out that the profound work of both Teilhard de Chardin and Thomas Merton is certainly compatible with an Orthodox interpretation. Their significance to the New Age thus lies perhaps not so much in the premises and conclusions of their opus, but in what use New Agers have made of these. The same cannot be said for the work of Madame Blavatsky or Gurdjieff. Jung, as will be witnessed throughout this book, may be seen as a liminal figure in this context, neither entirely compatible with an Orthodox Christian interpretation, nor entirely hostile to it.

19th century scientific materialism which otherwise dominated the intellectual climate of their day. Madame Blavatsky, for example, saw her occult theories very much as being the spiritual counterpart to Darwin's biological theory of evolution,[15] complete with an influential — and thoroughly racist — occult theory of the development of human races to boot. As we are still arguably in the thrall of these modernist debates at the end of the 20th century and the beginning of the 21st, it is not therefore surprising that New Age spirituality continues to have such enormous appeal.

However, the term 'New Age' is not only a philosophical label; taken on its own terms, it can also refer to a much more specific cosmic change that is being mooted: it is an astrological reference to the end of the Age of Pisces — the Fish — which roughly corresponds to the Judeo-Christian era. Astrologers claim that every 2,000 to 2,400 years we move from one sign of the zodiac to another, from Taurus to Aries to Pisces and so forth.[16] Jung himself also announced this imminent cosmic change, seeing in it a profound transformation of the archetypes which are dominant in the collective psyche (cf. CW 10, pars. 589–90). The 'New Age' in this sense, is the Age of Aquarius, the Water-Carrier. Carr (1991) explains:

> "As with all astrology, dates are less certain than we might expect. But roughly the theory proposes a two-stage transformation of the world. The first is the period between 1846 and 1918, when the rise of the two great empires of the USA and USSR begins. The second phase is from 1918 to 1990, when something

[15] Characteristically syncretic, the second declared objective of her system of theosophy is to encourage the study of Comparative Religion, Philosophy and Science, which aims at "open-minded inquiry into world religions, philosophy, science, and the arts in order to understand the wisdom of the ages, respect the unity of all life, and help people explore spiritual self-transformation." Taken from http://www.theosophical.org/about/mission.php, accessed 28.03.08.

[16] Cf. http://logosresourcepages.org/Occult/na-dict.htm, accessed 15.12.08, and Powell, V. (2006), available online at http://astro-articles.blogspot.com/2007/03/astrology-big-picture.html (accessed 15.12.08) for just one example.

> will end. At the time of writing it is unclear what this could be.[17] By 2062, however, the transformation will be complete and the Age of Aquarius will have dawned" (p. 30).

In this scheme of things, the old 'patriarchal' religions and traditional social arrangements are said to be giving way to a new vision of a more 'feminine' world, in which past orthodoxies and sclerotic institutions will be refreshed by the cool water of Aquarius, a new spirituality. It can be seen that through the New Age, as its very name suggests, runs a thread of opinion which rivals orthodox[18] understandings of Christianity and the Christian Church as an institution, while — significantly perhaps — not necessarily always rejecting the figure of Jesus as a moral teacher, or an avatar of cosmic significance. The scope of this New Age vision for humanity is simply immense. In her now-classic work in this field, *The Aquarian Conspiracy*, Marilyn Ferguson narrates that

> "For the first time in history, humankind has come upon the control panel of change - an understanding of how transformation occurs.[...] The paradigm of the Aquarian Conspiracy sees humankind embedded in Nature. It promotes the autonomous individual in a decentralised society. It sees us all as stewards of all our resources, inner and outer.[...] Human nature is neither good nor bad but open to continuous transformation and transcendence. It has only to discover itself. The new perspective respects the ecology of everything: birth, death, learning, health, family, work, science, spirituality, the arts, the community, relationships, politics" (cited in Bloom, 1991, p. 7).

[17] This statement today seems remarkable in its prophetic accuracy, considering the imminent collapse of the Soviet Union which followed it.

[18] Where a small 'o' is used for the word 'orthodox,' this refers to ideas which would be generally acceptable to all mainstream Christian churches, whether Protestant, Roman Catholic, or Eastern Orthodox. When a capital 'O' is used, this refers to the Eastern Orthodox confession in particular.

2 CHARACTERISTICS OF THE NEW AGE. The text quoted above could serve as a brief summary of some of the salient characteristics of the New Age. As Heelas (1996) discusses, the New Age is a creature with two faces, and is hence so difficult to characterise, being essentially both anti-Enlightenment and anti-Tradition. Its emphasis, as suggested above, on the primacy of Nature and the possibility of transcendence, places it politically in a 'reactionary' frame; its emphasis on continuous transformation makes it politically 'radical.' The Roman Catholic psychologist Paul C. Vitz (1994, pp. 113–4), in a study which focuses on the religious character of much contemporary psychology, includes a chapter on the New Age, and offers seven such defining characteristics:

1. *Philosophical Monism*—the collapse of ontic boundaries into a vision of the absolute unity of everything; "all is one."
2. *Pantheism*—a tendency to attribute divinity to all that exists, "all is God."
3. *Human Divinity*—the assertion that we ourselves are Gods,[19] and free to develop this inherent divinity away from servile bondage to any deity outside us.
4. *Transformation of Consciousness*—required by the belief that we are blocked from recognising our inner divinity, often termed the Higher Self, by the illusion of ignorance. This calls for a change of consciousness through the acquisition of esoteric knowledge.
5. *Religious Syncretism*—the assertion that the same universal Truth underlies all religions, and can be captured in such notions as cosmic oneness or "Christ Consciousness."

[19] This understanding of human divinity may be compared and contrasted with that of John 10:34 ("You are gods"), where Jesus indicates the human right and vocation to aspire to divinity *through grace*, in contradistinction to His own inherent divine Sonship. As St. John Chrysostom wrote: "If those who have received this honour by grace are not guilty for calling themselves gods, how can He who has this by nature deserve to be rebuked?" (quoted in *The Orthodox Study Bible*, p. 1445).

6. *Cosmic Evolutionary Optimism*—the belief that, through our God-consciousness, humanity is about to enter a new stage in its evolution, which will herald a new era of peace, unity and bliss—we are about to become suprahuman.[20]
7. *Right Brain Thinking*—the rejection of the analytical stance and all "left-brain" activity. This feeds back into the first point of philosophical monism.

It is not hard to see why these ideas may be attractive to the complex, pluralistic society in which we live, where world religions and political ideologies with equally fervent claims both to utilitarian pragmatism and to the absolute truth, often contend uncomfortably for supremacy, while at the same time the relentless advance of technology leaves thinkers little time to catch up with the social implications of major changes and rearrangements of life patterns at home and at work. In fact, in his seminal academic study of the New Age, which carries the telling title *The New Age Movement: The Celebration of the Self and the Sacralization of Modernity*, Paul Heelas (ibid.) offers in an appendix the same characteristics of the New Age as Vitz (*ibid.*), together with some further elaborated ones. He also convincingly suggests that the New Age is a reaction to the uncertainties of modernity, and he personally stands in an ambivalent relationship to it, both celebrating it as an era of individual liberation and attempting simultaneously to offer a spiritual alternative to the grosser materialistic aspects of secularisation. For all its surface optimism and

[20] The rise of 'transhumanism' as a cultural phenomenon, or the enhancement of human aptitudes by means of science and technology, appears to cohere with this New Age characteristic. Interestingly, transhumanism has its roots in the Russian Orthodox contextual background of Russian Cosmism, especially the heretical aspirations of Nikolai Fyodorovich Fyodorov (1828–1903) to extend human life by scientific means and achieve immortality and resurrection of the dead artificially. It might be said that like the medieval alchemists seeking the elixir of life, and ultimately perhaps via the same spirit in which the serpent offered knowledge to Eve, Fyodorov also naively sought to achieve divine goals by human means, which makes him yet another forerunner of the New Age movement.

convenient philosophical monism, however, an implicitly world-negating and dualistic attitude can simultaneously be seen as characterising New Age thought. This becomes apparent when comparing it to the numerous ancient Christian heresies which together came to be termed 'Gnosticism'—which Jungian psychology also officially adopted as a historical antecedent. Indeed, Gnosticism may be at the root of all occult and esoteric thought.

Perhaps the most important characteristic of New Age thought, which may also be seen as having the centrality of a 'doctrine' (if one may use such a term for a movement so openly hostile to 'dogma' in any form) is the notion of a 'Higher Self.' This notion is similar to that of a "divine spark" in a corrupt body, and belongs to a set of beliefs that for Christians lies much closer to home. Ovsiannikov (*ibid.*) explains that

> "Like the classic Gnostics, some representatives of New Age believe that the Higher Self is a divine spark in man, a divine light caught up in matter, that is, in the human body" (ibid, p. 14).

The dualistic premise on which this notion is based is that:

> "All life, as we perceive it with the five human senses or with scientific instruments, is only the outer veil of an invisible, inner and causal reality. Similarly, human beings are twofold creatures—with (i) an outer temporary personality; and (ii) a multi-dimensional inner being (soul or higher self)" (Heelas, 1996, p. 225).

This anthropological teaching can be shown to have very ancient origins indeed. Consider, for example, the similarities of the above assertion with the reflections of the Eastern Orthodox theologian Nicholas Arseniev on Plato's[21] religious message:

[21] It is interesting in this context that occult philosophers like M. P. Hall (1998)

> "To preach, to proclaim the *real Reality* [...], as opposed to our deceitful and shadowy world, as the light of the real Sun is opposed to the illusory images (which are only shadows of shadows, reflection of reflections seen by the poor prisoners of the dark cave and considered by them to be the only reality: see *Republic*, book VII): this proclaiming, this opposition, this inspired witness to the real Reality and the call to lift the mind's eye towards it—this is the ultimate purport, the soul of Plato's philosophy [...]" (1982, pp. 67–68).

The assertion of an inner, causal, and ultimately Higher Reality than the one confronting our senses, is an idea that has puzzled humanity for much longer than the New Age alone can lay claim to. This tendency in religious thought, to assert the illusory character of the world accessible to our senses, is known as "platonising," and the theology of such eminent Orthodox Church Fathers as Clement of Alexandria has been seen as sharing it; and while it has been argued that the Alexandrian school inasmuch perhaps also digressed from Orthodoxy, it is surely more accurate to see in this approach the Christian transformation of Plato. Bearing in mind these platonising tendencies in the New Age, however, tendencies which Christianity itself has been accused of and has had a long experience of dealing with, the third point given by Vitz (1994) above, namely the assertion of human divinity, may nonetheless serve as an entry into the place where Christianity, Jungian psychology and New Age thought can begin their dialogue—for the assertion of divinity, or the Higher Self (a concept which is actually very different from the Christian understanding of the word 'soul,' despite Heelas' suggestion of their categorical equivalence in the definition given above) may also be seen to be a relative of the Jungian 'Self' archetype, as of the 'divine spark' of Valentinian, Cathar and Rosi-

emphasize the fact that Plato was an initiate into the classical Mystery religions, who was however criticised for revealing many secrets to the uninitiated.

crucian Gnosticism: a piece of God Himself imprisoned within the human body. In the words of the sinister occultist Aleister Crowley, "every man and woman is a star" (*Book of the Law*, 1904). Crowley's famous '*law of Thelema*' ('do what thou wilt'), is probably a telling consequence of this distorted way of perceiving human greatness, and stands in remarkable contrast to the humility of St. Augustine's "love, and do what thou wilt."

Nevertheless, the doctrine of a Higher Self does perhaps follow somewhat logically from the assertion of a Higher Reality. The assertion that we are ourselves essentially Divine in nature, rather than having the capacity to become *partakers* in the Divine by being sanctified in union with God through the action of the Holy Spirit, may appear quite preposterous to a traditional Christian believer, yet it entered the 'idolatry' of popular culture in the sixties and seventies quite forcefully.[22] An abundance of examples ranging from the simplistic to the tragic, seems to confirm the existence of a modern tendency towards the belief that we have a Higher Self within us, which is inherently Divine, and which seems to have had an enormous appeal to the popular imagination of the previous century. Vitz (*ibid.*) suggests that it is precisely this belief in a Higher Self which makes the New Age ultimately incompatible with Christianity. The belief that we *are* God, not just created in His image and able to be united

[22] Pop 'idols' are a case in point; one is reminded of examples of graffiti stating, albeit humorously perhaps, that "Eric Clapton is God"; also of David Bowie's flirtation with the teachings of Aleister Crowley, or Jimmy Page's purchasing of Boleskine House, Crowley's lair in Scotland. Characteristic comments such as the following about Jim Morrison, the iconised lead singer of the rock group, *The Doors*, who described himself as 'the lizard king' and whose self-destructive career led to an early demise, are also perhaps not coincidental: "My personal belief is that Jim Morrison was a God. To some of you, that may sound extravagant; to others, at least eccentric. Of course, Morrison insisted we were all gods and our destiny was of our own making. I just wanted to say I think Jim Morrison was a modern-day god. Oh hell, at least a lord" (Hopkins & Sugerman, 1979, p. vii). Morrison's grave in the *Pere Lachaise* cemetery in Paris has since been decorated with the telling ancient Greek inscription KATA ΔAIMONAN EAYTOY, meaning 'according to his own daemon.'

to Him, is perhaps the most ancient delusion men have been prone to; it locks us into a circular, narcissistic spiral of spiritual grandiosity. In Vitz's own words:

> "... the thesis proposed here is that New Age spirituality is the transformation of psychological narcissism into spiritual narcissism. [...] The seven points enumerated earlier in this chapter [see above] all strongly support this interpretation of New Age. The idea that each person is divine [...] directly encourages self-worship. The notions that all is one, all is God, and all religions are one [...] also support narcissism by suspending distinctions between good and evil and between true and false. This allows religion, morality and truth to be self-defined. All particular laws, all struggles with internal sin or pride are ultimately meaningless if distinctions and polarities collapse into one vast undifferentiated category. [...] The rejection of reason — means that the New Ager is exempt from criticism. This exemption isolates the narcissist in his or her own self-confirming world, since criticism requires reason — words, speech and writing. [...] The need for a change of consciousness, assumes that each person is the source of this change and therefore of his or her own salvation. [Finally, the call] for "cosmic evolutionary optimism," reinforces and justifies the whole narcissistic system" (p. 125).

The Jungian analyst Donald Williams, echoing Christopher Lasch (1932–1994), concurs with a diagnosis of 'narcissism' for the New Age, and for our culture in general, and writes that we are now living in an age which is preoccupied

> "... with fantasies of unlimited success, power, beauty, and ideal love. Sometimes called a culture of narcissism, often we collectively seem unwilling or even unable to recognize the feelings and needs of others. Psychotherapy is designed to treat

> such pathological narcissism, not to make it a therapeutic goal. Therapists, however, also can be narcissists who skillfully exploit their patients. The tantalising solutions offered by therapists and spiritual guides in the New Age are varieties of seduction. Every virtue has its shadow, and the psychological and spiritual virtues of the "New Age" cast shadows of plain greed, shallowness, and self-aggrandizement" (1995, p. 3).

Yet, as mentioned earlier, Williams may be on shaky ground, since Jungian psychology has itself been classed as 'New Age,' paradoxically especially perhaps as it has been appropriated by its Christian proponents.[23]

As mentioned earlier, the idea of a Higher Self is not new. It is characteristically to be found in the diversity of faiths springing out of Hinduism and its derivatives; hence the popularity too, of such Eastern doctrines as the Law of Karma and reincarnation among adherents of the New Age. Blavatsky (1889) draws a direct link between Eastern philosophy and western Gnosticism, and hence defines the Higher Self in these terms:

> "The 'great Master' (sic) is the term used by *lanoos* or chelas [disciples] to indicate one's "Higher Self." It is the equivalent of *Avalôkitêswara*, and the same as *Adi-Buddha* with the Buddhist Occultists, ATMAN the "Self" (the Higher Self) with the Brah-

[23] Hence the Orthodox author Damascene Christensen (in Rose, 1999) writes that "Concurrently, there is now a movement in contemporary Roman Catholicism to assimilate the teachings of Carl Jung, one of the founding fathers of the New Age movement. Jung, who participated in séances and admitted to having "spirit guides," taught that the exclusion of the "dark side" is a fatal flaw in our religion, and that there therefore needs to be a fourth *Hypostasis* added to the Holy Trinity—Lucifer! His theories are now being extolled by Roman "theologians" [...] and his psychic therapy is being practised in some Roman Catholic churches, and by monks and nuns in some monasteries. Episcopal and Protestant (especially Methodist) churches have also entered this movement: a growing number of Protestant ministers also work as Jungian analysts" (pp. 204–5).

mins, and CHRISTOS with the ancient Gnostics" (pp. 73–4, italics and capitals same; words in square brackets mine).

In this syncretic theological framework, God becomes an impersonal 'force' or 'energy,' and human identity is eliminated in merger with this force, like a drop of water in a vast ocean. The implications of Western Gnosticism thus hold much in common with the tenets of Eastern religions such as Hinduism, and these different world-views often coincide and find a home in the same thinker, as they do frequently in the writings of Jung himself (cf. Clarke, 1992).

Just as the human body is in fact the 'prison of the soul' in Gnostic theologies, so too for the Gnostics, Jesus was only apparently a real man; in fact, to them He was an avatar of the Light in human form, come to lead humanity back to the Light. Given their relevance both to the New Age and to analytical psychology, it would perhaps be useful to examine here more closely some of the features of the Gnostic heresy which flowered in the 2nd century AD. This was the heresy which was probably being referred to already in the New Testament as the "falsely called knowledge" (1 Tim. 6:20). The following characteristics of Gnosticism, as given by Wilson (1993) may perhaps be fruitfully compared with the seven characteristics of the New Age given above by Vitz (*ibid.*):

1. *Cosmic Dualism*—a rejection of the world and all matter, and a vision of the body as a prison from which the soul longs to escape.
2. *The Demiurge*—the God of the Hebrew bible is seen as being essentially evil and self-serving, as opposed to the transcendent, true God. God the Father is given the name 'Demiurge.'
3. *Human Divinity*—the human race is essentially similar to the divine, being 'divine sparks' of light imprisoned in our bodies.
4. *The Fall*—a myth accounting for the current human predicament in terms of a premundane fall, but different, as we will see, from the orthodox Christian understanding of this event.
5. *Gnosis*—the doctrine that salvation comes not through God's merciful Grace sent to the repentant sinner, but through the acquisition

of an esoteric knowledge which lifts the veil of illusion and ignorance, making us aware of our true nature and heavenly origin.[24]

A closer examination of these characteristics may superficially suggest that Gnosticism has in fact, much in common with both orthodox Christianity and with the New Age, its only real 'difference' from New Age teachings being its emphasis on a radical ontological dualism between matter and spirit, darkness and light, which the New Age however, as we have seen, acknowledges implicitly in affirming the temporary character of the phenomenal world (see the first part of Heelas comment on page 6). The true difference from Christianity however, may be highlighted further when the characteristics of Gnosticism are seen from the perspective of Gnostic practitioners themselves. Stephan Hoeller, a bishop of the 'Gnostic Church' (*Ecclesia Gnostica*), and author of *Jung and the Lost Gospels* (1989), draws on the academic Hans Jonas in offering the following list of tenets, which, he suggests "may be considered normative for all Gnostic teachers and groups in the era of classical Gnosticism; thus one who adheres to some or all of them today might properly be called a Gnostic:

- The Gnostics posited an original spiritual unity that came to be split into a plurality. [This may now be compared with the underlying New Age assumption of philosophical monism].
- As a result of the precosmic division the universe was created. This was done by a leader possessing inferior spiritual powers and who often resembled the Old Testament Jehovah.
- A female emanation of God was involved in the cosmic creation (albeit in a much more positive role than the leader).
- In the cosmos, space and time have a malevolent character and may be personified as demonic beings separating man from God.

[24] As Holroyd (1994) explains: "there is a fundamental difference from Christian belief in that the Gnostic Christ brings salvation not from sin but from ignorance, offers not redemption but the knowledge that redeems, and demands not contrition but spiritual effort and diligence" (pp. 5–6).

- For man, the universe is a vast prison. He is enslaved both by the physical laws of nature and by such moral laws as the Mosaic code.
- Mankind may be personified as Adam, who lies in the deep sleep of ignorance, his powers of spiritual self-awareness stupefied by materiality.
- Within each natural man is an "inner man," a fallen spark of the divine substance. Since this exists in each man, we have the possibility of awakening from our stupefaction.
- What effects the awakening is not obedience, faith, or good works, but knowledge.
- Before the awakening, men undergo troubled dreams.
- Man does not attain the knowledge that awakens him from these dreams by cognition but through revelatory experience, and this knowledge is not information but a modification of the sensate being.
- The awakening (i.e., the salvation) of any individual is a cosmic event.
- Since the effort is to restore the wholeness and unity of the Godhead, active rebellion against the moral law of the Old Testament is enjoined upon every man."[25]

It is easy to see from this brief list, that Gnosticism and Christianity are ultimately radically incompatible, and lead to different conclusions and practices, which is of course the reason Gnosticism was designated a heresy by the mainstream Church in the early eras of its development. Yet the complexity of the relationship between Gnostic thought and orthodox Christian teachings was recognised early on by the Church Fathers. The idea of heresy did not arise, as is often tendentiously and anachronistically presented, to protect the professional 'interests' of the mainstream and more powerful Church, but was a result of the

[25] From 'What is a Gnostic?,' at http://www.webcom.com/gnosis/whatisgnostic.htm, accessed 2/4/08.

pastoral concern to distinguish those doctrines which were authentically passed on by Christ's apostles, from the numerous false claimants to this tradition; it was also a sincere pastoral attempt to separate out those doctrines which were self-serving and exploitative, from those which truly aided spiritual growth through the self-denying love of one's neighbour as taught by Christ. As Lossky (2002) writes:

> "Unlike gnosticism, in which knowledge for its own sake constitutes the aim of the gnostic, Christian theology is always in the last resort a means: a unity of knowledge subserving an end which transcends all knowledge. This ultimate end is union with God or deification, the *θέωσις* of the Greek Fathers. [...] All the development of the dogmatic battles which the Church has waged down the centuries appears to us, if we regard it from the purely spiritual standpoint, as dominated by the constant preoccupation which the Church has had to safeguard, at each moment of her history, for all Christians, the possibility of attaining to the fullness of the mystical union. So the Church struggled against the gnostics in defence of this same idea of deification as the universal end: 'God became man that men might become gods'" (pp. 9–10).

The introduction of the concept of heresy was hence as much a practical attempt to define the true limits of the Church's theological experience, as it was an attempt to purge what amounted to moral diseases from its body.[26] Gnosticism, though more often ascetic than libertine in its practice, actually encouraged an unhealthy contempt for the body as the 'prison of the soul,' and for creation as the abor-

[26] It may be said that much the same kind of practical controversy, both political and humanitarian, lies behind today's definitions of 'mental health' and 'illness' in secular society — definitions based on statistical and functional criteria which provide us with a useful set of rules (ideally only rules of thumb) about what constitutes pro- and anti-social behaviours. The history of homosexuality as a diagnosis is a case in point. What is different, of course, about secular controversies surrounding mental health issues, is that the definitions sought by the psychiatric profession are not necessarily relative to truth as revealed in Christ.

tive accident resulting from the evil actions of the Demiurge in the Gnostic cosmological world-view; and the Church Fathers hence legitimately recognised in this contempt an affront to the Christian sense of God's providential love and the goodness of creation. Nevertheless, it can be argued that this heavy emphasis on world-negation found its way into mainstream Christianity too, especially in Western Christendom, through certain aspects of the work of even such great Doctors of the Church as the formerly Manichean St. Augustine, and of course through the more direct influence of suppressed medieval sects such as the Cathars, Albigensians and Bogomils; and from these to modern sects and secret societies such as the Rosicrucians and Freemasons. Despite the optimistic gloss, the same streak of world-negating pessimism runs through New Age thought, which owes so much of its own existence to the post-Gnostic, Romantic thought of the 18th and 19th centuries, including figures as disparate as Voltaire, Goethe, William Blake, W. B. Yeats, Hermann Hesse and Aleister Crowley, who could all could be said to have been Gnostic in their basic spiritual style and message.

Taking one of the above figures as a rather extreme example, namely Aleister Crowley (1875–1947)—a man who personally identified with the scriptural beast with seven heads and ten horns from the Book of Revelation, and who acted as an intermediary between Britain and Germany during WWII,[27] thus earning the reputation of being a traitor; in his own time Crowley's exploits were sensationalised by the tabloid press, and he was reputed to have been so evil, that even saying his name was enough to bring bad luck. Together with Eliphas Levi, Papus, Madame Blavatsky and the Hermetic Order of the Golden Dawn, Crowley was responsible for the continuation of the 'Western Mystery Tradition'—the magical occult—into the 20th

[27] As suggested earlier, this cooperation was not coincidental or irrelevant to Crowley's occult aims; many upper-class Germans who later came to prominence in the Nazi Party, including Heinrich Himmler, were members of occult circles such as the Ordo Templis Orientis and the Thule Society. Crowley's Nazi sympathies were, therefore, also perhaps attempts to reinforce and strengthen the hold of the occult on European society.

century, ideas which influenced much modernist thought and art, from Symbolism and Surrealism to the New Age.

New Agers, however, especially those involved in Wicca, witchcraft and neo-paganism, are also often—despite vociferous public protests to the contrary—demon-propitiators or even demon-worshippers; they may, like William Blake, see the Judeo-Christian God as a tyrannical and egotistic authoritarian, and the Christian 'Devil' as a being unfairly punished by him—thereby inverting the moral essence of the Gospel and of Christian doctrine. The beliefs of Gnostic sects like the Sethians, which possibly date from even earlier than Christianity, can be seen to be at work here. From the 'Gospel of Judas' to Blake and Milton, to popular pulp novels like 'The Devil's Apocrypha' (De Vito, 2002), Satan is viewed sympathetically, sometimes as the friend and liberator of humanity, championing its rights against the 'tyranny' of the austere Hebrew God, the serpent offering us knowledge in the Garden of Eden which, rather than deceiving man to his demise, would open our eyes as to our condition of oppression. What Holroyd[28] (1994),[29] therefore says about Christian at-

[28] Holroyd (*ibid.*) goes on to outline schematically what Gnostics did, and still do, believe: "In the beginning there existed only the transcendent God, a male principle that existed for eternities in repose with a female principle, the Ennoia (Thought), until there emanated or was brought forth from their union the two archetypes Mind (male) and Truth (female). In turn, these principles emanated others, in male-female pairs to the total of thirty, known as Aeons, who collectively constituted the divine realm, known as the Pleroma, or fullness. Of all the Aeons only the first, Mind, knew and comprehended the greatness of the Father and could behold him, but the last and youngest Aeon, Sophia (Wisdom), became possessed of a passion to do so, and out of the agony of this passion and without the knowledge or consent of her male counterpart, she projected from her own being a flawed emanation. This abortion, the 'Demiurge' was the creator of the material cosmos and imagined himself to be the absolute God. The cosmos that he created consisted of a number of spheres, each of which was ruled by one of the lower powers, the Archons, who collectively govern man's world, the earth, which is the lowest of the spheres of the degenerate creation" (p. 4).

[29] Elsewhere a similar description may further clarify the above, and is worth quoting fully, because such elaborate cosmological systems as the one being described are an important feature of Gnostic thought, which entices followers

through the promise of privileged insight and elite knowledge: "Gnosticism was a religious system that flourished for centuries at the beginning of the Common Era, and in many regions of the ancient Mediterranean world it competed strongly with "orthodox" Christianity, while in other areas it represented the only interpretation of Christianity that was known. The Gnostics possessed their own Scriptures, accessible to us in the form of the Nag Hammadi Library, from which a general sketch of Gnostic beliefs may be drawn. Although Gnostic Christianity comprises many varieties, Gnosticism as a whole seems to have embraced an orienting cosmogonic myth that explains the true nature of the universe and humankind's proper place in it. [...] In the Gnostic myth, the supreme god is completely perfect and therefore alien and mysterious, "ineffable," "unnamable," "immeasurable light which is pure, holy and immaculate" (Apocryphon of John). In addition to this god there are other, lesser divine beings in the pleroma (akin to heaven, a division of the universe that is not Earth), who possess some metaphorical gender of male or female. Pairs of these beings are able to produce offspring that are themselves divine emanations, perfect in their own ways. A problem arises when one "aeon" or being named Sophia (Greek for wisdom), a female, decides "to bring forth a likeness out of herself without the consent of the Spirit," that is, to produce an offspring without her consort (Apocry. of John). The ancient view was that females contribute the matter in reproduction, and males the form; thus, Sophia's action produces an offspring that is imperfect or even malformed, and she casts it away from the other divine beings in the pleroma into a separate region of the cosmos. This malformed, ignorant deity, sometimes named Yaldabaoth, mistakenly believes himself to be the only god. Gnostics identify Yaldabaoth as the Creator God of the Old Testament, who himself decides to create archons (angels), the material world (Earth) and human beings. Although traditions vary, Yaldabaoth is usually tricked into breathing the divine spark or spirit of his mother Sophia that formerly resided in him into the human being (especially Apocry. of John; echoes of Genesis 2–3). Therein lies the human dilemma. We are pearls in the mud, a divine spirit (good) trapped in a material body (bad) and a material realm (bad). Heaven is our true home, but we are in exile from the pleroma. Luckily for the Gnostic, salvation is available in the form of gnosis or knowledge imparted by a Gnostic redeemer, who is Christ, a figure sent from the higher God to free humankind from the Creator God Yaldabaoth. The gnosis involves an understanding of our true nature and origin, the metaphysical reality hitherto unknown to us, resulting in the Gnostic's escape (at death) from the enslaving material prison of the world and the body, into the upper regions of spirit. However, in order to make this ascent, the Gnostic must pass by the archons, who are jealous of his/her luminosity, spirit or intelligence, and who thus try to hinder the Gnostic's upward journey" (Dailey & Wagner, 2001).

titudes to the Gnostics can sometimes hold equally true for some of these same neo-pagan adherents of the New Age, who are in fact far from naïve, starry-eyed optimists:

> "There is ... an alternative view [to the loving Christian God], namely that the world was imperfect from the start, that the blame lies not with man, but with God, the Creator. [...] It is said that the Devil has all the best tunes, and if we are to believe the orthodox Christian Church, Gnosticism was the work of the Devil" (pp. 1–2).

Just as Gnosticism was viewed as the 'work of the devil' by early Christians, many New Age beliefs are perhaps deserving of the same treatment by contemporary theologians. The popularity of recent films like *The Matrix* (Wachowski & Wachowski, 1999) possibly further attests to the currency of Gnostic thought in popular culture and imagination. Even a prestigious popular scientific magazine like *National Geographic* recently carried an edition of *The Gospel of Judas* as a special offer to its readership! Other recent cultural products, like the successful book and eponymous film *The Da Vinci Code* (Brown, 2003), have made Gnosticism even more widely accessible to the public. *The Da Vinci Code*, though a work of fiction, actually indirectly claims the historical veracity of its speculations. These speculations[30] contain many Gnostic themes, which have entered the con-

[30] The book is based on the premise that Jesus and Mary Magdalene were married, identifying Mary Magdalene with St. John as Jesus' true 'beloved disciple,' and even suggesting that St. Mary Magdalene was the real 'Holy Grail,' who carried Jesus' bloodline since she was pregnant at the time of the crucifixion. The book further suggests that the royal line of Jesus' descendants became the rulers of the Merovingian dynasty of Frankish kings (5th to 8th century AD); this 'secret,' discovered by the Crusaders and kept by secret societies until our day, was supposedly violently suppressed by the Roman Catholic Church for 2000 years, because of its desire to maintain the primacy of St. Peter, and, significantly, because of its fear of the sacred feminine. Groups like the Knights Templar and the Gnostic Cathars would, according to this view, have been persecuted

temporary popular imagination to such an extent, that many people are now confused as to which ideas represent the actual contents of the canonical gospels, and which derive from apocryphal or pseudepigraphal sources. The massive popularity of the *Da Vinci* book sadly suggests that it has 'hit a nerve' in the cultural *zeitgeist*.

Gnostic beliefs strongly proclaim an interdependence between masculine and feminine — with the emphasis on the creative power of the feminine — and are frequently negatively juxtaposed with the purportedly traditional, authoritarian, and hence 'imbalanced' patriarchal concept of divinity in Christianity. It is strange to notice how one metaphysical view of the world (Christianity) is denied on the basis of lack of empirical evidence, and another like Gnosticism, with its wild, almost baroque intricate complexity, then forcefully enters popular culture. One is almost reminded of Jung's late comment that "You can take away a man's gods, but only to give him others in return" (1993, p. 63), and even more of G. K. Chesterton's "when people stop believing in God, they don't believe in nothing — they believe in anything."

3 **Jung and Gnosticism.** Holroyd (ibid) refers to the 1945 discovery of the Nag Hammadi library, a collection of early Gnostic 'gospels' which have received great attention from western academics. Despite his protests to Martin Buber's accusation that he was a Gnostic, Jung's own enthusiastic embrace of Gnosticism as the historical antecedent of analytical psychology, was such that the Dutch theologian Gilles Quispel procured through the Jung Institute in Zurich in 1951, a codex containing five of the 52 Gnostic tractates discovered at Nag Hammadi, to be presented to Jung on his birthday. Although later returned to the Egyptian government, this codex is still known

---

by the Church for their possession of the radical secret of Jesus' royal lineage. The novel, if taken seriously, essentially renders Jesus into the male consort of the representative of the Mother Goddess (Mary Magdalene), their union being a *hieros gamos*, an occult concept Jung used as a symbol in his discussions of alchemy and the union of the opposites.

as the 'Jung Codex.' In spite of its disclaimers to having the status of a religion therefore, Jungian psychology can nevertheless be seen as a cultural heir to the history of the occult, a history which begins in primordial times with shamanism, and emerges in antiquity with Gnosticism and Hermetism and the practice of the occult sciences such as astrology, magic and alchemy, as well as the philosophical influences of Neoplatonism. This history continues in the West through Renaissance Hermetism in the 15th century, Kabbalah (as practiced in both Jewish and Christian settings), the theories of Paracelsus, Rosicrucianism, Christian Theosophy (Böhme), Freemasonry, Illuminism, then Swedenborgianism in the 18th century, followed by Mesmerism, 19th century Spiritualism, Theosophy, Ritual Magic, and leading on into the 20th century with Steiner's Anthroposophy and even aspects of the school known as Traditionalism (or Perrenialism).[31]

In his response to Buber's description of him as a modern Gnostic however, the father of analytical psychology adopted the posture of being an empirical scientist, whose interest is "to investigate facts and make them more generally comprehensible" (Buber-Agassi, 1999, p. 60). Of the Gnostics themselves, Jung says that his "[...] en-

[31] Cf. Jung (CW 11, pars. 138–149): "When Carus, von Hartmann, and in a sense, Schopenhauer equated the unconscious with the world-creating principle, they were only summing up all those teachings of the past which, grounded in inner experience, saw the mysterious agent personified as the gods. [...] The hypothesis of invisible gods or daemons would be, psychologically, a far more appropriate formulation, even though it would be an anthropomorphic projection. [...] If the historical process of world despiritualization continues as hitherto, then everything of a divine or demonic character outside us must return to the psyche, to the inside of the unknown man, whence it apparently originated." In a paragraph such as this, Jung could be said to be eliding metaphysical commitment by using the word 'apparently' in an ambiguous manner: do deities 'apparently' originate in the psyche, or do they only seem to do so, but in fact have independent existence? Nevertheless, his reference to 'all those teachings of the past,' and his association of the unconscious as explored by analytical psychology with the *anima mundi* or 'world-creating principle' as outlined in these teachings of the past, suggests how aware he was himself of writing within, or after, a certain historical tradition of esoteric spirituality. Godwyn (2007) refers to this tradition as the "Golden Thread" of Western esoterism.

thusiasm arose from the discovery that they were apparently the first thinkers to concern themselves (after their fashion) with the contents of the collective unconscious" (*ibid.*, p. 60). Jung then goes on to suggest that

> "If Buber misunderstands my empiricism as Gnosticism, it is up to him to him to prove that the facts I describe are nothing but inventions. If he should succeed in proving this with empirical material, then indeed I am a Gnostic. But in that case he will find himself in the uncomfortable position of having to dismiss all religious experiences as self-deception. [...] If I hold the view that all statements about God have their origin in the psyche and must therefore be distinguished from God as a metaphysical being, this is neither to deny God nor to put man in God's place. [...] Considering the fearful paradoxicality of human existence, it is quite understandable that the unconscious contains an equally paradoxical God-image, which will not square at all with the beauty, sublimity, and purity of the dogmatic concept of God" (*ibid.*, pp. 63–6)

Here again, Jung takes care to distinguish his own 'paradoxical God-image'—noting also that he does not deny the existence of a transcendent God—from that of both the Gnostics and orthodox Christianity, and he then importantly goes on to conclude that

> "It is inevitable that the adherents of traditional religious systems should find my formulations hard to understand. A Gnostic would not be at all pleased with me, but would reproach me for having no cosmogony and for the cluelessness of my gnosis in regard to happenings in the Pleroma. [...] As for an orthodox Christian, he can hardly do otherwise than deplore the nonchalance and lack of respect with which I navigate through the empyrean of dogmatic ideas." (*ibid.*, p. 67)

Strictly speaking, it is fair to suggest that Jung's notion of God does differ from the evil Gnostic demiurge. God, as Jung depicts Him in his writings, is an unconscious totality which is both totally good and totally evil.[32] This unconscious totality seeks to become conscious through man, in a process known as the 'transformation of the God-image' (eg. Edinger, 1992). Contrary to the Christian understanding of redemption, it is Jung's belief that God redeems Himself through His continuing incarnation in men like Job, whom as will be shown below, Jung compares to God's 'suffering servant' in Isaiah 53.[33]

Hence, too, the true definition of 'divine service' in Jung, is in the act of enabling God, the unconscious, primal and amoral life-urge, to become aware of Himself. This is of course, nothing less than a complete reversal of the direction of salvation according to traditional Christian soteriological teaching, which implies a 'reciprocal indwelling' (Ware, 1996, p. 54) between man and Christ, made possible by Christ's descent to our fallen condition. It is also, importantly, not a scientific or empirical statement, but a clear theological thesis, despite Jung's protests to the contrary, and his neo-Kantian distinction between God *an sich* and the *imago Dei.*

Jung was also not merely critical of 'conventional' morality as derived from Christian principles; he suggested a complete theological alternative to it, urging the individuating person to its transcendence. For Jung, the vocation to selfhood sometimes means that we have to 'sin' in order to grow. Hence Jung's theology is not only elucidated and explored further by his disciples, like Edward Edinger (1992) and Lawrence Jaffe (ibid), but is also still being appropriated by such an-

[32] Although this description of God differs from the evil Demiurge as presented by other Gnostic groups, it nevertheless resembles greatly the theological characteristics of the Basildeian Abraxas, who is a singular and henotheistic deity, but not all-good; and it can be no coincidence that Jung makes Basilides the central speaker in his *Septem Sermones ad Mortuos.*

[33] This in contrast to the traditional Christian interpretation of the 'Song of the Suffering Servant' as a prophecy of the coming of Jesus 700 years prior to the Incarnation. Could Jung have been unconsciously identifying both with Job and with Jesus in this role-reversal?

tinomian spiritual movements as neo-Sabbatean kabbalism,[34] which completely reverse the direction of salvation, by suggesting that anyone who becomes a vessel for God's self-realisation is a continuing incarnation. According to these teachings, remarkably similar in some ways to those of the Gnostic Khlysty which influenced Rasputin, and to the earlier libertine Carpocratians, spiritual law is fulfilled though its violation; in this understanding, one does not exactly become holy through sinning as such, but through liberating the grace which is 'trapped' in sin — in other words, sinning in order to redeem sin itself, thereby returning the imprisoned 'sparks of holiness' to God.[35] These teachings and movements may sound complex and obscure, but authors like Jeffrey Mehlman have suggested that via Georges Bataille's influential theories of transgression and the sacred, "the whole pantheon of French postmodernism — from Jacques Derrida to Julia Kristeva to Michel Foucault to Jean Baudrillard [...] can be seen as a late manifestation of this heretical, Jewish messianism" (Weingrad, 2001, p. 113).[36]

Returning to the New Age as a cultural phenomenon, all of the above descriptions of Gnostic beliefs show clearly that some of the very roots of the modern New Age movement are, from an Orthodox Christian point of view, entirely incompatible with Christian doctrine. The Demiurge of the Gnostics is a demonic tyrant, and his cosmos, far from being a "jewel" as the Greek word *κόσμημα* from which 'cosmos' is derived, suggests, is an offensive lump of lifeless and evil matter. It is ironic then, that the New Age 'twist' on Gnosticism has turned to precisely this creation it philosophically should consider 'evil' — if it was consistent in its beliefs — for worship, in a pantheistic

[34] Cf. http://www.donmeh-west.com/incarn.shtml.

[35] Perhaps this lamentable doctrine is an inevitable theological consequence of ascribing substance to evil, and objecting to the *privation boni* Christian formulation as Jung did.

[36] Hence, too, the Orthodox theologian David Bentley Hart can describe modern continental philosophy as being "[...]very much the misbegotten child of theology, indeed a kind of secularized theology [...]" (2003, p. 30). As Hart implicitly acknowledges, it is not the absence of spirituality which characterises postmodern thought, but its 'misbegotten' or distorted view of the spiritual.

sense. The figure of Jesus in the New Age movement, when He does appear, takes the form which is known (*via* a distortion of Teilhard de Chardin's ideas) as the 'Cosmic Christ' (Peters, 1991), in whom all dichotomies and oppositions are dissolved, including good and evil. Rhodes (1999) confronts the New Age 'Cosmic Christ' as counterfeit, being a vision not of the Son of God, but of one Master among many 'Ascended Masters'[37] who will lead the human race into the New Age of enlightenment and harmony. The 'Aquarian Christ' is merely Jesus, a man who has achieved 'Christ Consciousness,' as any other ordinary man can. Can this be such a far cry from Jung's own reduction of Christ to a symbol of the archetypal Self?

And yet, even among traditional Christians, the drive to accommodate the needs of a complex pluralistic society has led to brushing over the radical and uncompromising aspects of their faith, or even trying to incorporate doctrines into it which are clearly blasphemous and heretical, if not intentionally, then out of a misguided enthusiasm to respond to the modern condition. This is perhaps more often a sign of some awareness of past mistakes that have been made in the faith, than a result of pure ignorance or any active wish to subvert Christian teachings. Also, some Gnostic ideas which are compatible with New Age teachings have made their way into the controversial religio-philosophical fringes even within Eastern Orthodox Christianity, particularly in the intellectual ferment of pre-revolutionary Russia: Sophianism and Sophiology, for example, caused much debate in the Church when it was argued that in effect they taught the doctrine of a fourth, female principle within the Holy Trinity which equates to the Wisdom of God (identified as both Christ, Mary, and as a separate

[37] 'Ascended Masters' are defined in Whelton (2002, p. 147) as "departed souls whose past lives have elevated them to the highest plateau of spiritual growth and beyond the necessity for further reincarnations. They now permanently inhabit the spiritual realm, ready to be channeled through an appointed medium and reveal the mysteries of life." The Theosophical and Arcane schools of Helena Blavatsky and Alice Bailey rest on the belief in such beings, clearly demonic from an Orthodox Christian perspective.

fourth hypostasis by thinkers such as S.N. Bulgakov (1871–1944).[38] This is a set of teachings which appeals both to Orthodox Christian theologians of the 'Paris School' such as Paul Evdokimov (1994), and Jungians such as Marion Woodman (1985). It is of course unsurprising to find that these very different thinkers are both influenced by Jung. And the cross-fertilisation of ideas between Christianity and the New Age also extends to the Christian process-theology known as 'Creation-Centred spirituality' of Matthew Fox (1990), for example, which has proved very popular with the New Age.

The simplistic and immediate equation of the New Age movement with Gnosticism, and its subsequent dismissal on the grounds of being heretical would probably be too rash and poorly considered a conclusion, but nevertheless perhaps, a justified concern for Christians. It has been suggested however, that the temptation is all too easy, to fall into the sort of intellectual cul-de-sac which rejects *all* New Age thought simply because it resembles an old heresy and challenges orthodox doctrines (Carr, *ibid.*). Examples of this kind of intolerance can be found across the Christian Churches — whether Protestant, Roman Catholic or Orthodox. Typically in the writings of evangelical fundamentalists such as Cumbey (1983), but also in the writings of some stricter Eastern Orthodox authors such as Rose (1990), Ovsiannikov (*ibid.*) suggests, "[T]hese writers are not aiming at an ecumenism that attempts to see 'the other' as he really is" (p. 18). This exclusivist attitude tends to throw out the proverbial baby with the bathwater. After all, if the New Age bases itself on the promise of salvation through privileged knowledge, this is not an entirely dumb assertion; Christianity (and most other religions) do also offer some promise of special knowledge and even of revealed Truth,

[38] It should be noted that the non-canonical nature of Bulgakov's sophiology, and also for the Russian philosophers in general, is a debatable point of controversy. Bulgakov wrote namely, not of a hypostasis, but of 'hypostasity' with respect to Sophia, and the feminine principle in his writings is not Sophia as such, but the Holy Spirit (cf. Valliere, P. (2000) *Modern Russian Theology: Bukharev, Soloviev, Bulgakov: Orthodox Theology in a New Key*, pub. T&T Clark, Edinburgh).

and the impulse to partake in this Truth needs to be recognised as still existing within popular culture, even in such a distorted form.

The question therefore arises of what the difference is, between an awareness of the importance of ecumenical and interfaith dialogue as an arena where Truth may be lovingly discerned, and a coarsely pluralistic New Age syncretism? Between true integration of philosophical and theological thought, and the denial and blurring of epistemological boundaries?

Apart from its insistence on the Higher Self and its resemblance to Gnosticism in its world-negation, another major difficulty in engaging the New Age in a creative dialogue with Christianity is a result of its philosophical monism. The assertion that 'all is ultimately one,' can be seen to lead to a sort of doctrinal nihilism, a state of affairs where something is no sooner asserted than disproved. As Carr (1991) suggests, New Age thinking "... may tend towards becoming anti-critical as its holistic assumptions minimise, and often specifically obliterate, the subject/object distinction" (p. 44). The Orthodox Christian understanding of God as the Uncreated, stands in direct contrast to the claustrophobic pantheism which monism can ultimately lead to. Whelton (2002) concludes that

> "On the spiritual level, Christians and New Age devotees are worlds apart. The common shared underlying premise of New Agers is Monism [...] which states the belief "that all is one," which is pure occult philosophy. All life and inanimate matter is derived from a single energy source or force. Thus, they deny any duality of mind or matter, good or evil, and reduce all reality to a single, unifying principle. This is diametrically opposed to the Christian biblical view of God as a distinct personal being who presides over the separateness and diversity of his creation. For, as Orthodox Christians, we are reminded in the Divine Liturgy that we all stand as individuals "before the dread judgment seat of Christ." We will not be able to dissolve and hide our souls or deeds in some giant cosmic soup" (pp. 58–9).

Thus, monism can be seen as dissolving both ontological and ethical boundaries and leading to a regressive state of merger, a loss of personal distinctiveness which is inimical to the Christian appreciation of personhood and hypostasis. From an Orthodox perspective, Vlagkioftis (2007) cites the Hebrew Kabbalah as the source of much occult thought, and compares the philosophical assumptions underlying occultism and the New Age to the ideas of Origen. He comments that

> "One of the consequences of the holistic model [of absolute monism] and the unified evolutionary scale [from the mineral kingdom to God and back], is the negation of subject-object duality, and of boundaries in general" (p. 39, translation mine).

Interestingly too, the absolute monism which underlies occultism is a philosophical tendency that can equally mislead the potentially devout as much as the unremittingly rebellious. Hence within Orthodoxy itself, the beliefs of the heretical[39] *imiaslavie* movement, consisting of those — originally Athonite monks — who believe that the Name of God is God Himself, can be paralleled with Buddhist and Kabbalistic emphases on the names of things being somehow primary with respect to their essential qualities, and hence carrying within themselves magical powers of incantation (it may be remarked here that Plato shared in this view, having claimed that the name of an object exists since before the object itself does). It is also not surprising that the *imiaslavie* proponents of this potentially pantheistic doctrine took their inspiration partly from the aforementioned Gnostic Khlysty movement through Grigori Rasputin, and found natural sympathizers in the Sophiologists Bulgakov (previously a Marxist) and Florensky (influenced by Kant), who perhaps through their ideas

[39] Again, there is some debate within the Orthodox Church as to the aptness of ascribing a heretical nature to these beliefs.

regarding Sophia idealistically tried to wed Hegelian dialectics and dialectical materialism with the realm of transcendent spirit.

The occurrence of movements like Sophiology and the *imiaslavie* within Orthodoxy might—were some of their more extreme implications and misinterpretations not recognized as potentially heretical by the Church—lend credence to the accusations of Roman Catholic opponents of hesychasm (e.g. Vailhé), who see this form of prayer as being both auto-suggestive and polytheistic. Similarly, there are those who claim that a Gnostic or Neoplatonic doctrine of emanationism, like that which can be found in Kabbalah, can also be found in the Palamite essence-energies distinction, which states that God is knowable through His energies, but not in His essence. Since for St. Gregory Palamas, the divine energies were not separate from God, but are themselves God, it is possible to consider them as similar to divine emanations, overflows from God's essence, as described in Neoplatonism and in the Kabbalistic sefirot (indeed, in the writings of Nikitas Stithatos, the nine ranks of angels together with humanity have been viewed as having an affinity with the ten sefirot of Kabbalah, cf. Lubheid & Rorem (eds.) (1987)). Although such ideas and comparisons can be interesting and informative from the intellectual perspective of comparative religion and the history of ideas, what is consistently ignored in all these accounts is the apophatic Orthodox principle of absolute divine transcendence, which renders the 'mechanism' of such divine operations ultimately unknowable.

The appeal of occultism and heresy is frequently based therefore, on the understandable human need to discern rational mechanisms at work in the universe, a sort of reduction of spirituality and theology to a pseudo-science of metaphysics. Fr. Alexander Elchaninov writes that

> "The practice of theosophy, occultism, spiritualism is not only harmful in its effect on the health of the mind, but has as its basis an illegitimate desire to peer through a closed door. We must humbly admit the existence of a Mystery, and not try to slip round by the backstairs to eavesdrop. Moreover, we have been

given a supreme law of life which leads us straight to God — love, a difficult, thorny path; but we must follow it, bearing our cross, with no excursions into byways" (1967, p. 43).

A psychoanalyst may speculate on the possible oedipal motives underlying the characteristic occult and New Age desire to 'peer through a closed door,' perhaps in the hope of a regressive merger with the Great Mother in a universe without laws or boundaries. Thus too, what is so often presented as 'science' and 'knowledge' then turns out, as in the numerous instances previously cited, to be scientifically unfounded, imprecise and unclear. The New Age is almost impossible to converse with theologically because, like Proteus, it refuses to take any specific shape when engaged in dialogue. Ouspensky, the Russian disciple of Gurdjieff, describes well — and sadly also employs in his own opus — this 'fuzzy' logic; in his 'third canon of thought,' *Tertium Organum*, he writes:

> "The axioms which *Tertium Organum* contains cannot be formulated in our language. But if we still try to formulate them, they will produce the impression of absurdities. Taking the axioms of Aristotle as a model, we may express the principal axiom of the new logic in our poor earthly language in the following way : *A is both A and not A*, or *Every thing is both A and not A*, or *Every thing is All.* But in fact these formulae are completely impossible" (1990, p. 221).

Given its embrace of an impossible logic, it seems that any interfaith dialogue between Christianity and the New Age, and importantly also for our study, between Christianity and many of the philosophical tenets and theological ramifications emerging from Jungian psychology, is going to be very restricted in its efficacy and outcome. Christians on one side and New Agers/Jungians[40] on the other may

[40] Jungians are not being equated here with 'New Agers,' the purpose of the ar-

not find that their difficulty in communication arises so much from their differing specific beliefs or hypotheses, but through the fact that, they are often speaking the widely different languages of analysis and synthesis, of reason and (individualised) mysticism; but the synthesis and mysticism of the New Age is closer to Hinduism and other Asian philosophies, than it can ever be to Christianity, which appreciates and includes mystical experience in a radically different way. Hence, while on the one hand Christianity sets mystical experience at the end of a path of purification from sin, followed by illumination to the degree that the individual can bear while sustaining their unique identity, New Age spirituality can sound similar to Christianity in its emphasis on mystical experience, yet at the same time have crucial points of difference due to its negation of sin and its monist assumptions. Blavatsky, who emerged from a Russian Orthodox social context though she was so hostile to Christianity, writes:

> "Seek for him who is to give thee birth, in the Hall of Wisdom, the Hall which lies beyond, wherein all shadows are unknown, and where the light of truth shines with unfading glory. That which is uncreate abides in thee, Disciple, as it abides in that Hall. If though would'st reach it *and blend the two*, thou must divest thyself of thy dark garments of illusion. Stifle the voice of flesh, allow no image of of the senses to get between its light and thine *that thus the twain may blend in one*" (1889; 1992 p. 7, italics mine).

The above description of the spiritual path could *almost* be acceptable to a Christian—but for the phrases in italics, suggesting a 'blending' of the human with the Divine. A "light" inherent to humanity, as Christianity acknowledges in the *Imago Dei*, yet also a 'blending' which merges the created with the Uncreated light of Di-

gument being alone to highlight some philosophical commonalities. Key differences between New Age ideas and Jungian psychology are discussed immediately below.

vinity. From the point of view of the Christian theologian this perspective on spiritual growth is unacceptable; man unites with God, yet remains a distinct person in Christian mysticism. Yet in the spirit of Christian discernment, New Age thought and Orthodox Christianity may continue to stimulate and influence each other through the scholarly examination of sources, through patient and thoughtful personal contacts, as well as by persuasive argument either way; indeed, given the cultural prevalence of New Age ideas, this process is not only necessary, but probably inevitable.

4 Implications for Contemporary Orthodox Spirituality. Despite its various dangers, the New Age as a social and religious phenomenon does, however, have several lessons to offer Christianity, especially in its broad appeal to the public at large at the end of this century. Carr (1991) suggests the following:

(a) *eclecticism*: that the Christian Churches could benefit by paying attention to the eclectic character of modern spirituality, particularly its dislike of dogmatism;
(b) *mysticism*: the emphasis on a mystical, rather than a rational, approach to spirituality may go hand-in-hand with eclectic tastes, hence rendering overly rationalistic, non-sacramental approaches to Christianity unappealing;
(c) *post-Enlightenment thought*: the New Age is taking into account in its spirituality the end-of-century fatigue with Enlightenment values, especially scientific materialism, and Christianity,[41] especially the Protestant Churches, could learn from this.[42]

[41] Writing as an Anglican, Carr (*ibid.*) is primarily addressing Protestant churches here; it is assumed that some of what is being said may be pertinent to Orthodoxy, with some important differences due to Orthodoxy's distinct theological heritage, which arguably has not suffered from Enlightenment biases in the same way.

[42] Nevertheless, the following argument from Ovsiannikov should be seriously considered in the light of the above historical discussion (*ibid.*): "I would like to suggest that New Age in general is a natural continuation of the Reformation and

(d) *disorientation*: the New Age phenomenon may well indicate the sense of loss of direction which Christian Churches have experienced as much as the other members of our complex society; and finally
(e) *undergirding wisdom*: it is clear that the Christian tradition contains elements which are both compatible with and attractive to the New Age, such as the wisdom literature, an emphasis on which may make the Christian message more relevant to today's audiences.

So far the focus has been mostly on describing the premises of New Age thought and its influence on contemporary culture. Bringing a Christian critique to bear on these premises has been shown to lead to important conclusions, while recognising that the influence is mutual, and that the Christian Churches have a lot to learn from New Age phenomena and several good reasons for engaging these contemporary notions in interfaith dialogue — while being cautious about ascribing to the New Age a potential status of theological clarity, which it neither claims nor indeed possesses.

But it is also honest to recognise that, if Christianity has something to teach the New Age, and hence to address to the popular *zeitgeist*, it must do so on the grounds that what it has to offer is truly different from New Age teachings themselves. Eastern Orthodoxy, while recognising the yearning for Truth in all religions, sometimes veers between a thoughtfully compassionate but nonetheless boundaried tolerance, and an exclusivism which appears to sharply reject all difference in dealing with other beliefs. Continuing with the example suggested by the Anglican Carr (1991) the following attitudes can be characteristic of Christians across denominations:

in its direct line of protest. Once criticism of tradition began, it developed the force of an avalanche and crashed onto its creators' heads. Each successive school has the right to question the tradition of its predecessor; and as protest hardens into tradition, so the 'old/new' tradition will, in its turn, be rejected — hence the multiplicity of Protestant sects. The logic of such a process leads to the belief that every individual has the right to create his own 'tradition'. New Age, the contemporary stage of the Reformation, completes a round of protest" (p. 18).

> "When Christians first encounter an apparently alien religion, their initial reaction is usually defensive. They emphasise differences and, depending to some extent upon their theological stance, either seek to baptise the religion by pointing to the presence of Christ within it or to convert it by bringing the light of Christ to bear upon it. Few aspects of New Age activity, however, are so clearly alien. For they deal with areas of life with which the churches aspire to deal and they use language which either has a Christian tinge or is even explicitly Christian in context" (p. 56).

Many Eastern Orthodox theologians cannot perhaps share this optimism, but in engaging with New Age thought, as with any other set of beliefs ancient or modern, the best Christian policy may be to attend to what Christianity itself has to learn from these beliefs and practices, and what they may mean to the people who engage with them, while also bearing witness to the transcendent, Triune God Who unites Orthodox Christians with others across denominations. The reasons for engaging New Age beliefs in interfaith dialogue with Christian theology can be seen to be manifold and significant ones, reaching as they do right into the heart of the (post)modern spiritual condition. In the search for a clearer definition and use of the word 'spiritual' it will remain, however, to the Eastern Orthodox theologian Paul Evdokimov to point out what is also risky about the sort of syncretism New Agers may sometimes be justly accused of engaging in, and to suggest what may be special about Christianity in relation to other faiths:

> "Considered on the vast plane of world religions, the spiritual life represents the Christian synthesis between the anthropocentric inwardness of the Oriental religions without God, and the transcendental and theocentric personalism of the biblical religions, Judaism and Islam. In combining the marvellous penetration of

> Hinduism into the abyss of human inwardness with the sacred fear of Jewish and Islamic monotheism before the absolute transcendence of the Creator, the Christian, nevertheless, creates an entirely new element. The divine "I" has spoken to a human thou. His word has established the one who listens to him, has brought him into existence in his image, and he continues to create and fill him by keeping him in living communion with the *Word made flesh*. [...] Another error is shown by syncretism. A psychologist easily crosses the frontiers of the various confessions, and supposes that all religions converge. Nothing is comparable, however, to the truth of the Gospel offered and lived in the Eucharist. It bears in Christ the accomplishment of the aspirations not only of men and angels, but of the three Divine Persons, for according to Nicholas Cabasilas, the Incarnation is the "pouring of God outside himself" (1998, pp. 57–8, 60).

The above statement is certainly not acceptable to everyone, nor is it within the scope of this book to elaborate on its validity. However, even from a Jungian standpoint, it would seem that today's spiritual condition as exemplified by the New Age does have a great deal to benefit from a more traditional Christian understanding of spirituality. David Tacey, in his book on Jung and the New Age (1993), poignantly points out that New Age spirituality involves mostly a regressive return to the Great Mother archetype, aspiring as it does to a prelapsarian Edenic condition which denies all suffering and conflict.[43] Although the New Age has claimed Jung for its spiritual father, Tacey fervently rejects this as a misappropriation, while acknowledging that certain (mis)interpretations of Jungian theory may nevertheless lead to New Age ideas. Certainly Jung inherited his monism from the thought of 19th-century Romantic figures like C.G. Carus, and

[43] Interestingly, C.S. Lewis in his book *A Pilgrim's Regress* also suggests that occultism seduces "[...] with fatal attraction: smudging of all frontiers, the relaxation of all resistances, dream, opium, darkness, death, and the return to the womb" (1943, p. 12).

his pantheistic tendencies from K. E. von Hartmann, perhaps passing such ideas on to the contemporary New Age milieu in turn; yet Jung, in concord with genuine spiritual teachers across time and culture, but especially in harmony in this instance with the Christian *weltanschauung*, in his writings on individuation also does not recommend any recipe for instant or magical bliss, as offered by many—if not most—New Age teachings. On the contrary, as will be seen in the following section, redemption through suffering is key to the process of individuation as Jung conceives it, exactly as it is for the Eastern Orthodox Christian (and other Christian denominations). Even in the thought of a quasi-prophetic modern figure like Jung, the ultimate implied spiritual aspiration is perhaps therefore not so much to naively deny the fallen character of existence by 'imagining figures of light,' but to facilitate instead the transfiguration of the world into the Kingdom of God by discerning and obeying His Will on earth as in heaven, however different the underlying images and associations to that 'divine realm' and 'divine Will' ultimately prove to be in Christianity and in analytical psychology.

The link between Gnosticism and the occult/human potential roots of the New Age spirituality which pervades popular culture has been described above. The political thinker Eric Voegelin[44] suggests a further association between Gnosticism and contemporary science itself, which brings together perhaps both the spiritual and the scientific aspects of Jungian psychology, and has wider implications for psychotherapy as a whole. As a political thinker, Voegelin suggested that the utopianism, escapism and selectivity towards facts which is characteristic of modern thinkers and ideological movements, is due to a desire to 'immanentize the eschaton,' a term introduced in his work, *The New Science of Politics* (1952). This 'immanentization of the eschaton' can basically be defined as a desire to establish the Kingdom of Heaven on earth through human means alone, or to create heaven on earth, but unaided by God or religious faith. Hence

[44] For his list of complete works, cf. http://press.umsystem.edu/voegelin.htm.

modern movements such as Marxism and psychoanalysis necessarily tend towards an overly optimistic assessment of humanity, ignoring the limits of human nature and social organisation. In contrast to the pessimism of ancient Gnosticism regarding mundane existence, the neo-Gnosticisms of modernity attempt to provide 'knowledgeable,' authoritative responses to the problem of alienation, which they view as involving a disconnection between the individual and society due to an inherent cosmic disorder, equivalent to the cosmic evil which the ancient Gnostics attributed to the creation of the Demiurge.

These new Gnosticisms share the assumption that alienation can be transcended through specialised insight and knowledge (e.g. scientism, positivism), or 'Gnostic speculation' as Voegelin called it, and also to a parallel drive to implement this learning and insight derived from the 'Gnostic speculation' into social policy. This means that there is also an inherent political totalitarianism implied in the neo-Gnostic systems which have been enforced on twentieth and twenty-first century society, from the extreme revolutionary totalitarianist ideologies of socialist states (Stalin's "you have to crack a few eggs to make an omelette") to the monstrous implementation of Nazi racial ideology in WWII Germany. Without the transcendent mystery of God, humans are perhaps forcibly 'squeezed' into their own categories and systems of knowledge, since a sort of *libido dominandi* appears to inevitably develop in the thinkers and historical actors who espouse and apply these new Gnosticisms, turning yesterday's rebel warrior into today's dictator.

The key characteristic of these modern systems of thought which do not acknowledge the limits of a merely human potential, is in this sense similar to the tendency in Jungian psychology which Papadopoulos (2006) refers to as 'Gnostic epistemology' (p. 45), the assumption of privileged knowledge which instigates a social knowledge / power nexus, and causes analytical psychologists to cling tenaciously to fundamental hypotheses such as that concerning the archetypal nature of the contents of the collective unconscious. Needless to say, similar points can be made about the tenets of Freudian psychoanalysis and those of all the other psychotherapeutic schools, which ironically cause postivist philosophers like Karl Popper to refer to Marxism, psychoanalysis and religion as the enemies of an 'open society'—as though the methods and discoveries of empirical science were themselves privy to the absolute Truth! Although the implications of Voegelin's research can be over-emphasized, and he himself moderated his perspective to include influences other than Gnosticism on modern thought, there may apparently be more than a grain of epistemological and sociological accuracy in this perspective.

Clearly, Jung was more than a New Age guru; yet, as we have seen, his psychological system is grounded in the same philosophical currents as so much of today's indeterminate New Age 'spirituality.' The rest of this book will deal systematically and in some detail with the epistemological and practical meeting and departure points between the Gnostically-influenced epistemology of Analytical Psychology, and the spiritual approach to human suffering in Orthodox Christianity.

CHAPTER TWO

Research Methodology and 'Scientific' Psychology

The currently widespread popular interest in what may be loosely termed 'new age' approaches to self-help and self-realisation (Bloom, 1991; Carr, 1991; Heelas, 1996; Tacey, 2001; Whelton, 2002; Haule, 1999), suggests that the contemporary psychospiritual *zeitgeist*, prophetically termed the 'age of Aquarius'[1] by Jung, may indeed be underway, at least in the sense of profound changes at the social and cultural levels. If nothing else, the proliferation of self-help literature informed by spirituality, suggests a deep-seated need for the sacred and the numinous in many people's lives.

Paradoxically, however, there seems to be an equal and opposite force operative in contemporary scientific culture, which can perhaps be seen as the direct descendant of 19th century Victorian materialism and modernist philosophical utilitarianism, which gave its impetus to the work of thinkers like Darwin, Spencer and Freud. In psychotherapy, this cultural force tends to find its expression in the paradigms of 'evidence-based practice' and the 'scientist-practitioner'

[1] Cf. Jung (CW 10, pars. 589-90): "It is not presumption that drives me, but my conscience as a psychiatrist that bids me fulfil my duty and prepare those few who will hear me for coming events which are in accord with the end of an era. [...] They are manifestations of psychic changes which always occur at the end of one Platonic month and at the beginning of another. Apparently they are changes in the constellation of psychic dominants, of the archetypes, or "gods" as they used to be called, which bring about [...] long-lasting transformations of the collective psyche. [...] We are now nearing that great change which may be expected when the spring-point enters Aquarius."

model or 'medical model' of clinical application (cf. Davison & Neale, 2001; Milton, Taylor & Gaist, 1998). Writing from a person-centred perspective, Thorne (2002) eloquently warns that

> Perhaps the greatest rationalisation of all [...] is the retreat into a pseudo-professionalism. This particular stance represents the detailed contract, the rigid observance of boundaries and the commitment to empirically validated (whatever that means) therapies as the necessary hallmark of a true professionalism appropriate to twenty-first century men and women. By implication, those approaches which view human beings as anything but predictable and remain open to the evolution of humankind through the journey into relationship and the mystical apprehension of a transcendental reality are in danger of losing their professional credibility and finding themselves pilloried as little more than endearing mythologies of yesteryear (p. 21).

In the context of psychotherapy this 'professionalising' force has been experienced through a medicalising, manual-based and diagnostic approach to the treatment of psychological difficulties, frequently constraining clinicians to work with clients within specified parameters of 'managed care'. The pressure to make therapy brief, targeted, structured, contractual, legally and financially viable (e.g. to be covered by health insurance, NHS budgeting etc.), and above all 'empirically supported,' can be paramount to any other concerns (Andrews, 2008; Khele, 2008). Taking into consideration the current economic crisis, this climate of quantity is likely to be reinforced.

As Thorne (*ibid.*) suggests, spiritual and depth approaches to the human person will be the first to suffer. The current climate of pragmatic endeavour can at best perhaps serve a purgative and chastizing function, through emphasising 'what works'; yet it can arguably also promote a restrictive attitude of 'professional audit' and 'accountability' which is inimical to creativity in the clinical field, setting up an artificial tension between 'process' and 'outcome' studies in the field of psychotherapy research. Psychologies which are not based on immediate symptom removal and behaviour change, but attempt to address the deeper causes of maladaptive experience and behaviour, can find themselves marginalised by an approach to therapy which is often more scientistic than scientific, and which treats isolated problems outside of their social—not to mention their spiritual—contexts. Jungian analyst J. Marvin Spiegelman seems correct in suggesting that, in this materialistic professional climate,

> The participatory approach, which involves the unconscious, will still find some place (the Division of Psychoanalysis is still an important one in the American Psychological Association), but the truly spiritual approach of many Jungians will probably enjoy a quiet life outside of all that, even though the professionalisation and popularity of Jungian societies increases greatly throughout the world. [...] This seems to be the direction of the United States, certainly, but I am aware that the European Union, with its demand for the collectivization of psychotherapy standards and of licensure, is going in the same direction" (Spiegelman, 1996: p. 145).

Indeed, this prophecy from over thirteen years ago currently appears to be materialising in the U.K., with legislation for the professional regulation of counsellors and psychotherapists having the support of bodies like the Health Professions Council, and only a few lone, but significant, voices of protest such as Andrew Samuels and Brian Thorne, among seasoned clinicians (Browne, 2009).

However, alternative attitudes and approaches to research in the humanities, which involve paying attention to the observer's effect on the process of observation and on the thing observed, have grown out of phenomenological critiques of the Cartesian subject-object dualism which underlies the traditional methods of Western science (Popkin & Stroll, 1986: pp. 356–7; Cooper, 1990: p. 35ff). These attitudes and approaches have been corroborated by an awareness of Oriental philosophies and perspectives such as Buddhism; but also developed as a result of the differentiated perception of what material reality *is*: an insight gained by research in the 'new physics,' which proposes new paradigms and scientific ideas, such as quantum theory, relativity, chaos theory, Heisenberg's uncertainty principle and Gödel's theorem, all of which are challenging to the Newtonian 'clockwork' understanding of the universe as espoused by 19th century materialism.[2] This new scientific paradigm (e.g. Zohar, 1991) has prompted psychotherapy research to give serious emphasis to the qualitative, since as King (1996) suggests,

> Qualitative research methods involve procedures that result in rich, descriptive, contextually situated data, based on people's spoken or written words and observable behaviour. Within this context, it is nowadays generally acknowledged… that *an understanding of the experiences not only of our participants but also of ourselves as researchers constitutes a fundamental part of the research process* (quoted in Richardson (ed.), 1996, p. 175; emphasis mine).

A fundamental notion underlying the new physics, is that we cannot eliminate the personal and subjective role of the experimenter; hence the nomothetic approach of experimental 'scientific' psychology, in its attempt to discover objective, universal laws of human behaviour as observed *ad extra*, is incomplete at best: Jung famously maintained that, far from being an impartial science, every psychology is, in fact, a 'subjective confession' (CW4, par. 774).

This research too, will necessarily involve the author's personal and professional individuation process,[3] while attempting to remain

[2] Thus, the famous Einsteinian formula, $E=mc^2$, suggests matter and energy are interdependent, but the issue of what energy is remains a riddle to modern physics.
[3] Cf. Romanyshyn (2007) for a post-jungian approach to the research process which takes account of the researchers' own individuation process. This archetypal approach is an innovative post-Jungian contribution to psychological re-

congruent in response to analytical psychology and Christian theology. Like the medieval alchemist searching for a method to turn base metals into gold, it is necessary for the researcher as an honest seeker after truth in psychological experience, to draw the *prima materia* of raw data from history, the arts, natural and social sciences, philosophy, religion and indeed from any field of human thought which has something of essence to bring to bear on the topic being researched; data then has to be distilled in the alembic of real-life, concrete individual and collective human experience which is gained in personal as well as professional settings, as it was for Jung. Quantitative research, when investigating something as intersubjective as the psychotherapeutic relationship, may be insufficient in describing the wealth of inner individual and collective experience — however useful the abstractions and comparisons of statistical results can indeed be, as heuristic aids to interpretation.

It seems logical, in a way, that a method ought to be designed to match the nature of its object of study. Von Franz's (1998) comments given below, precede the qualitative methodological approach as discussed by King (*ibid.*) and others by several decades, yet continue to sound relevant and timely:

> Although the coming generation shows a heightened interest in the human being and the human condition, and although young people are taking up psychology and sociology in ever greater numbers, these two disciplines give far more attention at present to statistically calculable, collective human behaviour than they do to the understanding of the individual. [...] Theories based on statistics formulate an ideal average, in which exceptions at either end are abolished and replaced by an abstract mean. In this way a psychology or an anthropology is developed which is "generally valid", it is true, but which gives us an abstract picture of the average man, from which all individual traits have

search, but will not form the methodological basis for this study.

> been erased. This method leads to scientific knowledge but not to understanding of the actual human being. The result is an increasingly unrealistic, rational picture of the world, in which the individual figures only as a sort of marginal phenomenon (pp. 253–4).

Regarding, therefore, the sources and methods used to articulate the dynamics of psychological experience and growth through suffering, and to further the understanding of its contribution to process in psychotherapy and spiritual direction, it can be argued that by combining the findings of systematic empirical science, using such methods as clinical observation, experiment, statistical analysis and encyclopaedic knowledge, with the more 'irrational' qualitative, heuristic sources and methods fuelled by creative instinct,[4] artistic inspiration and philosophical intuition, a more complete Jungian 'third' is born, casting the phenomenon of suffering in a new light through the prism of knowledge, imagination, creativity and experience, the whole gamut of which is needed to provide an adequate basis for sufficiently understanding or coming to terms with such global issues — and paradoxically this means, too, that the findings of this research will necessarily be circumscribed and propositional.

In what follows, it will be argued that human psychology cannot be reduced to impulses suggested by biological survival and reproduction. Post-Freudian object relations theorists are probably correct in suggesting that the economy of psyche operates on a basis of relationship rather than drive satisfaction, but humans need even more than to give and receive love from others. It may be that the profoundest human quest is for a connection to the life and structure of the cosmos itself — a 'cosmic consciousness' amounting to a personal relationship with an objective Other. Theology suggests that the deepest human need is the yearning to worship and be united to something greater than oneself, which amounts to nothing less than

[4] Jung thought of creativity as instinctual, as discussed below (ch. 9).

a total transfiguration of being and consciousness. The formulation of a Freudian death instinct (1920, SE 18:36) as a tendency for living organisms to return to the condition of inert, inorganic matter, is only half the story; we do not simply wish to cease upon the midnight with no pain (Keats, Ode to a nightingale, v. 36). Perhaps even more, humans desire to fertilise the soil through the decomposition of the body, to light up the universe and bring the cosmos into being through a *hieros gamos* of matter and consciousness, to give birth to the knowledge that love is as strong as death (Song of Solomon, 8:6), and to continually mediate the creation to the Creator through a universal sacrament of communion (Staniloae, 1984; p. 28). As the founder of the discipline of Pastoral Psychology in Greece, I. Kornarakis (e.g. 1958; 2009) realised early on, analytical psychology went further than Freudian psychoanalysis in this direction by pointing to the religious function of the psyche; but it did not perhaps go far enough, denying as it did the possibility of divine salvation, or as the Orthodox psychotherapist Jamie Moran suggests, being effectively closed to the operation of the Holy Spirit (cf. Moran, 1996). The dismissal of Jung from 'scientific' psychology on the grounds of being a 'mystic,' however, may be a sore loss to psychology as a human science. One does not have to agree with Jung's conclusions, to understand that an engagement with his problematic is in fact, essential to mental health.

CHAPTER THREE

Experience and Meaning in Psychotherapy

Brief discussion of research methodology has already suggested that investigation into the underlying theoretical framework for analysing the *whole* experience of the therapist within the psychotherapeutic process, constitutes an attempt to contribute — in a minor and necessarily limited sense — to the broad and epistemologically diverse opus of contemporary interdisciplinary research, which aims towards achieving a unified understanding of the bodily, psychological *and* spiritual experience of both the psychotherapist and their client. Such a unified understanding of physical, psychological and spiritual experience cannot be limited to the collection of quantitative data regarding diagnosis, therapeutic process and treatment outcome, important as such data is; it must also involve the active and ongoing personal effort of both parties engaged in the therapeutic relationship (or that of all the participants, in the case of therapeutic groups) to articulate their own sense of existential 'being-in-the-world' or within the cosmos (Cooper, 1990; p. 57) — simply put, to find positive meaning in life.[1]

[1] Frankl (1959; 1984), for example, writes: "The existential vacuum which is the mass neurosis of the present time can be described as a private and personal form of nihilism; for nihilism can be defined as the contention that being has no meaning. As for psychotherapy however, it will never be able to cope with this state of affairs on a mass scale if it does not keep itself free from the impact and influence of the contemporary trends of nihilistic philosophy; otherwise it represents a symptom of the mass neurosis rather than its possible cure" (pp. 152–153).

Though the above quest may sound idealistic and abstract, it is not a search which is restricted, as is stereotypically assumed, to adolescent stages of development (Jacobs, 1986), or to the vicissitudes of mental illness and social maladjustment in later life. As much as it does pertain to the struggles of those whom traditional psychiatry labels 'neurotic' and 'psychotic,' persons who suffer from self-estrangement through dysfunctional thoughts, feelings and behaviour, a profound and untiring quest for meaning may paradoxically also characterise the innermost yearnings of psychologically awakened individuals operating at the very highest levels of human potential, such as those whom Rogers (1980) described as 'persons of tomorrow.'

It seems significant therefore in terms of the cultural *zeitgeist* mentioned earlier, that following psychological research on the 'intelligence quotient' or IQ in the early part of the twentieth century, and research on 'emotional intelligence' or EQ in the mid-1990s (e.g. Goleman, 1998), there is currently an intuition among some social scientists that, as Zohar & Marshall (2001) write:

> The full picture of human intelligence can be completed with a discussion of our spiritual intelligence — SQ for short. By SQ I mean the intelligence with which we address and solve problems of meaning and value, the intelligence with which we can place our actions and our lives in a wider, richer, meaning-giving context, the intelligence with which we can assess that one course of action or one life-path is more meaningful than another. SQ is the necessary foundation for the effective functioning of both IQ and EQ. It is our ultimate intelligence (pp. 3–4).

Therapists are, of course, human; regardless of the level of personal individuation achieved, the actual behaviour of the client *or* the therapist at different times and in diverse situations may be characteristic of tendencies towards either health or dysfunction.[2] It is

[2] Hence, perhaps a significant qualitative distinction needs to be maintained

not being assumed here that healers are constant beacons of spiritual intelligence and moral integrity, but it *is* suggested that healing behaviour frequently involves the use of SQ (as well as IQ and EQ). Hence, another important predicate of this study is that, contrary to received opinion in some current therapeutic circles, the *overall* moral character of a therapist is pertinent to the kind and quality of healing that can be provided, even if this can only be poorly ascertained in scientific studies,[3] whether through judging individual actions in particular situations, or by measuring the efficacy of specific therapeutic interventions, according to the quantitative criteria which psychotherapy outcome research imposes.

---

between the compulsive and rigid, unconscious thirst for absolute and exclusive meaning which characterises undeveloped and neurotic, indeed fundamentalist, states of mind, and that inner state of flexible, meaningful creative play which comes as a result of genuine psychological growth and inner abundance. Jungian analyst Dale Mathers (2001) writes that:

> "Meaning comes from the no-man's land of dreams and synchronicities, which validate our experience to help us adapt to environmental change. This adaptive function is, I believe, a primary purpose of meaning: it confers developmental, evolutionary advantages. Open, fluent meaning systems are better able to adapt to environmental change than closed ones. The result of analysis [is the development of] different awarenesses [...] increased ability to tolerate uncertainty, to avoid premature closure and sustain ambivalence (pluralism). We can stay longer in transitional space (Winnicott), the 'third area' (Schwartz-Salant 1989), the 'intersubjective field' (Atwood 1994) — in *between*" (p. 15, words in square brackets mine, references in original).

In the spirit of this intersubjective 'in-betweenness' *pace* Plato's 'metaxy,' the author hopes this study will be actively co-constructed in meaning together with the reader, offering ideas, concepts and imagery which encourage constructive dialogue and a diversity of opinion.

[3] "The psyche is one of those things which people know least about, because no one likes to inquire into his own shadow. Even psychology is misused for the purpose of concealing the true causal connections from oneself. The more "scientific" it pretends to be, the more welcome is its so-called objectivity, because this is an excellent way of getting rid of the inconvenient emotional components of conscience" (Jung, CW 10:841).

While the importance of moral character is perhaps already implicitly acknowledged in the profession, through the formulation and adoption of general ethical codes of practice, as well as through the rigorous selection procedures of numerous therapy training courses, it is nevertheless alarmingly commonplace amongst practising therapists to hear suggestions — perhaps as a result of an overambitious but well-intentioned wish to be inclusive, democratic and pluralistic — that the personal lifestyle of the therapist is entirely a matter of private choice, and that such important areas of life as the therapist's politics and spirituality, do not bear significantly on client outcome, provided the therapy itself is ethically and ably carried out in terms of psychotherapeutic technique.

There is of course an element of truth in the above suggestions; but, while moral character is a dimension of personality which arguably cannot be measured objectively, it will nevertheless be implicitly and explicitly suggested in what follows that the personal lifestyle (including political and spiritual beliefs and practice) of a therapist *does have major bearing on client outcome.* It makes little sense in fact, on the one hand to argue that the client may only go as far as the therapist can take them,[4] and on the other hand to omit discussion of the therapist's overall personality and lifestyle when personal ethics and the source of meaning is at issue. Von Franz (1993) writes that

> Even the most comprehensive training program that is limited to the purveyance of the indispensable knowledge, as necessary as this doubtless is, cannot convey to people that "something" which creates in a person a healing emanation. It is true that moral integrity and the will to help are indispensable, but they alone cannot produce the result in question (p. 267).

[4] Cf. Freud (1910:145), "No psychoanalyst goes further than his own complexes and internal resistances permit."

Hence moral integrity is acknowledged as being fundamental to therapeutic practice from a Jungian perspective, yet there is a larger aspect to this than the responsibility and good will shown to the client in the session. Following Jung, Von Franz (*ibid.*) suggests

> If it is not possible to establish a relationship with the numinous, no cure is possible; [...] From this point of view, the work of the therapist can only consist in dismantling preconceptions and blockages to possible numinous experience. [...] But it is essential that the analyst himself have a connection with the numinous and have a belief in it that is based on his own experience; [...] For this reason the analyst must say to himself again and again, "I do not know what God wants from this person!" All he can do is help the patient hear better what the patient's own psyche is whispering to him (pp. 177–179).

Baldwin (2004), discussing the modern quest for meaning through psychotherapy, in contrast to the pre-modern reception of meaning through dogmatic religion, takes this requirement for therapists to have a personal relation to a source of ultimate meaning, even further:

> The experienced therapist and spiritual guide know that the basis of a happy, fulfilling life is based on the ability to form good relationships. All human suffering, whatever form it takes, can be traced to fractured relationships, with another, with oneself and, ultimately with some transcendent meaning, which some call God. Thus psychotherapy and religion are on common ground (p. 10).

And she immediately adds,

> Is there a common understanding of the ground pattern that impels the human being toward fulfillment and a meaningful

> life? I think there is. Jung [...] perceived the growth of the human personality as a gradual process toward becoming what we are meant to be: a process of realising the image left by a creator. It is as simple to understand as the image imprinted in an acorn, destined to become an oak (p. 10).

The existence of a possible link therefore, between individuation, personal growth and our relationship to a source of 'transcendent meaning' is being suggested. This idea of growth towards what one is meant to be, as an understanding of personal destiny, will also be explored further in a later section on human vocation, as it is of central importance to both psychotherapeutic work and spiritual direction.

Just as the therapist's moral character may be important in psychotherapy and spiritual direction, so too is his personal suffering. It may, in fact, be the ability to suffer *creatively* which most typically characterises the spiritual intelligence or SQ of healers in the way they empathise with and help solve the difficulties others face.[5] Nevertheless, suffering in itself, however much it invites our sympathy, is not necessarily productive; it becomes fruitful only when creativity, intelligence and imagination are used in its possible resolution and acceptance. Young-Eisendrath (1996) writes that:

> Many theories of development and spirituality draw some kind of distinction between useful suffering, which leads to development, and useless suffering, which leads merely to the repetition of suffering. Carl Jung talked about neurotic suffering as a bogus replacement for real suffering. In his writings he clearly separated the repetitive ruminations, worries, self-doubts, and anxious habits of the neurotic from the suffering that is an essential part of life. Honest confrontation with this deeper anguish over our

[5] Zohar & Marshall (2001) write that "to come into full possession of our spiritual intelligence we have at some time to have seen the face of hell, to have known the possibility of despair, pain, deep suffering and loss, and to have made our peace with these" (pp. 14–5).

> ordinary human limitations and imperfections, our inevitable loss, illness, decline, and death, wakes us to the significance of our lives (p. 9).

Suffering and evil are, as discussed below, woven into the fabric of human existence in such a way that only a genuine, courageous and creative response to these through struggle, through an *auseinandersetzen* with lived experience, can be at all meaningful and ultimately healing for both therapist and client. This response, seen from a Jungian perspective, implies a 'crucifixion,' a fertile suspension between the opposites such as ego and Self, conscious and unconscious, which patiently waits for the birth of the transcendent function, as Von Franz (1993) explains:

> The decisive point is always whether or not one is conscious of one's conflict and endures it consciously; but one should not indulge in the illusion that even in this way the evil is eliminated; [...] Since evil is for the most part a deviation from the *numen*, [...] repeated deviations of this sort are unavoidable, and the conflict between turning away from the numen and turning toward it is a long one, if not a life-long one. The image of the crucifixion is therefore an eternal truth, and therefore also analysis does not promise the patient happiness, but can only liberate him from the neurotic stagnation of his life, not from its authentic suffering (pp. 196–7; italics same).

This way of conceptualising therapeutic work, namely by emphasizing the role of suffering and its meaning for the therapist and client and for the relationship between them, does not therefore necessarily constitute an abrupt departure from a traditional Jungian (or perhaps even a post-Jungian) analytic view, nor indeed from most other psychotherapeutic orientations. However, the theoretical framework is perhaps extended by an implicit pluralistic assumption that there is inherent value in, or that at the very least there are lessons to be learned from, the positive contribution made to the difficult work of the psychotherapist by almost all systems of psychological thought regardless of school, as well as almost all religious, spiritual and secular philosophies—and that this positive contribution may have validity, even within the context of a firm commitment to a specific religion or philosophy of life.

Jungian analytical psychology will thus provide the main theoretical departure point and overarching conceptual framework for the psychological ideas discussed in this study, but ideas may also be borrowed liberally, wherever appropriate, from other psychological schools, systems and approaches, such as Freudian and post-Freudian psychoanalysis (especially object-relations theory), the existential-phenomenological school, the person-centred approach, family systems theory etc., as well as ideas from various other schools of spirituality and secular philosophical thought, ensuring that where such borrowing occurs, it will be identified and cited as such.

Jung himself could perhaps be seen as an early promoter of interdisciplinary research, drawing on ideas from numerous writers both ancient and modern, who were based in very diverse and often conflicting epistemological backgrounds and traditions. He was a widely read polymath in the natural sciences, anthropology, philosophy, literature, theology, alchemy and esoteric thought, and several other fields of study. Jung, being an original thinker, engaged with ideas in order to create his own unique psychological system, a system based on theoretical and practical synthesis-construction, as much as on analysis-reduction,[6] which is ultimately greater than the sum of its

[6] Cf. Sharp (1991): "In the treatment of neurosis, Jung saw the constructive method as complementary, not in opposition, to the reductive approach of classical psychoanalysis" (p. 44). In creating his psychological theory and method, Jung viewed the human psyche as a self-regulating system, and the principle of complementarity was therefore essential to his understanding. He thus purposely retained the Freudian, reductive/analytical approach to psychological formulation, because he felt that the psyche calls for different approaches at different times and stages in its development. The same could perhaps be said of his intentional use of equivocal language when discussing psychological issues,

parts. Jacobi (1962) characteristically writes that "Because of the generic nature of its material, Jungian psychology has always been compelled to draw on other fields." "But," she is also quick to add, "the objective observer will soon discover that these alleged encroachments are more apparent than real. Psychic phenomena, no matter whether they derive from the sound or the sick, can only be grasped through a total vision that considers every single detail from all sides at once, so that a widely ramified knowledge far beyond the ordinary is needed for their elucidation" (p. xii).

This is perhaps one reason why Jungian analysts are expected to be familiar in depth with a great deal of world mythology, and to also be well-versed in their knowledge of religious systems. As for the value of religious insights *sui generis*, in Jung's own words, "religions *are* psychotherapeutic systems" (CW 16:390). Hence treating religion and psychotherapy as totally separate disciplines with nothing constructive or significant to say to one another — an attitude which cannot be said to have been present in Jungian thought even at its inception — would also seem inappropriate in this context. As Jacobi (*ibid*) points out, nothing less than a 'total vision' is required for the full comprehension of the way in which phenomena affect the psyche.

It may be noticed that despite Jung's scientific aspirations and credentials, analytical psychology — like Freudian psychoanalysis, but more so perhaps — has come under much criticism from diverse authors concerned with its epistemological and cultural validity (e.g. Smith, 1984; Sherrard, 1998; Rieff, 1966), and even authors previ-

---

as Stephenson (2004) explains, in an effort *not* to be untrue to life's paradoxical and complex nature as Jung perceived it. This polyvalent ambiguity is an aspect of Jungian thought which poses problems to those who attempt to systematize it, but it might be a source of strength where similarity and contrast, compatibility and difference to other living disciplines, such as Orthodox spirituality, are being sought. While it is therefore simplistic and dangerous to reach facile conclusions about Jung's meaning on almost any issue, based on isolated quotations from his collected works, his psychology, when appreciated as a whole, invites active engagement, offering an integral prism through which other discourses may be perceived in a novel light.

ously sympathetic to it, have at times been alarmed by Jung's guru-like significance to his followers, and by the alleged potential for analytical psychology to become a dangerous religious 'cult' (e.g. Storr, 1996; Noll, 1994). Professional politics aside, this mixed reception may partially be the immediate *result* of the broad, eclectic learning which went into the formation of Jungian psychology: it sits uncomfortably between most schools of thought; it is not theological in any traditional sense, but also not strictly 'scientific' in a reductionistic or positivistic sense either.

The interdisciplinary academic nature of the metatheoretical approach discussed earlier, is a contingency which permits and encourages a non-partisan epistemological 'openness' (Papadopoulos, 1997), and could be said to offer a theoretical 'transitional space'[7] which allows (also in true Jungian fashion, it may be said) an emphasis on the therapists' own experience-based understanding, thereby acknowledging the experiential value there is in engaging with a diversity of different ways of knowing.

However, openness to epistemological diversity must not necessarily imply relativism. On the contrary, an attitude involving the suspension or 'bracketing' of preconceptions (similar to the phenomenological *epoché* as described by Spinelli (1994) and others), may be encouraged through their very acknowledgement. Hence Williams (2003) suggests that in fact an unethical bias exists in current therapeutic practice, which implies that religious interpretations and assumptions are often condemned,[8] whereas secular assumptions, secular indoctrination and the avoidance of religious issues go un-

[7] Cf. Winnicott (1965).

[8] Samuels (2005) humorously but accurately refers to spirituality as the 'S' word. The connotation of sex is not insignificant—just as Foucault (1990) refers to postmodern generations as the 'New Victorians,' talking openly about sexual matters in the manner of a *scientia sexualis*, but lacking any *ars erotica*, it is perhaps equally true to suggest that spirituality, especially in its explicitly religious expression, has become pathological and taboo in clinical settings. Might it not be the case, however, that much that passes for eroticism and sexuality today, is in fact suppressed spirituality?

challenged. When working with religious clients, the unethical implications of this practice are obvious, but even with non-religious clients they are present, though less explicitly. She writes:

> Assumptions are essentially what is taken for granted and the worst assumptions are often the hidden ones, the ones which ignore, gloss-over or simply miss out any reference to the client's religious faith and beliefs. Assumptions are often more powerful than beliefs because they are out of awareness. Counsellors without any religious belief or understanding and trained psychologically with a scientific, positivist and secular view of life, are most likely not to perceive when religious beliefs and values are relevant. Counsellors with a religious faith need to avoid making false assumptions or judgements about the particular faith of their client based on their own religious beliefs or a general knowledge of religion. A non-religious approach to life from a counsellor can be at best confusing and at worst conflicting for the religious client. Surely counselling is about making assumptions visible so they can be seen and if necessary challenged (p. 19).

Naturally this brings up practical questions regarding self-disclosure and ideological transparency from the therapist, as well as the need for therapists to familiarize themselves with more than one religious tradition in order to be aware of the client's reference points. Just as clients experience their lives and difficulties with their whole selves—through bodily, mental and, arguably, spiritual phenomena—therapists too can be encouraged not to leave these essential parts of their personal experience outside the consulting room, but to be as fully present and conscious of all aspects of self and client as the occasion of therapy and their own capacities permit. Therefore, while it is assumed that an absence of religious faith and personal commitment to a specific spiritual discipline in the therapist is not necessarily an impediment to effective clinical work, neither is its active presence in any way discouraged—on the contrary.

As discussed below, it may even be suggested that a certain compatibility in the quality of attentiveness exists between the supple mental alertness, or 'nepsis,'[9] traditionally required for spiritual contemplation, and the balance of 'evenly-suspended attention'[10] which

---

[9] 'Nepsis' is a term used in Orthodox spirituality to describe a state of alert watchfulness. Cf. Vlachos (1994a): "According to the holy Fathers, watchfulness (nepsis) is the presence of reason at the gateway of the heart, guarding against the entry of temptation and the creation of any precondition that might result in sin. Watchfulness is closely related to prayer [...] [since] attentiveness and prayer are the two spiritual weapons which constitute "philosophy in Christ." [...] True theology is neptic, and the real theologian is in essence neptic, since he must recognize all the secrets of the spiritual struggle and have discernment, which has been cultivated as a result of his own spiritual journey to health" (pp. 78–9). An important distinction between nepsis and evenly-suspended attention is that nepsis is used to discern the emergence of a chain of mental associations which enter the imagination, and subsequently to guard against the distraction it may cause; whereas evenly-suspended attention fosters these associations as 'clues' to what is going on in the unconscious.

[10] Bollas (2002) quotes Freud on this quality of listening required of the analyst, adding his own interesting comments:

> "*Experience soon showed that the attitude which the analytic physician could most advantageously adopt was to surrender himself to his own unconscious mental activity, in a state of evenly suspended attention, to avoid as far as possible reflection and the construction of conscious expectations, not to try to fix anything he heard particularly in his memory, and by these means to catch the drift of the patient's unconscious with his own unconscious.*" [...] In other words (Bollas continues), psychoanalysis works through unconscious communication. [...] Asking the analyst what he or she is thinking in the midst of listening to the patient would be akin to waking someone from a meditative state. [...] This [...] is a new form of creativity fostered only in the psychoanalytical space (pp. 12–14).

Although the above comments pertain primarily to process in Freudian psychoanalysis, active listening and relaxed attention can nevertheless be recognized as being generic to psychotherapy, employing perhaps the two hemispheres of the therapist's brain in equal measure. Jung borrowed a term from Janet, *abaissement du niveau mentale*, to describe the preparatory state which both patient and analyst need to enter into in order to engage with the process of ac-

encourages an imaginative engagement with the unconscious (as a response by the analyst to the analysand's free association), while at the same time it cannot be denied that on some level the psychoanalyst's ego does need to remain consciously with the client in the consulting room:

> The analyst sets himself the task of working 'without memory and desire' (Bion 1967), using 'free-floating' (Sandler 1992) or 'evenly suspended' attention (Freud 1912a) to listen effectively to his patient, to monitor his countertransference feelings and to address central concerns in a helpful way. He allows his mind to wander, reflects on why particular thoughts arise and tolerates feelings rather than avoids them. He tries in his self-monitoring to allow his thought patterns to be dynamic and fluid and to avoid intellectual rigidity. He oscillates between empathic primary identification … with the patient and objectivity, perhaps representing maternal and paternal roles respectively. He tries to strike a balance between silence and speaking and to vary the 'dosage' of interpretation appropriately (Bateman & Holmes, 1995: p. 159).

---

tive imagination in the transferential field. As Beebe, Cambray & Kirsch (2001) have pointed out,

> "Although Jung initially formulated his dialectical viewpoint to describe the way the conscious and unconscious interact in a person, he soon expanded this view to include the analytic process itself, in which he felt patient and analyst took turns being 'conscious' and 'unconscious'" (p. 232).

It is therefore also not surprising that Schaverien (2007) in a recent article speaks of 'countertransference as active imagination.' These dialectical skills and fundamental qualities of listening-attention, empathic relationship, and contact with what may be called the 'primitive,' 'mythopoetic' domain of consciousness are required from both psychological and spiritual practitioners.

What is immediately striking about the above description is the large number of tasks the analyst needs to employ in his inner dialogue between conscious and unconscious, his own and that of the patient. It may be expected, therefore, that a discipline which encourages the growth and cultivation of inner awareness — such as prayer, contemplation and meditation — will be facilitative of the analyst's / therapist's capacity for establishing and maintaining the deep, healing atmosphere of relationship with clients which is described above. It is then perhaps regrettable that few Freudian psychoanalysts may openly engage in these activities during their training analysis or with their analysands, as reported by psychoanalysts themselves (e.g. Simmonds, 2004).

CHAPTER FOUR

Jungian Psychology, Christian Theology and Other Discourses

The 'short and easy' answer to the question of examining Eastern Orthodox spirituality and Jungian analytical psychology in parallel, would simply be that the two disciplines ultimately meet at no point, and essentially have nothing constructive to say to one another. Eastern Orthodoxy is a traditional, and to some a conservative — even reactionary — form of Christianity, with a set of accepted doctrines and a defined, well-articulated body of dogma, founded on an unshakable belief in a transcendent God, a triune personal spiritual being Who nevertheless lives among us and within us and acts, intervening in everyday affairs through a spiritual process of cooperative synergy with humans. For Orthodox Christians, such categories as miracles, life after death, sacraments, etc. — are all words and concepts which signify ontologically real, historically current and future events and persons, and not the mere 'symbols' or 'metaphors,' as some Christians from other denominations, as well as some critics of religion, psychologists not least among them, like to suggest.

Jungian psychology on the other hand is, to quote a well-known writer on Jungian thought, at the very most only a sort of 'religion' *in statu nascendi* (Shamdasani, 1999)[1] — but one with a methodical, scholarly and above all *scientific* remit and framework of opera-

[1] Interestingly, writing from a post-Freudian psychoanalytic perspective Symington (1993) seems to mirror this idea of psychoanalysis being a 'religion in the making' — albeit a "natural religion" (p. 50) which addresses itself more to questions of how man should live, than to the worship of any revealed deity in particular.

tion, as understood and bequeathed by Jung, who himself could be seen as adopting a neo-Kantian empiricist philosophical position.[2] Where Orthodoxy sees the revelation of an absolute ontological reality, Jungian psychology will posit the 'psychically real,'[3] which makes no claim to the ultimate origin of phenomena, since all is seen to be mediated by the psyche:

> According to Jung, the psyche (and psychic reality) function as an intermediate world between the physical and spiritual realms, which may meet and mingle therein. [...] This means that the psyche appears to stand midway between such phenomena as sense impressions and plant or mineral life on the one hand and, on the other, intellectual and spiritual ideation [...]. Acceptance of the idea of psychic reality brings to an end the easy accep-

[2] Nevertheless, Lawrence Jaffe (1999) offers a good example of the way the Jungian 'myth' can replace traditional religion. He writes that:

> "The central idea of the Jungian myth is the redemptive power of consciousness. [...] *If we know ourselves we have an effect on God.* The relationship between the Jungian myth and depth psychotherapy now becomes clear, because depth psychotherapy promotes knowledge of ourselves more effectively than any other modern institution. Psychotherapy is an invention of the twentieth century; religions were the earliest psychotherapeutic systems" (p. 23).

Jaffe (*ibid*) calls the Jungian myth a "new religion of consciousness" (p. 24) and a "Psychological Dispensation," following on from the Hebrew Dispensation (Old Testament) and the Christian Dispensation (New Testament). This idea of a 'Third Age' is itself interesting, as it harks back to the heretical ideas of Joachim of Fiore, followed up by Eugene Vintras, and even the occult system of *Thelema* introduced by Aleister Crowley. It is present in Jung's own writings, such as *Answer to Job*, and Jaffe (*ibid.*) makes it a significant feature of the new religion, whose "major ritual" (p. 24) is depth psychotherapy.

[3] Cf. CW 8, par. 680, in which Jung states that "[a]ll our knowledge consists of the stuff of the psyche which, because it alone is immediate, is superlatively real." Jungian psychology may nonetheless be seen as having its own reluctant version of 'absolute reality'; Kelly (1993) identifies it as a 'complex holism' during which the wholeness of self is realized through the process of individuation.

tance of an inherent conflict between mind and matter or spirit and nature in which these are looked upon as radically different (Samuels, Shorter & Plaut, 1986, p. 118).

Despite these apparent differences, similarities have been pointed out in some of the assumptions underlying these divergent world-views. Archbishop Chrysostomos (2004) for example, discusses Jung's mysticism and suggests several significant structural similarities with Orthodoxy. These include:

1. Inclusive Cosmology:[4] striking a balance between the observable and the unknown ("transcendent," p. 98). Jung's use of the Kantian distinction between numenal and phenomenal may be compared to the Palamite[5] distinction between Divine essence and energies.
2. Use of Paradox: Jung conceives of the collective unconscious and of God as containing the sum of contrasting opposites, and speaks of *mysterium coniunctionis* and *coniunctio oppositorum*; Orthodoxy perceives God as both knowable and unknowable, both imminent and transcendent. In the Orthodox apophatic tradition of theology, God is known by contrast and paradox. Florensky (1997) offers perhaps the best theological expression of this, when *pace* Kant and Heraclitus, he articulates antinomy as the main principle of Christian dogma, perhaps predating Derridean reflections on identity (Collins & Mayblin, 1996) by several decades with his paraconsistent logical proof (cf. Letter 6, Contradiction; also Rhodes (2005)).
3. Ultimate Unknowability: Jung emphasized the unknowable nature of the archetypes; Orthodoxy holds religious images and symbols not to be in and of themselves the reality they

[4] The names for the categories of similarity are my own suggestions.
[5] Derived from Gregory Palamas (?1296-1359).

"bring into limited human cognition. Rather, they reach up to a real archetype [...]. Thus when the Holy Spirit descends as a dove, this is not a real "bird," though the image seen has spiritual properties, is perceived spiritually, and affects one in a spiritual way. These images are in the realm of spiritual energy, but are never isomorphic with the unknowable essence which is ultimately their source" (Chrysostomos, 2004, p. 99, see also further discussion on symbols below).

4. Fulfillment of Human Potential: in Jung, through individuation, in Orthodox theology through theosis (see below).
5. Transformation: In Jung, through expansion of consciousness by contact with symbols from the archetypal Self; in Orthodoxy through deep self-reflection in a process described as the 'mind entering the heart.'[6]
6. Spiritual Deception: in Jung, via the process of inflation; in Orthodoxy via *υψηλοφροσύνη* or spiritual pride in which one identifies oneself with a spiritual image.

To the above list may perhaps be added the similarity of such Jungian distinctions as 'personal' and 'collective' shadow, with 'personal' or 'ancestral' sin ('sin' and 'sinfulness' respectively) in Orthodoxy; and also between 'complexes' in Jungian psychology and 'passions' in Orthodoxy. Many other similarities in concepts may be suggested, some of which are perhaps generic to Jung's origins and general background in his broad reading of Christian theology; nevertheless, these particular concepts do also lend themselves to a comparison between their specialised uses in Orthodox spirituality and in Jungian psychology.

[6] E.g. St. Nicephorus of Mt. Athos, a 14th century solitary and spiritual father of St. Gregory Palamas describes this process in detail, and interestingly adds: "From the very fact that the [spiritual] director has suffered and been tempted himself, he will be able to explain to us what is required and will truly show us this spiritual way, which we shall therefore easily accomplish" (cited in Brianchaninov, 2006; p. 90). This connects strongly to the discussion below on creative suffering and the wounded healer.

Before going further however, it may be pertinent to outline some of the differences in the ways in which psyche or 'soul,' and 'spirit,' are respectively understood in theology and in analytical psychology. Abenheimer (1956) suggests that dynamic psychology bases its understanding of 'spirit' in what is experienced phenomenologically through the 'fundamental apperception' as "the dynamic interaction of animated subjects" (p. 1). According to this notion, we apperceive the world at a primitive psychological level as consisting of entities who are subjects with a will of their own. Hence, although we may know that anger is an emotion with specific psychophysiological correlates, when we get angry we do not experience ourselves primarily e.g. as being angry, but as being overcome at the experiential level by an entity called 'rage.' This entity, as Abenheimer describes it, is an hypostasization of the energy of anger. 'Spirit,' therefore, is the sum total of all these energy-entities:

> Just as in moral thinking every moral norm is experienced as the concrete application of the one summum bonum, so the Spirit is experienced as the subject of all the spiritual energies because it contains them all. It is their source and the symbol of their meaningful unity. Thus the Spirit becomes identical with the Godhead, e.g. with one Person of the Holy Trinity. A great many theological assertions on the Holy Spirit are true quite irrespective of the religious dogma; true in the sense that they are statements based on the inherent logic of the concept of the Spirit within the logical rules of fundamental apperception (Abenheimer, *ibid.*, p. 2).

According to this view, it can be seen that 'fundamental apperception' is perceived to be ontologically prior to any theological revelation, and indeed also to any scientific causal explanation, as Abenheimer notes. In a way, the spirit here is built up through a bottom-up process of sub-projections which are experienced as 'spiritual' energy-entities, but are in fact physiologically based. What then makes this manner of perceiving things more valid than spiritual illumination as described in religious writings, seems at best arbitrary. Abenheimer does acknowledge, however, that due to its theoretical commitment to the phenomenological mode of fundamental apperception, dynamic psychology is confined to a field of study which renders it incompatible with religion, or at best separate in its assumptions and conclusions, since it looks at phenomena from a different perspective. Hence also Samuels, Shorter and Plaut (1986) explain that:

> Jung applied the word 'spirit' to the non-material aspect of a living person (thought, intention, ideal) as well as to an incorporeal being detached from a human body (ghost, shade, ancestral soul). [...] In both instances, spirit is conceived of as the opposite of matter [...]. Spirit as the non-material aspect of man can neither be described nor defined. It is infinite, spaceless, formless, imageless. It lives of itself, neither subject to our human expectations nor the demands of will. It is *other* worldly or *non*-worldly, arrives unbidden, and the usual response is one of affect, whether positive or negative. [...] [Jung] gave credence to spirit but without stipulation of a creed (p. 140).

Giving credence to spirit without stipulation of a creed appears to lead, however, to the notion that a privileged position may be attainable with regard to interpreting the dogmatic spiritual positions held by others. Hence Lambert (1960) for example, suggests that, in contrast to the theologian, the analyst

> [...] is not handicapped by having his studies confined to the more collective phenomena of religion. Furthermore he gets involved personally in the religious development of the patient, sometimes finding himself treated as a divinity, and sometimes having his own religious position stimulated, activated, changed, enlarged, or even threatened by his relationship with the patient. Secondly, he has the opportunity of understanding and partici-

> pating in the personality development of the patient and sometimes he can gain an understanding of the intimate relationship between this and the patient's real religious position. Thirdly he is in the unique position of being able to realise how religious and "metaphysical" imagery and symbolism arise spontaneously from the unconscious of the patient, and cannot be regarded as mere contrivances of the conscious ego. [...] analysts can discern an intimate relationship between personality development and the spontaneous religious imagery of the person involved. This can be seen even when the profession of the person is theology itself, i.e. his spontaneous religious imagery may be found not to correspond to his conceptualized or dogmatic beliefs (p. 134).

Lambert (*ibid.*) does point here to an important variable in theological formation, namely that of personality development as a major influence on the ability to theologise. Far from being a notion which is new to theologians, however, this may actually be the reason why a strong emphasis has always been placed in Orthodox theology on 'purification of the mind' prior to the formulation of theological opinion.[7] The discrepancy which the analyst observes between 'subjective' religious imagery arising spontaneously in the patient, and the objective religious truths encased in dogmatic formulations, may in this sense be a phenomenon of the existing spiritual lack of clarity within the patient's own psyche, rather than any indication of radical theological truth being communicated by the collective unconscious. Indeed, given the stringency by which true theological insight is measured in the Orthodox Church (the title 'Theologian' only ever

[7] St. John Cassian, to quote just one example, writes that "The reason such great differences and mistakes have arisen among commentators is that most of them, paying no sort of attention towards purifying the mind, rush into the work of interpreting the Scriptures, and in proportion to the density of impurity of their hearts form opinions that are at variance with and contrary to each other's and to the Faith, and so are unable to take in the light of truth" (quoted in Pennock, 1973, p. 10).

having been granted to three saints[8]), this same ubiquitous observation, which is found throughout Orthodox thought, may equally call into question the analyst's psychospiritual state or condition and her ability to correctly assess the personal and collective parameters of the patient's imagery in a theologically discerning manner.

For his own good reasons, Jung strongly disapproved of, and resisted the transformation of his psychological system into a doctrine.[9] Many analytical psychologists, however, taking perhaps to a further extreme Jung's own ambivalent attitudes on the topic of religious dogma, are strong proponents of adopting a completely sceptical approach to *all* dogma, religious or otherwise, and advocate commitment to an ideological flexibility and intellectual rigour (or perhaps rigidity) which involves being critical in all matters of faith, to such an extent as to preclude the possibility of any religious belief informing psychological work. Mogenson (2005), for example, writes that

> Despite the comparisons drawn between the analyst's couch and the priest's confessional, the difference between the two is perhaps more significant. When he examines the engagement of

[8] St. John the Beloved, St. Gregory Nazianzen, and St. Symeon the New Theologian. No other Orthodox saint has been described thus, although of course both saints and non-saints have written coherently about God, each to the best of their ability. The rarity of the use of this epithet, shows the esteem in which theology is held by the Orthodox Church, and confirms the significance of scriptural passages such as Matthew 5:8.

[9] "It is a particular satisfaction to me that the author has been able to avoid furnishing any support to the opinion that my researches constitute a doctrinal system. Such expositions slip all too easily into a dogmatic style which is wholly inappropriate to my views. Since it is my firm conviction that the time for an all-inclusive theory, taking in and describing all the contents, processes and phenomena of the psyche from one central viewpoint, has not yet arrived, I regard my concepts as suggestions and attempts at the formulation of a new scientific psychology based in the first place upon immediate experience with human beings. This is not a kind of psychopathology, but a general psychology which also takes cognizance of the empirical material of pathology" (Jung, 1939, in his foreword to Jacobi(1962, p. ix)).

> theology, the psychologist cannot help wondering if theology has placed the needs of the soul secondary to its own need to justify the ways of its root metaphor "God." Even those theologians who fastidiously attempt to keep themselves open to the phenomenon of suffering work from an essentially closed perspective in that their thinking is committed from the outset to the service of what they already believe on instinct. For the theologian, the premier psychological question — "What does the soul want?" — takes a backseat to the premier theological question — "What does God demand? (p. 10).

It may be argued that the adoption of such an "essentially closed perspective" on *either* side of the psychology / theology debate would, in fact, inevitably result in a diminished ability to help others, whether one is a psychologist or a priest. Whether investigating human phenomena from the perspective of a psychologist or that of a theologian, there is therefore nearly always a need to keep oneself 'open to the phenomenon of suffering,' and it is, as mentioned previously, in this spirit of openness that an attempt is made here to respectfully navigate this complex theoretical territory, with due significance given to the underlying epistemological tensions already mentioned.

The explicit claim made in the above statement by Mogenson, moreover, concerning the presumptive character of theological thinking, may at least in part be due to a categorical reasoning error, in that the *tools* used to solve problems are by definition not the same as the *solutions* to the problems themselves. This logical principle may be said to apply equally to both theological and psychoanalytic categories of understanding. Theologians therefore may attempt to understand and explore phenomena such as human suffering using theological concepts such as salvation, the eschaton, sacrament, etc., or by referring to the particular teachings and experiences of saints and to the life of Christ, to the Theotokos, and other holy figures — but does this make theological conclusions regarding the nature and purpose of human suffering necessarily biased or untrue? If such is deemed to be the case, then a need arises to explain what it is that makes the utilization of theological concepts and the reference to historical religious figures or narratives, less 'scientific' or intellectually viable than the deployment of other such 'root metaphors'[10] as instincts, complexes and archetypes, the psyche or the unconscious. Indeed, Mogenson (1994) himself seems to acknowledge the weakness in his argument, when he writes that

> One grounds upon which the concept of the collective unconscious may nevertheless by criticized is that it is an abstract God or "God of Gods" and, as such, an impossibly higher order concept, illegitimately ontologized to be the realm of the others (pp. 132–137).

Is the explanation of phenomena with reference to the lives, activity and theoretical writings of near-legendary historical figures like Zosimos of Panopolis or Paracelsus, or actual psychologists such as Freud and Jung, or James Hillman, itself proof of scientific reliability or validity? In fact, was Jung's own wondering which myth he lived by (MDR, p. 195), not itself a covert indication of his awareness of the circumscribed historical relativity of his own perspective and theories?

Jung's friendship and correspondence with the English Dominican, Victor White (Arraj, 1988; Lammers, 1994) was strained to breaking point as a result of the latter's methodical attempt to connect

[10] The assault on classical ontology which Hillman's post-jungian archetypal psychology represents, is the tradition in which Mogenson (via Giegerich) writes of 'root metaphors.' In this perspective, 'concretistic thinking' is pathological, and the ability to think metaphorically is seen as the defining feature of mental health: "Psychopathology can be generally defined by one catchword: *concretism*, taking psychological events such as delusions, hallucinations, fantasies, projections, feelings, and wishes as actually, literally, concretely real" (Hillman, 1996, p. 240). As discussed below, apart from begging the question of its own ontic foundation as a theory of psychic life, this perspective cannot therefore respond to fundamental questions concerning the nature of existence; perhaps in this much it is philosophical heir to a dualistic Gnostic docetism within analytical psychology.

analytical psychology with Catholic theology. Indeed, although Jung, like William James, can be seen as one of the few pioneers of psychology who genuinely embraced the healing potential of the spiritual and religious dimension of human experience, nevertheless the ambivalence in Jung's writings towards metaphysical truth-claims has led to suspicion and mixed responses from religious scholars. Von Franz (1998) says of the numerous theological criticisms of Jung's opus, that

> Seen in a certain perspective it is striking that the criticisms [...] although coming from such different directions, nevertheless all come back to the same point: namely, to Jung's unwillingness to espouse absolute metaphysical truths (p. 194),

and she goes on to quote Jung himself:

> [...] It seems to me advisable [...] in view of the limitations of human knowledge to assume from the start that our metaphysical concepts are simply anthropomorphic images and opinions which express transcendental facts either not at all or only in a very hypothetical manner (CW14, par. 781).

The careful reader will notice here, however, that Jung does not discount the possibility of metaphysical truth—only the human capacity to comprehend it; in fact, Jung's subtle and complex attitude towards metaphysical truths, like Nietzsche's who preceded him (Storr, 1996b), can only be balanced by considering some of the other statements which number among those he frequently makes about metaphysics. Of the afterlife and the eternity of the psyche, for example, he writes:

> Now whether these are in the last resort absolute truths or not we shall never be able to determine. It suffices that they are present in us as a "bias," and we know to our cost what it means to

> come into unthinking conflict with these truths. It means the same thing as the conscious denial of the instincts – uprootedness, disorientation, meaninglessness, and whatever else these symptoms of inferiority may be called. [...] Deviation from the truths of the blood begets neurotic restlessness, and we have had about enough of that these days. Restlessness begets meaninglessness, and the lack of meaning in life is a soul-sickness whose full extent and import our age has not as yet begun to understand (CW8, par. 815).

Jung appears to be saying that whether or not religious claims are true, they represent basic tendencies in the human psyche which are ignored at a psychological cost to ourselves. And of the whole purpose of analytical psychology itself, he importantly states that

> [...] the main interest of my work is not concerned with the treatment of neurosis, but rather with the approach to the numinous.[11] But the fact is that the approach to the numinous is the real therapy, and inasmuch as you attain to the numinous experience, you are released from the curse of pathology. Even the very disease takes on a numinous character (Jung, 1976: Vol. 1, p. 377).

Jung does not by any means dismiss the reality of metaphysical truths, these "anthropomorphic images" which he nevertheless feels strongly enough about to call "the truths of the blood"; it is perhaps only the suggestion that the particular cultural human symbols to be found in individual religions can claim *to be identical to and sufficiently exhaustive of* the metaphysical truths they are attempting to express, which Jung criticises, and he therefore roundly proposes that only the psychological experience of the numinous, as expressed in symbols, is open to scientific study. As Fontana (1993, 2003) asserts however,

[11] It seems significant that the term 'numinous' which Jung frequently refers to, should come from the writings of the Protestant Christian philosopher of religion, Rudolf Otto (1958). See below for further discussion.

> If this explanation [of Jung's] sounds as if it reduces the gods — or God — to figments of our collective imagination, this is not so. For it does not deny that the collective unconscious may be in communication with an even deeper substratum of reality that represents the true creative source of our individual lives. Jungians say that we must recognize that this source, when discovered, can only reveal itself to us in a limited, and limiting, symbolic form (pp. 38–9).

It may therefore be said that Jung and analytical psychologists after him have not so much resisted the suggestion that God exists, as much as the 'temptation' to name Him; yet it seems vital to emphasize, that the idea of God is not necessarily 'merely' anthropomorphic imagery or projection as some psychoanalysts seem to suggest. Whatever the acknowledged philosophical objections, it is perhaps plain to any reasonable observer that *something* has existed before the self, exists outside the self, and will continue to exist after the personal self has passed away. We may imagine that we're dreaming it all up, and that it will all cease with us when we die, but what prevents us also asking how mature that is as a fantasy? Personal existence, Jung perhaps implicitly agrees, is patently contingent upon the hypostasis of this mysterious Being of a superior order to the personal self, however we choose to describe or designate It; therefore humans are both dependent, and mortal.

One may ask why this thought, namely that our possession of consciousness is purposefully structured, hard-wired, designed towards the production of some manner of a response[12] to the Being

[12] The relatively new field of neurotheology may be relevant to this discussion of the relation of religiosity to our animal nature. This special affinity of man to the animal kingdom is acknowledged in Orthodoxy, but viewed very differently from the way in which such scientific authors as, i.e. Dawkins (e.g. 1976; 1989) have viewed it. Writing in a pastoral context, Ware (1988) suggests that "The human animal is best defined, not as a logical or tool-making animal or an animal that laughs, but rather as an animal that prays, a eucharistic animal, capable of offering the world back to God in thanksgiving and intercession."

whose consciousness and identity surpasses our own, should be considered any less mature than the potentially solipsistic notion that, as far as humans are concerned, the universe exists because we exist to give it being and meaning through our conscious awareness of it, and what we call 'God' is in fact a projection of our own inner intelligence upon an otherwise quite silent, inanimate and indifferent screen.

Also with regard to anthropomorphism, psychoanalytic authors such as Jacoby (1985) have suggested that the presence of myths in many world cultures, relating to the existence of a perfect world which is free from conflict and suffering, is itself evidence for the existence of an archetype of Paradise, which is ultimately based on the symbiotic unitary reality experienced by the infant within the womb. What is to refute, however, the possibility that the fact that most cultures have an idea of 'paradise' may instead be due to a genuine longing for our true home, the Promised Land ordained by God? If 'Paradise' is a metaphor for the state of consciousness of the embryo in the womb, what is to say that this state of blissful symbiotic consciousness which we attribute to the embryo, is not itself a biopsychological metaphor and symbol for the condition of Eden which the actual phyletic memory of our soul recalls? Like the zen master who awoke wondering whether he was the butterfly he had seen in his dream, or the man dreaming of a butterfly, it may be that what we designate as *anthropo*morphism is in fact a result of the *theo*morphic nature of human consciousness!

Indeed, in many of his writings Jung arguably *can* be seen to have a notion of God, albeit a non-Orthodox one. Jung's 'deity' is an unconscious being:

> The naive assumption that the creator of the world is a conscious being must be regarded as a disastrous prejudice which later gave rise to the most incredible dislocations of logic (CW11; p. 383, fn. 13).

(p. vii). Nellas (1987; 1997) also reminds us of how the Church Fathers viewed man as a *zoon theoumenon*, or "deified animal" (p. 15).

Human consciousness for Jung is the 'eye' of creation, and necessary to God; yet God resists the insight man has to offer, as Jung goes on to clarify elsewhere:

> Existence is only real when it is conscious to somebody. That is why the Creator needs conscious man even though, from sheer unconsciousness, he would like to prevent him from becoming conscious (1954; 2002, p. 11).

This unconscious being is served by man, in that man offers 'it' the opportunity to become conscious; furthermore, man does this by increasing his own consciousness:

> That is the meaning of divine service, of the service which man can render to God, that light may emerge from the darkness, that the creator may become conscious of His creation, and man conscious of himself (MDR, p. 338).

Consciousness is clearly the supreme moral and metaphysical value here, both for man and for the deity, which Jung refers to as God. In his key theological work, *Answer to Job* (1954; 2002: CW11), Jung uses the story of Job as a paradigm in which man's moral superiority to his 'creator,' as suggested by his undeserved suffering, leads eventually to this unconscious being's increased self-knowledge. Jung writes that, after making Job suffer,

> There can be no doubt that [God] did not immediately become conscious of the moral defeat he had suffered at Job's hands (1954; 2002, p. 51).

It is difficult not to regard this image, of man being burdened with the responsibility of making God conscious, as a potentially self-serving philosophy for a person who is resistant to repentance. Man is perceived here, not as the sinner in need of redemption, but as the redeemer of God—divinity seeks 'its' own redemption in the form of self-awareness through the creature's awareness, and via a sort of Augustinianism-in-reverse, God then brings 'its' 'Original sin' of ignorance to man, who renders service by shedding light on God's own darkness for God. Though ultimately unfair, it is tempting to view the motivation behind this formulation through an *ad hominem* prism of biographical conjecture about Jung's own possible resistance to any unconscious guilt he may have felt, even in his mature years, with respect to his duplicitous private life, given his Swiss Christian background and early conditioning.

Man's mission in Jung's theological model is not therefore, as in Orthodox Christianity, to be the priest of creation—a living soul raising material creation up to God through his ascetic life, to be transfigured in a eucharistic sacrifice of praise; instead, man is to be the priest of God (or God's analyst perhaps), bringing 'it' in touch with a creation 'it' has unconsciously emanated—essentially 'it' *is* the creation, creation being best theologically conceived in Jung's understanding via a sort of polytheistic pantheism as *anima mundi*, a universe crowned by human consciousness, which becomes the 'tiny light' in Jung's dreams (MDR, pp. 107–8), the 'second creator of the world' which grants their existence to the 'silently eating' creatures in the African bush (see MDR, pp. 284–5). Consciousness for Jung is therefore both God and above God, indeed in a sense the whole of Psyche is God, the *anima mundi*, and everything is in the Psyche. Orthodoxy cannot accept this perspective on God at face value, since as Sophrony (1973) writes,

> God did not create the world in order to live the life of the creature: He created it in order to associate man with His own Divine Life. [...] Correspondingly, when man, conscious of his divine vocation, contemplates the work of the Creator, he is seized with a wonder which, while giving him a very vivid perception of everything in the created world, at the same time draws him away from every created thing for the sake of contemplating God (p. 99).

In Orthodox tradition, God is not viewed as being in need of anything from man. The service, e.g. of Divine Liturgy, is entirely for man's benefit, as are all the sacraments and prayers of the Church. While sacrifice is offered to God through Holy Communion therefore—by exception among all the sacraments (Kokkinakis, 1975: p. 110)—it is offered in full consciousness of the fact that "Thine own of Thine own we offer to Thee, in all (time) and for all (kindness to us)" (Elias, 1966; 1984: p. 165). Thus the priest first prays for God to make him "[...] worthy to offer these Gifts to Thee. For Thou art the Offerer and the Offered, the Receiver and the Received [...]" (*ibid.*, p. 135, 137), and it is God Who thereby makes the offering through His people, by the hands of the priest.

Man in Christianity is therefore viewed as a bridge, or link, between God and creation, being as it were the only personal hypostasis among his visible creatures. In a sense perhaps, Jung's understanding of human consciousness as the eyes, ears, and mind of nature, is from a Christian perspective correct; what differs is that the *telos* of human consciousness in Christianity is to participate in the glory of God, culturing the elements of a fallen and disordered nature[13] back into a harmonious garden by the living water of grace, which is itself unlike anything within creation. Creation is therefore saved alongside man, and this salvation is the work of God in synergy with human freedom (Gregorios, 1987).

In contrast, by rendering the relation between God and man on an intrapsychic level, Jung skirts close to solipsistic psychologism (e.g. Vitz, 1977; 1994: p. 4), and perhaps loses the very sense of the "wholly Other" which he borrowed from Otto (1923; 1950, pp. 25–30) since the "numinous" in Jung could thus be said to be rendered into a merely egoic experience, or more precisely, the result of an encounter between the ego and the psychic unconscious. Although Jung frequently describes the archetypes as having a numinous quality, this quality is

[13] "Because he is created in the image of God, man is [...] a person who is not to be controlled by nature, but who can himself control nature in assimilating it to its divine Archetype" (Lossky, 2002; p. 120).

primarily the result of their encounter with the limited resources of the ego, the 'sparks that fly' as the archetypes meet consciousness — there is thus, in terms of logical necessity, nothing *inherently* numinous about the collective unconscious, since nothing is really "wholly Other," everything being ultimately only perceptible within the psychic reality. Jung perhaps eludes being placed in the category of pure psychologism through his formulation of such concepts as synchronicity, the *unus mundus* and the psychoid unconscious, which offer a potential bridge between psychology and physics, man and creation; yet is this appreciation for the empirically uncanny, comparable in its depth and its affirmation of the transcendent and the wholly Other with Orthodox theology, or is it almost a form of modern psycholatry,[14] a worship of the soul, its operations and its properties? The question may concern both whether and what the soul can perceive beyond itself, and a religious perspective usually affirms both. Indeed, writing from a perennialist perspective, a philosophically distinct approach to universal metaphysics which does not share either Orthodox or Jungian assumptions, Stoddart (2005) states that:

> The central fault of Jung and other modern psychologists is their confusion of Intellect and soul (or indeed their complete exclusion of Intellect) (p. xii).

What Stoddart refers to as 'Intellect' above, may be equated to what will be discussed later as the *nous* in Orthodox tradition. This ultimately anthropological question is perhaps controversial, and the claim that Jung's formulation does not fully appreciate the depth and otherness of the numinous is dismissed by most Jungians, who

[14] A term used by Max Müller (1882; 2000: p. 119) to describe reverence for the spirits of the departed; it is being used here in its etymological sense as worship, *latreia*, of the soul. As Moran (1996) writes, Jung's "conflation of psychic forces with genuine mysticism," means that "[h]is solipsistic psyche-ism [sic] condemns him to the contemplation of his own inner universe. There is no Other to bring risk, vulnerability, and the dynamic of personal love" (p. 143).

point to the archetypes as the very source of numinosity, since they effectively identify the collective unconscious with 'God'[15] in asserting that there can be no practical distinction between 'God' and the *imago Dei*. Nevertheless, regardless of the human capacity to perceive it, numinosity in Otto's sense derives from the inherently "wholly Other" nature of God's being,[16] so it is this author's contention that the word 'numinous' as used by Jung, is semantically differentiated from Otto's original term in this context.

> [...] from Jung's perspective, commerce with divinity, removed from the skies, is now to become a wholly intra-psychic reality describing the interior dialectic of the ego with the unconscious under the orchestration of the self. When Jung's total work is weighed and considered [this understanding] prevails. The unconscious creates the Gods and spirits wholly out of is own archetypal resources, and the evolution of human religious consciousness and its attendant spirituality is presently coming to realize this fact (Dourley, 2006, p. 4).

Jung did not simply conclude that man is therefore the inventor of Gods, who themselves do not exist, as this would have been too unsophisticated a conclusion from a thinker of his stature. As Dourley (*ibid*) suggests, he instead replaced what he saw as the myth of monotheism, with a new myth for modern man:

> Jung's myth revisioned humanity's relation to the divine as the ground movement of the psyche in which both the divine and

[15] "The world of gods and spirits is truly 'nothing but' the collective unconscious inside me" (CW 12, par. 857, p. 525).

[16] The truly 'mysterious' object is beyond our apprehension and comprehension, not only because our knowledge has certain irremovable limits, but because in it we have come upon something inherently 'wholly Other' [...]. [...] By this 'nothing' is meant not only that of which nothing can be predicated, but that which is absolutely and intrinsically other than and opposite of everything that is and can be thought" (Otto, 1923, 1950, pp. 28–29).

> the human are inescapably implicated from the outset in the conferral of mutual redemption on each other. The dissolution of the distant and perfect Gods foreshadowed in the book of Job evolved into the growing contemporary realization that God and reality at some point coincide. Jung puts it this way, "It was only quite late that we realized (or rather, are beginning to realize) that God is Reality itself and therefore last but not least man. This realization is a millennial process (CW 11, par. 631, p. 402) (Dourley, *ibid*, p. 5).

God, therefore, for Jung is identical with Reality and with man. He is not "wholly Other" — indeed, in Jung's theology, the ancient Gnostic claim that we are all gods reemerges[17] — gods, but of the same substance, *homoousioi*, with Christ; we are *by nature* 'divine,' and at the same time we are called (or, more correctly in Jungian terms, driven by our religious instinct) to become more conscious of our innate divinity, just as so many New Age spiritualities proclaim today through the doctrine of the Higher Self (Heelas, 1996). Nevertheless, Dourley correctly — if rather begrudgingly — notes that "The extension of divinity to humanity universal and the implied extension of the sacred to all that is remains unacceptable to the Church" (2006, p. 9). It should be noted that Dourley, both a Roman Catholic priest and a Jungian analyst, himself represents perhaps the theoretical gulf which exists between an Orthodox viewpoint and some Western Christian perspectives, since his uncritical defense of the Jungian myth would not be tenable in Orthodox terms, and indeed it has not escaped the notice of Orthodox authors (cf. Christensen, 1999: pp. 204–5).

As has already been suggested and will be explored further later in this book, Jung's theological myth also impacts the significance of suffering in human lives, since as Dourley (*ibid*, pp. 19–20) explains from his Jungian perspective:

[17] Cf. also John 10:34.

> When this sweeping vision [Jung's description of the transcendent function in Answer to Job] is taken to the personal level it means that the most intense suffering in an individual's life is an incarnation in that life of some aspect of the divinity's self-contradiction seeking relief in that suffering. To the extent such suffering is well born and issues into a higher consciousness it redeems both the divine who suffers in it and the human who suffers through it.

While always ambiguously negotiating the boundary between a metaphysical and a psychological world-view in his writings, Jung believed that the reason man experiences moral conflict is because God Himself is somehow divided. Below is a characteristic remark from one of his letters, indicating Jung's rich but idiosyncratic analogy of his own spiritual experiences to those of the 11th century Orthodox Christian saint, Symeon the New Theologian:

> I had to wrench myself free of God, so to speak, *in order to find that unity in myself which God seeks through man*. It is rather like that vision of Symeon, the Theologian, who sought God in vain everywhere in the world, until God rose like a little sun in his own heart ... The outcome [of conflict within God] may well be the revelation of the Holy Ghost out of man himself. Just as man was once revealed out of God, so, when the circle closes, *God may be revealed out of man* (italics mine; reference untraced, but see also CW 11 par. 267).

From this paragraph alone, it can be seen that Jung considered God to be divided in himself, and seeking resolution to his divine inner conflict through the human individuation process. Therefore, where traditional Christian theology has maintained that man grows by becoming more aware of God, Jung seems to reverse this by suggesting that God grows by becoming more aware through the increased consciousness man alone can offer in service to him. As Anthony Stevens (2001) writes:

> Jung's whole life was an expression of a truly protestant quest — a spiritual journey away from the moribund church of his clergyman father to encounter the living God as a personal revelation in the Self. He believed that by committing himself to his individuation through engaging the symbols emerging from his dreams and 'active imagination' he was not merely extending his own consciousness but enabling God to become more conscious of what he created! 'That is the meaning of divine service, of the service which man can render to God, that the Creator may become conscious of his creation, and man conscious of himself' (Jung, 1963) (p. 112, reference in original).

What, however, is the mechanism whereby increased consciousness in man becomes an increase in consciousness also for God? How is the new awareness communicated from the human mind to the divine? The answer to this may come from considering the significant semantic and philosophical difference which exists between Jung's evolutionist, 'bottom-up' approach to the concept of God, and the traditional Christian theological understanding of man's 'top-down' creation by and origin in God.

The evolutionist approach represents in some ways a characteristically 19th century conflict, which assumes the greater could somehow emerge from the lesser, and has carried over into our own times in the 'integral' theories of Teilhard De Chardin and Ken Wilber. From an Orthodox philosophical perspective, Bp. K. Ware states Sherrard's (1998) objection to this point of view, namely that:

> [...] Jung went astray [...] in accepting the presuppositions of Darwinian evolution; in affirming, that is to say, 'From below, upwards' rather than 'From above, downwards.' Instead of seeing human personhood as God-sourced, Jung interpreted it in terms of the unconscious; and this he regarded as our 'prehistory,' the 'earliest evolutionary stages of our conscious psyche,' to use his own words. Thus, whereas in the Christian view human

> consciousness has its roots in the divine, for Jung it is rooted in the animal world; and so, when he uses the word 'archetype,' he does so in a sense profoundly different from that ascribed to it by Christian Platonists (in Sherrard, 1998: p. xxxiii).

As will be discussed below, the question of an answer to the specific problem of suffering — his own and that of the whole world — greatly influenced Jung's implicit theology. A very different response to the question of suffering may be obtained, depending on whether one views it from the perspective of an evolutionist collective unconscious seeking resolution of internal contradiction through the transcendent function of consciousness, or via an awareness of our human response to the intentional creative will of a personal deity. Jung's thought addresses an important area of theological concern, by offering responses to such traditional theological puzzles as why God, the sum of all perfection, created human beings whom He foreknew would fall from His grace — in other words, why did a Perfect Being create an imperfect being? If our freedom is part of His Image in us, then why didn't God also give us the wisdom to know how to resist temptation, and the emotional strength to do so on every occasion? Indeed, Lucifer was also His most splendid angel — why did God create him in such a way, that Lucifer would abuse his freedom through susceptibility to pride? Why didn't God create a cosmos that was perfect and never went wrong in any way?

C. S. Lewis (2001, p. 225) suggests that God didn't want to create beings which run like robots or clockwork, unable to love freely. God's nature being boundless Love, it was therefore impossible for Him not to permit the option of falling, even though in His omniscience He knew this would happen. Indeed, as the Orthodox author Thomas Hopko (2006) boldly writes:

> My personal view is that the Bible speaks of God's providential activity as being his *will* in the sense that God *willed* to have a world in which creatures corrupt His good creation. He *willed* to make

> angels who He knew would make themselves demons. And He willed to make human beings who He knew would deform their humanity and that of their children and neighbours, and who would corrupt the world as a whole. God knew all this and He did it anyway. In doing so, the Lord decided to use wicked creatures, both human and demonic, as well as evil acts and events, for His beneficent providential purposes (p. 46, italics same).

If freedom is truly free, then the option of sin is *necessary* to it, even if it is never recommended or beneficial in itself. Nevertheless, there is admittedly something almost casuistic about such arguments; they don't satisfy the (proud?) need for complete understanding, and they send naturally questing minds like Jung's into spiralling cycles of ambivalence and doubt.

Perhaps simple faith is another way of accepting the sorry state of affairs which is the human condition, the 'argument from authority' being that God doesn't have to share all his secrets with us, His children. This argument was closer to Jung's father's approach to faith,[18] but it not only frustrated his intelligent son's need for explanations, it also perhaps caused Jung to later hold the view that "[p]eople who merely believe and don't think, always forget that they expose themselves to their own worst enemy: doubt" (CW 11:170). Fideism generally seems to encourage a certain attitude of dependence on our

[18] Stein (1999) writes that "[Jung] grew up in a parsonage, but his early experience of Swiss Reformed Protestantism left him cold. To him it seemed like a lifeless institution without either much intellectual honesty or spiritual vitality. While he maintained a correct relation with the Reformed Church throughout his life — being baptized, married and buried in it, having his children do likewise, etc. - he did not seek to find any further spiritual benefits from this source. [...] Perhaps a different parson father would have been a greater positive influence on him" (pp. 10–11). It may be interesting too, to note that Schuon (in Soares de Azevedo (ed) 2005, p. 18) suggests that, among protestant denominations, the Lutheran, Calvinist and Anglican Communion could, with some reservations, be "covered by a valid archetype," whereas the Zwinglians and liberal Protestants are characterized by "ambiguous intentions" and "human arbitrariness."

behalf as humans, whereas it can reasonably be asked whether that is what God wants — or does He want us to stand on our own two feet, while loving Him and depending on Him in an adult way? However mature humans become, of course, Christian theologians remain aware that we are still His children, and therefore in a sense never 'equal' with Him, since as mentioned above, in Orthodox theology He is not understood as needing anything from anyone (though He may want something). With us created beings, however, it is different; so a 'mature dependence' — to use a psychoanalytical term (Fairbairn) — would seem an appropriate response to God, but does this mean 'ask no questions'?

In his work taken as a whole, Jung can be seen to have asked: could God possibly be 'working on it'? Did he create an imperfect creation ('very good,' but not perfect), because it was His first time round? Does He need our assistance in order to now perfect the work He started? Also, if God gave us trials, as Christianity suggests, so that we can love Him back truly, not automatically, is He then so insecure, that He needed to make sure we wouldn't just worship Him because He had created us that way? Or is it only 'for our own good,' so that we may freely love Him in return for His love, rather than being compelled by 'nature' to do so? Jung's questions are indeed probing and profound, and reading between the lines of such works as *Answer to Job*, it may be tentatively suggested that, in contrast to Job who refused to curse God and die (Job 2:14–15), Jung felt quite angry at God's mysterious ways, and his 'protestant quest' led him both to a rejection of traditional Christianity and to a renewed examination of the origins of faith.

It is interesting therefore to compare the Jungian understanding of 'spirit' as discussed above, with an equivalent Orthodox set of definitions from *The Orthodox Study Bible* (1993).[19] The concept of 'soul' for example, is defined as

[19] But see also Chirban (1996). Definitions from the OSB are selected here for their simplicity and popular use, bearing in mind the considerable academic discussion of these terms in theological literature.

> SOUL: A living substance, simple, bodiless, and invisible by nature, activating the body by which it brings life, growth, sensation and reproduction. The mind is not distinct from the soul but serves as a window to the soul. The soul is free, endowed with will, and the power to act. Along with the body, the soul is created by God in His image. The soul of man will never die (Gen. 1:26; 2:7; Matt. 10:28). (p. 808)

Immediately below 'soul' in the same text, 'Spirit' is then defined as:

> (Gr. *Pneuma*) Literally "breath"; that which is living but immaterial. *Spirit* is used in three ways in Scripture: (1) The Holy Spirit is one of the three Persons of the Trinity (John 4:24; 20:22). (2) The angels are called spirits (Ps. 104:4). (3) The human spirit possesses the intuitive ability to know and experience God (Rom. 8:16; 1 Cor 2:10–12). (*ibid*)

Finally, it may be relevant to look also at the Orthodox definition of 'symbol':

> In Orthodox usage, the manifestation in material form of a spiritual reality. A symbol does not merely stand for something else, as does a 'sign'; it indicates the actual presence of its subject. For example, the dove is the symbol which brought to Jesus the descent of the Holy Spirit (Matt. 3:13–16). (*ibid.*)

It can immediately be seen that there is much in the above three definitions which is similar to the equivalent ones provided by Jungian psychology; perhaps the essential point of difference, however, is that where Orthodox theology posits the ontological reality of the entities it describes, analytical psychology aims to confine itself to their phenomenological description alone. Hence 'symbol' in Jungian psychology is, as in Orthodox theology, more than a sign; but rather than placing emphasis on its function as the manifestation in material form of an underlying spiritual reality, Jungian psychology assigns to the symbol "the best possible description or formulation of a relatively unknown fact, which is nonetheless known to exist or is postulated as existing" (Jung, CW 6:814). And whereas for Jung, intuition is the irrational function which apprehends possibilities in the present via the unconscious, in Orthodox spirituality it offers immediate spiritual knowledge and experience of God.

The question of which came first however, God or the psyche, seems more than anything else to delimit the boundary between a theological appraisal of human being, and one couched in terms acceptable to analytical psychology. Indeed, in her discussion on the role of fantasy in religion, Bregman (1975) draws attention to the interpreter/experiencer divide which characterises the psychological approaches to religious symbolism, and humorously but pertinently points out how:

> The specific contents assigned to fantasies, what they are *really* about, seem determined by the theoretical bias of the psychologist. Monotonously, Freudian thought on religious symbols or any other symbols discovers sexual organs and longed-for parents everywhere. Jungians, who see fantasies expressed through archetypes, guiding the person towards individuation, are equally monotonous in substituting "the Self" for every religious symbol of divinity or totality (p. 724).

Additionally one may perhaps ask, if analytical psychology simply points to the unknown and leaves it thus, as in Jung's above definition of the symbol, by what authority does it then *dis*qualify the assertions of Christian dogma? Indeed, how can it assert that the psyche is 'real'? If the unconscious is the prime arbiter of everything consciousness is capable of realising, what is to preclude a future collective disclosure that Christian dogma is, in fact, the correct interpretation of things? Ulanov (2008) may therefore correctly suggest that

> The image lies at the heart of the symbol, and symbol lies at the heart of faith, as we celebrate in every recitation of creed or ritual action (in Ulanov & Dueck, 2008: p. 38).

It also becomes clear from the above, that what passes the strictly 'scientific' criteria for knowledge according to the current consensus in the 'hard sciences,' such as the notions of experimental validity and reliability, and even the stringent Popperian standards of falsification, come up against serious epistemological obstacles when the 'data' of both Orthodox theology and of analytical psychology is under investigation. In a chapter of seminal importance on Jungian epistemology, Papadopoulos (2006) highlights the tension which exists in Jung, between an open-ended 'Socratic-ignorance' which is empirical and phenomenological in character, and a closed, pre-established approach to knowledge which Papadopoulos terms 'Gnostic epistemology. He writes:

> It is not difficult to identify Jung's 'Socratic ignorance' as it coincides with Jung's own way that he characterised himself and with the way he has been characterised by almost all Jungian authors. What has not been examined often is Jung's opposite epistemological stance that he also followed, evidently without him being aware of its antithetical direction; this was termed 'Gnostic epistemology' [...]. According to this epistemology, Jung was by no means open and his researches followed his own pre-established ideas about phenomena and, although he always waved the empiricist 'Socratic-ignorance' banner, in fact, his approach also included closed and predetermined epistemologies (p. 45).

It seems important from a metatheoretical perspective to hold on to the epistemological tensions which may arguably characterise most living bodies of human knowledge—if not all—despite frequent claims to the contrary, and may especially underlie the genuine but naïve belief that no assumptions are being made (as in Socratic ignorance, phenomenological epoché, etc.). Hence there are perhaps four possible general attitudes one can adopt in the contemporary understanding of the relationship between psychology and religion[20] (Gaist, 1998, unpublished):

1. *Psychology vs. Religion*: Psychology has superseded religion in its understanding of human development and potential, and all religious anthropology is now therefore a defunct set of ideas from an ignorant, superstitious past.[21]
2. *Religion vs. Psychology*: Psychology having failed to offer a unified central paradigm for man, leaves religion as still the

[20] To some extent this whole debate may be viewed as artificial since, as Bodhakari (2008) writing from a Buddhist perspective explains, concerning 'psychology,' 'philosophy' and 'religion' "It is also worth bearing in mind that these three distinct categories are a relatively modern conceptual division" (p. 30); this would certainly also apply to research in a Christian context.

[21] Perhaps as a result of the troubled relationship of science and religion in the West, even eminent contemporary scientists and public figures continue to negate and devalue religious experiences. In *The Man who Mistook his Wife for a Hat* (1985), Oliver Sacks dedicates a whole chapter to explaining away the visions of Hildegard von Bingen (1098–1180) as "indisputably migrainous" in origin. Of religious visions in general he writes: "it is impossible to ascertain, in the vast majority of cases, whether the experience represents a hysterical or a psychotic ecstasy, the effects of intoxication, or an epileptic or migrainous manifestation" (p. 160). It would almost seem as if science here finds itself inadvertently committed, with an almost fundamentalist insistence, to explaining everything through the principle of parsimony, to the invalidation even of the possibility of true religious experience. William James (1982) referred to this reductionist tendency as 'medical materialism,' already in his 1902 classic, *The Varieties of Religious Experience*: "Medical materialism seems a good appellation for the too simple-minded system of thought which we are considering. Medical materialism finishes up Saint Paul by calling his vision on the road to Damascus a discharging lesion of the occipital cortex, he being an epileptic. It snuffs out Saint Teresa as an hysteric, Saint Francis of Assisi as an hereditary degenerate. George Fox's discontent with the shams of his age, and his pining for spiritual veracity, it treats as a symptom of disordered colon. Carlyle's organtones of misery it accounts for by a gastro-duodenal catarrh. All such mental overtensions, it says, are, when you come to the bottom of the matter, mere affairs of diathesis (auto-intoxications most probably), due to the perverted action of various glands which physiology will yet discover" (p. 13).

only authentic and permissible way to address the question of human nature, personal integrity and destiny.

3. *Psychology and/or Religion*: The findings and insights of psychology and religion confirm each other without any serious conflict, or alternatively are addressing entirely separate areas of human experience that do not need to be in dialogue.
4. *Psychology with Religion*: Psychology and religion can inform and enrich each other by each providing a separate but connected and cross-fertilising arena of informed opinion, and different methods for consideration of each other's paradigms.

This study hopes to demonstrate that although it may be currently intellectually legitimate and permissible to hold any of the first three attitudes above, in the light of a fully contemporary and postmodern understanding of the human situation, all three are untenable in the final application. The more complex fourth approach described above, leaves perhaps many questions unanswered, but it is also arguably more open and epistemologically sincere. It can offer psychotherapists who try to expand the theoretical vocabulary with which they aid and facilitate psychological growth in their clients, a useful heuristic, cultural and hermeneutic conceptual tool and a source of inspirational perspective in the discipline of theology. Simultaneously, it can equip theologians and clergy of all denominations with the language and ways of talking about the human self[22] that are appropriate for communicating spiritual hope to a psychologically sophisticated intellectual culture, without the unquestioning importation of logically unclear, ahistorical, and philosophically

[22] Taylor (1992) persuasively argues that the modern turn inwards to subjective experience does not inevitably lead to solipsism or nihilism, and is in fact rooted in ideas of human good, providing a viable alternative to traditional notions of reason which were based on social hierarchies of birth and wealth. Perhaps analytical psychology and other modern ways of talking about the self, may therefore be to some extent compatible with traditional religious perspectives, if not with traditional social arrangements.

incompatible 'psychobabble' into Christianity. In the poetic words of Clement (2000):

> Contemporary man is an orphan. He has no roots outside of time and space. He feels lost in an infinite universe. Having descended from primates he moves towards nothingness (p. 6).

Both psychology and religion, being addressed to the human condition, therefore may be said to share in the ethical responsibility to help orphaned contemporary man find a home in the modern world. Yet it would be impossible to do this without first becoming aware of the spiritual climate in which modern man finds himself.

1 **Pre-Revolutionary Russian Religious Philosophy.** Those Russian religious philosophers whose creative intellectual activity began in the years prior to the Communist Revolution of 1917, included such major thinkers as Vladimir Solovyev (1853–1900), Sergius Bulgakov (1871–1944), Pavel Florensky (1882–1943), Nicolai Berdyaev (1874–1948), and others such as Nicholas Lossky (1870–1965) and Semen Frank (1877–1950). Their ideas involved a meditation on the implications of Western post-Enlightenment thought meeting with Orthodox Tradition, but also a philosophical articulation of that tradition which simultaneously sought to extend, develop and enunciate some of its latent theological trends—trends which these great intellectuals recognized as being of significance to the modern world. In their bold attempts to reconcile apparent opposites, they often veered towards unconventional theological views, and some, like Bulgakov, were even condemned by certain groups of their contemporaries.[23] Nevertheless, they can be seen today as

[23] In 1935, the Council of Sremsky-Carlovtsy, attended by several bishops and convened and presided over by Metropolitan Anastasius, condemned Sophiology as preached in the Parisian school by Bulgakov. Sophiology was understood as the doctrine that *Sophia* does not refer to Christ alone, but is a separate feminine personality, the soul of the world, a fourth hypostasis in the Holy Trinity,

late precursors of "liberal Orthodoxy" (Sergeev, 2003), and unquestionably some of the most creative theologians of the twentieth century—and it is fair perhaps to add that some of their philosophical speculations should be read with caution as to their dogmatic implications by devout Christians, especially those new or not fully established in their understanding of the faith. Notwithstanding such implications, these rich and powerful ideas, set within an appropriate framework, can still be very relevant to the possibility of dialogue between Orthodoxy and contemporary thought.

2 **The Influence of Boehme.**[24] The Jungian analytical perspective in particular, especially in its ontological implications (such as Jung in his empiricist zeal consistently resisted articulating), lends itself remarkably well to comparative study with the works of these philosophers, and not without historical reason. Solovyev, who introduced the concept of Sophia as a central preoccupation of this branch of religious philosophy, was familiar with the work of the protestant mystic Jakob Boehme (1575–1624), who was also an important influence on Jung.

Boehme, a shoemaker in the East German town of Görlitz, experienced visions when still in his mid-twenties which he felt revealed to him the spiritual structure of the cosmos, and prompted him to write on mystical themes using bold notions which caused his work to be perceived as heretical. Boehme was a theosophist, following in the vein of Gnostic spirituality. He was influenced in his theological speculations by alchemy, Paracelsus, and Neoplatonic philosophy, and his writings subsequently influenced the spirituality of such nonconformist religious groups and teachings as the Society of Friends

---

even replacing God the Father with a "mother-goddess" based on an amalgam of Platonic philosophy, cabbalistic teachings, and Valentinian Gnosticism. This was taken so seriously that the council declared the Parisians (under the Ecumenical Patriarchate) to be bereft of grace; these historical interpretations however, are perhaps contestable from a pan-Orthodox perspective.

[24] Spelling used as given in Hinnells (1984;1995: p. 78).

(Quakers, via George Fox, their founder) and Theosophy,[25] but also importantly, another significant influence on Jung, the German Romantic philosophers such as Schelling.

Wilson (1984) vividly describes the first of Boehme's spiritual visions:

> When he was twenty-five, he had his first great experience of mystical insight. His gaze was attracted by a dark metal dish, whose polished surface reflected the sunlight; the brilliance of the reflection sent him into an ecstasy, and a strange sensation overpowered him; it seemed that he was looking into the heart of all nature, and could suddenly understand the world and the whole meaning behind it. He went out into the fields, and the same vision remained with him; he felt as if he could see into the heart of the trees and the grass, as if they were made of glass and lit from within. [...] Paracelsus had taught that the essence of things could be seen by the visionary: 'we may look into Nature in the same way that the sun shines through a glass' (pp. 153–4).

Generically, theosophy is the knowledge of divine things, or literally "the wisdom of God." As a term in the history of religion and philosophy, it designates a group of several different and sometimes cognate bodies of thought, experience and ideas originating in Late Antiquity. The Greek term is found on early magical papyri, and also appears in Neoplatonism; Porphyry, in De Abstinentia mentions "Greek and Chaldean theosophy" (*θεοσοφία*). The adjective *θεόσοφος*, "wise in divine things," is significantly applied by Iamblichus to the Gymnosophists, i.e. the Indian yogis or sadhus. The 6th century Orthodox saint and Bishop of Athens, Dionysius the Areopagite, also

[25] H. P. Blavatsky founded the Theosophical Society in 1875 with Henry Steel Olcott, William Quan Judge, and others. The word 'theosophy' was revived by her to designate her religious philosophy, maintaining the foundational New Age tenet that all religions are attempts by humanity to approach the absolute, and that each religion therefore has a portion of the truth.

uses the term in his Theologica Mystica (1.1), which is sometimes regarded as a neoplatonist-influenced text. The *Penguin Dictionary of Religions* (Hinnells, 1984; 1995: 523) defines theosophy as

> [...] any system of thought concerned with divine revelation as its basis and whose central experience is of an inward illumination by the spirit of God. The wisdom takes God as its principle and seeks to apprehend the universe, in all its aspects as they are in God. It claims to embody these truths as belonging to all religions, but many manifestations of theosophy fall short of this ideal [...]. The word sometimes refers to esoteric philosophy known as 'the ancient wisdom' or theosophy. It can describe any articulate mystical system; it has been applied especially to Kabbalah, Neoplatonism and the system of Jakob Boehme (p. 523).

The word was revived early in the 17th century (in Latin, *theosophia*) to denote the Renaissance occultism of Cornelius Agrippa, Paracelsus, Robert Fludd and others. As the above definition suggests, the name 'theosophy' was applied specifically to Boehme's writing, who showed at least stylistic influence by the Renaissance "theosophists"; Boehme's writing shows the influence of neoplatonist and alchemical writers such as Paracelsus, while remaining, arguably, within a Christian tradition. It was also an important source for German Romantic philosophy, as well as Enlightenment theologian Emmanuel Swedenborg. In the Canadian psychiatrist's Dr. Richard Bucke's (1905) influential treatise on cosmic consciousness, special attention was given to the profundity of Boehme's spiritual enlightenment, which seemed to reveal to Boehme an ultimate nondifference, or nonduality, between human beings and God.

A cursory glance at Boehme's teachings will make their influence on Jung's thought immediately apparent, since Boehme appeared to depart from more orthodox theology in his description of the Fall as a necessary stage in the evolution of the universe. In Boehme's cosmology, it was necessary for humanity to depart from God, and for all original unities to undergo differentiation, desire, and conflict—as in the rebellion of Satan, the separation of Eve from Adam, and their acquisition of the knowledge of good and evil—*in order* for creation to evolve to a new state of redeemed harmony that would be more perfect than the original state of innocence.[26] This also allowed God, thought Boehme, *to achieve a new self-awareness by interacting with creation* (vide *Answer to Job*), which is both part of, and distinct from God Himself. In Jung's own words:

> The visionary genius of Jacob Boehme recognised the paradoxical nature of the God-image and thus contributed to the fur ther development of the [Jungian] myth. The mandala symbol sketched by Boehme is a representation of the split God, for the inner circle is divided into two semicircles standing back to back (MDR, 1995, p. 366; words in brackets mine).

Boehme saw the incarnation of Christ, not as a sacrificial offering to cancel out human sins, but as an offering of love for humanity, showing God's willingness to bear the suffering that had been a necessary aspect of creation. He also believed the incarnation of Christ conveyed the message that a new state of harmony is possible. This was somewhat at odds with Lutheran dogma, and his suggestion that God would have been somehow incomplete without the creation was even more controversial, as were his emphasis on faith and self-awareness rather than strict adherence to dogma or scripture. Almost all of these theological notions can be found in Jung's own speculative works, particularly later texts such as *Answer to Job* and *Mysterium Coniunctionis*. Boehme, an original thinker, nevertheless drew on existing philosophical and mystical streams, and this influence came to bear on Orthodox Christianity both directly, through the work of philosophers like Solovyev, and indirectly through Kant (1724–1804)

[26] The Orthodox Bishop Irenaeus (d. 202) also wrote of the primary state of innocence as immature, but did not perceive the Fall as a necessary stage in the growth of humanity.

and neo-Kantian German idealist[27] influences on Russian thought.

Influenced by the Romantics, as well as leaning towards the Roman Catholic faith, the religious philosopher Vladimir Solovyev did not merely import Boehmian ideas into Orthodoxy, but actually experienced visions of Sophia himself, first when he was a boy aged 9, then twice in a single year as a young man in his twenties. In his later work, he came to understand these "3 Meetings" (the title of one of his poems) as being experiences of encounter with the Mother of God, whom he came to identify with the figure of Sophia; this brought his mature thinking somewhat further in line with Orthodox tradition. His earlier attempts to convey the nature and character of Sophia, however, certainly touch graphically on Jungian notions concerning the role of the anima in the human psyche, as well as the *anima mundi* in the cosmos, especially if Jung's notions of psychic reality, the psychoid level and the unus mundus are contextualized within their philosophical status as having an ontological value beyond the metaphorical.

3 **Dogma, Science and Psychoanalysis.** While not everyone in contemporary western society may, by any means, subscribe to the New Age movement, chapter 1 nevertheless aimed to outline some of the ways in which the neo-Gnostic formulations of New Age spirituality have been influential on the prevailing parameters of the spiritual *zeitgeist* in postmodern societies. One important factor which lends spiritual kudos to New Age-style spiritual ideas, is perhaps precisely their perceived lack of dogmatism, which is frequently contrasted by both scientists and adherents of heterodox spiritualities to the purportedly inflexible dogmas of traditional religion.

As an important response to the frequent objection that religion is circumscribed in its helping potential and its theoretical significance by its allegiance to credal dogma, it may be useful to note here

[27] "[...] historians of philosophy usually declare that Boehme was the father of German Idealism — especially Hegel's variety" (Wilson, 1984, p. 156).

that Jung, while being himself an opponent of doctrines and dogmatism in science as suggested above, is rarely as critical of actual religious dogma as some of his disciples[28] and also his critics have been; at least not in the same way. His enthusiastic response to the Roman Catholic proclamation of the dogma of the Assumption of the Virgin Mary by Pope Pius XII in 1950 is a case in point.[29] In this proclamation Jung detected an increasing popular awareness and appreciation of the mother archetype, as it has been encased in Christian dogma[30]

[28] "If, therefore, in what follows I concern myself with these "metaphysical" objects [archetypes], I am quite conscious that I am moving in a world of images and that none of my reflections touches the essence of the Unknowable," (CW 11:556). Jung remains open to spirit, since, as previously suggested, for Jung the psyche actually lies at the interface of matter and spirit, however idiosyncratically—from a theological perspective—he actually interprets both these terms. It seems therefore an oddly disloyal development of Jungian ideas on behalf of some post-Jungians like Giegerich (2003) to proclaim the 'end of meaning' by suggesting that "as long as the symbol is alive its meaning is still unborn" (p. 2), hence interpreting Jung as proclaiming the necessity for symbols, which are by definition rich in ambiguity, to 'die' in order for their meaning to be born. Giegerich likens the spiritual 'womb' of "myths, meanings, ideas, images, traditions" (p. 4) to "another state of unborness, another childhood" (p. 5); in its place he suggests 'extending' the classical Jungian position concerning the value of symbolic existence, to a set of "truth, norms, values, [which are] fundamentally contingent, subjective, human, all-too-human" (p. 20). It may be legitimate to ask where this post-Nietzschean, post-Hegelian philosophical manoeuvre—albeit itself arguably based on a scriptural metaphor (cf. Jn. 12:24), and certainly involving an implicit metaphysic—would leave any room for the fertile ambiguity in symbolic imagination which Jung himself is an advocate of. Giegerich's theory seems to leave no window open for spirit to enter the chamber of the heart.

[29] "The Christian nations have come to a sorry pass; their Christianity slumbers and has neglected to develop its myth further in the course of the centuries. [...] The only ray of light is Pius XII and his dogma" (MDR, p. 364).

[30] This observation appears to be borne out in contemporary writings on popular spirituality such as the following passage from Harvey & Baring (1996):

> "In her humanity, in her human suffering as the mother of Jesus, Mary brings the divine world closer to human experience, closer to human longing and human suffering. Only Demeter in the Greek world is as human as Mary. As all the Great Mothers did before her, Mary embod-

(Samuels, Shorter & Plaut, 1986). Indeed, of Christian dogma in general, Jung has written that:

> "The edifice of Christian dogma [...] undoubtedly stands on a much higher level than the somewhat wild 'philosophoumena' of the Gnostics. Dogmas are spiritual structures of supreme beauty, and they possess a wonderful meaning which I have sought to fathom in my fashion. Compared with them our scientific endeavours to devise models of the objective psyche are unsightly in the extreme" (Buber-Agassi, 1999, pp. 65–66).

As Stephenson (2004) suggests, Jung's own writings were often intentionally ambiguous, skirting the issue of metaphysical reality, while not rejecting it outright.[31] Moreover, they offer some evidence that he

---

> ies the principle of relationship, the relatedness of the whole of creation to every aspect of itself and to the divine ground that enfolds it. As the Divine Mother, she speaks for the values of the heart, the values that spring from the deepest instincts and feelings in all humanity. So Mary is, in the Christian experience of her, the most intimate and human of Mothers, as the offerings to her in thousands of shrines bear witness. Mary's suffering as a human woman who has given birth to a son, seen him grow to maturity, and lived through the terrible experience of seeing his life sacrificed to human cruelty makes her the sharer of the suffering of all women who have been through the same agonizing experience. Mary's experience makes human suffering bearable because she, as intercessor, is present with it. But if we look at the Christian myth in a deeper sense, we can understand that as the Divine Mother, Mary endures the suffering of the whole of humanity, her "child," until at last we return "home" to her in the divine spheres" (p. 12).

To what extent such writings, and those following the publication of *The Da Vinci Code* (Brown, 2003) are themselves the result of the popular propagation of Jungian ideas is pertinent to the discussion on Jung as an ancestor of the New Age movement (see section below).

[31] "The psychologist can criticize metaphysics as a human assertion, but he is not in a position to make such assertions himself. He can only establish that these assertions exist as a kind of exclamation, well knowing that neither one nor the other can be proved right and objectively valid, although he must ac-

did see value in religious dogma, especially for its role as the cultural manifestation of archetypal psychic reality. For example, Jung states that

> "The archetypes of the unconscious can be shown empirically to be the equivalents of religious dogmas. In the hermeneutic language of the Fathers the Church possesses a rich store of analogies with the individual and spontaneous products to be found in psychology" (CW 12:20).

Jung as a free-thinking democratic Swiss, feared dogma for the rigidity he perceived in its proponents, considering that this rigidity can act as a barrier to the spontaneous play of imagery in the human psyche. Nevertheless, on another level he also appreciated and in his own manner actually demonstrated a more thoughtful approach to dogma, one which does not shun the tension of opposites contained in paradox, or reject this spontaneous play of imagery. Elsewhere he therefore states:

> "We simply do not understand anymore what is meant by the paradoxes contained in dogma; and the more external our understanding of them becomes the more we are affronted by their irrationality, until finally they become completely obsolete, curious relics of the past. The man who is stricken in this way cannot estimate the extent of his spiritual loss, because he has never experienced the sacred images as his inmost possession and has never realized their kinship with his own psychic structure. But it is just this indispensable knowledge that the psychology of the unconscious can give him, and its scientific objectivity is of the greatest value here. Were psychology bound to a creed it would not and could not allow the unconscious of the individual that

---

knowledge the legitimacy of subjective assertions as such. Assertions of this kind are manifestations of the psyche which belong to our human nature, and there is no psychic wholeness without them, even though one can grant them no more than subjective validity" (CW 10:845).

free play which is the basic condition for the production of archetypes. It is precisely the spontaneity of archetypal contents that convinces, whereas any prejudiced intervention is a bar to genuine experience" (CW 12:19).

Jung's complex thesis regarding dogma seems to reflect on the need for a natural and organic psychological understanding of the place of dogma in religion itself. Theologians also know and realize that dogma is useful in delineating the boundaries of truth, but simultaneously appreciate that the mystery of God — the *numinosum* in Jungian terms — is actually experienced as an inner phenomenon by the saints and mystics at the level of spirituality, a phenomenon taking place far beyond the conceptual level of human language in which traditional dogma is couched and formulated. Elder Sophrony, for example, writes that:

> "Every human being is a unique and original phenomenon. Every ascetic's course is likewise unique and original. [...] We cannot penetrate into the mystery of the spiritual life of a man. All we are able to do is to observe certain phenomena in the inner life of a religious man, when these phenomena materialize into psychological expression. We may note certain external characteristics but we can determine nothing of the essence, since the root of each and every Christian psych-religious fact is the absolutely unrestricted action of the Spirit of God" (1973, p. 20).

What we know, and are able to formulate in the language of Church dogma, about spiritual experience, is already therefore at one remove from the event itself, an *a posteriori* psychological fact. Hence, too, the Orthodox author Andrew Louth (1976; 1983) argues that academic theology and spirituality *necessarily* meet and inform one another in the process of contemplation. He writes that:

> "[...] much of the division in theology is simply a reflection of the division in our culture: the specialization in theology, the

remoteness of theologians—often complained of—from the Church and the believing Christian [...] are all part of a phenomenon we see much of elsewhere and have come to regard as inevitable. One way in which the division in theology manifests itself is in the division between theology and spirituality, the division between thought about God and the movement of the heart towards God. It is a division of mind and heart, recalling Eliot's 'dissociation of sensibility,' and a division which is particularly damaging in theology, for it threatens in a fundamental way the whole fabric of theology in both its spiritual and intellectual aspects. [...] Even if God can be reached by reason, even if natural theology is possible, real theology could never be confined within such narrow limits" (1983, pp. 2–3).

If Christian dogma therefore, is articulated in precise, academic 'textbook' formulations which are seemingly experience-distant,[32] this impression is probably the result of a failure on behalf of theologians to bring across the full extent of the practical implications of their discipline, as it is experienced in contemplation and prayer. This 'dissociation of sensibility,' to use Eliot's term as suggested above by Louth is, or should be, far from the case in Eastern Orthodox theology, where, as Lossky writes (2002)

> "The eastern tradition has never made a sharp distinction between mysticism and theology; between personal experience of the divine mysteries and the dogma affirmed by the Church" (p. 8).

The categories of 'theology' and 'mysticism' in fact do not even make sense when they are opposed to each other in Orthodox thought, where the apophatic character of all spirituality essentially

[32] It is perhaps fair to add here that such exercises in systematic theology have been much more prevalent in Western Christianity, particularly since the writing of the *Summa* of St. Thomas Aquinas, than they have ever been in the East.

implies that God becomes more *in*comprehensible, the more He is known. Lossky (*ibid.*) immediately continues:

> "The following words spoken a century ago by a great Orthodox theologian, the Metropolitan Philaret of Moscow, express this attitude perfectly: 'none of the mysteries of the most secret wisdom of God ought to appear alien or altogether transcendent to us, but in all humility we must apply our spirit to the contemplation of divine things.' To put it another way, we must live the dogma expressing a revealed truth, which appears to us as an unfathomable mystery, in such a fashion that instead of assimilating the mystery to our mode of understanding, we should on the contrary look for a profound change, an inner transformation of spirit, enabling us to experience it mystically. Far from being mutually opposed, theology and mysticism support and complete each other. [...] If the mystical experience is a personal working out of the content of the common faith, theology is an expression, for the profit of all, of that which can be experienced by everyone. Outside the truth kept by the whole Church personal experience would be deprived of all certainty, of all objectivity.[33] It would be a mingling of truth and of falsehood, of reality and of illusion: 'mysticism' in the bad sense of the word. On the other hand, the teaching of the Church would have no hold on souls if it did not in some degree express an inner experience of truth, granted in different measure to each one of the faithful" (pp. 8–9, italics mine).

Jung is therefore probably correct in identifying the primal, experiential basis of all dogma;[34] where he radically departs from the

[33] This use of the word 'objectivity' on behalf of a theologian, may be interestingly compared with Jung's above claim for the scientific objectivity of the psychology of the unconscious, CW 12:19. Lossky refers to the 'whole Church' for the source of objectivity; Jung's reference is to 'scientific objectivity.'

[34] It is well to recall that the word 'dogma' derives from Greek, *dokein*, which

Christian understanding of dogma however, is in granting ontological *priority* to the archetypes themselves, by suggesting that the contents of theological dogma are only expressions or particular instances of underlying archetypes. Effectively, therefore, for many interpreters of Jungian psychology, such figures as Jesus and the Buddha constitute only particular cultural symbols of an underlying and much broader *typos* or imprint, and are thus interchangeable for one another in the objective, 'scientific' understanding of human experience. Even if this is in some sense true at a psychological level, it is not acceptable to Christians at an ontological level, a level of being which itself transcends[35] the psyche and can only be accessed, in Christian terms, through a lived relationship with and commitment to God. Sherrard (1990) clarifies this point further, and suggests what may be part of the Orthodox response to the Jungian notion of the primacy of the psyche, where he writes that:

> "'The presence of God is [...] the initial and ultimately unique presupposition of the sacred, for the simple reason that without that presence there is no sacredness anywhere. This means that if, for instance, earth, nature, life, art or anything else is sacred, this is because it is the expression or revelation of something infinitely more than itself, something which it but discloses or manifests. It is not because it is sacred in its own right, apart from this Other that it enshrines, still less because we make it sacred" (pp. 1–2).

In the Christian understanding, therefore, the power which underlies theological dogma is none other than that of the Divinity in which this dogma has its ultimate origin, and not any characteristic intrinsic to the human psyche. Sherrard continues:

means 'to seem,' 'to appear.'

[35] "For if our heart condemns us, *God is greater than our heart*, and knoweth all things" (1 John 3:20, italics mine).

> "If, then, something in the physical or psychological realm — the realm in which we experience the greater part of what we do experience — is sacred, this is because God, the wholly Other, has irrupted into or ingressed upon it. [...] This posits a theme crucial to the understanding of the sacred: the theme of the transcendent" (p. 2).

In fact, in his espousal of archetypes as the *primal* organizers of meaning in the human psyche, Jung runs the risk of divesting the psyche of the broader cosmic environment in which it operates — a path leading perhaps into the solipsism Jung has been accused of,[36] and which a close reading of his work nevertheless negates, through the careful appreciation of his formulation of the concept of the Self as central archetype and organizing principle in the psyche; hence Jungian analyst Ann Ulanov is able to write with insight that

> "More than three decades of clinical work have brought me to the clarity that the Self, in Jung's jargon, is not God, but is that within us that knows about God. Another way to put this is that the Self in us is one of the complexes that make up the psyche, and it functions as a bridge to reality that transcends the whole psyche" (Ulanov & Dueck, 2008, pp. 33–34).

Despite his attempts to be clear on the issue, the lack of clarity which Jung introduces through his writing on the concept of the Self — collapsing it at times with the 'God-image'[37] — suggests a theoretical difficulty in maintaining the important distinction between the

[36] Vitz (1994), for example, writes convincingly that "Jung's discovery of religious symbols is important, but there is with all this focusing on one's inner life a real danger of substituting the psychological experience of one's religious unconscious for genuine religious experience that comes through a transcendent God who acts in history. Those who make this mistake have truly treated psychology as religion" (p. 4).

[37] 'As the highest value and supreme dominant in the psychic hierarchy, the God-image is immediately related to, or identical with, the Self' (CW 911, par. 170)

imago Dei and God as such; in fact, three different notions seem to be at the root of the confusion: God as man perceives Him, man as God's image, and God as He truly is. Hence too, the very interesting proposition of analytical psychology that the 'God-image' undergoes transformation with the passage of aeons, becomes an assumption that gives precedence to the cultural zeitgeist, constructs of the time based on the spontaneous manifestation of archetypes, as if the actual deities themselves were interchangeable, and any claim to their objective truth value is simply excluded as untenable. Overemphasis on archetypes as the exclusive sources of meaning and experience also places analytical psychology dangerously close to the same category of disembodied spirituality as that taught by Plato and Origen (cf. Vlagkioftas, 2007), whose realm of Platonic Ideas the Orthodox Church responds to with severe censure, and for precisely the same reasons as Sherrard (*ibid.*) suggests above. Hence Vlachos (2008) writes:

> "'The 'Synodikon of Orthodoxy' does not stay on a theoretical plane but also proceeds to concrete topics which it condemns. And, as will be discovered, it refers to basic teachings of philosophy, of so-called metaphysics. Among these is Plato's teaching about ideas. According to this notion, there are the ideas, and the whole world is either a copy of these ideas or a fall from these ideas. According to Plato, man's salvation lies in the return of his soul to the world of the ideas. In the 'Synodikon of Orthodoxy,' the holy Fathers condemn this view and those who accept 'the Platonic ideas as true.'"[38]

The world seen in Christian terms is not a copy of eternal ideas, and Christianity cannot be reduced to Idealist philosophy, even if this philosophy can occasionally be useful in elucidating certain themes pertaining to it, but which lie outside the focus of the current inves-

[38] Fromhttp://www.pelagia.org/htm/b12.en.the_mind_of_the_orthodox_church.09.htm, accessed 7/04/08.

tigation. God's creation, including the human psyche, in the Christian understanding is fundamentally *real*, not a figment of the human imagination, nor even a projection of the Divine mind—however much theologians do perceive the cosmos as being dependent on God's sustaining providence. Hence, writing on the Platonic element in St. Augustine, Stamps (2008) further describes how:

> "Against all heretics ancient and modern, the Orthodox Church has argued that the dividing line between the Uncreated and what the Triune God has created ex nihilo is the most fundamental distinction in the universe, not the Platonic difference between what is intelligible and what is sensible. St. Gregory certainly didn't share Augustine's enthusiasm for Platonic forms! Recall also that the Eastern Orthodox Church condemns Plato's Ideas ("Anathema, anathema, anathema!") during the Sunday of Orthodoxy."[39]

The dividing line between Uncreated and created is objective and macrocosmic, whereas that between what is intelligible and what is sensible is subjective and ultimately microcosmic. As Moss (2004) explains,

> "For the Platonists, reality is immaterial; so that matter must be unreal. For the Stoics, reality is matter; so that the immaterial must be a refined kind of matter. [...] Christianity has solved these dilemmas by teaching that the immaterial God created the material universe out of nothing, which both preserves the reality and the goodness of that universe, and distinguishes it from God Himself. As a result of the fall, created reality tore itself away from union with uncreated reality, God, and corrupted itself; but through the incarnation of the Word the different realities of the Creator and His creation were reunited without divi-

[39] From http://conciliarpress.pinnaclecart.com/index.php?p=page&page_id=again_stamps_augustine, accessed 7/04/08.

> sion or confusion in the Person of Jesus Christ. And at the end of time all men who have received and retained Christ in themselves will be united in the whole of their transfigured natures, including their bodies, with the immaterial God" (p. 8).

Far from being experience-distant therefore, a lived relationship between man and God in the Christian understanding cannot at all be based on cognitive or even depth psychological events alone; the whole objective being—body, soul and spirit—is necessarily involved. Yet this is a sacramental, transfiguring experience which obviously cannot be communicated in purely verbal terms; therefore, Christians are in a sense obliged to assert its truths verbally in terms of belief:

> "If there is a collective subconscious that points in the direction of a transcendent being, if there are teachings about avatars or incarnate divine beings, other "sons of God," if there are other myths about creation and fall, other myths about cataclysmic floods, other stories about virgin births, then all of these are like strings that resonate, sometimes more, sometimes less, with one grounding note, whom we *believe* to be none other than Jesus himself, the eternal Son of God, in whom all things hold together" (Bouteneff, 2006, p. 18; italics mine).

In the above paragraph, the word 'believe' does not suggest that Christians take it on trust alone, that all the spiritual phenomena being described here are based in the miracle of the Incarnation, just because the Bible, or their interpretation of it, tells them so. Instead, what is being witnessed through such accounts is the genuine communal and personal experience which Christians share amongst themselves within the community of the Church, of Jesus Christ as anointed saviour of the world: God Himself is experienced as the source of faith in the Orthodox Church. Orthodoxy believes that God has revealed Himself to us, most especially in the revelation of Jesus

Christ, whom Orthodox Christians really come to know personally as the Son of God. This revelation of God, His love, and His purpose, are constantly renewed and made manifest in the contemporary life of the Church by the power of the Holy Spirit. The Orthodox faith does not therefore even view itself strictly as a 'religion,' in the sense that it is not premised on human religious speculations, or on "proofs" for the existence of God (however much a coherent rationality and solid basis for faith can in fact be found in such philosophical arguments), nor on any other kind of human quest for the divine. It is the understanding of the whole Orthodox Church that God approaches mankind first, and subsequently it is in the prayer and sacramental life of the Church where He can be most fully encountered.

The origin of the Orthodox Christian faith itself is therefore appreciated as being nothing less than the self-disclosure of God.[40] Each day the Church's Morning Prayer affirms this and reminds

[40] Although God's self-revelation in history through the chosen people of Israel — a revelation which culminates in the coming of Christ the Messiah — is of primary importance to the Orthodox, it is, as suggested above, also the doctrine of the Orthodox Christian Church that all the genuine strivings of men after the truth are fulfilled in Christ. Truth is indeed to be found outside the Christian Church, because it is written into human nature, but every genuine insight into the meaning of life is perceived to find its perfection and completion in the Christian gospel. Thus, several holy fathers of the Church taught that the yearnings of pagan religions and the wisdom of many philosophers are also capable of serving to prepare men for the doctrines of Jesus, and they are indeed valid and genuine ways to the one Truth of God, if not destinations in themselves. Furthermore, connected to this understanding is the fact that Orthodoxy teaches that if we want to hear God's voice and see God's actions of self-revelation in the world, we must purify our minds and hearts from everything that is wicked and false, we must strive to love the truth, to love one another, and to love everything in God's good creation; therefore, according to the Orthodox faith, purification from falsehood and sin is the way to the knowledge of God (notice again, practical mysticism and propositional theology are not in conflict with each other). If we open ourselves to divine grace and purify ourselves from all evils in this way, then Orthodox theology promises we will be able to interpret the scriptures properly and come into living communion with the true and living God who has revealed Himself and continues to reveal Himself to those who love Him.

Christians of it by declaring: "God is the Lord, and He has revealed Himself unto us. Blessed is He that comes in the name of the Lord."[41] While the inner Being of God always remains unknown and unapproachable, God has manifested Himself to mankind; and the Church experiences Him as Father, Son, and Holy Spirit. He has shown Himself to His creatures, and while He has not disclosed His very innermost being—since as was previously suggested, this innermost essence of God, the Uncreated, cannot be grasped by creatures—God has nevertheless truly and demonstrably shown what men *can* see and understand of His divine nature and will, each (as the above quote by Lossky also suggests) according to his own capacity for this.

The doctrine of the Holy Trinity, for a particular example, which is so central to the Orthodox Faith, is held not to be a result of pious speculation or rhetorical invention and philosophical argument, but the overwhelming outcome of the *experience* of God, even if it was only fully articulated by the Cappadocian Fathers (Basil, John Chrysostom and Gregory Nazianzen; cf. Meyendorff, 1987, pp. 44–45). As is well known, the doctrine affirms that there is only One God in whom there are three distinct Persons. In other words, when we encounter either the Father, or the Son, or the Holy Spirit, we are truly experiencing contact with God, and the presence of one of the Persons implies the presence also of the other two. While the Holy Trinity is acknowledged as a mystery which can never be fully comprehended, Orthodoxy believes that we can truly participate in the life of the Trinity through the life of the Church, especially through our celebration of the Eucharist and the sacraments, as well as in the non-sacramental services and through personal prayer.

In Orthodox Christianity, dogma therefore can be seen to be not simply a set of codified beliefs which the faithful must adhere to, but is instead the actual lived experience of the saints, the fathers and mothers of the Church, confirming the truth revealed in Holy Scrip-

[41] Matins Service, from Ps. 118:26–27.

ture and in the person of Jesus Christ. The emphasis for the Orthodox is on this lived experience, which a person freely and organically grows into, through a deepening of their spiritual life in prayer and ascetic effort. A whole vocabulary of inner life exists to address the experience, for example, of hesychastic noetic prayer as taught by Gregory Palamas, which is described, i.e. by Rogich (1997) thus:

> "In turning inward to the heart, the intellect which has become quiet or calm, now seeks personal integration or "unified recollection." Beholding itself, which is not only a vision "of the inherent luminosity of the human intellect," but also a shift to the "image of God" as a focus of concentration, allows one "positively" to experience the mirrored presence of God which exudes *from* the image. This cataphatic experience is a form of "relaxation of heart" which becomes a necessary condition for sustaining the intellect's seeing the grace of God. In order to maintain this *awareness* of the "otherworldly" dimension of human life — called "sobriety" (*nepsis*), "attention" or "guarding of the heart" — the hesychast begins to repeat the Jesus Prayer. At this point an interpenetration takes place between the image within the human — as the image best corresponds to the human person — and the Archetype Image, the *person* of Jesus Christ. Different from some practitioners, Gregory Palamas often sees this prayer not as one of the instruments or techniques to attain grace — a type of "Christian mantra" — but primarily as a product of what the grace of God "does" to the explorer, or as a result of what happens to the hesychast when one becomes "alert" or fully conscious. The Jesus Prayer is "Christ praying within the believer," or the "Spirit bearing witness with our spirit," which permits the prayer-adept to enter into the dynamic of trinitarian experience and personal relationship by sharing in Jesus' experience of the Father in the Spirit. Participation means then that human beings begin to become fully "alive," not at a loss to their humanity or absorption of it in the Divine, but rath-

> er as an "authenticizing" of the human self—becoming a real person again—proximating Jesus as portrayed in the gospels" (p. 32, italics same, quotation marks same).

In noetic prayer there is then, an 'interpenetration' of the divine image in us with the 'Archetype Image' which is the divine person of the Son of God. This is not a magical effect achieved by the technique of the prayer, but itself a working of the prayer in us. Once again, it is not man, but God Who makes the moves. The above passage is worth quoting in full, because despite its usage of some specialized terminology, it reveals much about the affinity, at a profound level, of Christian spirituality to psychotherapy, and even in particular to a Jungian approach to selfhood and individuation—yet at no point does Orthodox hesychasm ever contradict Christian dogma or refute the objective transcendence of God.

This search for authentic selfhood within Christian spirituality cannot of course be realized through reading or theological discourse alone. An attempt to do so may be likened to a person using a map to navigate, which was drawn up by others who have previously explored a certain area; one can rely on the prior knowledge and experience of map-makers to indicate the right direction, but still has to make the actual journey for oneself in order to reach the desired destination, and still experiences the whole of this journey in a unique, entirely personal way. The 'map' can thus offer general information about the landscape, but it cannot substitute for the actual travelling which must be done. Jung perhaps recognized something of this, when he characteristically wrote that

> "Religious experience is absolute. It is indisputable. You can only say that you have never had such an experience, and your opponent will say: 'Sorry, I have.' And there your discussion will come to an end. No matter what the world thinks about religious experience, the one who has it possesses the great treasure of a thing that has provided him with a source of life, mean-

> ing and beauty and that has given splendour to the world and to mankind. He has pistis and peace. Where is the criterion by which you could say that such a life is not legitimate, that such experience is not valid and that such pistis is mere illusion?" (CW 11:113).

A point which also follows from using the above image of a map, is that it also makes sense to say, that since there is one actual country—*one* actual underlying reality behind the map—then a truly correct map of this territory must convey all the necessary information accurately; maps which fail to do so are therefore to greater or lesser extents misleading, and may even lead the traveler to potential danger, though of course it should equally be borne in mind that the map is not itself the territory, and true maps may be drawn up in a number of differing, equally efficient or effective ways.

All this is both rational and probably true, and there is undoubtedly much in Orthodox spirituality, particularly as formulated by modern writers, which is compatible with a wide variety of religious and secular world views, as Rogich (*ibid.*), Arseniev (1982) and numerous other Orthodox authors have attested. It is also true however, that Orthodox spirituality has found through experience that the dogmatic teachings of the Church do provide a crucial point of reference for all attempting spiritual growth. It was perhaps for this reason that when late in life the modernist Russian Orthodox composer Igor Stravinsky regained his childhood faith, he still felt prompted to say that "the more one separates oneself from the canons of the Christian church, the further one distances oneself from the truth" (Kavanaugh, 1992, p. 186).

It is also simplistic therefore, to reduce those teachings about right living which follow on from the articulation of Christian dogma, to an authoritarian set of fixed rules, an image so often conjured up in modern minds upon even hearing the word 'dogma.' Since in actual Christian practice dogma is an experience to be lived into, in a sense, theology and analytical psychology are therapeutic sciences which reach different conclusions based on similar premises (Vlachos, 1994; Chrysostomos, 2007). Jungian psychology may be said to take the existing religious dogmas of particular cultures, and then try to distil and elaborate these into rendering conscious the 'eternal' archetypes pertaining to universal human experiences through the psychology of the unconscious; whereas Orthodox Christianity tries to relate its faith and practice to these same archetypal foundations of the whole of human existence and experience, rendering them conscious through its carefully formulated dogma of revealed eternal Truth.[42] Hence for one example, Jungians may speak of possession by the personal and collective shadow, by relating this concept to the same or similar underlying experience which Christians would describe as an act of sin.

Roman Catholic priest Fr. Aidan Nichols (1990), being both a student and a critic of Orthodox theology, ably introduces the conceptual basis of dogmatic formulation in the Orthodox Church to western readers who may be unfamiliar with it, writing that

> "In Eastern Orthodox theology, the idea of dogma possesses specific characteristics of its own — owing to its special relationship with the doctrine of the Spirit, with the Orthodox teaching on Tradition, with the theology of the Councils, and with the notion of the infallibility of the Church as a whole. In this, Orthodox theology has, most notably, preserved one vital feature of the primitive Christian concept of dogma, namely, its inseparable relationship with the liturgical life of the Church."

[42] This also partly accounts for the place of Scripture in Orthodox theology. Scripture is understood as the written record, divinely inspired but expressed in human words, of the Truth which was revealed to the Apostles through Christ about the life in God. The New Testament is therefore not understood in an inevitably literal and fundamental way, but is appreciated as being a reliable basis for teaching all that follows from the Christian revelation which preceded it (The Old Testament is also seen as the inspired writing of the people of God). Jung's Kantian influence however, possibly prevented him from recognising revelation as a legitimate cognitive phenomenon (Smith, 1996, p. 115), despite having had his own visionary experiences.

Through the special contribution of its scholastic intellectual heritage, Roman Catholicism has used classical philosophical skills in developing and extending Christian doctrine, in ways which, as will be seen shortly, the Orthodox Church has purposely not done — thereby preserving doctrine, albeit at the cost of much that has proven otherwise useful in its philosophical elaboration in the Roman Church. Orthodoxy believes the fullness of the revelation has been delivered in the Incarnation and Resurrection of Christ, and thus doctrines do not 'develop'; instead the whole truth is already present in the Church, and theology may perhaps be said to 'highlight' or articulate differing aspects of it. For the Orthodox, there is no linear notion of 'progress' in the Church's understanding through this highlighting of truth — every articulation of truth being seen as a renewal of what is already known, rather than an innovation or a discovery. Hence Fr. Nichols is correct when he goes on in the same text to explain that, for Orthodox Christianity, therefore, dogma, tradition and the lived experience of sacramental and ethical Christian life must inevitably accompany and inform each other[43] through the course of history:

> "Tradition is not a second source of revelation, parallel to the Bible. Rather is it that reality thanks to which, and owing to the presence of the life-giving Spirit, the Church transmits the sense, and the unity, of Scripture. The Holy Spirit, who, by the inspiration of the biblical authors, embodied revelation in the Bible, now assists the Church to remain rooted in the biblical message and to accommodate herself to the exigencies of each epoch by preaching, by the issuing of dogmatic statements, by the teaching of Church fathers, by iconography, and by liturgical worship. Dogma lives in the stream of Tradition, and acts as its witness. It enables believers to accept the truth, as transmitted by living Tradition, and, in case of necessity, separates it from

[43] Cf. Sophrony (2002), pp. 41–50 for a summary of Starets Sophrony's Orthodox gnoseological views, which adumbrate this perspective.

> error. Formulated dogma becomes for believers the rule of faith, separating orthodoxy from heresy."

Even scripture is not perceived as being prior to the Church, the community of Christians in which the books of scripture (the New Testament) arose and were written. This community is guided by the Holy Spirit today, as it was then; thus Orthodox Christian dogma is by necessity also not a 'closed book':

> "The Orthodox Church does not exclude the possibility that she may proclaim fresh dogmatic definitions at some future ecumenical council, should the need to preserve the integrity and purity of faith require it. If, however, the Church extends the rule of faith by new definitions, this does not entail any augmentation or development of Tradition, but rather a deeper knowledge of the truth, within Tradition's stream. The task of dogma, indeed, is not only to protect the truths of faith against error, or to define them in a conceptual manner (as an organic part of the Church's life). That task is also *to furnish direction for spiritual and moral living*" (italics mine).

Taking as one famous example a doctrine which is pertinent to both Christians and Jungians, it is interesting in this discussion of dogma, therefore, to note that, in contrast to Roman Catholic doctrine, while the Orthodox Church does share the belief—by way of Tradition and at the level of all the laity—that the Theotokos was indeed assumed bodily into heaven, it has nevertheless not felt the need to formulate any dogma concerning what Western Christians know as the Assumption of Mary. Vladimir Lossky writes:

> "It is hard to speak and not less hard to think about the mysteries which the Church keeps in the hidden depths of her inner consciousness... The Mother of God was never a theme of the public preaching of the Apostles; while Christ was preached

> on the housetops, and proclaimed for all to know in an initiatory teaching addressed to the whole world, the mystery of his Mother was revealed only to those who were within the Church ... It is not so much an object of faith as a foundation of our hope, a fruit of faith, ripened in Tradition. Let us therefore keep silence, and let us not try to dogmatize about the supreme glory of the Mother of God" (V. Lossky, quoted in Ware (1993), pp. 260–1).

This 'inner consciousness' of the Church concerning the spiritual meaning of the life of the Mother of God is perhaps reflected also in the fact that August 15th is celebrated in the Orthodox calendar as the Feast of the Dormition, and not the Assumption, though her bodily assumption is implied, related in the hagiography and shown in icons. There is a specific reason for this difference between the churches, which flows directly from the Roman Catholic trend of developing doctrine: since Roman Catholicism coined the doctrine of the "Immaculate Conception," which suggests that the Mother of God was conceived without original sin, then it becomes automatically impossible for the Theotokos to die a normal human death—death being the consequence of sin, albeit only generic, ancestral, collective sin as the Orthodox understand it in Mary's instance. Thus Roman Catholicism through formulating novel doctrine has created a confusion about the nature of the Dormition, by suggesting that the end of Mary's life and her natural death are in some way distinct.

Jung nevertheless enthusiastically detected what he thought was a tendency in Roman Catholic doctrine to elevate the 'feminine principle' into the divine. The Sophian controversy aside (Meyendorff, 1987), even if the mystery of gender has in recent years received increased attention in Christian theology across denominations, including the Orthodox (cf. Belonick, 1983; OCA, 1980; Puhalo, 1996), this tendency nevertheless would not be described by Orthodox Christians in the manner Jung proposes, when accounting for a variety of associated spiritual phenomena relating to the feminine, and hence it is not coincidental that it has also not required any such articulation in official Orthodox dogma either. Indeed, even among Jungian-influenced authors, the modern tendency to assign deity to the feminine, evidenced by the popular rise of neo-pagan belief in Goddesses, is sometimes intelligently critiqued. Helen Luke, for example, herself trained by Jung, writes that

> "The symbol of Mary bodily assumed, but precisely *not* a Goddess is surely a deeper thing than any other. She is Mother of God, Queen of Heaven, but she is not God. She remains completely human. Somehow it is a greater image than that of any mere Goddess. The primitive had to deify the feminine principle, because he did not know humanity redeemed, matter taken up into Heaven but remaining forever itself—"This is my Body"—but it is still a fragment of bread. The Trinity of the Godhead does not simply enter into the material elements, join itself to the bread and wine, as God did not simply operate through man in Christ. It actually *becomes* the bread and wine—Christ actually was God and Man in one Person. Earth and Heaven, time and eternity, are not two but one reality. So potentially with every detail of life on earth, once it is offered in its wholeness to the Divine. The life of the Mother of God was the perfect offering, so complete that God was born of her flesh. 'Figlia del tuo Figlio.' But to say that she was actually God is immediately to be landed in a kind of pantheism. Every mystic has said in effect that in the state of union man becomes God by participation. But as long as the Reality is expressed by image or concept at all it remains false to say that he is the same essentially as God, i.e. uncreated.—Christ alone is begotten, His Mother, she who gives Him birth, is created and taken up again into her Creator through union with this her Son. 'Figlia del tuo Figlio.'"[44]

[44] Taken from http://www.applefarmcommunity.org/THE%20ASSUMPTION.pdf, accessed 16.05.08.

In many less explicit ways perhaps, a 'feminine principle' of sorts is not entirely absent from Orthodox Christianity where the 'feminine' qualities of God are encouched in numerous scriptural and liturgical metaphors, and where the Theotokos, whose *cultus* as Lossky suggests and Paul Evdokimov augments elsewhere, is a more introverted, paradoxical[45] and less declarative one than that of her divine Son, is considered first among all saints — the 'Panaghia.' Chryssavgis (1996) writes that:

> "Orthodox doctrine stresses the Theotokos' double aspect as virgin and mother — as virgin she heals the brokenness of the

[45] The famous holy mountain of Orthodox spirituality, Mt. Athos, is dedicated to the Mother of God, to the permanent exclusion of all other women, and even female animals, from the monastic republic! Those who fail to understand Orthodox spirituality may detect a hostility to the 'feminine principle' in such regulations, and may even take offense. Nevertheless, the following anecdotal story suggests that such judgments do not take into consideration the monks' own view of things:

> "About a hundred years ago, said the monk — but like all good Athonites time meant little to him — the mountain suffered from a constant plague of snakes. Cats were needed to deal with them. But they had to be tom-cats; and the supply was always having to be renewed, and the cat-merchants of the mainland kept raising the price higher and higher till the monasteries could no longer afford to buy any more. The Holy Synod met and decided to dedicate an evening of prayer to the Mother of God to ask for her assistance. This was done; and a few mornings later it was found that all the tom-cats on the Mountain had given birth to kittens. Great was the rejoicing until it was revealed that half of these kittens were female. What was to be done about them? The holy Synod met hastily again. Some monks maintained that the females must be drowned at once. Others suggested that they might be sold; as miraculously born kittens they would fetch a high price. But the oldest and the wisest of the monks pointed out that it was the Mother of God herself who had provided them. She therefore could have no objection to them. Besides, if the monasteries got rid of them the same crisis would arise again in a few years' time; and the Mother of God might not be willing to perform the miracle twice. So we permit she-cats, said the monk" (from a sory told by S. Runciman, at http://www.mountathos.co.uk/perceptions.html, accessed 15/04/08).

> world, as mother she fulfills the barrenness of creation. No wonder that she is so esteemed by the celibate and married alike. [...] Orthodoxy's liturgical and mystical writers have developed the tradition of the eternal motherhood of Mary, while its iconography endorses this mystery in images" (p. 352).

That God Himself may be well described as having 'feminine' qualities is also not avoided or denied in Orthodoxy, but it is ultimately recognised as making little sense when ascribed to the inconceivable otherness of the Uncreated essence, just as the ascription of 'masculine' qualities do not pertain to the divine essence[46] as such. Hence, too, the direct ascription of such qualities to the Transcendent in the form of *theologoumena* such as those put forward by the Sophiologists, while they can and do occur, even among the Orthodox, to the religious imagination — which as we will see is not always perceived as a reliable source of information in Christian anthropology — ultimately such notions can find no place in mainstream Orthodox theology, which is a product of the ascetic, apophatic and mystical vision of God, the *theoria* experienced by saints.

[46] St. Justin Martyr, for example, suggests the names 'Father' and 'Son' do not pertain to the essence of God, and even the humanly-derived title 'God' is only symbolic of an ultimately unknown underlying reality: "The Father of all has no name given to Him, since He is unbegotten. For a being who has a name imposed on him has an elder to give him that name. 'Father,' and 'God,' 'Creator,' 'Lord' and 'Master' are not names but appellations derived from His benefits and works. His Son (who alone is properly called Son, the Word who is with God and is begotten before the creation, when in the beginning God created and ordered all things through Him) is called Christ because He was anointed and God ordered all things through Him. The name Christ also contains an unknown significance, just as the title 'God' is not a name, but represents the idea, innate in human nature, of an inexpressible reality." This passage clearly shows that Orthodox theologians write about God using the cultural materials surrounding them, but the theology itself is based on a direct, ineffable experience words can only partially communicate.

4 Historical Considerations, Freud and Jung. The differing value assigned to the formulation of dogma in Orthodox Christianity and in Jungian psychology may reflect a broader set of differing cultural and historical circumstances and antecedents. Indeed, the issues presented by the history of the conflict and cooperation between religion and science are perhaps in many ways the central themes underlying the structural arrangements of the whole modern world.

Early Christianity addressed an already highly educated and philosophically refined pagan Greek world, involving itself from the beginning in an *auseinandersetzen* with the intellectual disciplines and sciences of its day.[47] The dominant medieval view of the world and the whole of reality in Western Europe was based on an understanding of the Christian religion as it developed in the politically and culturally collapsed Western half of the Roman Empire. Until pagan philosophy and science was reintroduced by way of the fall of Byzantium in the Italian Renaissance, in the ensuing historical crisis of the Reformation in the 16th century and in the subsequent Age of Reason in the 17th century, the cultural *modus operandi* of Western Christianity, despite having its own its illustrious intellectual heritage,[48] sometimes nevertheless did veer towards a manichean du-

[47] St. Basil famously advised the youth of his era to collect from Greek learning the best, setting aside the worst, much as a bee flies to certain flowers for their nectar, leaving other plants aside: "For just as bees know how to extract honey from flowers, which to men are agreeable only for their fragrance and color, even so here also those who look for something more than pleasure and enjoyment in such writers may derive profit for their souls. Now, then, altogether after the manner of bees must we use these writings, for the bees do not visit all the flowers without discrimination, nor indeed do they seek to carry away entire those upon which they light, but rather, having taken so much as is adapted to their needs, they let the rest go" ("Address to Young Men on the Right Use of Greek Literature," *Yale Studies in English*, 1902, p.100).

[48] As found in the work of such authors as Augustine, John Cassian, Jerome and numerous others. Although the 'embarrassment of riches' found in Orthodox theology of the first millennium extends much further than what Rome produced, it would certainly be unrealistic to suggest that the fullness of Tradition was in any

alism, and thus operated in unenlightened, regressive and repressive ways, especially where church doctrine was felt to be at risk.

Challenges to this Christian world-view came from the natural sciences, such as astronomy, physics, and particularly in later developments from biology: Darwin's (1809–82) theory of evolution shook the foundations of much contemporary and future Christian belief, by suggesting that human beings evolved from lower species, rather than having been created by God. As a result, the whole of 19th century society was gripped by theories of evolution and phylogenetic development. Issues of 'higher' and 'lower' forms of life, social arrangement, culture and mental organisation were the concerns of most serious thinkers of the time. It may be significant also in historical terms that this was, for Britain and some other European nations, a time of Empire, when such ideas of scientific and technological progress were used in justifying colonialism. Karl Marx (1818–83) and Sigmund Freud (1865–1939), two major thinkers writing in these Victorian times, one a psychologist and the other a philosopher and economist/sociologist, significantly perhaps both being Jewish gentlemen from a central European background, left their imprint on their own time and the global history which followed it in the 20th century.[49]

Typical accounts of the split between Freud and his younger disciple Jung, suggest that Jung disliked Freud's materialistic and reductionistic views: namely, that religion is a collective obsessional neurosis, that the need for God is little more than an idealized projection of and infantile wish for a protective father-figure,[50] and that mystical experience is nothing more than "the restoration of limitless narcis-

sense absent from Western theological writings in this era of Church history.

[49] Although this study will focus primarily on discussion of the thought of Carl Gustav Jung (1875–1961), these two thinkers, and other related 19th century intellectuals such as the philosopher Friedrich Nietzsche (1844–1900) and the psychologist William James (1842–1910) do continue to be part of the general intellectual climate in which the current epistemological tensions and conflicts are contextualised.

[50] Cf. Freud (1907; 1911; 1919; 1923; 1927; 1930; 1937). All works cited in Ward (ed.) (1993).

sism" (Freud, 1927). It is also pointed out that Jung disagreed with Freud's view and his patriarchal insistence that the origins of human motivation lie exclusively in the energy of the sexual instinct, which Freud called libido, whereas Jung instead believed that humans are motivated by a thirst for meaning and self-realisation fuelled by 'psychic energy,' an essentially 'spiritual' drive towards the integrity of personality which he termed individuation. Therefore it is often suggested that, in contrast to Freud, Jung believed religion lay not at the infantile base, but at the mature pinnacle of human endeavour.

These claims are correct generally speaking; it is also true that the gulf in understanding between the two men widened even further among their respective followers, so much so that religiosity itself came to be perceived as inimical to psychoanalysis, as psychoanalyst (and former Jungian) David Black (1993) writes:

> "Because of Freud's uncompromising rejection of it, subsequent analysts tended to take for granted that religion was antithetical to analytic seriousness. [...] The one big exception, among the early analytic generations, was the heretical Jung; and the fact that Jung espoused religion no doubt further contributed to the determination of mainstream psychoanalysis to reject it" (p. 9)[51]

[51] An important aside is that in the same text, Black (*ibid.*) also suggests a way in which Object Relations theory, having moved past Freud's rigid rejection of religious experience, is now able to "[...] allow certain sorts of experience, often called "mystical," to be contained, valued and understood" (p. 13). Basically, while offering no opinion on the metaphysical reality underlying religion, Black sees psychoanalysis as capable of accounting for both a valuable and a pathological potential in the cultivation of "an emotional engagement" (p. 12) to "objects-of-religion" (p. 12). Thus, a healthy religiosity can become a source of strength in one person's life, whereas in an unhealthy religiosity the religious object may "[...] be ignored or hi-jacked into the service of personal pathology in the ways Freud indicates" (p. 12). Contemporary Object Relations theory may even make further space for positive religious experience, since as Field (2005) suggests, "More recently, thanks to the late work of the most radical of the post-Kleinian analysts, W. R. Bion, psychoanalysts are presented with the prospect that, by following the true path of psychoanalysis, they will come

However, the Freud/Jung case is not so simple; theoretical factors alone do not account for the split, and on a purely sociological and biographical level it may be suggested that, as a Gentile, Jung belonged to the racial and religious majority of the German-speaking world; hence it should not be surprising that he felt more comfortable about the issue of 'religion' than the Jewish outsider Freud, who came from an Austro-Hungarian empire where antisemitism was a very powerful and oppressive social force.[52] Nicholi (2002) writes that

> "Freud's early experiences with anti-Semitism critically influenced his attitude towards the spiritual worldview. In Austria over 90 percent of the population registered as Catholic. Freud said that in this environment 'I was expected to feel myself inferior and an alien because I was a Jew.' One can understand Freud's motivation to discredit and destroy what he called the 'religious *Weltanschauung*' and why he referred to religion as 'the enemy'" (pp. 21–22).

Moreover, Jung increasingly came to feel that he had found his own intellectual heritage in a Gnostic Christian past and in the opus of alchemy, but continued to have serious personal doubts throughout his life about the existence of any transcendent deity, as this is conventionally understood in many world religions—despite his famous misleading claim to 'know' that God exists in an interview with the BBC.

---

closer to the mystical knowledge of God" (p. xvii). The work of Michael Eigen (1998) is a step in this direction.

[52] On Freud's attitude to gentiles and to religion in general, Gay (1987) a historian and psychoanalyst, argues that for Freud the project of psychoanalysis was entirely atheistic. Freud's attitude to gentiles from the majority Christian culture, like Oskar Pfister and Jung, was one of amiable tolerance, greatly (but not entirely) motivated by his desire that psychoanalysis avoid being tarnished with the label of being a 'Jewish science.' Much to the chagrin of his more devoted Jewish disciples, such as Karl Abraham, Freud made an effort to grant a special status to Jung, who introduced the also Swiss Pfister to psychoanalysis, within psychoanalytic circles. Gay significantly also combats the notion put forward by thinkers such as Roback (1929) that the character of psychoanalysis as a school of thought is essentially Jewish.

Nonetheless, in many of his writings Jung arguably *can* be seen to have a notion of God, albeit a heterodox one. Jung's 'deity' is an unconscious being:

> "The naive assumption that the creator of the world is a conscious being must be regarded as a disastrous prejudice which later gave rise to the most incredible dislocations of logic."[53]

Human consciousness for Jung is the 'eye' of creation, and necessary to God; yet God resists the insight man has to offer, as Jung goes on to clarify elsewhere:

> "Existence is only real when it is conscious to somebody. That is why the Creator needs conscious man even though, from sheer unconsciousness, he would like to prevent him from becoming conscious" (1954; 2002, p. 11).

This unconscious being is served by man, in that man offers 'it' the opportunity to become conscious; furthermore, man does this by increasing his own consciousness:

> "That is the meaning of divine service, of the service which man can render to God, that light may emerge from the darkness, that the creator may become conscious of His creation, and man conscious of himself" (MDR, p. 338).

In his key theological work, *Answer to Job*, Jung uses the story of Job as a paradigm in which man's moral superiority to his 'creator,' as suggested by his undeserved suffering, leads eventually to this unconscious being's increased self-knowledge. Jung writes that, after making Job suffer,

---

[53] CW 11, p. 383, fn. 13

> "There can be no doubt that [God] did not immediately become conscious of the moral defeat he had suffered at Job's hands" (1954; 2002, p. 51).

It is difficult not to see that this philosophy, of man being burdened with the responsibility of making God conscious, can perhaps become self-serving to a person who trenchantly persists in what 'conventional' religion would view as a life of sin, refusing to repent. Man, in this philosophy, is not the sinner in need of redemption, but God is; God seeks 'its' own redemption through the creature, in the form of self-awareness, and through a sort of reverse monotheism, God brings his/its 'sinful' ignorance to man, who then sheds light on his/its own darkness for God. It is also almost too tempting to resist viewing this philosophy through the interpretative prism of a biographical conjecture about Jung's own resistance to the unconscious guilt he may have felt, even in his mature years, with respect to his duplicitous private life in light of his Lutheran background and upbringing.

Man's mission in Jung's theological model is not therefore as in Orthodox Christianity, to be the priest of creation - a living soul raising material creation up to God through his ascetic life, to be transfigured in a eucharistic sacrifice of praise; instead, man is to be the priest of God (or God's analyst perhaps), bringing 'it' in touch with a creation 'it' has unconsciously emanated—essentially 'it' *is* the creation, creation being best theologically conceived in Jung's understanding via a sort of polytheistic pantheism as *anima mundi*, a universe crowned by human consciousness, which becomes the 'tiny light' in Jung's dreams (MDR, pp. 107–8), the 'second creator of the world' which grants their existence to the 'silently eating' creatures in the African bush (see MDR, pp. 284–5). Consciousness for Jung is therefore both God and above God, indeed in a sense the whole Psyche is God, the *anima mundi*, and everything is the Psyche.

In skirting this close to total solipsistic psychologism, Jung perhaps loses the very sense of the "wholly Other" which he borrowed from Otto (1923; 1950, pp. 25–30) in his appreciation of the numinous, since the "numinous" in Jung could be said to thus be rendered into a merely egoic experience, or more exactly the result of an encounter between the ego and the unconscious. Although Jung frequently describes the archetypes as having a numinous quality, this quality is primarily the result of their encounter with the limited resources of the ego, the 'sparks that fly' as the archetypes meet consciousness—there is, in terms of logical necessity, nothing inherently, essentially, numinous about the collective unconscious, since nothing is really "wholly Other," everything being ultimately only perceptible within the psychic reality. Jung perhaps eludes being placed in the category of pure psychologism through his formulation of such concepts as synchronicity, the *unus mundus* and the psychic unconscious, which offer a potential bridge between psychology and physics; yet is this empirical appreciation for the uncanny comparable in its depth and its affirmation of the transcendent and the wholly Other with that of Orthodox theology? This question is perhaps controversial, and the claim that Jung's formulation does not fully appreciate the depth of the numinous is of course not accepted by most Jungians, who point to the archetypes as the very source of numinosity, since they effectively identify the collective unconscious with 'God'[54] in asserting that there can be no practical distinction between 'God' and the *imago Dei*. Nevertheless, numinosity in Otto's sense derives from the inherently "wholly Other" nature of God's being,[55] so it is this author's contention that the word 'numinous' as used by Jung, and Otto's original term are in this context semantically incompatible.

[54] "The world of gods and spirits is truly 'nothing but' the collective unconscious inside me" (CW 12, par. 857, p. 525).

[55] The truly 'mysterious' object is beyond our apprehension and comprehension, not only because our knowledge has certain irremovable limits, but because in it we have come upon something inherently 'wholly Other' [...]. [...] By this 'nothing' is meant not only that of which nothing can be predicated, but that which is absolutely and intrinsically other than and opposite of everything that is and can be thought." (Otto, 1923,1950, pp.28-29)

> "[...] from Jung's perspective, commerce with divinity, removed from the skies, is now to become a wholly intra-psychic reality describing the interior dialectic of the ego with the unconscious under the orchestration of the self. When Jung's total work is weighed and considered [this understanding] prevails. The unconscious creates the Gods and spirits wholly out of is own archetypal resources, and the evolution of human religious consciousness and its attendant spirituality is presently coming to realize this fact" (Dourley, 2006, p. 4).

Jung did not simply conclude that man is therefore the inventor of Gods, who themselves do not exist; this would have probably been too unsophisticated a conclusion from a thinker of his stature. As Dourley suggests, he instead replaced what he saw as the myth of monotheism, with a new myth for modern man:

> "Jung's myth revisioned humanity's relation to the divine as the ground movement of the psyche in which both the divine and the human are inescapably implicated from the outset in the conferral of mutual redemption on each other. The dissolution of the distant and perfect Gods foreshadowed in the book of Job evolved into the growing contemporary realization that God and reality at some point coincide. Jung puts it this way, 'It was only quite late that we realized (or rather, are beginning to realize) that God is Reality itself and therefore last but not least man. This realization is a millennial process' (CW 11, par. 631, p. 402)" (Dourley, ibid, p. 5).

God, therefore, for Jung is identical with Reality and with man. He is not "wholly Other." Indeed, in Jung's theology, the ancient Gnostic claim that we are all gods emerges "gods are ye," but of the same substance, *homousioi*, with Christ—we are by nature divine, and at the same time we are called (or, more correctly in Jungian terms, driven by our religious instinct) to become more conscious of our innate divinity, just as so many New Age spiritualities proclaim today. Nevertheless, Dourley (2006, p. 9) correctly reminds that "The extension of divinity to humanity universal and the implied extension of the sacred to all that is remains unacceptable to the Church."

As has already been suggested and will be explored further later in this book, Jung's theological myth also impacts the significance of suffering in human lives, since as Dourley (*ibid.*, pp. 19–20) explains:

> "When this sweeping vision [Jung's description of the transcendent function in Answer to Job] is taken to the personal level it means that the most intense suffering in an individual's life is an incarnation in that life of some aspect of the divinity's self-contradiction seeking relief in that suffering. To the extent such suffering is well born and issues into a higher consciousness it redeems both the divine who suffers in it and the human who suffers through it."

While always ambiguously negotiating the boundary between a metaphysical and a psychological world-view in his writings, Jung believed that the reason man experiences moral conflict is because God Himself is somehow divided. Below is a characteristic remark from one of his letters, indicating Jung's rich but idiosyncratic analogy of his own spiritual experiences to those of the 11th century Orthodox Christian saint, Symeon the New Theologian:

> "I had to wrench myself free of God, so to speak, *in order to find that unity in myself which God seeks through man.* It is rather like that vision of Symeon, the Theologian, who sought God in vain everywhere in the world, until God rose like a little sun in his own heart... The outcome [of conflict within God] may well be the revelation of the Holy Ghost out of man himself. Just as man was once revealed out of God, so, when the circle closes, *God may be revealed out of man*" (italics mine; reference untraced, but see also CW 11 par. 267).

From this paragraph alone, it can be seen that Jung considered God to be divided in himself, and seeking resolution to his divine inner conflict through the human individuation process. Therefore, where traditional Christian theology has maintained that man grows by becoming more aware of God, Jung seems to reverse this by suggesting that God grows by becoming more aware through the increased consciousness man alone can offer in service to him. As Anthony Stevens (2001) writes:

> "Jung's whole life was an expression of a truly protestant quest—a spiritual journey away from the moribund church of his clergyman father to encounter the living God as a personal revelation in the Self. He believed that by committing himself to his individuation through engaging the symbols emerging from his dreams and 'active imagination' he was not merely extending his own consciousness but enabling God to become more conscious of what he created! 'That is the meaning of divine service, of the service which man can render to God, that the Creator may become conscious of his creation, and man conscious of himself' (Jung, 1963)" (p. 112).

What, however, is the mechanism whereby increased consciousness in man becomes an increase in consciousness also for God? How is the new awareness communicated from the human mind to the divine? The answer to this may come from considering the significant semantic and philosophical difference which exists between Jung's evolutionist, 'bottom-up' approach to the concept of God, and the traditional Christian theological understanding of man's 'top-down' creation by and origin in God; this is in some ways a characteristically 19th century conflict, which has carried over into our own times in the 'integral' theories of Teilhard De Chardin and Ken Wilber. From an Orthodox perspective therefore Sherrard (1998) points out that, as Ware (*ibid.*) explains:

> "[...] Jung went astray [...] in accepting the presuppositions of Darwinian evolution; in affirming, that is to say, 'From below, upwards' rather than 'From above, downwards.' Instead of seeing human personhood as God-sourced, Jung interpreted it in terms of the unconscious; and this he regarded as our 'prehistory,' the 'earliest evolutionary stages of our conscious psyche,' to use his own words. Thus, whereas in the Christian view human consciousness has its roots in the divine, for Jung it is rooted in the animal world; and so, when he uses the word 'archetype,' he does so in a sense profoundly different from that ascribed to it by Christian Platonists" (p. xxxiii).

As will be discussed below, the question of an answer to the problem of suffering, his own and that of the whole world, greatly influenced Jung's implicit theology. His thought addresses an important area of theological concern, by offering responses to such questions as: why did God, the sum of all perfection Himself, create a being that He foreknew would fall from His grace? In other words, why did a Perfect Being create an imperfect being? If our freedom is part of His Image in us, then why didn't God also give us the wisdom to know how to resist temptation, and the emotional strength to do so on every occasion? Indeed, Lucifer was also His most splendid angel — why did God create him in such a way, that Lucifer would abuse his freedom through a susceptibility to pride? Why didn't God create a cosmos that was perfect and never went wrong in any way?

In his introductory text, *Mere Christianity*, C. S. Lewis (2001) suggests that God did not want to create beings which run like robots or clockwork.[56] God's nature being boundless Love, it was therefore impossible for Him not to permit us the option of falling,

[56] "Why, then, did God give them free will? Because free will though it makes evil possible, is also the only thing that makes possible any love or goodness or joy worth having. A world of automata — of creatures that worked like machines — would hardly be worth creating" (p. 225).

even though in His omniscience He also knew this would happen. As Hopko (2006) writes:

> "My personal view is that the Bible speaks of God's providential activity as being his *will* in the sense that God *willed* to have a world in which creatures corrupt His good creation. He *willed* to make angels who He knew would make themselves demons. And He willed to make human beings who He knew would deform their humanity and that of their children and neighbours, and who would corrupt the world as a whole. God knew all this and He did it anyway. In doing so, the Lord decided to use wicked creatures, both human and demonic, as well as evil acts and events, for His beneficent providential purposes" (p. 46, italics same).

If freedom is truly free, then the option of sin is necessary to it, even if it is not recommended. Nevertheless, there is perhaps something almost casuistic about such arguments; they don't satisfy the (proud?) need to understand completely, and they send questing minds like Jung's into spiralling cycles of ambivalence and doubt.

Perhaps another way of accepting the sorry state of affairs we seem to have been placed in, could be the 'argument from authority': God is the big Parent and CEO, and he doesn't have to share all his business secrets with us, his children and employees! This latter argument, was closer to Jung's father's approach to faith,[57] but it did not satisfy his intelligent son's need for explanations, and it generally seems to encourage a certain attitude of dependence on our behalf as humans — it can be asked, is that what God wants, or does he want

[57] Stein (1999) writes that "[Jung] grew up in a parsonage, but his early experience of Swiss Reformed Protestantism left him cold. To him it seemed like a lifeless institution without either much intellectual honesty or spiritual vitality. While he maintained a correct relation with the Reformed Church throughout his life — being baptized, married and buried in it, having his children do likewise, etc. — he did not seek to find any further spiritual benefits from this source. [...] Perhaps a different parson father would have been a greater positive influence on him" (pp. 10–11).

us to stand on our own two feet, while loving Him and depending on Him in an adult way? However mature humans become, of course, Christian theologians are aware that we are still His children, and therefore in a sense never 'equal' with Him: in Orthodox theology He is not understood as needing anything from anyone (though He may want something). With us created beings it is different; so a 'mature dependence'—to use a psychoanalytical term (Fairbairn)—would seem an appropriate response to the Almighty. But does this then mean 'ask no questions'?

In his work taken as a whole, Jung can be seen to have asked: could God possibly be 'working on it'? Did he create an imperfect creation ('very good,' but not perfect), because it was His first time round? Does He need our assistance in order to now perfect the work He started? Also, if God gave us trials, as Christianity suggests, so that we can love Him back truly, not automatically, is He then so insecure, that He needed to make sure we wouldn't just worship Him because He had created us that way? Or is it only 'for our own good,' so that we may freely love Him in return for His love, rather than being compelled by 'nature' to do so? Jung's questions are probing and profound. Reading such works as *Answer to Job*, it may not be over-reaching to suggest that Jung may have been angry at God's mysterious ways, and felt perhaps that he may well have been spared this particular lesson in love!

5 **Psychotherapy and Philosophy.** Sigmund Freud (1856–1939) entered the University of Vienna in 1873 as a 17 year-old medical student, and the General Hospital of Vienna as a young neurologist nine years later, in 1882. In 1885 he went to Paris to study with the neurologist Jean-Martin Charcot, whose work with patients classified as 'hysterics' introduced Freud to the possibility that mental disorders might be caused by purely psychological factors, rather than by organic brain disease. Since the end of the 19th century when this young and brilliant aspiring medical doctor and neurologist turned his attention to understanding hysteria and those 'functional' disorders which could not be shown to have a straightforward somatic

neurological basis, there has been much speculation, hypothesis, and scientific research on the ways disease may be caused by mental factors and healed through the interaction between a doctor and his patient. The introduction of psychological factors to the disease model of western medical science meant the simultaneous introduction of the medical epistemological model to psychology, which until then had been primarily an experimental discipline with its roots both in philosophy and the psychophysical laboratories of pioneers such as Wundt, Fechner and Helmholtz.

Contemporary psychotherapy is the historical child of an extremely broad intellectual heritage, beginning in prehistory with animistic shamanism, continuing on to the sages and philosophers of Mesopotamia, ancient Greece and India, and through both medieval Christian and occult antecedents (e.g. Franz Mesmer, Abbot Faria, the Marquis de Puységur (Morrison, 2004; Carotenuto, 1991)) reaching its current scientific stature. It has as a result also been a very diverse field of human activity, and in the historical context of psychotherapeutic healing over the past century, a very broad spectrum of philosophical questions have been reconsidered by psychotherapists and applied to what may viewed as the quintessentially modern and post-modern way of studying the perennial art of living, which the discipline of psychotherapy has come to represent.

In trying to understand human behaviour and mental life, and thereby to help people overcome mental illness and live in more satisfying and adaptive ways, psychotherapists have been prompted to ask and reframe fundamental ancient philosophical questions such as what consciousness is, and how it relates to reality; what is the nature of personhood and personality; they have been prompted to seek to determine if there is a relationship between the soul, psyche or mind of a person and their body; to ask what is the nature of suffering and of trauma, and whether they are meaningful or purposeful in some way as human experiences; to investigate whether some relationships or experiences can help to heal psychological — and even somatic — trauma and distress, and if so, then what the characteristics of such healing relationships and experiences are; and to explore the connection between the healing relationship and other intimate relationships — such as those to family, friends, erotic partners, work colleagues, society, the environment, even (though conspicuously less frequently) to God:[58] "We thus come to those ultimate questions," writes Jung in acknowledgement of the limits of empirical knowledge and the importance of philosophical engagement, "where does consciousness come from? What is the psyche? At this point all science ends"[59] (Jung, 1932).

As Jung's above remark suggests, all these are bold questions indeed. They indicate the limits of science, and the indispensability of having, not only the practical and empirical knowledge which will act as the foundation of therapeutic technique;[60] also needed is the thorough philosophical grounding which is arguably a *sine qua non* for the professional psychotherapist who is confronted with human suffering on a daily basis. This necessity has been pointed out, for example, by Macaro (2003) in discussing the moral dilemmas which may occur in counselling. She suggests that, in offering assistance to the client,

> "... it is important for counsellors to understand their own moral positions, to have explored alternative moral views, to be able to question and assess beliefs. In short, counsellors should have some training in philosophy" (p. 13).

Macaro in the same article also cites LeBon (2001), who believes that philosophical understanding, far from being an intellectualisation or rationalisation as some psychoanalytically-minded thinkers may claim, "... would not only help counsellors to be of assistance to their clients in cases of moral dilemmas, but also to deal with their

[58] Cf. Fromm (1989) pp. 56–71.

[59] CW 11, par. 533.

[60] Practical knowledge is often — and of necessity — emphasized in psychological training courses, where time pressures and results are paramount; but sadly perhaps this happens to the exclusion of a broader perspective, and to the detriment of the intellectual growth and depth of trainees graduating from such courses.

own dilemmas arising from clinical practice" (pp. 13–14). Furthermore, this kind of philosophical basis in training, "... has been identified as being needed in order to prevent professional abuse and promote ethical practice" (p. 14). Jung himself took a similarly positive early view of the philosophical skills needed for psychotherapists, stating in a presentation at a conference in Zurich in 1942 that

> "I can hardly veil the fact that we psychotherapists ought really to be philosophers or philosophic doctors — or rather that we already are so, without wanting to admit it, since an all too glaring difference gapes between what we pursue and what is taught as philosophy in the colleges" (quoted in Shamdasani (1999), p. 543).

The development of philosophical counselling as a distinct profession, further indicates an increasing awareness of the very practical significance of philosophical training. The mission statement of the American Association of Philosophical Practitioners (APPA), for instance, reads:

> "The APPA is a non-profit educational corporation that encourages philosophical awareness and advocates leading the examined life. Philosophy can be practiced through client counseling, group facilitation, organizational consulting or educational programs. APPA members apply philosophical systems, insights and methods to the management of human problems and the amelioration of human estates."[61]

In a professional social climate which increasingly forces universities to tailor their courses, even in the arts and humanities, to the applied needs of corporate business and the job market, it may be that it is no longer practical application which is undermined as a source of

[61] Accessed 29/02/04 at http://www.appa.edu/.

knowledge, but the crucial "luxury" of time-consuming philosophical deliberation. In fact, it is not only ethics, but also epistemology, metaphysics, aesthetics, logic, which all can be seen as interdependent philosophical fields of study and which always are, to a greater or lesser extent, implicitly or explicitly, involved in the generation of a psychological system or a psychotherapeutic theory. As in the case of Macaro and LeBon, quoted above, Spinelli (1994) is another author from the existential-phenomenological school of psychotherapy who makes the case very graphic for the necessity of developing a critical, philosophical awareness in *any* approach to therapeutic work:

> "Increasingly, a number of authors have pointed out the potentials for, as well as actual incidents of, physical and sexual abuse of clients by their therapists [...]. While I share those authors' concerns, I am convinced that there exists a much more subtle and prevalent problematic area that has not been sufficiently analysed. Generally speaking, it has to do with the distinct form of subtle (and sometimes not so subtle) potentially debilitating influences engendered by a variety of assumptions held by psychotherapists and counsellors regarding their role and function, their employment of specialist skills, and their (sometimes unquestioning) reliance upon, and belief in, the 'truths' of their theories" (p. 14).

Without fostering the illusion that complete or ultimate answers to the perennial philosophical questions of human life can ever be provided, the pertinence of these questions continually urges psychotherapists to respond in novel and unique ways. If this challenge is not undertaken *consciously* by practitioners, then, as Spinelli suggests above, nothing less than a subtle and less than conscious form of abuse of the client can take place.

The theme of making assumptions conscious — and making conscious assumptions — will be important in the countertransference-based understanding of therapeutic work developed in this study; it has been previously developed by Guggenbuhl-Craig (1971), who shows in his excellent short book titled *Power in the Helping Professions* how implicit and unexplored assumptions held by teachers, priests, social workers, and psychotherapists can lead to the misuse of entrusted power. In a characteristically humorous essay, for example, comparing the normative assumptions about family life made in contemporary social work to the activities of the Holy Inquisition, he pertinently demonstrates how crucial it is to appreciate that our current ideas of right and wrong, our ethics, change together with our changing views of what is real, or ultimately our metaphysics. After all, the Holy Inquisitors genuinely believed their activities were beneficial to the souls of those whom they persecuted; why then are our assumptions about normative, adaptive or 'healthy' social or psychological functioning necessarily any more objective than theirs?

As suggested above, Jung himself realised the importance and value of philosophical critique. Smith (1996) writes that:

> "Unlike Freud, Jung readily acknowledged the function of philosophy in calling attention to unacknowledged assumptions. As he wrote [in *Modern Man in Search of a Soul,* p. 118]: "It was a great mistake on Freud's part to turn his back on philosophy. Not once does he criticize his premises or even the assumptions that underlie his personal outlook ... I have never refused the bittersweet drink of philosophical criticism, but have taken it with caution, a little at a time ... At any rate, philosophical criticism helped me to see that every psychology — my own included — has the character of a subjective confession" (p. 111).

Being a psychotherapist, like being a philosopher, is in many ways about loving the questions themselves, while recognising that *there can be no* final answers for all time and for all cultures — uncertainty, as existential philosophers like Kierkegaard[62] have shown, is simply

[62] Popkin, R.H. & Stroll, A. (1986) *Philosophy Made Simple*, pp. 352–353, Heinemann.

a part of the human condition; therefore it is something basic and primary, and suppressing it comes at a price. Consequently, Watts (1951) also demonstrates that a conscious embrace of uncertainty is actually an advantage and a characteristic of true wisdom, since, as the 'law of reversed effort' (p. ix) suggests, psychological insecurity is the paradoxical result of *trying to be secure*, the outcome of grasping needily at security. Perhaps too, this is another aspect of what is meant in the New Testament when Jesus says "he who finds his life[63] will lose it" (Mt. 10:39). Psychotherapists are required to embrace uncertainty with courage and calm, and grasping at certainty (or even the more frequently and less vocally cherished certain*ties* of psychotherapeutic schools, 'pet' theories, etc.), only frustrates their efforts to understand clients, and communicates to clients the very sense of insecure attachment from which they themselves may be suffering.[64]

More controversially, it can be argued that it is usually the 'establishment' forces—whose motivation is in preserving a certain political *status quo*—which tend to avoid the uncertainty which results from restating and reviewing the fundamental questions underlying their belief systems, and as history has repeatedly demonstrated, the bigger these questions are, the more forcibly they tend to be avoided by those in power. It is beyond the scope of this study to furnish this claim with specific historical and sociopolitical references, but it may nevertheless be important to point out how such saturnine forces,

[63] The word 'life' here is sometimes also rendered as 'soul.'

[64] Wilkinson & Campbell (1997) write that "The general claim that emanated from Bowlby's writings that early relationships, particularly the mother-child relationship, are the *key* to explaining later difficulties does not hold" (p. 165). Nevertheless, while taking on board criticisms of the oversimplified mother-centred views of early attachment theory, and the need to consider other influences on the developing child such as those of the father, siblings and the extended social network, a body of scientific research (e.g. Thompson & Lamb (1986), Shaver et al. (1988)) clearly suggests that a person's attachment history is hugely important to the inner sense of security in later life, a security psychotherapy should nourish and protect in clients, while simultaneously encouraging openness of mind, flexibility and an inquiring attitude.

whether they are found in psychotherapy or religion, may be useful in the preservation, consolidation, and dissemination of a particular set of teachings, yet they often tend to obstruct necessary innovations, greedily swallowing their children by inflexibly insisting on the entrenched dogma and doctrine in a fundamentalist way. A sort of intellectual game is played out, whereby the entrenched belief system is made out to be entirely rational, and therefore true. Hoffer (1951), for example, writing on the nature of mass movements, points out that the creation of doctrine *itself* leads to fanaticism, the phenomenon of the "true believer," who prefers obfuscation and mystification to simplification and clarification. Paradoxically, he explains how items of belief are thereby presented as 'reason':

> "When a movement begins to rationalize its doctrine and make it intelligible, it is a sign that its dynamic span is over; that it is primarily interested in stability. [...] If a doctrine is not unintelligible, it has to be vague; and if neither unintelligible nor vague, it has to be unverifiable. [...] When some part of a doctrine is relatively simple, there is a tendency among the faithful to complicate and obscure it. Simple words are made pregnant with meaning and made to look like symbols in a secret message. There is thus an illiterate air about the most literate true believer. He seems to use words as if he were ignorant of their true meaning. Hence, too, his taste for quibbling, hair-splitting and scholastic tortuousness" (p. 81).

It has been previously mentioned that Jung has been frequently and understandably accused, even by authors who themselves make extensive use of his ideas (e.g. Storr, 1997), of being a 'guru' and encouraging blind devotion. Despite the frequently correct identification of Jung's many flaws as a thinker of his time and as a conscious actor on the stage of world events, this label seems like a misinterpretation of everything Jung stood for, since it has been already shown that from his intellectual beginnings he actively rejected these kinds of inflexible doctrines, like what he perceived as the brand of Swiss Reformed Protestant theology which strangled the Christian faith of Reverend Paul Achilles Jung, his father. Indeed, far from seeking devotees, the originator of analytical psychology famously wrote, regarding those who wished to professionalize his theories, "I can only hope and trust that no one becomes 'Jungian,'"[65] also famously exclaiming elsewhere "Thank God, I'm Jung and not a Jungian" (Main, 2003).[66]

Jung loved and embraced paradox as much as he recognized the creative tension it produces, and demonstrated this in his vast opus, which is itself characterised by a venusian fecundity, pliability and vitality which stimulates hypothesis, conjecture, and imaginative theorizing through patient engagement with paradox:

> "The inordinate number of spiritual weaklings makes paradoxes dangerous. So long as the paradox remains unexamined and is taken for granted as a customary part of life, it is harmless enough. But when it occurs to an insufficiently cultivated mind (always, as we know, the most sure of itself) to make the paradoxical nature of some tenet of faith the object of its lucubrations, as earnest as they are impotent, it is not long before such a one will break out into iconoclastic and scornful laughter, pointing to the manifest absurdity of the mystery. Things have gone rapidly downhill since the Age of Enlightenment, for, once this petty reasoning mind, which cannot endure any paradoxes, is awakened, no sermon on earth can keep it down. A new task then arises: to lift this still undeveloped mind step by step to a higher level and to increase the number of persons who have at least some inkling of the scope of paradoxical truth" (CW 12:19).

---

[65] McGuire ed. (1973), *Letters* vol. 1, p. 405, Princeton University Press.

[66] Quoted by Sheila Wilson in Main, R. (2003), "An Interview with Kathleen Raine," in *Harvest*, vol. 49, no. 1, p. 144.

"People who merely believe and don't think always forget that they expose themselves to their own worst enemy: doubt,"[67] he wrote in 1942, and interestingly added that "[T]he fact that a dogma is on the one hand believed and on the other hand is an object of thought is proof of its vitality."[68] Intellectually therefore, Jung was ever reluctant to turn his ideas into a rigid and unquestioning dogma, being a great philosophical synthesist seeking after truth, who tried to respond to the intellectual crises of the 20th century by providing religion with a scientific interpretation, and simultaneously exposing the religious foundations of science; he recognised the necessity to remain manly and courageously open to the big questions, rather than undergo a *sacrificium intellectus*,[69] the phenomenon Wilson (1990) elsewhere refers to as 'mind suicide' (p. 82). For Jung, both reason and faith must be tempered by imagination, since reason alone is incapable of appreciating the paradoxical nature of truth, and faith in the form of entrenched beliefs taken for granted, only breeds doubt.

"Eternal truth," Jung wrote when referring to the doctrinal inflexibility of the Catholic and Protestant Christian Churches, "needs a human language that alters with the spirit of the times,"[70] and his reluctance to make a doctrine of his own system of analytical psychology, accompanied by his general emphasis on the discovery of individual and personal truth has been well documented elsewhere (Papadopoulos & Saayman, 1984). This attitude of complex struggle with the truth, a simultaneous desire to formulate and to test 'dogma' is characteristic of so many serious thinkers as to be beyond enumeration. Contrary to popular misconceptions of religion and religious thinkers, it is an exploratory attitude which characterises many theologians as much as any other thinkers, a fact which which will become apparent in later sections of this book when theological research is discussed.

[67] CW 11, par. 170.

[68] *ibid.*

[69] *Answer to Job* (1952), p. 68 Routledge Edition.

[70] CW 16, para. 396

It may nonetheless be significant that Jung himself knew practically very little about the Orthodox Church, and hence referred in his writings exclusively to (Roman) Catholicism and Protestantism as the two branches of the Christian faith. In a talk he gave in 1939, he asserted in response to a question from the audience, that the ritual of the Church of England "absolutely" met his criteria for offering believers a ritual in which "Man expresses his most fundamental and most important psychological conditions [...]" (1964, p. 10), yet he goes on to have the following dialogue with the audience:

> "*The Bishop of Southwark*: [...] Have you ever come across the Orthodox ritual? Does the Russian ritual have the same effect?
>
> *Prof. Jung*: I am afraid that, owing to historical events, the whole thing has been interrupted. I have seen a few Orthodox people, and I am afraid they were no longer very orthodox.
>
> *The Bishop of Southwark*: I meet a good number of Russian exiles in Paris, in a colony there, who are very deliberately trying to keep alive, with as little change as possible, the old Russian religious life.
>
> *Prof. Jung*: I have never seen a real member of the Orthodox Church, but I am quite convinced that, inasmuch as they live the symbolic life in that church, they are all right" (*ibid.*, pp. 23–4).[71]

As an intuitive thinker, Jung recognised the psychological value which is present in the 'magic' of the symbolic rituals of the (Ro-

[71] Archbishop Chrysostomos writes: "I have often lamented that Jung never came into contact with the traditional mysticism of the Eastern Orthodox Church — though there are those doctrinaire Jungians, religiously convinced that their "father" knew all there is to be known about things spiritual, who naively and at times rather tenaciously hold that he exhaustively studied the roots of Eastern Christianity. He did not. He was hampered by the same limitations that obtained for his contemporaries in general, both in the East and the West. Had he done so, he would have found in the West (for indeed Eastern Christianity is a Western phenomenon)- as he did in the spiritual traditions of the Far East — much to support his mystical notions about the human being and the cosmos" (2004, p. 95).

man) Catholic Church, yet in his paternal Swiss Reformed Church this 'magic' was felt to be absent; perhaps due to his own early sense of a lack of much-desired spiritual experience, his spirituality took a different direction altogether from the orthodox teachings of Christianity. It is therefore perhaps also of some significance, given Jung's emphasis on the fact that children are profoundly affected by the unlived life of their parents, that one of Jung's own daughters much later wrote books on Eastern Orthodox iconography, seriously exploring its meaning and implications.[72]

Jung's relationship to the Christian religion is of fundamental significance to the overall theme and argument of this study, and will therefore frequently recur throughout. Mention is made below of Fr. Victor White, the Dominican priest who Jung had an extended correspondence and collaboration with, in what amounted to perhaps the most serious attempt by these two thinkers to bridge Christian theology and analytical psychology. Fr. Victor White, being a Thomist, was a natural heir to the scholastic philosophers of 12th to 16th century Europe; his school of theology belonged to the catholic scholastic revival of that era. As a result, it is argued that he was not well-placed to offer a cogent response to Jung's profound craving and demand for primordial religious experience, for a sense of healing through encounter with the numinous.

In a sense, both White and Jung were sufferers of the same ailment, since Jung himself indirectly drew on the scholastic approach to philosophy through his implicit use of dialectics and Hegel, in his attempt to understand how the human psyche utilizes its encounter with Otto's primal *mysterium tremendum et fascinans*, and then goes on to make sense of, or to derive meaning from its experience. It is submitted that in White, Jung only found a latter-day replica of his fideistic father, more robust and theologically convinced perhaps, but nonetheless merely discursive and ratiocinative, where Jung still thirsted with almost adolescent naivety at times after the living spirit,

[72] Cf. Hoerni-Jung (1995).

raw experience and its 'blood-truths.' White could sadly only offer Jung what he had already tasted and rejected as the son of a protestant pastor.

This is also perhaps why Jung was drawn to spiritualism and to the Gnostic, the theosophic and the occult for his spiritual point of reference: he, perhaps correctly, identified that it was the only alternative he could turn to in order to fully experience a living, authentic source of spiritual power that his particular Western European 'Christian' environment could offer him, regardless of—or perhaps precisely because of—its heretical, unauthorized and even demonic influence; it remains an exercise of conjecture, but one of tremendous interest, to surmise what Jung may have become had he been brought up in an Orthodox country, where the very starting-point of theology is totally different in essence and approach, despite important external similarities and some major basic points of continuing historically-derived agreement with Roman Catholicism. In the place of scholastic logic, the *lectio* and *disputatio* of medieval schoolmen, Orthodox Christianity refrains from wrangling at the level of the discursive intellect.[73] It offers instead the original 'early' Christian understanding of the intellect as the *nous*, of reason as *logos*; where theoretical scholasticism abides, Orthodoxy proposes hesychasm

[73] It should be emphasized that the strong wording used here is not directed as a criticism of scholastic philosophy, or of Roman Catholicism *per se*, but is deployed purposely and in a tendentious manner, only in order to highlight some important, and in the author's opinion quite fundamental, differences between a mostly discursive and a primarily experiential approach to theology. Despite areas of conflict, it has been already suggested that Orthodox Christianity and Roman Catholicism actually share the history of the whole first millennium of the Church, venerate mutual saints and observe similar feast days—in practise and on an everyday level Roman Catholicism is not really all that different to the Orthodox Catholic Church. Also, with respect to scholasticism in particular, it would be callous, ignorant and ahistorical to suggest that a theological approach which produced Thomas Aquinas, Anselm of Canterbury, Angela of Foligno, Francis of Assisi and Hildegard of Bingen, could be anything but most fertile and creative in fact. It is simply suggested here that this may not have been the approach to suit Jung's particular nature.

and the sumptuous asceticism of its liturgical life. Jung's attraction towards Roman Catholic ritual also attest to his need to experience this sumptuousness, but as a union of the sensual and spiritual which Orthodoxy could have perhaps provided in a healthy way. Is it a coincidence that modern occult schools in the west — such as the Gnostic Catholic Church, which is nothing other than a quasi-ecclesiastical arrangement for magical practices — themselves drew on the Russian Orthodox liturgy and vestments for imitation (though sadly not for inspiration) as it is described in Crowley's Liber XV (1918)?[74]

Lying at the opposite spiritual pole from the occult, and separated from it by a wide gulf, the Orthodox Church is fully scripture-based, but in its life and worship it includes the body and all the senses — the whole man, *totum hominem* as Jung so fervently demanded: "We knew not whether we were in heaven or on earth," wrote the 10th-century emissaries from Prince Vladimir of Russia upon observing the Divine Liturgy in the Hagia Sophia, "for on earth there is no such splendor or such beauty and we are at a loss to describe it." Almost in response to their observation, Dostoyevsky remarks through the character of the Prince in his novel *The Idiot* centuries later, that "... the world will be saved by beauty. I am a believer because Christianity is that beauty."

[74] Cf. Wikipedia article, "According to William Bernard Crow, [Alistair] Crowley wrote the Gnostic Mass 'under the influence of the Liturgy of St. Basil of the Russian Church,'" at http://en.wikipedia.org/wiki/Ecclesia_Gnostica_Catholica. Interestingly and as can be expected, however, the actual content of the 'mass' is directly influenced by the reprehensible practices of such ancient Gnostic sects as the Sethian Borborites (or Phibionites), whom the Orthodox bishop Epiphanius of Salamis (d. 403) described in his *Panarion* over 1600 years ago. The Satanist 'Black Mass' (Le Vey, 1972), a parody of the RC Mass which is aimed at profanation of the Host, nevertheless probably has a related historical pedigree in Gnostic practices, as witnessed by its similar structure.

CHAPTER FIVE

Paul Evdokimov on Depth Psychology

It would be a glaring omission to discuss Orthodox Christianity and Jungian psychology, without mentioning the writings of lay theologian Paul Evdokimov (1901–1970). In the Paris of the 1920s and 30s and the aftermath of the Russian Revolution, Evdokimov was Professor of Moral Theology at the St. Sergius Orthodox Institute, home to the famous "Paris School" of Orthodox theologians which included such illustrious religious philosophers as Bulgakov (a formative influence on Evdokimov) and Berdyaev. Nevertheless, he was, in the words of his biographer Fr. Michael Plekon, "quintessentially a man of the world" (2001, p. 3). A married father of two, widowed and remarried, as a student he supported himself by being a chef's assistant, working in the factory at Citroen, cleaning railway cars; outstandingly intelligent and resourceful, he wrote a doctoral dissertation on Dostoycvsky at thc Sorbonne while his wife worked, and he looked after the children. During WWII, he also worked for the French Resistance, hiding people who were fleeing the Nazis. Although a lay person, he was respected enough to serve as official Orthodox observer at Vatican II, and in his wide embrace of western life and culture he may today act as a bridge between Eastern Orthodox tradition and Western Christianity.

Unlike more disciplined professional theologians, Evdokimov writes spontaneously and unsystematically, but his erudition and familiarity with both Christian theology and the major philosophical currents of his day, from Marxism to existentialism to psychoanalysis, sparkle brightly through his texts. With respect to Jung, Evdokimov was particularly fond of analytical psychology, yet he used Jungian concepts in an idiosyncratic way which often may not be perceived by the reader as being immediately 'correct'; behind his writing lies not so much a misreading of Jungian psychology, as a reinterpretation of it, one which Evdokimov nevertheless characteristically leaves to the reader to deduce. Thus Evdokimov demonstrates a good awareness of the Jungian psychological 'system,' but at the same time he does not limit himself to its terminology; he understands it, but after having digested its meaning he transcends it in his own theological thought. He writes for example that

> Carl Gustav Jung drew attention to the fundamental psychic energy. His "Depth Psychology" discovered the "collective unconscious" alongside the individual subconscious. The inductive archetypes, remnants of all mythologies, live in the human psyche, and awaken a variety of analogous associations. The identification of the tendencies of extroversion and introversion in the structure of the human being is also important, as is bipolarity, where the *animus* is the polarization of the feminine soul toward the man, and the *anima* the polarization of the masculine soul toward the woman. The normality that is sought after lies in the balance between these various tendencies; it is achieved by means of psychic energy, the well-directed intensity and intentionality of which are closely correlated (1994, p. 81).

Paragraphs such as these demonstrate that Evdokimov possesses a good grasp of the structure and function of the psyche according to Jung, and also recognises fully the Jungian equation of health with balance, yet Clement (1985) is also correct when he suggests that, in his own theological writing, Evdokimov uses "not the system of Jung, but only its symbolism" (p. 9).

Taking his famous essay on marriage, *The Sacrament of Love* (1985) for an example, Evdokimov demonstrates his awareness of both Freudian and Jungian psychoanalytic systems, but simultaneously employs an Orthodox understanding of nuptial chastity to offer a critique relevant to both. Thus he writes:

> As long as psychoanalysis confines itself to contend with the irrational and the subconscious by the sole light of reason, it will remain unproductive. One may well consider sin and sickness, fasting and a vegetarian diet, asceticism and sports hygiene to be identical; such treatment falls far short of the power to command ("Rise, go and sin no more"), whether it be directly ("today you will be with me in paradise") or by degrees ("be perfect as your Father in heaven is perfect"). In order to change the very nature of man, one should turn to charismatic means and to the sacramental power of absolution (pp. 170–171).

Evdokimov asserts here that psychoanalysis is actually limited in its capacity to treat "the irrational and the subconscious," because the weapon it uses against the powerful forces in man is in the final instance merely human reason, in the sense of instrumental rationality. He offers as an alternative the ascetic and sacramental character of ecclesiastical being, as the powerful instrument by which "the very nature of man" is transformed. Therefore, he also suggests that Christian discernment and the awareness of professional boundaries is important in delineating the functional operational range of psychological analysis:

> To be sure, the office of a psychiatrist is not a sanctuary, but the Christian psychiatrist knows the limits of his science and what extends and completes it under the action of grace (*ibid.*, p. 171).

Modern studies carried out on the interface between psychotherapy and Orthodox spirituality, such as that on marriage by Muse (2001), appear to build on this insight; Evdokimov therefore does not eliminate the need for psychological intervention, but while implicitly recognizing its importance, he suggests that *grace* is the ultimate healing factor which actually completes and extends the psychotherapeutic opus. This is intimately related to the mystery of the person - the truth Evdokimov intuitively feels modern society has forgotten, so that in the current example of marriage, which Christianity elevates to the status of a sacrament, instead a mere social institution, a contract with specific rights and duties is perceived. Evdokimov's essay suggests that society thereby further eliminates and undermines the mystery of the person and of personal love,[1] and modern psychology also reflects this increasing depersonalisation in its formulations and concepts: a depersonalised condition which blocks the possibility of any genuine *metanoia* occurring, which would be the essential feature of truly personal being. Evdokimov uses the Freudian concept of the superego as an example in discussing this phenomenon:

> Modern psychology uses the term *über sich* or *superego* to designate the collective consciousness. The latter possesses enormous influence; by means of ancestral atavisms, it bears down with all its weight on each individual consciousness. The archetypes and complexes act with their mysterious charm. The *superego* keeps watch over the apparent balance of accepted ideas. It expertly thrusts aside all "metanoia" (i.e. change of mind, conversion), having become capable of awakening anguish and pained awareness in the presence of adulterated values. Every spirit that dares run counter to conformity, that wonders whether it

[1] Clement (1985) explains: "Christianity has fought to maintain the transcendence of the person against the blind impulse of the species and the idolatry of impersonal pleasure. This transcendence is achieved in the mystic union, where "desire returns to its origin" as St. Gregory Palamas says" (in Evdokimov (1985), p. 7). It is also clear that the transcendence being discussed here is unrelated to the sentimental notion of 'love' presented in box-office films and popular romances.

> belongs to those that "can accept this word" of the Lord, is at once suspect in its orthodoxy (*ibid.*, pp. 15–16).

The final sentence in the above paragraph demonstrates how Evdokimov is not only critical of psychology as a human science with limits it does not always acknowledge, but also of the "collective consciousness" which bears down heavily within the Church itself, passing itself for Holy Tradition when in fact it is the "customs of men," 'traditions' with a lower-case 't,' that are being propagated. Evdokimov does not value a tradition on the basis of its antiquity alone, but evaluates human practices *sub specie aeternitatis*, from a perspective outside time, 'in the beginning,' "in the mind of God ever present and new" (*ibid.*, p. 16).

Theologians vary in their appreciation and understanding of the events of the Fall and of God's material creation, as much as psychologists vary in their estimation of, for example, the relative importance of innate and acquired tendencies in the human psyche. Sometimes disagreement between differing schools of thought can be perceived as irreconcilable, as the history both of religious heresy, and of the splits of secular psychological schools, probably attests to. Thus Hughes (2005), writing on the differences in doctrine between 'Ancestral Sin' as taught in the early Church and in the Orthodox Church today, and 'Original Sin' as taught by St. Augustine in the fourth century and remaining dominant in the Western Churches today, explains how the notion of ancestral sin can lead to a focus on human death (as inherited corruptibility) and Divine compassion, whereas the doctrine of original sin can shift theological attention instead to human guilt and Divine wrath. Hughes (*ibid.*) says:

> In simple terms, we can say that the Eastern Church tends towards a therapeutic model which sees sin as illness, while the Western Church tends towards a juridical model seeing sin as moral failure (p. 5).

Also, it needs be indicated that the Orthodox understanding of the effects of the Fall as understood through the writings of the Greek Fathers, is at some variance from the Western notions of 'original sin' inherited via St. Augustine. The Western emphasis on 'justification' is not of central importance to Orthodox Christianity, because man is not understood *pace* Luther, as having become 'totally depraved' and incapable of freedom as a result of the Fall. Man in Orthodoxy retains some of his initial paradisal glory, and is able to act freely and in synergy with Divine Grace. Grace itself is the uncreated divine energies of God, and the sacraments are seen as means of partaking in these energies because God works through His Church, not just because specific legalistic rules and rituals are followed; grace is the working of God Himself, not a created substance of any kind that can be treated like a commodity. There is also no distinction made in Orthodoxy, between mortal and venial sins, no doctrine of Purgatory (this was a recurring controversy partly contributing to the Great Schism between the West and the East), and no "treasury of surplus merit." Instead, the Eastern Church has emphasized the role of acquiring the Holy Spirit in the Christian's practical life, and with this purpose in mind has maintained ascetical disciplines such as fasting and almsgiving — not so as to make penance for past sins, or to build up merit, but as a healing means of spiritual discipline to help reduce sinning in the future, to exercise self control, and to avoid being enslaved to one's passions and desires. The therapeutic purpose of this activity is, therefore, seen to be paramount.

While Hughes (*ibid.*) recognizes the temptation towards oversimplification of such issues and the tendentiousness of some theological writing, it is probably true to say that Evdokimov is informed in his appreciation of marriage and of nuptial chastity by this open, therapeutic pastoral spirit of the Orthodox Church, never assessing the human condition or human relationships in legalistic terms. Thus Evdokimov (1985) characteristically states: "The concept of chastity, *sophrosyne*, points out above all a spiritual quality, complete "knowledge," the power of the integrity and of the integration of all the elements of life" (*ibid.*, p.169). He adds elsewhere that "A sophrosynic being is one who is chaste in the structure of the spirit, integrated" (*ibid.*, p. 279). And thus too, of sexuality, Evdokimov writes, "Sexuality is surpassed by its own symbolics; as a symbol of unity it transcends itself toward the spiritual integrity of the one being" (1985, p. 169), calling to mind the image of the Jungian *coniunctio*, but earlier on in the same work he points out that this is achievable only in marriage, and through the transfiguration of the passions: "St. John Chrysostom saw in the crown [worn during the Orthodox wedding service] the symbol of nuptial asceticism, in order to obtain chastity, integrity of being.[...] The prayer for nuptial chastity is the opposite of every concept advancing "a remedy for concupiscence"; it asks for something entirely different, the miracle of the transfiguration of Eros" (*ibid.*, p. 155). Marriage is not a cure for lust, but its opposite: the arena of its transformation towards true integrity of being. The person who resists sexual temptation is not repressing his sexuality, according to Orthodox theology, but discovering it. Finally, of the sexual freedom of modern times Evdokimov writes:

> The sexual freedom of the modern world, paradoxically and through violent contrast [to marriage] points to a secret desire for purity and covering. The grandeur of the nuptial community calls for the victory not of a tyrant who measures out and weighs love and ends by suppressing it, but for a master and lord who has the power to transform it. Against the drab background of modern eroticism, surfeited and sunk in gargantuan boredom, love once again stands out as the one, great, fascinating adventure through which man touches heaven not simply in poetry, but ontologically, through the charism of nuptial holiness (p. 155).

Sexuality, therefore, finds its meaning in Evdokimov, and in Orthodox thought, within the context of the relation between the human and the divine, reflecting man's true nature and destiny as theology defines them. Is there too, an implicit recognition of sacred eros, within the ethical injunctions against sexual acting-out in psychotherapy? Jungian analyst J. R. Haule (1996) suggests that effective therapists need to adopt a stance of empathic "distance-amid-union" (p. 169) to the client, while knowing that "Deeply and essentially understood, every therapy is a love cure" (p. 173). The importance of the sublimation, if not the transfiguration, of eros, cannot be overestimated.

A detailed discussion of sexuality and eros lies outside the scope of this study; however, the issue does highlight the differing modes of existential being which are articulated in Orthodox spirituality and Jungian psychology, despite a common emphasis on the transformation of instinct or passion in both disciplines. Theologians perceive love crucified in Christ's sacrifice on the cross; psychodynamically speaking, the jouissance (e.g. Lacan,1994) implied in the image of crucified eros may in fact symbolize the hidden archetypal and transpersonal aspects of suffering, which has been described as "the inner side of love" (Ratzinger, 2002). Hence the capacity to respond creatively to the mystery of suffering, as discussed below, emerges as the deeper meaning of eros—that characteristically human and personal mode of sacramental participation in creation—suffering being the stimulus prompting man towards that creative fullness which alone can respond to the lack at the heart of desire.

1 A CAVEAT. In having considered briefly the thought of Paul Evdokimov, and before moving further on in applying this work and the work of other Orthodox theologians to the issue of creative suffering, an important caveat needs to be made concerning most of the Russian religious philosophers who contributed to the religious revival of the late 19th and early 20th century. As discussed, the sophiology of Boehme was crucially important in the formation of their world-view, and thus it is entirely true to write that Evdokimov had certain Gnostic influences in common with Jung—noting however, that strikingly, radically different conclusions are arrived at despite these common influences. Regarding the issue of sexual relations, for example, Berdyaev (1930) says the following of Boehme:

> Boehme is remarkable in this, that although the metaphysical profundity of sex stands at the centre of his contemplation, his teaching about Sophia is distinct by its heavenly purity and detachment, fully free from any vileness. Sex becomes fully sublimated. And amidst this in him, there is not that clipped-wing aridity which results in sexlessness of thought. Boehme strives not toward the negative sexlessness, characteristic to arid ascetic teachings, but to a positive virginal integral-wholeness, i.e. to a transfiguration of sex, to a transfiguration of man, as a sexually sundered being. Virginity is not sexlessness, but deific sex. Integral wholeness and fullness is connected not with negation of sex, but rather by a transfiguration of sex, with the alleviation of the yearning of sex as regards integrality. In this is the mystical meaning of love, which Boehme himself did not adequately reveal (p. 8).

Although this is reminiscent to some extent of Jung's suggestion that persons are less likely to fall in love in a romantic way as they age, because the unconscious anima and/or animus is gradually integrated into consciousness (e.g. Hyde & McGuinness, 1992), it is significant in terms of the contrasting application of similar sources, that in the Orthodox philosophers something deeper and more pervasive is being suggested. It is clear that Evdokimov's thinking on marriage and Berdyaev's thinking on sexuality is in entire alignment with this controversial school of thought emerging from Sophiology however, and these can be seen as attempts, following Vladimir Solovyev and in parallel with Sergius Bulgakov—Evdokimov's own mentor—to "adequately reveal the mystical meaning of love." Evdokimov's formulations regarding chastity as spiritual integrity have a mystical foundation which, despite being Orthodox in its intent and formulation through Evdokimov's own thought, is nevertheless admittedly partially Gnostic in origin, and in fact very unconventional with respect to much equally Orthodox religious thinking and language of his time.

Evdokimov's thought therefore offers an opportunity to briefly examine further the contextual particularities of this influential late Russian approach to Orthodox theology. Hoeller (1990) writes that Russia in the early 19th century was influenced by the spiritual inclinations of its leaders, and Czar Alexander I (1777–1825) was

> Deeply attracted to mystical religiosity and the occult, he welcomed the Hermetic and Neo-Gnostic currents reaching him from Germany and France, and also immersed himself in the magic and mystery of the Slavic soul. [He] drew on the thought of Jakob Boehme as interpreted by the brilliant Roman Catholic Hermeticist, Franz von Baader (p. 30).

Hence too, Hoeller describes how

> Mystical theologians associated with the Orthodox Church increasingly turned their gaze toward a mysterious yet potent image initially inherited from Byzantine theology. This image was an Orthodox adaptation of the Gnostic Sophia, envisioned as a *hypostasis* of God, i.e. as a purely spiritual feminine being, not to be identified with the also greatly revered Virgin Mary, the human mother of Jesus (*ibid.*, p.30).

Sophiology therefore lends itself to non-Orthodox thinking about the feminine in spirituality, but also perhaps to the peculiar Russian mentality itself, as a practitioner of the Western mystery traditions, Caitlin Matthews (2001) suggests:

> Russia is a motherland where the concept of divine motherhood is irreversibly ingrained. [...] The spirit of the goddess [*sic*] of the land in Russia is devouring and possessive, in the way of the Black Goddess. [...] Perhaps here the extreme patristic spirit of Orthodoxy is partnered by an equally strong matristic spirit of ancient religion (pp. 293, 296).

Hence, too, it is not surprising that where St. John Chrysostom saw in the crowning of the wedding ceremony a sign of martyrdom in ascetic self-sacrifice, Matthews (*ibid.*) detects vestiges of the sacred marriages of pagan antiquity, and writes that

> The Orthodox wedding service preserves a vestige of the early sacred marriage [*hieros gamos*, between the Goddess and her male consort, the king] in that it places crowns on the heads of husband and wife during the marriage ceremony in token of the joy of union and the self-sacrifice that care of each other brings with it (*ibid.*, p.296, words in square brackets mine).

It is in this cultural context that Solovyev saw Sophia, the Divine Wisdom, as that purely spiritual feminine hypostasis of God, "the expression of cosmic, creative impulses, bearing all Nature in her innermost being, as well as the eternal, archetypal idea of humanity itself" (Allen, 2008: p. xiii). A closer look at what the idea of Sophia meant to these philosophers may therefore help untangle some of the conceptual difficulties leading to this theological controversy, which also lies however beyond the scope of this study and has been carried out elsewhere (e.g. Allen, 2008; Kornblatt & Gustafson, 1996). For current purposes, it is perhaps a happy accident that these same difficulties can suggest a significant point of encounter between Orthodox theology and analytical psychology. Arguably, from an Orthodox theological perspective, this cultural and intellectual heritage does not necessarily render the writings of the Russian philosophers null, and indeed they may have more influence in the contemporary Church than is perhaps generally admitted. There can be value in theological speculation, given the useful distinction made in Orthodox theology between theological thought *per se*, and 'theologoumena' or ideas related to and deriving from theology, but not necessarily ones which are dogmatically approved. At the very least, this strand of Boehmian Russian thought does perhaps explain much of the surface affinity that is to be found between Evdokimov's thinking and formulations such as those of Jung, his intellectual cousin in this respect, although admittedly some Orthodox theologians may not choose such terminology and concepts to formulate their ideas. This area of theological controversy will therefore need to be borne in mind, as it informs some of the themes discussed below.

PART TWO

Psychotherapy, Suffering and Evil

Introduction

In this world, suffering is inevitable. This ancient religious truth, profound in its implications, is known in the Far East as *dukkha*, the Buddha's first Noble Truth (Brazier, 1997; p. 36). In Western culture, this truth is predominantly understood as an inevitable consequence of the fallen condition of man, following the original sin of Adam and Eve as recounted in the Judeo-Christian tradition. In his later writings, however, Jung increasingly drew on Eastern spirituality to comprehend the phenomenon of suffering in his patients,[1] and it is significant that Jung's attraction to Eastern thought derived from his reading of Schopenhauer.[2] Jung felt that Schopenhauer was the first among western philosophers to give serious attention to the issues of suffering and evil, and this he correctly attributed to Schopenhauer's influences in Eastern religions like Buddhism. Hence Smith (1996) writes:

---

[1] "Observations made in my practical work have opened out to me a quite new and unexpected approach to Eastern wisdom ... when I began my career as a psychiatrist, I was completely ignorant of Chinese philosophy, and only later did my professional experience show me that in my technique I had been unconsciously following that secret way which for centuries had been the preoccupation of the best minds of the East" (CW 13:10).

[2] Schopenhauer was such a major influence on Jung, that, as Smith (1996) writes: "After his break with Freud, Jung returned to Schopenhauer and Von Hartmann. Schopenhauer's great treatise was *The World as Will and Representation* (1818,1958), 'representation' also being translated as 'idea.' Of it Jung was to comment, 'I would ask the reader to replace the word "idea" by "primordial image," and then he will be able to understand my meaning' (CW 6:446)" (p. 104) .

> Schopenhauer's view of life, reflecting to some degree the Eastern cycle of rebirth, was for Jung a needed corrective to the Western rationalism of his age. He wrote that Schopenhauer was "the first to speak of the suffering of the world, which visibly and glaringly surrounds us, and of the confusion, passion, evil — all those things which the others hardly seemed to notice and always tried to resolve into an all-embracing harmony and comprehensibility" (MDR, p. 69). At the same time Schopenhauer stressed the inexorable aspects of ceaseless striving in which the blind will is realized through us and in spite of us. For him man's life is permeated with illusion in much the same manner as Hindu *maya.* [...] Doubtless, Schopenhauer was to stimulate Jung's later interest in Eastern religions, since he and they took suffering seriously (p. 105).

Jung also relied on Schopenhauer's ideas for his own future elaboration of such notions as the principle of individuation (*principium individuationis*) and the teleological function of the unconscious. In a way, Jung's entire view of divinity coincided with Schopenhauer's, as mentioned above, since both thinkers viewed 'God' as blind will, sheer dynamism of a purposive yet also raw, amoral nature. This concept of the divine is more in tune with the impersonal nature of the divinities of the far East, than it is with western theology. Hence, it is also likely that the Jungian understanding of suffering is coloured by this impersonal character of Eastern theodicy. Indeed, Jung wrote of Schopenhauer that

> He spoke neither of the all-good and all-wise providence of a Creator... but [of the] blindness of the world-creating Will (MDR, 69).

It may be, however, that Jung's disaffected turn from his Christian background[3] to Schopenhauer and Eastern religions blocked him

[3] A Calvinist background, where the doctrine of predestination is important. Perhaps the combination of the idea of a personal God, and the evident suffering Jung clearly perceived in the world, produced such rebellion in him as

from seeing the whole picture of the purpose of suffering *and* its cure which exists within Western religion itself. As the Russian Orthodox philosopher Vladimir Solovyev suggested:

> However these three religions [Hinduism, Buddhism and Christianity] may differ, all of them have this in common, that, in principle, they have a *negative* relation to the present reality and see as their essential task the *liberation* of humanity from the evil and suffering that are necessary in the existing world. They are religions of salvation (Solovyev, 1996: p. 158, italics same).

Solovyev also offers a response to the attribution of the phenomena of the world to the mind, which Schopenhauer—and Jung after him—sees as a product of the above-mentioned 'will to life' (*Wille zum Leben*). Schopenhauer asserted that this cosmic will 'suffers' an eternal hunger or yearning, drawing humans ultimately towards death, which "must conquer, for we become subject to him through birth, and he only plays for a little while with his prey before he swallows it up" (from *The World as Will and Idea,* 4:57, quoted in Smith, 1996, p. 105). Solovyev noticed what amounted to reification in Schopenhauer's ideas, and offers a rebuttal to this notion:

> The second chief alogism of Schopenhauer's philosophy is his assertion that will as such suffers. Suffering in the objective or logical sense is the name given to the determination of one thing by some other thing, external to it. From the subjective or psychic side this corresponds to unpleasant or morbid sensations of any kind. But it is clear that will as such—an all-one substance, not having anything outside of itself—cannot be determined by anything external, and thus cannot suffer in the objective sense (or therefore in the psychic sense, since this is only the other

a result of this, from an Orthodox perspective, imbalanced doctrine implying that a God Who knows each by name, may nevertheless predestine persons to suffer, yet also condemn them to eternal punishment.

> side of the same thing). Therefore all that Schopenhauer so eloquently says about the suffering of the will actually refers exclusively to the suffering of limited subjects with volition, insofar as they are limited (p. 100).

Solovyev clarifies in the above statement the fact that the 'blind will' mentioned in Schopenhauer is precisely blind because it cannot suffer—*subjects* do, precisely as a result of their limited, contingent being. Therefore, Solovyev rescues the notion of suffering from the realm of the impersonal:

> From the essential suffering of will follows the necessity of its self-negation. And here the very same contradiction appears. The question is asked: In the ascetic negation of the will to life, *who* is the subject of negation? According to Schopenhauer, will itself "is converted and negates itself." But since it is, in essence, only the willing of itself, only self-assertion (*Wille zum Leben*), how can will stop willing? That is, how can it lose its immediate nature? It is obvious that not will itself, but only the *willer* can stop willing. [...] It is clear that universal, metaphysical will can as little be the *object* of negation as its *subject*. The real subject of negation is the *person* of the ascetic, while the real object of negation is his *personal, particular* will (1996, pp. 100–101, italics same).

Solovyev thus returns the subject, and the suffering of the subject, to the personalistic basis it traditionally has in Orthodox Christian thought.

There is therefore a pull away from the personal, Christian understanding of suffering in Jung's opus, as a result of the influence of Schopenhauer; it should be pointed out in fairness to Jung, however, that

> Jung's attitude towards the East [...] was far from one of enthusiastic emulation, and despite his evident fascination for the

> philosophies of India and China he remained firmly and consciously rooted in the Western Christian traditions in which he had been reared. Indeed he urged considerable caution over what he called the 'imitative urge,' the growing fascination of people in the West to 'possess themselves of outlandish feathers and deck themselves out in exotic plumage' (CW 12:126). At one level such a tendency may be purely superficial, applying, as he put it, magical ideas like an ointment, and failing therefore to address the fundamental problems of loss of direction and meaning that beset our culture (Clarke, 1992, pp. 84–85).

Jung realised therefore, that the philosophical problems behind the riddle of suffering and the related problem of evil, are neither new nor simple to analyse, since they address the entirety of the human condition. In fact, they have probably troubled and perplexed theologians, philosophers, sages and ordinary people since the dawn of consciousness, stimulating *homo sapiens* to produce countless responses to what are certainly some of the most important and vital issues regarding the nature of our existence on the planet. Indeed, if a single overall aim could unite the diverse caring professions we find in modern societies — such as doctors, nurses, priests, teachers, social workers and psychotherapists — it would be, in fact, *to alleviate human suffering* through knowledge and care.

It seems inevitable that not only great thinkers, but all intelligent and sensitive participants in the precarious, difficult process of living will come to ask, *why do we suffer*? Why do people die? Why do they get ill? Why do they experience failure, rejection, injustice, loneliness, emptiness? Where is the sense in the horror of bringing a stillborn child into the world, or a severely handicapped baby? What is the purpose of disease?

If the perplexed person asking these questions also turns their attention to their inner healer (cf. Sharp, 1991: p. 150) they will then feel compelled to add: *what can be done to end this?* And perhaps, as the biographies of countless healers of the human race testify, and as will be discussed below, a life purpose may be found in attempting to formulate a personal response to human suffering.

The etymology of the word 'suffering' offers many clues as to the nature of the phenomenon. It derives from the Latin *subfero*, which literally means 'to bear under,' to put up with. The corresponding Greek verb is *υποφέρω*, which is alike in both form and meaning to the verb 'to suffer,' i.e. to bear under (in fact, the Latin *subfero* is probably a calque of the original Greek). Long*suffering*, a word used in Christian theology to describe the ability to put up with unpleasant states and events over long periods of time, is commonly called *patience*, a word which is itself a derivative of the Latin *passionem*, meaning 'endurance of ill or illness, suffering,' and from which the English word 'passion' and the medical term 'patient' also derive. Again, the Greek *πάθος*, which means both 'suffering' or 'affliction,' but also 'passion' in the more modern sense of 'strong emotion,' shows the intimate semantic connection which etymologically exists between our outer experiences of suffering and their transformation into inner psychological events, or passions. Furthermore, the noun *πάθος* gives the Greek verb *πάθειν*, to suffer, which is akin to *πάσχειν*, to be afflicted, and to *πένθος*, or sorrow, mourning. *Πάθος* is to also be found at the root of such words as 'pathetic,' 'pathology,' 'empathy.' Also, the root of all words containing *pat-*, *–pat-*, or *–pass-* such as the aforementioned *pat*ience, *pat*ient, but also *pass*ive, com*pat*ible, com*pass*ionate, is the Latin *pati*, which, as already indicated, means to suffer, to endure, to be patient. The Indo-European *pa-* has the variation *pē-*, but also *po-*, as in Greek *πόνος*, pain, punishment, and *ταλαίπορος*, unfortunate, and in Latin *paenitet*, regret or remorse, and Sanskrit *pāpman*, harm. Spiegelman (1989) confirms that

> The shorter Oxford English Dictionary informs us that the word "passion," from the original Latin, *passionem*, means "suffering." It further gives three senses in which "passion" can be understood: (1) the suffering of pain, as with some bodily affliction, or the Passion of Jesus Christ (spelt with a capital P); (2) be-

> ing passive, or affected by outside forces; (3) an affection of the mind: any vehement, commanding, or overpowering emotion; in psychology and art, any mode in which the mind is affected or acted upon, as ambition, avarice, desire, hope, fear, love, hatred, joy, grief, anger, revenge. The latter two uses also arise from the Greek *pathos*, which also means emotion or deep feeling. And, from these comes our word "patient," one who bears pain, enduring and long-suffering (p. ii).

The term 'temptation' is also conceptually related, in a theological sense, to suffering; 'temptation' derives from the Latin *temptare*, meaning to touch, to feel experimentally, to try. And since suffering can also be described as 'trial' or 'tribulation,' it is interesting to note that the Greek translation of 'temptation' is *πειρασμός*, a derivative of *πειράζω*, which initially meant 'to try' or 'to test.'

Although illustrious, numerous and, some may argue, sufficient historical attempts to discover the causes and purposes of suffering may have been proposed, it nevertheless remains the unique individual responsibility of each person in his own lifetime to try to find some more or less satisfactory answers to these issues. As even this brief discussion of the origins and some of the philosophical implications of the terms suggests, the fact of suffering and the evil associated with it is central to the whole experience of being a human subject; as Solovyev suggests above, "the real subject of negation is the *person* of the ascetic," a limited but separate volitional being with the capacity to assent to or decline from life's challenges. Hence the significance of these facts is profoundly existential, and in order to arrive at any sort of response, some further clarification of the value and importance of personal and collective suffering is due.

CHAPTER SIX

The Value of Suffering, Strength and Weakness

The quest for the reasons behind the phenomenon of suffering is accompanied by the consideration of whether this phenomenon has any ultimate utility or meaning; if it does, it may be possible to trace what this use or meaning may be through investigating closely the phenomena which precede, accompany and ensue the myriad particular ways in which human beings suffer. Of all the modern 'healing arts' therefore — a term which may include the broadest reaches of medicine, religious and spiritual ministry and even education — psychotherapy is perhaps best suited to the pursuit of such an investigation, since psychotherapists are not only daily witnesses to real human suffering, but also offer their help and expertise to others by bridging knowledge and wisdom from science, the arts and humanitics, and also from religion, though not all care to admit it.

The centrality of the phenomena of suffering and evil to both collective and personal human experience would suggest then, that psychotherapy, the modern paradigm *par excellence* for alleviating psychological distress, would already be sated with such investigation in depth from all schools of psychotherapeutic thought. However, even a cursory glance at the relevant literature, too extensive to mention here, would confirm that this does not appear to be the case. It can be surmised that many psychotherapists have their own reasons for feeling perhaps uncomfortable or unqualified when they have to address the generality of such an 'abstract' issue as suffering, thereby frequently leaving attempts at resolution to other disciplines, such as philosophy or theology.

Among the forerunners of modern psychotherapy it seems fair to say however, that it was Jung, and analytical psychologists after him, who devoted the most serious attention to the complex problems of suffering and evil, even offering a new philosophical perspective on them. In 1932, for example, Jung wrote: "[…] we psychotherapists must occupy ourselves with problems which, strictly speaking, belong to the theologian. But we cannot leave these questions for theology to answer; challenged by the urgent psychic needs of our patients, we are directly confronted with them every day" (CW11, par. 532). The problem of suffering in particular, as he witnessed it in the neurotic struggles of his patients, seems to have intensified Jung's awareness of the limitations of a reductionistic, 'purely' scientific approach to the psyche such as Freudian psychoanalysis aspired to be:

> Ordinary reasonableness, sound human judgment, science as a compendium of common sense, these certainly help us over a good part of the road, but they never take us beyond the frontiers of life's most commonplace realities, beyond the merely average and normal. They afford no answer to the question of psychic suffering and its profound significance. A psychoneurosis must be understood, ultimately, as the suffering of a soul which has not discovered its meaning. But all creativeness in the realm of the spirit as well as every psychic advance of man arises from the suffering of the soul, and the cause of the suffering is spiritual stagnation, or psychic sterility (CW 11, par. 497).

It can be seen that Jung saw psychic suffering as being at the very core of neurosis. The aim of psychotherapy for Jung is to aid the suffering soul in discovering its meaning, a quest which science and common sense alone cannot complete. The soul of the neurotic has become 'sterile,' their spirit stagnates — a condition which calls for a creative response from both the doctor and, more importantly, the patient; indeed, this condition, this "loss of soul," lies at the root of all human creativity. Suffering and creativity are thus, for Jung, inextricably intertwined. The power of Jungian psychology to shed light on these complex and multifaceted existential issues, lies partly in its inheritance of the dynamics of Hegelian dialectical philosophy, as Kelly (1993) explains in his excellent study of the relation of the process of individuation to the absolute. Hegel's appreciation of the creative potential of conflict via a process of thesis, antithesis and synthesis is reformulated in Jungian thought as the tension of psychic opposites being resolved via the transcendent function. This appreciation of the creative potential in conflict is shared, in different ways and with certain qualifications,[1] by both Christian and Jungian approaches to suffering, evil, and to that archetypal psychic structure which Jung called the personal and collective 'shadow.'

Jungian psychology appreciates that human beings grow through the mystery of suffering; in fact we

> [...] become persons through dangerous experiences of darkness; we can survive these difficult initiations [...] Care of the soul sees another reality altogether [to that offered by conventional psychotherapy]. It appreciates the mystery of human suffering and does not offer the illusion of a problem-free life (Moore, 1992, p. 20; words in square brackets mine).

Suffering introduces us to the limits of our conscious powers. Plans are interrupted, goals left unfulfilled, expectations disappointed. When unpredictable suffering occurs, it seems first of all to be irrational, shocking, and a preposterous obstacle to our free will and our chosen direction in life. The very fact that we suffer, is experienced on a primal level as an affront to our dignity and a source of

[1] Christianity is by no means committed to a Hegelian historicism or phenomenology of spirit, ideas which can implicitly be found in modern thinkers from Marx to Kazantzakis. As will be discussed in a later section, the Uncreated, personal Christian God cannot be constrained to a determined process.

injury to our self-esteem, or a 'narcissistic wound,' to borrow a term from psychoanalysis (Rycroft, 1968: p. 107). We are painfully forced to abdicate our past conquests, and to surrender heretofore cherished images of our importance and capability. Yet, from a Jungian alchemical perspective, Edinger (1987) explains that "[t]orture and humiliation belong to the mortificatio phase of individuation. [...] The ego must be *relativized* to make room for the Self. The totality of the Self brings with it the shadow, encounter with which is always a painful humiliation" (Edinger, 1987; p. 91).

Especially in modern cultures, persons value having a sense of near-total control over their lives, but suffering incontestably challenges the capacity of the conscious ego to structure and make sense of life by using the familiar faculties of reason and free will. Paradoxically therefore, in reminding humans of their limitations, suffering can be also understood as an opportunity to become aware of forces at work in life which are *more powerful* than those of the conscious ego—for to suffer creatively is an art, as Herman Hesse's fictional characters show in their difficult journeys towards individuation; there may even be an art of a particular "soul's way through suffering," as Linda S. Leonard suggests in her discussion of Dostoyevsky (Leonard, 1989; 2001: pp. 83, 305). For this reason alone, suffering has also been a very important tool in introducing both ordinary and extraordinary humans to the spiritual life.

For example, in the Pauline epistles, the view is expressed that suffering, as an affront to pride and reason, does have a purpose in revealing the power of grace (2 Cor. 12:7–10). The second letter to the Corinthians begins with reminding this early community of Christians of the consolation for affliction that is to be found in God, who is capable of rescuing humans from all suffering—even from death, a recurring theme in the New Testament. St. Paul therefore unequivocally maintains, that suffering, this 'thorn in the flesh,' exists as a check on human pride and a reminder of our dependence on God; and he also directly links the problem of suffering to the problem of evil, when he describes his suffering as a 'messenger of

Satan.' He advocates therefore that human beings should place their trust in a power higher than themselves when confronted with the problem of suffering. In the Christian world-view, what we perceive as our human weakness and fragility when confronted with life's afflictions, is in fact an opportunity for God to demonstrate graceful strength in helping us through. Metropolitan Anthony of Sourozh (1970) comments that the term 'weakness' here "is not the kind of weakness which we show by sinning and forgetting God, but the kind of weakness which means being completely transparent, completely abandoned in the hands of God. We usually try to be strong and we prevent God from manifesting his power" (pp. 34–5).

In Jungian terms, the ego, represented in the epistle by St. Paul's conscious 'I,' is relativized when the Self—of which Christ is a symbol—makes its appearance *through* the ego's experience of weakness and suffering. St. Paul does not directly explain why a loving God would wish to demonstrate his power over us in such a seemingly cruel way, except as a way of keeping us from becoming 'too elated'—from forgetting, that is, our place in the creation as His subjects, thereby committing the hubris of wanting to become God ourselves. Hollis (2001) however, writes that the "Greek positing of hubris is paralleled by the Judeo-Christian concept of sin, though they are not the same thing. Etymologically the word sin derives from an archery term which means to miss the mark. As the archer is flawed, as the wind of fate shifts the flight of the arrow, imperfect achievement is virtually inevitable" (p. 13).

Another way of seeing this, is that the purpose of suffering in Christianity, but also in Jungian theory, is educational; in reminding us how distant we are from the perfection of the Creator, God incites us to continue the unending task of bridging the gap between ourselves and Him through our faith and works, or virtuous action. The particular cardinal virtue which is required to accept the role of suffering in our lives, is known as humility. Metropolitan Anthony explains the meaning of humility, with which a Christian can counter his hubris, and keep from becoming 'too elated':

> The word 'humility' comes from the Latin word 'humus,' which means fertile ground. To me humility is not what we often make of it: the sheepish way of trying to imagine that we are the worst of all and trying to convince others that our artificial ways of behaving show that we are aware of that. Humility is the situation of the earth. The earth is always there, always taken for granted, never remembered, always trodden on by everyone, somewhere we cast out and pour out all the refuse, all we don't need. It's there, silent and accepting everything, and in a miraculous way making out of all the refuse new richness in spite of corruption, and a new possibility of creativeness, open to the sunshine, open to the rain, ready to receive any seed we sow and capable of bringing thirtyfold, sixtyfold, a hundredfold out of every seed. (*ibid.*, p. 37).

The Christian spiritual teaching on suffering is therefore clear: we suffer not in punishment, but in order to become transparent to the forces of the Divine at work in our lives; and in order to suffer creatively, we need to acquire an attitude of genuine humility, suffering voluntarily and transmuting our experience of pain into growth, which for the Christian means growth in Christ. There is also an understanding that the very *extent* to which we suffer is determined by God, that our particular individual suffering is both necessary and sufficient to our salvation.

This can be related to the Orthodox concept that each person's 'cross' has been designed to fit their life and personality exactly. Bakoyiannis (1999)[2] explains that, in the Orthodox Christian perspec-

[2] Bakoyiannis (1999) narrates a story which illustrates this concept and is worth quoting here: "A believer once said to God: "Lord, why have you given me such a heavy cross? Why?" Then he fell asleep, and he had the following strange dream. He was in the most enormous room. All around the walls there were hanging all kinds of crosses: large, small, wooden, iron, marble and so on. And he heard a voice saying to him: "Give up your cross, my child. Choose which ever one you think suits you." The poor fellow cast off his heavy cross with much joy and started desperately looking for the cross that would suit him. One seemed to

tive, as long as we view our suffering as an unnecessary burden, the imagination exaggerates its intensity, making it unbearable. But when we take up the same 'cross' with joy, voluntarily, the same suffering then seems light (Matt. 11:30).

Orthodoxy maintains furthermore, that self-imposed suffering through the ascetic practice of virtue, strips us of the inner resistance which accrues through sinfulness, and prevents us from experiencing God. Through voluntary suffering, as well as the acceptance of involuntary suffering, we come to understand suffering, and understand too the meaning of Christ's suffering for mankind. Christ did not open the gates of heaven with a triumphant chorus of angels, but with the cross; Christians learn therefore, to sacrifice themselves and to suffer for the sake of higher things, a very important stage of spiritual development known as purification (and followed by illumination and union). Suffering in this case leads to health, and to happiness—paradoxically, that is, to the cessation of suffering, which was never God's initial intention for mankind. Suffering is thus inextricably related to healing, and is rewarded with the happiness that comes from the goodness of practising the virtues.

Orthodox Christian writers point, too, to ancestral—if not personal—sin as the cause of suffering, and the willing embrace of suffering is thus associated with the struggle to be free from sin and the sinful tendency (Matthew 7:14). Although suffering is never a direct punishment for sin, it has nevertheless been inherited by humanity as a consequence of ancestral sin; inasmuch as according to Orthodox understanding, in this world all are subject to ancestral sin, our obedience in suffering is a remedy against our own inherited sinful

---

him too heavy, another he couldn't lift at all, one was for a child, another for an old man, yet another for a baby. One had thorns, another had needles that pricked. He looked and looked, trying them all. None of them would do. In his disappointment, he glanced round at a corner and saw one that had been abandoned. He ran to it, tried it, and it suited. Not too heavy, not too light. Just the right size for him. "At last I've found the cross for me," he said. But, to his surprise, he discovered that it was the very cross he had worn before and had seemed such an unbearable burden" (pp. 23–4).

tendency, if not — it cannot be stressed enough — in itself any sort of exculpation for guilt. Indeed, Orthodoxy does not keep a tally of sins, or see sin in terms of guilt - rather as illness demanding a cure. The ascetic struggle to bear suffering is thus compared to the training of athletes for contests, where suffering and effort leads directly to reward (Romans 8:17). Suffering is therefore also perceived as only temporary, but nonetheless necessary for salvation.[3]

However, even this account leaves unanswered to a degree, the crucial related question of what exactly the relationship of suffering is to the presence of evil in the world. The question of why God allows people to suffer, though ultimately irresolvable, can to some extent be addressed in the above arguments — how can God, who in Christian theology is considered all-good, a *summum bonum*, permit his children's suffering to take place? The second letter to the Corinthians is not the only place in the scriptures where God is mysteriously seen as, if not directly cooperating with Satan, then at least giving him permission to send suffering to humans.

From the point of view of the theory of opposites, one may ask: if there were no failures, what would successes measure themselves against? If there were no disease, how would we measure health? If no night, what would day be? James Schultz (1997), therefore, points out the Jungian response to the question of evil: that good and evil are opposites, and the reality of one therefore requires the reality of the other. 'Good' and 'evil' have no meaning without each other in analytical psychology, with its emphasis on the importance that *meaning* has — even more so than happiness — for human beings;

[3] It can be noted that the Roman Catholic idea of redemptive suffering is slightly different, since it tends to view suffering *itself* as a virtue, as opposed to a phenomenon leading to virtue. Purgatory, for example, is a place where suffering alone purifies souls — an idea alien to the Eastern Church. The four Noble Truths of Buddhism mentioned above, on the other hand, lead in the exact opposite direction away from suffering, but still perhaps remain on the same level of understanding, since it may be maintained that escape from suffering in traditional Buddhism is attained by impairing the human faculty for feeling, a fact which Buddhist psychotherapist David Brazier (1997) understandably reacts against.

it is well-suited to giving evil in human life and in the cosmos the respect and even the appreciation it realistically deserves. Controversially however, Jung parted with traditional Christian theology on this issue, because he attributed both a good and an evil aspect to God. From his early childhood dreams and his religious upbringing, Jung became increasingly aware of this apparently ambiguous nature of God (Von Franz, 1998). Noticing a peculiar 'alliance' between God and Satan in the Bible, Jung understandably questioned the idea that God is the '*summum bonum*' of Christian theology. Certainly, a cursory glance at non-Christian mythologies offers a wealth of examples of the dark side of the heavenly Father; this verse, for example, from the shamanic call to Bai Ülgän, the highest god of the Altaians of Central Asia:

> Father Ülgän, thrice exalted, […] Deliver us not to misfortune,
> Let us withstand the Evil One! (Von Franz, 1998; p. 101),

may be compared to the well-known sixth and seventh petitions from the Lord's Prayer, 'lead us not into temptation, but deliver us from evil,'[4] which becomes intriguingly analogous. How 'good' is a father who knowingly delivers his children to evil? Indeed, in *Answer to Job* (1954; 2002), Jung states that

> God is asked not to entice us outright into doing evil, but rather to deliver us from it. […] Christ considers it appropriate to remind his father of his destructive inclinations towards mankind and to beg him to desist from them. Judged by human standards it is after all unfair, indeed extremely immoral, to entice little children into doing things that might be dangerous for them, simply in order to test their moral stamina! […] The incongruity of it is so colossal that if this petition were not in the Lord's Prayer one would have to call it sheer blasphemy, because it re-

[4] But compare James 2:13–15.

ally will not do to ascribe such contradictory behaviour to the God of Love and Summum Bonum (1954: 2002: pp. 60–61).

In the Freudian psychoanalytic interpretation, Rycroft (1968; 1995: p. 155) explains that belief in God is seen as a response to the recognition of human helplessness. Freud conjectured that the child's terrifying sense of helplessness brought about a need for protection through the father's love, which is given adult expression in religious devotion. Perhaps it could be that the 'good' side of the father-god projection inspires worship and love, but the 'evil' side indicates a fearful need to propitiate a potentially wrathful and even seductive paternal deity, one who mysteriously 'leads into temptation,' and vengefully 'delivers into misfortune,' as suggested above (Makrakis, 1993). Perhaps then, ultimately the transcendent reality of God contains both good and evil aspects, and is beyond each — as Jung *pace* Nietzsche attested.

Writing from an Eastern Orthodox perspective however, a more accurate translation from the Aramaic of the petition in the Lord's Prayer not 'to be led into temptation,' as Kokkinakis (1975) explains, renders it a request "not to enter into temptation," rather than a plea for God to "lead us not" into it, and this, according to Kokkinakis, "... is in agreement with Christ's enjoinder to His Disciples before His Crucifixion, 'Pray not to come into temptation'" (p. 95). This suggests that God does not in fact 'lead' us into temptation, but on the contrary, His help is sent to strengthen our resistance. This is further corroborated by Jas. 1:13, "God tempts no one and he who is tempted must not say that God tempts him." More accurately speaking, therefore, this final petition in the Lord's Prayer means "do not allow us to enter into temptation, lest we be carried away by it." We are asking God to deliver us from our *own* misguided choices. Even logically, it would make little sense to request of the same Being Who we think has just tempted us, to now rescue us from the temptation He has purportedly set before us.

The Orthodox understanding of the 'cooperation' between God and the devil is therefore that the devil, himself being God's creature, *cannot* in fact tempt us, or do anything else, except by God's permission. God does grant him permission to tempt us, as in 1 Cor. 10:13: "No temptation has overtaken you except such as is common to man; but God is faithful, *who will not allow you to be tempted beyond what you are able*, but with the temptation will also make the way of escape, that you may be able to bear it" (italics mine). In this sophisticated understanding of the relationship between temptation and salvation, it is implied that God allows for us to be tempted, but always according to our strength and always providing at the same time a way out of the temptation — so that, just as physical athletes become stronger through resistance training, spiritual athletes also mature through their successive victories over temptation, with God's help. In a sense, therefore, God does expose us to temptation, since He permits it to enter our lives; but He does so out of respect for our freedom, and through a paternal desire for us to come to know Him as responsible adults: "Behold, I send you out as sheep in the midst of wolves. Therefore be wise as serpents and harmless as doves" (Mt. 10:16). In this sense also, it is clear that, despite the devil's constant primary motive to destroy us, God is using him to render goodness out of evil, sabotaging the enemy's plans, making it possible for humans to co-operate with God, acting in synergy with His divine will.

The idea that God has such light and dark aspects is not novel — and there are hints at a 'dark' aspect of God even in orthodox patristic theology, where the metaphor of darkness is used frequently to describe God's otherness and unknowability. Bishop Kallistos Ware (1998) points out that

> "Darkness" language, as applied to God, takes its origin from the Biblical description of Moses upon Mount Sinai, when he is said to enter the "thick darkness" where God was (Exod. 20:21). It is significant that in this passage it is not stated that God *is* darkness, but that He *dwells* in darkness: the darkness denotes, not the absence or unreality of God, but the inability of our human mind to grasp God's inner nature. The darkness is in us, not in Him (italics same; pp. 126–7).

However, Bishop Ware also makes explicit here the Orthodox Christian belief that there is no 'darkness,' in the sense of evil, *in* God. Sophrony (1973, p. 100) states categorically that "God is not 'beyond good and evil,' for He is Light in which there is no shade of darkness." In fact, darkness in the sense of evil and sin in Orthodox Christianity is located only, by way of the devil, inside man's soul through our fallenness and consent to his evil promptings. This has been perceived by many modern psychological thinkers, especially Jungians, as having enormous negative consequences for Christian psychology. As Brother David Steindl-Rast, a Benedictine monk and Jungian analyst, suggests,

> In contrast to some other traditions, Christians have not done particularly well in cultivating a practical method for integrating the shadow. This is part of the reason we have some of the problems that plague us today. In its enthusiasm for the divine light, Christian theology has not always done justice to the divine darkness. [...] On the level of religious doctrine, it's a God that is totally purged of anything that we call dark. Then we try to live up to the standards of a God that is purely light and we can't handle the darkness within us. [...] But the more we suppress it, the more it leads its own life, because it is not integrated. Before we know it, we are in serious trouble (Zweig & Abrams, 1991; pp. 131–132).

The apparent duality in the Godhead suggested by the metaphor of darkness and the complexity of the relation between temptation and salvation, is an issue addressed at some length by Jung in his classic essay already mentioned, *Answer to Job* (CW11), a book which led the Jewish theologian Martin Buber to accuse Jung of espousing Gnosticism (an accusation which Jung denied despite his intimate acquaintance with Gnostic beliefs, and his view that Gnosticism, hermetic philosophy and alchemy were historical forerunners of analytical psychology). Job, a righteous man, is the biblical personality which offers an answer to the perennial question 'why do bad things happen to good people?' Job is seen in the Old Testament to become the suffering pawn in a seemingly capricious contest between God and Satan to test the strength of Job's faith. God, Jung argues, is therefore seen in this ancient story not to be characterised by goodness alone. Jung here obviously considers the problem of suffering to be central to the understanding of the Christian faith, but also of analytical psychology; and he links the figure of Job with Christ Himself, a symbol of the Self, as God's 'suffering servant' (Is. 53:3–5), in his autobiographical *Memories, Dreams, Reflections*:

> [...] Job is a kind of prefiguration of Christ. The link between them is the idea of suffering. Christ is the suffering servant of God, and so was Job. In the case of Christ the sins of the world are the cause of suffering, and the suffering of the Christian is the general answer. This leads inescapably to the question: Who is responsible for these sins? In the final analysis it is God who created the world and its sins, and who therefore became Christ in order to suffer the fate of humanity (p. 243).

The key controversial idea here, from a Christian perspective, is that 'in the final analysis it is God who created the world *and its sins*.' Perhaps a superficial reading of Jung could suggest that, like the Marquis De Sade, Jung holds God accountable for human sin, thereby denying our human responsibility to do good. However, a closer reading may suggest Jung's approach was more subtle; Bishop (2002) points out that there is a crucial distinction in *Answer to Job* between the God image — the *imago Dei* — in man, and the transcendent reality of God. As Rowland (2002) explains:

> The narrative form of such an elemental drama [as in 'Answer to Job'] is the individuation of God as one pole of the evolution of human consciousness. God, or the divine archetype, is afflicted by overwhelming unconsciousness, hence the torture of

> Job. The answer to Job's pain comes in repeated crises of divine-human relations. Christ's incarnation and agony on the cross is a notable example, but one that does not end the dialectic of heaven and earth. For in writing about the biblical portrayal of God and humanity, Jung is also looking at what he regards as a long cultural record of ego-self dynamics.

Orthodox Christianity would not attribute such operations to the intentions of the Creator, in which it discerns an inexplicable but profound mystery; yet it definitely recognises God's ability to use *everything* for the fulfilment of the Divine plan. Breck (2007) writes that

> [...] there is nothing that happens — no event or occasion, however tragic it may be — that does not in some mysterious (sacramental) way, serve His purpose for our salvation and the salvation of all creation. This does not mean that God creates tragedy or encourages sin. These are consequences of human freedom in a fallen world. Nevertheless, whether we can perceive it or not, there is no such consequence that God cannot and does not use for His purpose and to His glory. When it is assumed with faith, however shaky, there is ultimate meaning to *all* our suffering, no matter what its cause or how great its intensity. With the apostle Paul, we can have absolute confidence that our anguish "completes what is lacking in Christ's afflictions," and does so by God's grace "for the sake of the Body, that is, the Church" (Col. 1:24) (p. 2).

Hence, too, Clement (2000) writes that

> Evil flies in the face of God, like the scourging of the blindfolded Jesus. The cries of Job can still be heard and Rachel weeps for her children. But the answer to Job has been given and remains given: *it is the Cross.* It is God crucified upon all the evil in the world but causing an immense power of resurrection to burst forth in the darkness. Pascha is the Transfigu-

> ration taking place in the abyss. "Deliver us from evil" means: Come, Lord Jesus; come, you who said that you "saw Satan fall like lightning from heaven" (Lk 10:18). This victory is present within the depths of the Church. We receive its strength and its joy whenever we receive communion. If Christ keeps it secret it is in order to bind us to it. "Deliver us from evil" is an active prayer intended to challenge us (p. 39).

Despite the shock value of Jung's suggestion then, that God has a 'shadow' of which He needs to become conscious, Orthodox teaching as described in the Pauline epistles and elsewhere may be said to concur remarkably in places with Jung's description of the *human* unconscious, and subtly suggest an understanding that the source of evil is not only outside us, but also within. James Hollis (2001), for example, explains that "[a] more recalcitrant feature of the human psyche is hinted at by St. Paul when he admits that though he often knew the good, he did not always, or often, choose the good. The Pauline qualification of missing the mark introduces a more sinister dimension to the matter, much closer to that intimated in hubris. *Something within us seeks destruction*" (p. 13, italics mine). The problems of suffering and of evil in practice have no ultimate resolution then, even in analytical psychology. James Schultz (1997) explains:

> The distressing struggle of integrating the shadow side of ourselves, of wrestling with the dark angel within, is ongoing and never ending for those who are willing to take it on. Jung considers it a moral task of the first magnitude… [T]he battlefield of choice is within ourselves. The enemy is evil. The enemy is us. God has made it so.

This may appear to be a pessimistic teaching about man and God, but it is, on one level, simply pointing out the implication of understanding that *in practical terms*, the shadow of good is evil, and that of evil, good. Orthodox theologian Clément (2000) almost seems to offer a direct response to comments such as Schultz's when he writes that

> We must not forget that when we speak of the Evil One, it is not to our neighbour that we must look but first to ourselves. We must not forget either that the greatest, most realistic spiritual masters — Saint Isaac of Syria, for example [...] did not only pray saying "deliver us from evil" or "from the Evil One," but also "if it is possible, deliver the Evil One from evil, for he is also your creature..." (p. 40).

The acknowledgement of evil is a precondition of goodness. Good and evil do seem indispensable to and inseparable from one another in this world, and however much soul and spirit may yearn for absolute goodness or appear to be possessed by unadulterated evil, neither condition is in fact realistically possible. It is indeed almost as if, as Jung sometimes imagined (cf. CW 9i par. 66; CW 9ii, par. 24), in practical terms some daimonic force of life pursues its inexorable and undefinable course, pitilessly crushing any human attempt to capture it once for all time, within any single scientific theory or philosophical definition of existence. As Buber (1996) has pointed out in a Jewish theological context, in fact *the very belief* that one has acquired some 'finite good' — be it nationality, art, power, knowledge, money, the subjugation of woman — is itself a form of idolatry:

> He who has been converted by this substitution of object now 'holds' a phantom that he calls God. But God, the eternal Presence, does not permit Himself to be held. Woe to the man so possessed that he thinks he possesses God! (p. 136).

Similarly, Berdyaev (1937) explains that the paradox of ethics is the fact that the distinction between good and evil is a result of the Fall. Before the Fall, according to Berdyaev, man did not experience the categories of 'good' and 'evil,' so

> It is bad that the distinction between good and evil has arisen, but it is good to make the distinction once it has arisen; it is bad to have gone through the experience of good and evil, but it is good to know good and evil as a result of that experience [...] Man has chosen the knowledge of good and evil through experience, and he must follow that painful path to the end; he cannot expect to find Paradise half-way. The myth of the lost paradise symbolizes the genesis of consciousness in the development of the spirit (pp. 49–50).

Perhaps much of the New Age misappropriation of Jungian thought, and of the Gnostic epistemology underlying so many 'isms' of the modern *zeitgeist* which seek a 'finite good' in man-made theories and solutions (socialism, capitalism, existentialism, etc.), lies precisely in the tendency to 'find Paradise half-way,' an artificial escape from suffering, or its denial in a fantasy of prelapsarian innocence. Therefore, as both analytical psychology and Orthodox spirituality suggest, it is necessary to engage and confront the causes and sources of suffering in a practical struggle.

CHAPTER SEVEN

'Suffering' and 'Passion' in Eastern Orthodoxy

Orthodox Christianity expresses itself in and through Holy Tradition, which has five sources: apart from the primacy of place it gives to scripture, which it views as the inspired word of God couched in human language, Orthodox theologians arrive at their formulations by looking to the transformational experience of liturgy (the seven sacraments, or 'mysteries,' which include baptism, chrismation, ordination, marriage, communion, confession and holy unction); the doctrine and canons produced by the first seven ecumenical church councils, beginning with the first at Nicea in AD 325 and ending with the seventh, again at Nicea, in 787 AD; the lives of the saints, accepted by the church to be men and women who lived exemplary Christian lives and who were graced with eternal life; and, last but not least, Church art, which includes iconography, music and architecture.

One group of saints of particular importance are the Church Fathers. Anderson (1997) explains that

> By a Father of the Church, we mean one who by his (or her) wisdom in teaching or defending Church doctrine, often at the cost of his life or in the face of great suffering, bore witness to the tradition of the Church. When we read the Gospels, we say yes, what is written in the Gospel here is what the Church has always believed. In the same way, when we read the writings of the great Fathers, we can find in them a faithful and true testi-

> mony to what the Church has always believed and experienced about God (cited in OSB, pp. vi–vii).

With its vast, ancient literary heritage of patristic writings, Eastern Orthodoxy offers a wealth of historical resources on human psychology, which can be of use to all the professions whose vocational concern is human wellbeing. The Church Fathers are not empirical scientists in any modern sense, nor even systematic philosophers, although many had excellent philosophical training in the classical Hellenistic tradition of antiquity; like Christ, however, they often teach using parables, brief stories, metaphors, allegories, analogies, sayings, and references to scripture. Although not all Church Fathers analyse the human person in exactly the same way or use the same terms or concepts, the acquisition of an Orthodox *phronema*, or mind-set, through the study of patristic texts (the writings of Church fathers) can nevertheless lead to profound insights into the operation of the human soul. The relevance of the Church Fathers to contemporary analytical psychotherapy will be explored below in more detail, with particular reference to the work of a 6th century monastic saint, St. John Climacus. The immediate objection may understandably be raised, that since fourteen centuries have elapsed since St. John wrote the *Ladder of Divine Ascent*, the change in contextual factors between now and then is so great as to render such ancient texts practically irrelevant to our (post) modern research into human nature; yet as will be shown, the study of patristics is of direct relevance to modern life and thought. Indeed, in the bold words of Orthodox theologian Paul Evdokimov (1994),

> The creative assimilation of the thought of the Fathers, the restructuring of elements of the Christian tradition and of various branches of learning into a strong synthesis, will probably be the major work of the twentieth century (p. 31).

Certain recurring themes related to the meaning of suffering in Orthodox spirituality are of central importance to the study of patristic psychology, such as the relation of illness and sin, the nature of the body, the significance of evil and the fall, the roles of passion and dispassion in the spiritual life. Spiritual growth in the Orthodox tradition, as will be shown here, is in fact synonymous with psychological understanding and transformation through suffering; and theology in the Eastern Church cannot be an abstract exposition of ideas, a θεωρία (theory) without a πράξις (practice), separated from its ascetical beginnings in the monasticism of the Egyptian desert in the 3rd century. Evagrius (346–399 AD) quotes St. Neilus as saying, "If you are a theologian, you pray truly; if you pray truly, you are a theologian" (Louth, 1997; p. 20). In fact, it would be correct to argue, as Vlachos (1994) does, that Orthodoxy sees itself not so much as a religion, but as a therapeutic science. Ascetic Orthodox Christian spirituality proposes an understanding of creativity and human freedom which actively restructures the experience of suffering, bringing out both its teleological purpose and the source of our capacity to be transformed by it. This deep understanding of the role of creative suffering in our lives is partly based on and informed by the particular meaning of personhood in Orthodox theology.

There is a reductionistic tendency in western scientific thinking about the human person, which tends to maintain the thesis that 'person' is a superordinate construct which can be, indeed ought to be, more usefully broken down into simpler parts and analysed. In Orthodox Christianity this is not how the human person is perceived or understood; persons are known to be irreducible. In the theology of Fr. Sophrony (Sakharov), for example, the human persona[1] is nothing less than equivalent to the human spirit, the immaterial identity in man which transcends human nature and relates it to the Divine: "God is Spirit[2] and man-hypostasis is spirit" (Sakharov, 1998; quoted

[1] The use here of the term 'persona' may be confusing to Jungians. Fr. Sophrony is not referring to the Jungian archetype of social interaction; he is using the latin word 'persona' as the equivalent of the Greek term, *hypostasis*, roughly translated as "essence."

[2] Cf. Hopko (2006): "We must note here as well that God is not 'a spirit.' God

in Sakharov 2002, p. 78). It may even be the case, some Orthodox authors suggest, that the western scientific view of man as basically an animal with a mind, actually derives from a similar tendency within the western Christian tradition itself:

> [...] Western Christian theology in general [...] presupposes an anthropology different from that of the Greek Patristic tradition. In western theology, man by nature — as he is created 'in the image' — is a union of the animal or organic life and the intellectual life. The animal or organic life is not superadded to man as a consequence of the fall. On the contrary, it is the spiritual life which is superadded to man's natural state. Man is not spiritual by nature, as he is in the eastern Christian tradition. He is spiritual through a supererogatory act of grace (Sherrard, 1995, p. 8).

As man is the image of God, the human persona (in Fr. Sophrony's sense) escapes definition and remains hidden to empirical investigation; it can only be known in the way we know other people, so that f.e. one may know factors X, Y, Z pertinent to Mr. Smith and his life, but not really *know* him until Mr. Smith is met, and chooses to reveal himself. Hence for Fr. Sophrony and other Orthodox thinkers like V. Lossky (e.g. 2001, 2002) and N. Berdyaev (e.g. 1977) the human person is ultimately non-definable, and is the very source of the human freedom and creativity which liberates us from being determined — and, therefore, also limited — by our human nature. This maximalistic understanding of personhood stands in contradistinction to those tendencies in psychoanalysis (itself a body of thought

is completely different (*totaliter aliter*) from creatures in every way. To refer to God as 'spirit' is as anthropomorphic as to speak of God's eyes or hands. In St. John's Gospel, Jesus says 'God is Spirit' to indicate that God is not located anywhere, and must be worshipped 'in spirit and truth' (John 4:24). The Lord here is not making a metaphysical statement about God's being, which according to the Orthodox church fathers' interpretation of the Bible, as well as their personal mystical experience, is 'beyond being [*hyperousios*]' and even 'beyond divinity [*hypertheos*]'" (p. 19).

deriving largely from the Western philosophical tradition) to reduce the person into simpler elements. Sakharov (2002) explains:

> [The human person] is sometimes seen as a natural product of physical processes. These attempts revive the principles laid down by psychology. Freud seems to have emphasized the *biological dimension* (i.e. instincts and drives) as it interacts with the intrapsychic and interpersonal. Jung's approach is more complex insofar as he introduced the *archetypes* as playing a central role in the development of personality. Archetypes are elaborate constructs that, although they have a biological basis, also belong to the societal realm of culture and language. Though Jung attributed a positive role to spirituality in the well-being of the person, his position tends to psychologize religion and to reduce spirituality to a "psychic phenomenon." Both Freud and Jung limit their idea of personality to various combinations of intrapsychic and interpersonal causality, ignoring God-like freedom and self-determination of the human hypostasis (pp. 78–9, italics same).

In a very interesting study comparing Orthodox anthropology in John Zizioulas and the archetypal psychology of James Hillman, Melissaris (1997) uses a dialogical conception of truth to compare the writings of these two authors on personhood. He finds that "both authors agree that human beings are unique, unrepeatable, and inexhaustible entities" (p. 145); also, significantly in terms of its implications for theology, Melissaris suggests that the "categorical understandings rendered by either theological or psychological categories violate this quality of personhood and can lead to anthropological reductions" (p. 145). Finally he concludes that:

> [...] the two authors [...] disagree on the ontological basis of personhood. Zizioulas grounds personhood in ontology, for only then may otherness be relational and unshakable. Hillman,

> on the other hand, rejects ontology altogether, fearing that ontology not only reduces the person to a fixed point, but also creates grand metaphysical systems, which sacrifice personhood and otherness to abstract ideals. (*ibid*., pp. 145–146)

Hillman's 'fear' of ontology may be a direct descendant of Jung's ambivalence towards metaphysics. Hillman justly praises the appreciation for the complexity and multiplicity of life which the ancient Greek polytheistic view of the world represented; yet he neither espouses polytheism, nor of course the Christian faith. Hillman's avoidance of ontology is well-argued in his own oeuvre, yet it doesn't answer the basic question of ontology, since as Carter (1990) explains:

> We are addressing ontological issues when we ask whether something is *real* or whether something *exists* (p. 3, italics same).

Christian theology, on the other hand, does furnish us with an answer, albeit a paradoxical one perhaps, Melissaris suggests:

> It is because Zizioulas sees the person as *Who* and not as *what*, that he wishes to ground personhood in an absolute ontology, so that not only may otherness no longer be challenged and compromised, but personhood be given an ultimate core, resistant to deconstruction and/or reductive classification. This ontological content to personhood, claims Zizioulas, is the philosophical achievement of the Cappadocian Fathers, whose Trinitarian formulations first stressed the incontestable otherness and diversity manifested in the Trinitarian Persons, and then applied it to the human being, God's living icon on earth. Thus are overcome, in Zizioulas' view, the dilemmas of unity or diversity and individuality versus relatedness. Hillman, on the other hand, seems quite content with openness to multiplicity as such, stripped of ontology and metaphysical grounding (*ibid.*, pp. 141–142).

Personhood and otherness,[3] therefore, are seen to require an ontological basis in Christian theology. To an extent, this returns to the issue of the very purpose and compatibility of psychology and theology. Some Orthodox authors, like Avgoustidis (2004) have suggested that the continuing misunderstanding between the disciplines may be due to the fact that

> The main limitation on the way in which Orthodox pastoral practice can benefit by the science of psychology, is found in the anthropological assumptions which determine the aims and rationale of each of the two disciplines. Psychology ignores the meaning of man's prelapsarian condition. It considers the mode of being of fallen humanity as the only anthropological datum, and the anthropological consequences of the Incarnation of the divine Logos lie outside its field of interest. [...] (a) Orthodox anthropology differs from that underlying the contemporary human sciences. Caution is therefore required when engaging in dialogue with these sciences, so that anthropological views which are incompatible with Orthodox Tradition are not adopted. (b) Without the neptic experience of those who are gods by grace, i.e. the saints of the Church, it is impossible to articulate any substantial teaching on what man really is (pp. 17–18, my translation).

From an Orthodox perspective therefore, the fact that psychodynamic psychologists have focused on the irascible and appetitive aspects of the human soul, as taught by the Church Fathers hundreds of years ago, but reinterpreted these as the 'basic instincts' of sexual-

[3] Papadopoulos (1991) brilliantly discusses the development of the concept of otherness in Jung's opus from a metatheoretical perspective, defining the 'problematic' of the 'Other' as "the pivotal phenomenon of the composition and dissociability of the psyche" (p. 54). Papadopoulos demonstrates how Jung reached his appreciation of the Self as a superordinate psychic centre — *the* centre of the psyche, in fact — via his gradual engagement with the problematic of the 'Other' at different stages of his life (in Papadopoulos & Saayman, 1991).

ity and self-preservation, is suggestive of the secular error of not distinguishing between the pre- and post-lapsarian condition of man, as Avgoustidis (*ibid*) indicates. Elsewhere, Metropolitan Euthymios (2005) explains that, according to Orthodox tradition, the human body was created by God in three different 'phases,' only adding 'garments of skin' in the final, postlapsarian phase. It is during this phase of somatic creation that man's nature took on an 'animal' aspect, and the faculties of the soul began to be expressed *contra naturam* as passions. As Gregory of Sinai (Kadloubovsky & Palmer, 1992) explains:

> [...] [W]hen He created the body, He did not first include therein anger and unreasoning lust. It was only later, through transgression, that death, corruption and bestiality were added. [...] [T]he body was created incorruptible and [...] such it will be resurrected, just as the soul was created passionless. Thus both of them, body and soul, became corrupted and compounded together, in accordance with the natural law of combining and interacting with one another. [...] [T]he body became akin to beasts devoid of reason and was plunged into corruption. Thus joined together, the forces of the two formed one animal being, unreasoning and senseless, subject to anger and lust (p. 52).

Although necessarily also critical of the merely psychological approach to the person, Sakharov (*ibid*) nevertheless acknowledges the significance of psychology in reviving interest in and ideas, regarding the human person in contemporary theology:

> A significant reestimation of the issue of personal identity in theology is also due to the impact of research in psychology. Freud and Jung enhanced the interest in the inner processes of self-awareness (p. 69, ibid).

Yet for all its hiddenness and indefinability, in Christian practice the human persona is that aspect of personal identity which is nevertheless recognized by Fr. Sophrony to be "the very 'hidden man of the heart' (1 Pet. 3:4)" (cited in Sakharov, 2002; p. 72). It is, therefore, the core of our personhood, the 'ultimate core' Melissaris refers to above; also that part of us whereby we can be united to God. Metropolitan Anthony (2005) explains:

> There is no separation between the physical, the psychological and the spiritual, although each of them has got its function and place. They are interrelated, they penetrate one another. But we have power over the central core — that aspect of our bodies, our feelings and emotions, and our wills of which we can consciously become aware. If we the open this central core of ourselves to the action of God's power, his grace will overwhelm us, change us, and truly transfigure us (p. 292).

It may be interesting from a psychological perspective that although this 'central core' is voluntarily opened up to God in Orthodox spirituality, the operation of the will does not limit the reach of the divine spirit into the person to a conscious level alone. As Fr. Sophrony (1973) writes:

> The battle-ground of the spiritual struggle is, first and foremost, man's own heart; but 'the heart is deep.' The real life of the Christian is lived in this deep heart, hidden not only from alien eyes but also, in its fullness, from the owner of the heart himself. He who enters those secret recesses finds himself face to face with the mystery of being. Anyone who has ever given himself up with a pure mind to the contemplation of his inward self knows how impossible it is to arrive at a complete understanding even of a few moments of his life; knows how impossible it is to detect the spiritual processes of the heart, because in its profundity the heart touches upon that state of being where there *are* no processes (pp. 7–8).

This may also be the reason why, when praying for forgiveness of sins, Orthodox Christians do not only acknowledge sins they have consciously committed, but also those of which they are still unaware. Hence, St. John Chrysostom's prayer of preparation for Holy Communion asks God to

> ... absolve, remit and pardon me my transgressions, as many as I have committed in sins of word or deed or thought, wittingly or unwittingly, in knowledge or in ignorance ... (MEOP, p. 76).

Or as a second example from the Order of Confession (according to the Slavonic use), where the spiritual father leads a person towards the icon of Christ and says:

> Lord, loose, remit, forgive the sins, transgressions and iniquities, whether voluntary or involuntary, whether of willfulness or of ignorance, which have been committed unto guilt and disobedience by these thy servants (*ibid.*, p. 58).

The abundance of other such examples from Orthodox prayer life, may indicate both the acknowledgement of non-conscious thought and behaviour as a part of Christian anthropology,[4] as well as a tendency in Orthodox prayer (e.g. prayer of the heart; Chariton, 1966) to work on the person from consciousness *into* less conscious parts of the personality, in contradistinction to analysis, which tries for example to work on the person directly via the avenue of dreams and other unconscious material.[5] The famous words of St. Paul from

[4] Of course, it cannot be concluded that Christianity views the underlying processes and contents of the human psyche in the same manner as suggested by the Freudian or Jungian psychoanalytic unconscious.

[5] This distinction cannot be rigidly maintained, since both Orthodox spirituality and psychoanalysis can be understood to employ both 'conscious' and 'unconscious' elements in helping persons, viz. the use of the senses and bodily participation in Christian sacraments, and the conscious aspects of the frame and working alliance in psychoanalysis.

his epistle to the Romans (7:14–25) offer further acknowledgement of the struggle Christians must undertake with the two 'laws,' that of the flesh and the spirit. This very vivid first-century description of inner conflict could perhaps be described as a graphic instance of what Jungians call 'tension of opposites,' a crucifixion of the mind. Christians need to struggle not only with specific sins, but also with the deep-seated psychic debris of the inner inclination towards sinfulness, which all have inherited as a result of the Fall. Because the Fall was a result of the misapplication of human freedom through the misuse of our ancestors' free will, it is *this selfsame will* which is recognized as the very first aspect of our humanity in need of reparation. This is the reason the spiritual life in Orthodoxy begins with the virtues of humility and obedience to God, usually through a spiritual elder.

Christian spirituality therefore naturally includes the fortifying of conative powers, in such a way that we become more conscious of our thoughts, deeds and words – psychoanalytically speaking, a stronger 'ego' is achieved, but not at the expense of, or in spite of, the demands of the inner self or soul, nor with an aim to the fulfilment of selfish desires, as colloquial use of the word 'ego' implies. It is fully recognised that the soul itself is in need of healing; in sin, it is divided against itself, alienated (but not completely divorced) from its true nature, and needs to become whole. Like psychoanalysis, but less explicitly, Christian spirituality offers a method of treatment which indirectly includes the realm of the unconscious. Fr. V. Thermos (1996) explains:

> The term 'unconscious' or 'subconscious' is familiar to us all. And it would be correct to define it as that area of psychic life which is not under the control of our knowledge and will. Indeed, there do exist psychic regions which we do not know, and whose influence on our thought and behaviour we do not suspect. This fact obliges us to keep alert and continually exercise self-knowledge.

And Fr. Thermos then significantly adds,

> Only the saint is free of such dark spots, since the light of grace has flooded all regions of psychic life. And we also reduce the influence of the unconscious, the more we journey towards holiness (pp. 23–4, translation mine).

Thermos' above comment may be interestingly compared with Sumner (1950; cf. section on St. John Climacus), who writes from a Roman Catholic perspective, and suggests that

> It has indeed been found that an analytical process which opens out the deeper layers of the psyche and brings to the light of consciousness the innermost secrets of life leads to a richer and more vivid religious experience. The psyche, cleared of repressions and complexes, will provide a more suitable soil for for the supernatural (pp. 6–7).

Combining the two perspectives given above, it would seem there is some agreement that the freedom from psychological difficulties and increased consciousness which Jungian analysis and other psychotherapeutic approaches offer, in fact also both *lead to*, and are *the result* of genuine spiritual experience.

1 **Deification.** It needs to be emphasized from the outset however, that ascetic struggle alone is purposeless; it can only be made meaningful if put in the context of man's overall aim, which in Eastern Orthodoxy is the acquisition of the Holy Spirit. Seraphim of Sarov (Ware, 1993) is quoted as saying:

> Prayer, fasting, vigils, and all other Christian practices, however good they may be in themselves, certainly do not constitute the aim of our Christian life: they are the indispensable means of attaining that aim. *For the true aim of the Christian life is the acquisition of the Holy Spirit of God* (p. 230, italics mine).

Hence, it would be a serious misrepresentation to offer a summary of how Eastern Orthodoxy responds creatively to the theme of human suffering through its ascetic practices, without making reference to asceticism as *only a means*, the 'true aim' of the ascetic Christian life being what is variously called sanctification, divinization, deification or in Greek *θέωσις*, theosis. The Eastern Orthodox Christian aims at nothing less than to respond to God's self-emptying, kenotic, *philanthropic* act of incarnation — God's Word becoming flesh through the *Theotokos* in Jesus Christ — by emptying himself of his own human nature in order to become one with God, a *microtheos*, to become by grace what God is by nature. As Ware (1984) elsewhere explains,

> In the Orthodox understanding Christianity signifies not merely an adherence to certain dogmas, not merely an external imitation of Christ through moral effort, but direct union with the living God, the total transformation of the human person by divine grace and glory — what the Greek Fathers termed "deification" or "divinization" (*theosis, theopoiesis*) (p. 7).

Sanctification in the Orthodox Church is being set apart for God, being cleansed of sins and made holy by Christ in the Holy Spirit (Conciliar Press, 1988). Although it is a gift from God, and cannot therefore ever be magically coerced, Christians are nevertheless required to cooperate synergistically with Him in their transformation, by making correct use of their freedom.

John Climacus only refers briefly to this aim in his *Ladder* (see below), perhaps because it is to him so obvious what the sometimes austere spiritual exercises he offers, are ultimately for. Gregory Palamas (Meyendorff, 1998) offers a more complete description of the process of theosis in his theology — as good a description as possible, of something which words can only fail to describe — and would therefore probably provide another valuable primary source in the investigation of the purpose of human suffering in the Orthodox faith, although this is generally true of so many saints and Church Fathers as to be something of a truism.

2 **The Orthodox Approach to Suffering in John Climacus.** For the purpose of offering a concrete example of the operation and cure of the psyche in Orthodoxy, particular reference will be made to the theme of creative suffering through the ascetic struggle with the passions. Prior to discussion of the cure of the psyche through creative suffering however, a classic text of orthodox ascetic literature, namely St. John Climacus' *Ladder of Divine Ascent* (e.g. Climacus, 1982), will be briefly referred to as an instance of patristic thought. This work is so highly esteemed among Orthodox, that it is read every Lent in the refectories of monasteries, while the monks or nuns consume their spare fasting meals in silence. Archimandrite Isaias Simonopetritis even writes that

> [St. John] provides an authentic Orthodox response to every Western school of Psychology and Psychoanalysis, by mercilessly exposing the origin of the passions, to release the human soul from the tyranny of delusion and the seething emotions of the unhumiliated ego (Simonopetritis, 2008).

Elsewhere Vlachos (1994) also writes of the same Church Father that:

> St. John Climacus introduces true theology in many places in his spiritually delightful 'Ladder.' "Total purity is the foundation of theology." "When a man's senses are perfectly united to God, then what God has said is somehow mysteriously clarified. But where there is no union of this kind, then it is extremely difficult to speak about God." On the contrary, the man who does not actually know God speaks about him only "in probabilities." Indeed, according to patristic teaching it is very bad to speak in conjectures about God, because it leads a person to delusion. This saint knows how "the theology of the demons" develops in

> us. In vainglorious hearts which have not previously been purified by the operation of the Holy Spirit, the unclean demons "give us lessons in the interpretation of scripture." Therefore, a slave of passion should not "dabble in theology" (pp. 31–2).

It is beyond the scope of this study to analyze in detail the *Ladder* itself, taking extracts from it and discussing their meaning in the context of Western psychology, though this would certainly be useful and interesting as the topic of a separate study. Avgoustidis (1999) does in fact undertake such a task, in an important study on human aggression as it is approached in the *Ladder*.

Climacus obtains the image of a ladder from Jacob's ladder (Gen. 28:12), which stretches from earth to heaven. The spiritual life is represented as a series of thirty ascending steps, or rungs on the ladder (one step "for each year in the hidden life of Christ prior to his baptism" (Ware, 1982, p. 11)). St. John's path of spiritual development may be broken down into three stages: (i) a break with the 'world' (Steps 1–3); (ii) practise of the virtues, or *praxis* (Steps 4–26); and (iii) the final steps lead to union with God, or *theoria* (Steps 27–30), the very last step being love. Other Orthodox authors have also used the image of a ladder as a metaphor for the spiritual life; for example, St. Isaac the Syrian revealingly writes:

> The ladder to the Kingdom is hidden within you, and within your soul. Dive down into your self, away from sin, and there you will find the steps by which you can ascend ([Hom. 2, B12; quoted in Brock (1997)]).

A wealth of such quotations indicate that self-knowledge and Christian praxis and theoria, of which purification through suffering is an important part, are intimately interwoven in Orthodox spirituality. As the definition of the word 'passion' (1), offered by Spiegelman (1989; see above) suggests, suffering is a central theme of the Christian faith, a faith which has at its very core a suffering God, and employs the cross, nothing less than the cruel instrument of His torture and execution, as its central symbol. The theme of responding creatively to suffering and evil, and the significance of suffering in Christian life experience, far from being one of Christianity's theoretical weak points, or—as it is sometimes presented—a question which confounds and alarms the startled Christian theologians, who then comically proceed to stumble over it in various acts of intellectual contortionism, can be seen to actually run right through mainstream Orthodox Christian theology.

While considering suffering to be to be of inherent value in the event of martyrdom, however, the Christian religion is also not, as some have claimed, masochistically enamoured of suffering for its own sake, however pointless or arbitrary. In fact, Mack (1999) points out,

> As Christians, we are not masochists. All of our spiritual struggles have as their goal the joy and true celebration of union with Christ. In a very real sense, we are the ultimate hedonists. We seek true and lasting joy—joy which will never end and joy which can never be taken away. [...] By God's grace, we have been enlightened, and so have come to understand that the joys of this world are fading and never last. [...] true joy is only found in the everlasting Kingdom of our God and Saviour Jesus Christ (p. 10).

The impermanence and transience of worldly pleasures is what drives Christians to reject them and seek true, lasting joy. Pleasure in itself, however, is not only *not* evil, but a natural psychological aim; it is only the quality and manner of 'pleasure' that determines whether it is sinful (i.e. misses the aim of theosis). As Mack (*ibid*) suggests above, true pleasure is the bliss of union with God in His kingdom, experienced here and now by the devout Christian. Ware (2004) further explains that

> In itself suffering is an evil. It is not part of God's original plan for His creation: He made us not for sorrow but for joy—as

> St. John Climacus puts it, not for mourning but for laughter. Upon some people the effects of suffering are utterly destructive, leading to nothing but bitterness and despair. We are not to say that suffering as such is a blessing from God. And yet, by the divine mercy what is in itself evil can be turned to good. [...] suffering can be used. Something can be made of it (p. 116).

Suffering, therefore, has redemptive value for Christians, not for its own sake, but because repentance, the awareness of sin and of the possibility for change, is recognized as the beginning of spiritual life. Christians are encouraged to become aware of sinfulness, both their own and that of collective humanity, not through some morbid, neurotic guilt complex, but because of the revelation of what is true, beautiful and good, sinfulness being the distance from it through participation in what is ugly, false and evil. Guilt, too, is therefore of no inherent value to Christians, and not really part of the psychology of the saints. Its only use is in awakening the voice of conscience and motivating a sinner towards repentance and change; substitute methods for becalming the pain of contrition, ranging from the excessive use of tranquilizers to certain approaches in psychotherapy and political ideology, are recognized to be ineffective, offering false consolation by putting conscience to sleep, the 'sleep of sin.' In fact, the achievement of a genuine state of 'blessedness,' in which one's relationship with God as Creator is based on sincerity, involves acquiring *parrhesia*, boldness before God,[6] not guilt.

In Christ, perfection is seen and desired; therefore, suffering — which He voluntarily and without sin embraced — is not seen

[6] It is suggested below that a peculiar characteristic of many saints, is that they hold themselves responsible not only for their own sins, but also for those of others. Theologians maintain this is not due to the excessive growth of a dysfunctionally harsh superego, but is more correctly regarded as a direct consequence of understanding that blaming others has been a human failing since the time Adam blamed God for giving him Eve as companion, and Eve blamed the serpent. Humility, and therefore repentance, suggests the assumption of increasing personal responsibility.

by Christians as something to be avoided, much less a source of complaint against God, the universe and everything. On the contrary, suffering is voluntarily embraced and accepted with 'joyful sorrow,' χαρμολύπη (step 7 of the *Ladder*), as it thereby offers Christians the opportunity to participate in Christ's own suffering (Passion) and to pay for sins and redeem sinfulness, cleansing the eyes of the soul, making God's glory visible even during this life. In the *Ladder of Divine Ascent*, St. John Climacus explains:

> Repentance is cheerful renunciation of every creature comfort. Those making some progress in blessed mourning are usually temperate and untalkative. Those who have succeeded in making real progress do not become angry and do not bear grudges. As for the perfect—these are humble, they long for dishonor, *they look out for involuntary sufferings*, they do not condemn sinners and they are inordinately compassionate. The first kind are acceptable, the second praiseworthy, but *blessed surely are those who hunger for suffering* and thirst for dishonor, for they will be filled to abundance with the food that cannot satiate them (1982, p. 136 italics mine).

St. John clearly suggests that there is a connection between repentance and suffering. Furthermore, he outlines three stages in which one may deepen in repentance, the 'hunger for suffering' belonging to the final stage, a characteristic of those whose repentance has been perfected.

The Roman Catholic Benedictine author Dom M. Oswald Sumner (1950) presents a Jungian perspective on St. John Climacus. He says of the *Ladder of Perfection* that

> The advantage of choosing this book is that, coming as it does at the end of the "Desert" period [of the history of Christian monastic spirituality] it is a kind of *Summa* of the Wisdom of the Desert: and also it was very greatly used during the whole of the Middle Ages throughout the West (p. 5).

Sumner (*ibid*) is particularly concerned with the question of whether Western spirituality (i.e. Christianity) has anything similar to offer to yoga and the Eastern meditative practises which fascinated Jung, and he turns to St. John as a natural option, for his contemplative teaching. Of Jungian psychology, Sumner (*ibid*) writes that

> It turns out to be an introverted attempt to provide a *Heilsweg* for the psychic ills of our day. In this attempt it has drawn close to the religious realm represented by the yoga of the East and the symbolic and contemplative life of the West (p. 6).

Sumner (*ibid*) describes how, in direct contrast to yoga and Eastern meditative practices, there are no detailed directions on meditation, posture, breathing exercises, or indeed any "phantasmata to be formed in the imagination" (p. 7), or "surprising effects such as levitation, clairvoyance, clairaudience, self-heating and cooling of the body" (p. 7) to be found in the *Ladder*. Instead,

> What we do find in John Climacus is a certain type of life — hours of solitary meditation, recitation of offices or psalms, the weekly attendance at the great Liturgy in the common church — hours of manual labour, Scripture reading, fasts, penances, vigils. All this is done under the direction of a Master and is accompanied by a striving to quieten the passions and exercise certain virtues (*ibid*, p. 8).

Sumner goes on to discuss the master-disciple relationship in Climacus, comparing it to the analyst-patient relationship in Jungian analysis. He writes:

> Both the analyst and the ascetic have the master-disciple relationship as part of their disciplines. But, as their tasks differ, so does the concept of this relationship. The analyst has no theological or ethical task before him, though ethical questions will

> certainly present themselves. He is primarily concerned with the neuroses of his patient and his aim will be, first of all, to help the patient to *live* and then to achieve wholeness or integration. [...] The analyst does not have to take the position of the great infallible master at all (*ibid*, p. 9).

In this latter comment, Sumner shows surprising ignorance of the true nature of the function of the elder-disciple relationship in Orthodoxy. The whole point of this spiritual relationship is not a celebration of the wisdom and infallibility of the 'master,' but lies in the *act of obedience* itself. There are numerous accounts of cranky, unreasonable and downright wrong elders in the discipline, whom disciples are requested to follow and obey nonetheless, not through some masochistic urge, but because of the fruits of humility. The only area where the master-disciple obedience may be productively challenged, is if the elder asks the disciple to do something which transgresses the Lord's commandments.

Sumner (*ibid*) goes on to suggest that the 'master' is different to the analyst also in that he *leads* the way because he "knows the way from experience and because he has qualities that will enable him to bring out the potential virtues of the disciple" (p. 9). For Sumner, the analyst is "the companion on the road, the other is quite definitely the Master-his to command, the disciple's part to submit and obey [...]" (p. 10). Despite these inaccuracies concerning the role and psychology of the spiritual elder, Sumner does identify correctly that, where the analyst aims at the emergence of the Self, the ascetic elder guides the disciple to "transforming union" with God. He correctly quotes from St. John that the elder should be a man who has attained victory over his passions, who is not "sick himself instead of a physician" (*Ladder*, p. 92, 1982). Sumner also suggests that the elder should be chosen by the disciple "according to the [Jungian] principle of compensation" (*ibid.*, p. 11), since St. John advises prospective disciples to judge and discern what superiors are proper for them, according to the passions they are most susceptible to, for example a corporally austere master is suited to those who are susceptible to passions of the flesh, a rude and severe elder for those inclined to pride. In pointing out this element of choice by the disciple, however, Sumner inadvertently begs the question of whether the Master-disciple relationship is as autocratic as he implies earlier.

Sumner then turns to the interesting question of whether a transference relationship is set up, between master and disciple. He concludes that "the master-disciple relationship is not based on transference" (*ibid*, p. 14), and does so on account of the fact that St John urges disciples to remember and inscribe on their hearts the good deeds which they see their elders perform; St. John does so in order to ensure that the disciple can recall these positive memories when the temptation to judge their elder arises on a later occasion. Sumner suggests that because St. John praises obedience and warns against the temptation to judge an elder, transference cannot be set up because the elder is God's "ambassador" (*ibid*, p. 14), and "therefore only the mediator and not the end in itself" (*ibid*, p. 14). Once again, the understanding here is only partially correct; while an elder would be first to admit that he/she is 'only a mediator,' of itself this does not prevent the setting up of transference in the elder-disciple relationship. In fact, it may be suggested instead that when St. John warns against the sin of judging one's elder, it is precisely the distortion of the relationship by transference projections which we could say he is, in modern terms, trying to prevent. The fact that something is counted a sin, does not imply that Christians will therefore not do it! All that St. John may be doing therefore, is calling a sin by its name. Sumner (*ibid*) seems to contradict himself when he later suggests that

> The Master is expected to care not to accept this projection of heroic archetypes, and, by humility, he is to leave the disciple as free as may be (p. 15).

If a transference relationship is not set up between elder and disciple, then why is the 'Master' being described in the process of dealing with the risk of illusory countertransference through humility? Sumner puts it down to 'rapport' that an elder may set a disciple 'free' (was he/she not free during his discipleship?) to seek another elder if he can no longer be of assistance for a specific problem — yet how does this differ in essence from the occasion when a responsible therapist refers a client to a more suitably qualified practitioner? Sumner consequently discusses differences between confession and psychoanalysis, the danger of not having an elder in the spiritual life as compared with the risks of psychological self-analysis, libido or psychic energy, the humility with which the shadow must be confronted, and the topic of dreams; in all of these matters he compares and contrasts the teachings of the *Ladder* with analytical psychology, with greater or lesser success.

It is also of interest that in his study of the New Age movement, Jungian analyst J. R. Haule (1999) devotes several pages to St. John Climacus (whom he amusingly refers to as 'Ladder Man'). Haule writes the following almost in response to Sumner's above misinterpretation of obedience in St. John:

> Based on the biblical image of Jacob's vision of angels ascending and descending between Heaven and Earth, the *Ladder of Divine Ascent* is a thirty-step catalog of the virtues a monk must attain and the vices he must overcome. It reveals John Climacus as a consummate Director of Souls, whose central concern is the personal obstacle each individual has to surmount in order to climb that ladder and gain union with the One. He begins with, and returns constantly to, the virtue of obedience — an emphasis that may perplex a modern reader inclined to pre-judge "perfect obedience" as a kind of infantilization. But John's notion of obedience can only be understood when we remember that a monastery is an entirely voluntary institution (p. 31).

Haule (*ibid*) thereby correctly identifies the supreme importance given by Orthodoxy to the freedom of the person. Ware (2004) uses the tonsuring ritual to explain how significant the voluntary nature of monastic obedience is:

> At the tonsuring — the decisive moment in the monastic profession service — the abbot places the scissors on the Gospel Book, saying to the candidate, "Take the scissors, and give them to me." When the candidate does so, the abbot replaces them on the Gospel Book, repeating the same words. This happens yet a third time; and only after that does the abbot proceed to cut the novice's hair. Underscoring the significance of this threefold ceremony, the abbot says "See, no one compels you to be clothed in the habit. See, you have freely chosen to receive it." No one has taken away the new monk's freedom, but he has himself offered it to Christ (pp. 115–116).

Of the novice monks, Haule (*ibid*) writes:

> Why did people join? [St.] John gives three reasons: some have hit bottom in their sinfulness and are searching for a higher principle on which to ground their lives, others are convinced of the reality of the Kingdom of God and enter a monastery to devote themselves to it, and a few are after oneness with God in love. All of these people are convinced of the reality of *soul*, but find that they are soul-people only intermittently. They wish to live in and through their souls more consistently. They want their gaps opened so they can *see*[7] the eternal cosmos every day and every moment of their lives (pp. 31–32).

[7] Haule (*ibid*) uses the verb 'see' to mean visionary imagination, as distinct from normal sensory vision, which implies the existence of a heightened, shamanic-like altered state of consciousness, rendering access to levels of reality which cannot be immediately detected with the senses or scientific instruments, but which are nonetheless real, like the "imaginal realm" referred to by Sufis as in Corbin (1972; cf. Samuels, 1989).

Continuing, Haule (*ibid*) goes on to suggest that what St. John did was to "accurately *see* the people whose souls he directed" (p. 32), opening the eyes of their souls through the assignment of tasks and the ascetic lifestyle of the monastery. "Climacus," writes Haule, "recommends an obedient attachment to a director uniquely suited to free us from the flesh world and open our eyes to the world of soul" (p. 32).

Haule's understanding of the meaning and purpose of obedience and the struggle against the passions in John Climacus, comes much closer to the way it is understood by Orthodox Christians. Even his declaration that St. John dedicated his life to the pursuit of gnosis is not entirely mistaken:

> Gnosis did not die [...].[8] Indeed, it could be mentioned again by name. For, although the Ladder Man devoted his life and his book to the pursuit of that mystical knowledge, he dared not use a word reeking of heresy and paganism. Gnosis remained, but in the second half of Pisces, it has gained a connection with matter (p. 36).

Haule's whole framework of presuppositions is clearly different from an Orthodox Christian one, yet what is contestable here is whether the understanding of 'gnosis' necessarily refers to heretical or pagan gnosis, or whether there is in fact, a Christian gnosis.[9] Also, the so-called ascetic 'denial' of the body may be a war against the *flesh*, but is it a rejection of matter as such? These issues are addressed elsewhere (e.g. Ware, 1998), but it may suffice here to quote from the introduction to the *Ladder*, where Ware (1982) writes that

[8] After the Renaissance reawakened classical antiquity's interest in nature and the body, rendering the Christian ascetic 'denial' of the body and instincts 'unhealthy,' according to Haule.

[9] In the special instance of the *Ladder*, Ware (1982) points out how "In contrast to Evagrius, [St. John Climacus] holds that the supreme end of the spiritual way is not contemplation or *gnosis* but love" (p. 12). Without contradicting this observation, it may nonetheless be added that, on the level of practical spirituality, Christian gnosis and love are often interdependent, the one flowing from and accompanying the other.

> The dialectical stance displayed by St. John Climacus in his treatment of repentance and tears is to be seen equally in his attitude to the human body. The body is both adversary and friend: adversary inasmuch as it has been marred by the fall, friend inasmuch as it remains God's creation and is called to share in the resurrection glory. To appreciate John's attitude aright, and to avoid unjustly accusing him of anti-Christian body-soul dualism, it is important to determine on what level he is speaking in each particular passage: whether of the body in its true and natural state, as formed by the Creator, or of the body as we know it now, in its contranatural or fallen condition (p. 28).

When the Athonite elder Porphyrios was sixteen years old, he used to come out from celebrating the Holy Liturgy in church, feeling so grateful for God's generous gift of Holy Communion and so indebted to God for the gift of salvation, that he would ask God in a prayer to give him "a serious illness, a cancer, so that I would suffer for His love and glorify Him through my pain" (Porphyrios, 2005; p. 224). Fr. Porphyrios did not do this out of hostility to his body, or due to some masochistic or depressive frame of mind, nor even consciously indulging in the spiritual grandiosity of seeking martyrdom — although his own elder did tell him to stop saying this prayer, explaining to the young monk that

> ...this was egotism and that I was coercing God. God knows what he is doing. So I didn't continue with this prayer (*ibid*, p. 224).

This wish, certainly pathological by contemporary psychiatric standards[10] — and especially in a young person — is perhaps more appro-

[10] Hence Sophrony (1973) writes: "What the spiritual man sees or hears, his emotions, his whole experience, may often seem folly, or the fruit of a psychopathological state, to the 'natural' man who, ignorant of the reality of the spiritual world, rejects what he does not know. [...] if a man fixes his will on

priately conceived within its own context, as a direct result of the clarity with which Fr. Porphyrios perceived his own and other's sinfulness, and the fervent desire to bear Christ's suffering in his own body, for the life of the world. If Christ has emptied and humiliated Himself for us, voluntarily renouncing his divine omnipotence to become a mortal man, and offer up his body to be broken as a sacrifice, it becomes imperative to the saint who progresses in the spiritual life, to do something for God in return; to share in the Lord's suffering (Rom. 8:17), to complete what is lacking in it (Col. 1:24) and thereby to get as far away as humanly possible from sinfulness, transcending the human inclination to evil through the correct use of the free will. Far from having a diagnosable mental illness, Elder Porphyrios was in fact a gifted counsellor and protector of the mental and physical health of numerous spiritual children.

In later life, Fr. Porphyrios did in fact develop cancer among a host of other illnesses,[11] and considered that God had demonstrated his love to him in this way, granting his early prayer and giving him the opportunity to share in Christ's suffering:

> Now I do not pray for God to take away from me the thing I asked Him for. I am glad that I have it so that I can participate in His sufferings through my great love. I have the chastisement of God: *for God chastises the one he loves* (Heb. 12:6). My illness is a special favour from God, who is inviting me to enter into the mystery of His love and to try to respond with His own grace. But I am not worthy. [...] I pray for Him to make me good [as opposed to making him well]. I'm certain that God knows I am

material things and physical satisfactions, he becomes blunted and spiritually insensitive" (p. 20).

[11] One of his spiritual children, cardiologist Dr. G. Papazachou, diagnosed Fr. Porphyrios with the following: myocardial infarction, chronic kidney disease, duodenal ulcer, operated cataract, facial herpes zoster, staphylococcus dermatitis, inguinal hernia, chronic bronchitis, pituitary cancer (Porphyrios, 2005, p. 224).

> in pain. But I pray for my soul, for God to forgive my transgressions. (*ibid*, pp. 224–5, words in square brackets mine).

It can be seen that the problem of suffering, viewed from an Orthodox perspective, is inextricably interwoven with our freedom and our struggle against the passions, and with the way we use our bodies and souls in our relation to the divine. The example of Elder Porphyrios demonstrates how Orthodoxy is characterised by a very keen awareness of sinfulness (Zernov, 1999); sin is the only thing an Orthodox Christian is encouraged to hate, the real purpose of the soul's irascible part[12] being to motivate us against this, our only true enemy. God's holiness is perceived as being such, that there is no distinction — as is to be found in Roman Catholicism — between 'mortal' and 'venial' sins: *all* sin, however 'slight' it may appear, is a serious departure from Him who cannot coexist with sin (Spidlik, 1986; p. 187); a loss of grace, a 'missing of the mark' for ourselves. Hence a seemingly 'small' sin may have greater spiritual implications than one which is more apparent in its gravity. Sophrony (1973) writes that

> Sin is primarily a metaphysical phenomenon whose roots lie in the mystic depths of man's spiritual nature. The essence of sin consists not in the infringement of ethical standards but in a falling away from the eternal divine life for which man was made and to which, by his very nature, he is called. Sin is committed first of all in the secret depths of the human spirit, but its consequences distort the whole individual. A sin will reflect on a man's psychological and physical condition, on his outward appearance, on his personal destiny. Sin will, inevitably, pass beyond the boundaries of the sinner's own life to burden all humanity and thus affect the fate of the whole world. The sin of

[12] The soul in Orthodoxy is considered to have a rational aspect (λογικόν), a desirous aspect (ἐπιθυμικόν) and an irascible aspect (θυμικόν). Each aspect has its particular use and purpose; this tripartite structure involves a theological development of Platonic theory.

> our forefather Adam was not the only sin of cosmic significance. Every sin, secret or manifest, committed by each one of us, has a bearing on the rest of the universe (p. 22).

Sin, therefore, can be seen as having catastrophic ramifications not just for us and our fellow human beings, but for everything, ultimately for the (dis)order of the entire cosmos, as the elder Zosima eloquently reminded his disciples in Dostoyevsky's novel, *The Brothers Karamazov.*[13] Sin is never an isolated event (Antonopoulos, 2007), and therefore everyone is responsible for their own as well as their neighbour's sins.[14] Again, properly understood, this perception is not the result of inappropriate or diffuse personal boundaries, or some pathological identity moratorium resulting from personal grandiosity or a hypertrophied superego; on the contrary, in the experience of the saints it is the fruit of a sense of profound humility which gives birth to self-awareness, such that our failure to fulfil the commandment to "be perfect" (Matt. 5:48) is a painful reminder, of our responsibility and share in all that is evil.

It is, therefore, generally accepted in Orthodox spirituality, that the sense of sin and personal responsibility increases with holiness, so that saints eventually come to feel themselves personally responsible for everyone's sins. Hence, it is naturally taken for granted that:

---

[13] The character of Elder Zosima is based on the real life elder, Starets Amvrosy of the Optina Pustyn monastery in Kozelsk (Dunlop, 1988)

[14] Of the Athonite Elder Paisios (d. 1993) for example, it is written that: "He believed that the grace of God was the only cause of every good; for every evil, he blamed himself out of his deep sense of humility. When he saw someone falling into sin, refusing to repent, or having no faith in God, he thought: "It is my fault that one of my brothers has found himself in this difficult situation. If I were acting according to Christ's will, then He would listen to my prayers and my brother wouldn't be in this unpleasant state; my wretchedness is causing my brother's misery."[...] He constantly prayed to God to help all the people who [...] suffered due to his own negligence and spiritual indolence" (Priestmonk Christodoulos, 1998, p.12)

> However just and pure a man may be, there is always an element of sin in him which cannot enter the Kingdom of God and which must be burned up. Our sins are burned up by our sufferings (Elchaninov, 1967, p. 27).

Although suffering is never a direct consequence of sin in Orthodox theology, when responded to through faith, it acts to purify the human person. Indeed, the same author explains how the sense of sin does not in fact, decrease with increasing sanctity, but on the contrary becomes even keener:

> The sense of deep sinfulness experienced by saints is caused by their nearness to the source of light — to Christ (*ibid*, p. 34).

Hence, the closer to holiness we come, the more clearly visible our sinfulness becomes. This metanoic awareness is very different to the variety of guilt experienced in the various psychoneuroses (Singh, 2000), which is ultimately egotistical because it is enclosed within the self, and not truly seeking relation to another. Similarly masochism[15] and algolagnia actively seek suffering, but once again with primary reference to the self, as a morbid side-effect perhaps, of the underlying pride behind the same unconscious psychological guilt complex. This perspective concurs with psychoanalyst Neville Symington (2001), when he writes that:

> I think there are two modes of human action. Either we act on impulse, or we act freely. [...] Whenever people act on impulse,

[15] As regards accusations of masochism, De Beausobre (1940; 1999), whose theory of creative suffering is discussed below, humorously writes that: "[M]any educated and most half-educated people of all countries [...] being used to consider the whole subject of suffering morbid, would dub any discussion of its brighter side, of its creative possibilities — masochistic. Well, after living a long life which has followed a rather curious pattern, I think I can say quite firmly that I am not a masochist" (pp. 2–3).

> they are guilty. Why are they guilty? Because it damages them, whereas if they act freely, after things have been processed, it is enriching to the personality (p. 84).

The guilt of neurosis is tied in with an arrested psychological development; in contrast, the "guilt"—or more appropriately, the remorse and repentance of saints deepens, as they become more fully themselves, acting with greater freedom, but also becoming more aware of the true dimensions of responsibility.

Sophrony (1973) also correctly contrasts sin with mere 'ethical infringement' in the paragraph given above. Yannaras (1996) even suggests that neurotic guilt may itself be a symptom of the legalistic approach to sin permeating culture, which sometimes Western theology is prone to:

> The idea cultivated in western Christendom, which identified sin with legal transgression and salvation with individual justification and atonement, linked Christian ethics in people's minds with a host of psychological complexes offering no way of escape. [...] The egocentric fear of transgression, and the tendency to gloss over sin or to reach an accommodation with it are extensions and consequences of the psychological guilt complex, and neither has any place in the spiritual climate of Orthodox ethics.[...] Thus the Christian does not fear sin with the psychological fear of individual guilt, the complex of depression over individual transgression which lessens the "moral worth" of his individual self. [...] *He fears sin only as deprivation of the potentiality to respond to the love of Christ.* But a fear such as this is already a first step toward love (pp. 38–42, italics mine).

Although it is viewed with such gravity, sin is therefore not perceived as primarily being a barrier to our individual moral 'justification,' but as an incapacitation of our ability to respond to Christ's love. The 'joyful sorrow' (*χαρμολύπη*) of John Climacus is suffering accepted, and transformed creatively into the profound joy of man's resurrection. Christians know true bliss and spiritual pleasure do not come from shirking worldly pain, but they also do not relish pain for its own sake. Hence Nicodemus the Hagiorite enjoins Christians to

> Make firm in yourself the conviction and faith, that all things happening to us happen according to God's will and for our profit, so that we may gain thereby a certain spiritual fruit (Nicodemus the Hagiorite, 2008).

And he continues, in the same passage, to suggest that in a certain sense there is a place allocated *even to our particular sins* in the divine economy, through seeing in the shape of our destiny — even in its wrong turns — an ever-present opportunity to deepen our relationship to God through repentance:

> Although we cannot suppose that some things, such as our sins and those of other people, are the direct result of a willed action of God's, yet even they do not happen without God's leave, as a means of admonishing and humbling us (*ibid*).

Nicodemus then explicitly declares that our sufferings and afflictions are sent by God as an instrument whereby we may acquire virtue:

> As regards sufferings and afflictions which are our own fault or due to malice of others — God Himself sends them, desiring us to suffer and be tormented by them, in order to gain the blessing of virtue, which we are bound to earn if we calmly endure as we should the trials He has sent us (*ibid*).

Nicodemus does not imply here, that there is any sadistic satisfaction for God in witnessing our suffering, but he expressly links the permission given for us to suffer, to God's desire for us to grow in virtue — and hence in the spiritual life — through the suffering.

Finally, Nicodemus reproaches even the human tendency towards feeling resentment for the wrongs done to us, suggesting that it is a sort of secondary, self-inflicted trauma, an adding of insult to injury, which amounts to nothing less than a rejection of God's ordinance, and thereby also of the inner peace which results from accepting things with a good heart:

> [...] Thus, convinced that God Himself wishes you to endure hardship and grief, which assails you, either arising from the evil nature of other people, or invited by your own wrong action, you will cease to think [of the wrong done to you]. By this they [who think of the wrong done to them] want to justify their lack of patience [...] and the feelings of revenge they feel at the sight of injustice; but in actual fact the only thing they achieve is to rebel against God's ordinance and to attempt to cast off their life-saving cross, imposed on them by God for their own good, instead of shouldering it with a good heart, which would undoubtedly be pleasing to Him. And what do they get? They cannot cast off their cross, they offend God, and still they gain no peace. On the contrary, to grief they add contention and useless irritation and render their state unbearable; whereas had they borne what happened with good heart, they would have peace and would have attracted God's benevolence, and would have eaten richly of the fruit of the spirit (*ibid*).

The cross of suffering cannot be cast off without repercussions, nor should we wish its expulsion from our destiny. Suffering, even the self-inflicted kind for which we alone are culpable, therefore acquires meaning in the furnace of patient acceptance of God's will, and through our learning from experience:

> If a man supposes that life should be one long, luxurious "vacation," then any amount of suffering that comes to him is unbearable. But if a man views life as a time of sorrows, correction,

> and purification, then suffering and pain become not only bearable, but even useful (*The Teaching of the Holy Fathers on Illness*, 1986, p. 1).

It is largely, then, a question of perspective. The general meaning and purpose of suffering is inevitably of prime concern, not only to the academic theologian, but also to the priest or minister who is trying to offer pastoral care to distressed and hurting members of their congregation on the spiritual path, and — it is here argued — should also be of equal concern to the practising psychotherapist, who aims to help their client's wounds heal, so that they may move on in life with a greater sense of inner freedom. It is also widely acknowledged that suffering, left untreated and unresponded to, can blunt and simply damage the heart — whereas the great challenge for the Christian and for everybody seeking help, is to maintain clarity, innocence and sensitivity even in the face of great suffering. The growth of compassion and the growth of virtue are hence mutually reinforcing.

Nonetheless, despite what has already been said about the centrality of its significance, suffering *per se* is not a preoccupation of the Church Fathers, or indeed a major theme for meditation in Orthodox spirituality, or for doctrinal or dogmatic development in Orthodox theology — as it sometimes can be in Roman Catholicism (cf. Grassi, 2000; John Paul II, 1984), and thereby also in much Western spirituality and thought concerning God. As suggested above, this is not because the Orthodox are indifferent to suffering, or unaware of its impact, but is perhaps a result of the emphasis placed in Eastern Christianity on God's holiness: His incomprehensible majesty, His unfathomable mystery and otherness, but above all his profound love. As Maximus the Confessor (580–662 AD) writes:

> God is one, unoriginate, incomprehensible, possessing completely the total potentiality of being, altogether excluding notions of when and how, inaccessible to all, and not to be known through any natural image by any creature (Louth, 1997; p. 10).

It is as though the glory and power of God and the reality of His Kingdom — where all suffering ceases to exist, "where there is neither sickness, nor sorrow, nor sighing, but life everlasting" (MEOP, 1999, p. 27) — are so evident and clear to the vision of the Fathers, and hence to the whole Orthodox Church, that human suffering in this context is but a means to an end, a passing incident in the brief darkness of our mundane existence, which is soon followed by bliss in the eternal day of the coming Kingdom of God. Not only is human suffering thus seen as temporary, but correspondingly Orthodox theology emphasizes the Transfiguration and Resurrection of the Lord, as opposed to His Crucifixion.[16] God's suffering, in the Eastern Church, is seen as being in a sense proof of his divinity; St. John Chrysostom characteristically says, "I call Him King, *because* I see Him crucified"[17] (italics mine). There is an emphasis on Christus Victor, but one which does not imply that the meaning of Christ as sacrificial Victim is ignored or forgotten.

Nevertheless, some modern Orthodox writers mostly in the context of pastoral care, do deal explicitly, both briefly and in more extensive treatments, with the theme of suffering in human life (e.g. Aleksiev, 1994; Papakostas, 1998), and their work is useful in expanding and consolidating the way in which John Climacus in the *Ladder of Divine Perfection* responds to the issue of suffering, as well as all the other Church Fathers who also wrote a great deal on the spiritual struggle with the passions. The connection between suffering and the human passions may seem strange initially; but it can be argued that there are two dimensions of suffering: the external circumstances, and the internal events they trigger. Illness, temptation, loss of loved

[16] Ware (1993, p. 226) and others point out, this does not mean His humanity or His suffering and death on the Cross are being overlooked — there are as many representations of the Crucifixion in Orthodox Churches as in Western ones, and veneration of the Cross is *more* developed in the Byzantine than in the Latin rite. It may be more appropriate to say that the pleroma of experience in Orthodoxy includes the Crucifixion and Resurrection simultaneously.

[17] PG xlix, 413.

ones, professional or social failure, relationship breakdown or stress, accidents and disasters—all manner of tribulation can beset a human person. As Aleksiev (*ibid*) writes:

> The question of suffering is one of the most sensitive questions. Many ask themselves: why has God created us to suffer in this world from different diseases, sorrows, calamities, troubles and misfortunes; *from passions on the inside, from bad people on the outside*, from the envy of neighbours, from the menace of enemies? (p. 17, italics mine).

Hence inner passions are considered as much part and parcel of our total suffering, as external misfortunes, and there is also a further recognition that, in order to process the experience of suffering, inner or outer, it is the ascetic struggle with our passions that needs to be undertaken. The battle-ground, as the Elder Sophrony (1973) suggests, is the human heart; no matter where suffering is coming from, it is the manner in which it is borne by the suffering subject (Gr.: πάσχον ὑποκείμενο, loosely translated as "that which passively lies underneath"), which is important.

CHAPTER EIGHT

Creative Suffering

Despite recognising the traumatic repercussions of the suffering humans are exposed to however, Orthodox Christian spirituality is an advocate of emotional sobriety. In contrast to the 'cathartic approach' (Bateman & Holmes, 1995; p. 5), it attaches no value to grief, rage, despair, regret, or indeed to any purposeless, sterile suffering for its own sake.[1] Instead, it invites the person to respond creatively to such events.

Iulia De Beausobre (1940; 1999) first suggested the term *creative suffering* to describe an Orthodox manner of responding to life's vicissitudes in 1938. Allen (1984) writes of this concept that it:

> [...] is the concept of a total event [...] in a book published in 1938 entitled *Creative Suffering*, by Iulia de Beausobre. She was arrested and tortured during the Stalinist purges and farm collectivization of the 1930s when some ten million peasants perished. She points out that the suffering inflicted on a person is not a complete event, but that a complete or total event must include a person's *response* to the suffering (and indeed the response of other people). The way a person responds affects the

[1] Sophrony (1973) writes: "mention may perhaps be made here of the difference between ascetic and emotional weeping which is as radical as that between heavenly wisdom and earthly wisdom. For the spiritual warrior emotional tears are an inadmissible weakness; but the other form of weeping which comes from on high and accompanies true prayer, when the mind is united with the heart, is essential if the spirit would be lifted up to God" (pp. 18–19).

> meaning and significance of the act. A person, for example, who responds to torture with fear, self-pity, and hatred, and in no other way makes the total event worse (Allen, 1984).

St. Ilias the Presbyter wrote: "Suffering deliberately embraced cannot free the soul totally from sin unless the soul is also tried in the fire of suffering that comes unchosen. For the soul is like a sword: if it does not go 'through fire and water' (Psalm 66:12, LXX) — that is, by suffering deliberately embraced and suffering that comes unchosen — it cannot but be shattered by the blows of fortune" (Ilias the Presbyter, Palmer et al., 1986: p. 35). To struggle against temptation and one's own tendency to sin is 'suffering deliberately embraced'; but to also cheerfully accept whatever comes as God's will, is to be 'tried in the fire of suffering that comes unchosen.' In patristic quotations like this, the understanding of 'creative suffering' can be seen to be, not a latter-day innovation of De Beausobre, but a teaching which, as has been suggested above, runs through the whole of Orthodox theology like a golden thread, even if it is not the object of dogmatic formulation. The graphic metallurgical image St. Ilias uses, is of the soul being like a sword which is tempered in the 'fire' of suffering deliberately embraced (vigils, prayer, resistance to temptation, obedience to a spiritual director, may all be understood as such voluntarily undertaken sufferings), and in the 'water' of suffering that comes unchosen (which includes everything that may belong in the category of 'the slings and arrows of outrageous fortune' (Hamlet, IIIi) — St. Ilias himself refers to "sickness, material losses, and slander" (*ibid.*, p. 35) as the causes of involuntary sufferings).

Like a modern psychologist, St. Ilias appears well aware of the fact that, if suffering is not creatively embraced, it can 'shatter' the soul, leaving only the exposed wounds of psychic trauma as the broken shards of personal experience; hence St. Mark the Ascetic, too, can write that "[t]here is a breaking of the heart which is gentle and makes it deeply penitent, and there is a breaking which is violent and harmful, shattering it completely" (Palmer et al. 1979, p. 111). Yet although for these saints, as for today's psychotherapists, there is an awareness of the symptoms of a post-traumatic condition, the treatment they offer as a cure for suffering differs in crucial respects from a strictly psychological approach, in that suffering is not regarded so much as part of the problem, as it is part of the solution.

Interestingly for an Orthodox Christian, De Beausobre (*ibid.*) juxtaposes the Byzantine ascetic *phronema* against the Russian mystical temperament, and casts the former in quite a negative light. She suggests that the Byzantine ascetic mentality, though alien to the mystical Russian temperament, was highly influential as the spirituality of the learned Greeks who brought Christianity to Russia. Yet, in De Beausobre's estimation, this austere ascetic 'temper of mind'[2] (p. 4) stands in direct contrast to the common attitude of the majority of the Russian people, which is inherently mystical in that

> [...] their longing was for grace, for illumination, irradiation, redemption, for a oneing of the many — of all; and for the achievement of this they looked to the self-sacrifice of the greater to the less, to the coming down out of heaven of the greater, to the transfiguring of the less, to an elevation of the whole (p. 6).

Articulating this 'innate philosophy' (p. 9) of the Russian people via authors such as Dostoyevsky and Berdyaev, De Beausobre tries to indicate the attitude by which Russians dealt with the oppression and suffering they have experienced throughout history, and especially in the captivity to Bolshevism. The Russian attitude, she argues, implicitly takes for granted the fact that freedom is a central feature of spiritual life. She says Berdyaev articulates this well when he concludes that:

[2] As an interesting aside, De Beausobre also links the ascetic temperament to the revolutionary Bolshevik tendency to subordinate the one to the many, as well as to the capitalist frugality and work-ethic in its post-puritan Anglo-American historical expression. She appears to have adopted some of Berdyaev's less Orthodox ideas on this theme, suggesting that asceticism by itself *can* become sadomasochistic and anti-Christian, when not counterbalanced by mystical joy.

> [...] the paradox of evil [...] is that [...] evil is the outcome of freedom, which itself is an inseparable attribute of spirit, and thus engenders both good and evil. [...] 'the paradox of suffering and evil is resolved in the experience of compassion and love' (*ibid.*, p. 12).

Not only is involuntary suffering of great value to spiritual growth therefore, but when embraced, it also functions as an appropriate response to wickedness and evil. St. Isaac the Syrian writes:

> Remember that Christ died for the wicked, as Scripture says (Rom. 5:6), and not for the good. Consider it a much greater thing to suffer on behalf of evil people and to do good to sinners, than to do this for the righteous ([Hom. 50, B 348], quoted in Brock (1997)).

Since suffering however, is meaningful only when it is freely accepted, faith and salvation can never be coerced; this is also, according to De Beausobre, the reason why

> [...] Christ's suffering was never decreed or accepted in view of its being a possible inducement for men to follow him and do his will; not even if some of us do find in his suffering an additional reason for being practising Christians (*ibid.*, p. 14).

It may be that the reason Russians cannot, according to De Beausobre — or indeed the Orthodox as a whole perhaps cannot — accept coercive methods for restricting evil, and for inducing the imitation of Christ, is because the doctrine of substitutionary atonement did not take root in the same way in Orthodox Christianity as in the West. At least since Anselm and Abelard, the Western understanding has been that Christ sacrificed Himself, so that humans may be saved from the punishment which sin deserved (Yannaras, 1996, p. 35). The Orthodox understanding of the atonement would not entirely disagree with the above rationale, yet the different emphasis on original sin in the Orthodox Church (as previously discussed) affects also the understanding of how the death of Christ impacts the redemption of mankind. John the Evangelist affirms divine love for mankind in the giving of His Son (John 3:16). In the Orthodox understanding too, Christ's voluntary sacrifice on the cross was not to satisfy God's vengeance, a desire to see sin punished (which is a frequent misunderstanding of the doctrine which Western theologians call "substitutionary atonement"[3]). Rather, for the Orthodox, Christ's death on the cross enabled Christ to enter death and to destroy it, harrowing hell itself, as evidenced by rising from the dead once and for all. In His sacrifice, the profound act of divine love for mankind is emphasized:

> The entire purpose of our Lord's death was not to redeem us from our sins, or for any other reason, but solely in order that

[3] Once again, it can be remarked that church polemics often overstate differences between East and West on these issues. The danger of the language of substitutionary atonement, is of seeing Christ's sacrifice as something completely externalized: we sin, and Christ 'fills in' for us, satisfying the debt we owe the Father. Left entirely like this, it becomes something Calvinist, and from an Orthodox perspective theologically imbalanced, since the whole element of our personal effort disappears—we need do nothing at all to be saved, except to 'acknowledge' Christ. But all through the Patristic period and beyond, such language was meant to convey a deeper truth that also included *our* efforts towards salvation. Although expressed differently than in the East, the Western Fathers placed more stress on the relationship between human sin and Christ's 'economia' of redemption. In the writings of Augustine, for example, he ponders the mystery of his sinfulness and God's evident mercy on him. Augustine's resolution is to stress Christ's mercy entirely, that in approaching Christ there is always an entirely undeserved aspect on our part in receiving this mercy. There is something intensely personal in how he understands Christ's redemption; it is worth pointing out, therefore, that while the Western way of conveying Christ's redemption *can at times* degenerate into something legalistic, and occasionally in Christian history it has been made to be thus, this almost certainly was not the intention of those, like Augustine or even later western Fathers like Abelard, who went a step further in expressing Christ's substitutionary sacrifice. Viewed objectively, there is no theological problem with this kind of language, and behind it there is still considerable reverence for the mystery concerning Christ's redemption of mankind.

> the world might become aware of the love which God has for creation. Had all this astounding affair taken place solely for the purpose of the forgiveness of sin, it would have been sufficient to redeem us by some other means (St. Isaac the Syrian, [Keph. IV.78], quoted in Brock (1997)).

Understandably, differing emphases in interpreting Christ's sacrifice, will have pastoral implications for the way sin is treated. Where the emphasis is on substitutionary atonement, sin will be viewed primarily as juridical offence for which penance, often with set penalties (*epitimion*), must be made; but when the atonement is perceived as an act of divine love, the pastoral emphasis will be on sin as disease or *hamartia*, "missing the target," with spiritual healing and regeneration of divine-human relations as primary objective (Ware, 1993; pp. 289–290). It may be interesting to speculate, whether the 'darker' image of God the Father suggested by the Western emphasis on substitutionary atonement, may have predisposed Jung's view, as Main (2006) states, that

> God's experience with Job prompted God to incarnate as Christ. [...] [H]is evil side continued to be projected onto his creatures (quoted in Papadopoulos, 2006; p. 307).

To return, however, to the issue of creative suffering as De Beausobre understands it, the powerful link in the Russian mind between suffering and freedom, incapable of being considered apart from one another, together with the tendency not to separate social classes or areas of life into manichean dualistic terms of 'good' and 'evil', but to see both as dividing each and every human heart, leads to the remarkable fact of

> [...] our profound conviction that evil can be overcome by man only through knowledge, the knowledge of evil; and it seems to the Russians that man can know a thing, as man, only through participation (1940; 1999: p. 17).

De Beausobre is not advocating, in the manner of the Gnostic Khlysty sect to which Rasputin reputedly belonged, that in order to be saved we *have* to sin.[4] What she is suggesting instead is that it is by nature of our inevitable personal participation in evil, by way of the sad fact of our shared fallen sinfulness, that we are able to empathize with others who are suffering. She brings the example of the *yuródivy*, an itinerant 'holy fool' figure who can be found all over Russia,[5] and is much loved by the people despite his tendency to express his views — often in chant and rhyme — on everything both worldly and spiritual, and to live on charity. She says:

> The aim of the *yuródivy* is to participate in evil through suffering. He makes of this his life's work because, to the Russian, good and evil are, here on earth, inextricably bound up together. This, to us, is the great mystery of life on earth. Where evil is at its most intense, there too must be the greatest good. [...] the *yuródivy* sees godliness and spirit shining out from all that is lowliest and 'worst'; from the dust of the highway, the sharp stones that cut his feet, the thorns that tear his flesh, the biting winter frost, the intolerable heat of summer, the stench of the doss-house; from the most degraded types of men and women. He participates in all the badness and degradation, and believes fervently that in so doing he helps in the great drama of redemption (*ibid.*, p. 18).

Interestingly, the spiritual labour of the holy fool may, to some extent perhaps, be compared to the paradoxical alchemical transfor-

[4] A view of sin which Jung — *pace* Carpocrates — nevertheless found useful since it is compatible with his view that it is the consciousness which characterizes human acts which is the redeeming factor (or lack of it, cf. CW11, par. 130–4) .

[5] Holy Fools are in fact found in all Eastern Orthodox countries, as saints whose intentionally unconventional and sometimes shocking behaviour is directed at hypocrisy and the pride of worldly wisdom. In Greek, these figures are known as *διά Χριστόν σαλοί*, 'Fools for Christ.' In the West, such figures also occur, as in the famous example of St Francis of Assisi.

mation involved in changing the *prima materia* through nigredo to albedo—psychologically speaking, those shocked by this saint's participation in evil could be said to be invited to a process of 'washing' out their own projections on him (Von Franz, 1980; pp. 220–222). From a theological perspective, however, just as Christ entered hell on Great Saturday and harrowed its realm, the *yuródivy* 'enters' the whole of earthly squalor, firmly believing all the while in its redemption:

> The intuition [...] is that evil must not be shunned, but first participated in and understood through participation, and then through understanding transfigured (*ibid.*, p. 19).

The Fool-for-Christ then, is a moving example of how true religiosity transcends conventional morality and behaviour, and redeems evil through a certain way of participating in it. Most dramatically, however, De Beausobre calls to mind the moving example of the sort of attitude that Russian prisoners in Soviet concentration camps developed through their intense experiences.. She suggests that sadistic prison officers[6] only stopped torturing those who did not react to the pain; one way their victims could achieve this was by passively turning themselves into unfeeling objects (St. Ilias' shattered 'sword'). This however, De Beausobre explains, can only lead to a morbid apathy in need of psychiatric treatment. The active way of coping with the inflicted suffering instead, she suggests is much more difficult:

> It exacts of the victim who undertakes it a heightening of consciousness, which is inseparable from the pain that goes with any expansion of awareness. It demands simultaneous participation, by an intense effort of sympathetic insight, in the particular and

[6] Jung, writing in the late 1950s, says concerning these conditions in Russia that "The Christian world is now truly confronted by the principle of evil, by naked injustice, tyranny, lies, slavery, and coercion of conscience. This manifestation of naked evil has assumed apparently permanent form in the Russian nation; but its first violent eruption came in Germany." (MDR, 1995, p. 360).

> the general context of the [torturing] action; insight into the entirety of your present situation; clear perception of all the most trivial details that are occurring around you; penetration, as far as possible, into the mind of the men who have staged the 'cross-examination', and insight into the breadth of God's composition for this particular event on earth. [...] it is imperative that this heightening [of awareness] should be brought about in a mood of complete selflessness.[...] All this is very hard. But the point is, that once it is achieved, you realize that you have been privileged to take part in nothing less than an act of redemption. And then you find that, incidentally and inevitably, you have reached a form of serenity which is, if anything, more potent to counteract sadistic lusts than any barren impassivity could be (*ibid.*, pp. 21–22).

In order to comprehend this advice, it needs be said that Orthodox Christianity is an inherently dynamic faith, which maintains that man in his present condition is incomplete, and in search of completion. Furthermore, although as seen above, Orthodox spirituality promotes a profound surrender to the divine Will, and a condition of expanding spiritual growth through inner peace, it does not assume any static image of the 'end of suffering' or the 'cessation of struggle' as in, i.e., the state of detached awareness of the eternal present which is achieved in Buddhist experiences, such as nirvana or satori (Hope & Van Loon, 1994: pp. 34, 37).[7] Man, for Orthodox Christianity, is by nature 'hard-wired' as a eucharistic being in search of ever greater completeness, an expansion of ontic boundaries through the increased or enhanced consciousness achieved in prayer and wor-

[7] Needless to say, this is not meant as an argument against the profound wisdom offered by Eastern philosophy or Buddhist spiritual teaching; Christian authors such as Thomas Merton and David Steindl-Rast have attested to the complementarity of Buddhist and Christian spirituality, and within Orthodoxy monk Damascene Christensen has written a favourable comparison of Christianity and Taoism. However, perhaps the Orthodox criterion concerning differences between religions, would be the extent to which they actually offer adherents a reliable and effective route to union with God.

ship. This increased state of awareness may be achieved by legitimate means through prayerful union with God, or via illegitimate means, such as substance abuse or sociopolitical ideologies, including religiosity itself when it becomes fundamentalist (Bouteneff, 2006; p. 12).[8] In fact, it is interesting that most major religions do discourage their adherents from the use of mind-altering substances which are harmful to the person, and also from espousing totalitarian political ideologies. The same search for a 'transformation of consciousness' may even underlie the endemic urge to satisfy the passions by worldly means, e.g. through food, sex or power — so that, even in the full grip of his fallen condition, man may nevertheless be viewed as exhibiting the motivation to transcendence latently operating within him.

Incredible as it sounds therefore, the abstract-sounding suggestion that creative suffering results in a transformation of consciousness, is coming from someone who herself experienced torture. Born into an aristocratic family in St. Petersburg in 1893, Iulia de Beausobre married a patriotic Russian diplomat who was imprisoned under Stalin in the notorious Lubyanka prison in Moscow, and in 1933 was shot. She was then sent to a concentration camp, which she survived only because she was ransomed out of Soviet Russia by the English woman who had been her governess. Iulia neither turned her heart to stone, nor tried to 'slur over' (*ibid.*, p. 22) her tormentors' acts. Upon arriving in England she wrote a book called *The Woman Who Could Not Die*, which was one of the first accounts in the West of what was really happening in Soviet Russia. Comparisons may be drawn to Solzhenitsyn (1973; 2003), Fr. Arseny (Bouteneff, 1998), but also to Frankl (1959; 1984) in another context. Solzhenitsyn's attitude to evil perhaps most closely resembles that of De Beausobre, when he writes:

> If only it were all so simple! If only there were evil people somewhere insidiously committing evil deeds, and it were necessary

[8] Interestingly, Jung also saw this link between intoxication and ideology, when he suggested that "Every form of addiction is bad, no matter whether the narcotic be alcohol or morphine or idealism" (MDR, 1995, p. 361).

> only to separate them from the rest of us and destroy them. But the line dividing good and evil cuts through the heart of every human being. And who is willing to destroy a piece of his own heart? (quoted in Zweig & Abrams, 1991, p. iv)

De Beausobre's view of the division between good and evil is expressed thus:

> [...] the line of cleavage that divides humanity seems to run vertically, cutting through the whole of human life. Indeed it does not divide humanity alone; it is a wound that mars the whole of creation; it severs the world of spirit too between good and evil so that the whole world we know, both for thought and action, is split, from top to bottom between good and bad, between joy and wretchedness (*ibid*, p. 16).

The complexity of the Russian soul is illustrated further, in a verse by St. John of Kronstadt (1829–1908), echoing these complex but mature views on the nature of good and evil within us:

> The heart can change several times in one moment
> — to good or evil,
> to faith or unbelief,
> to simplicity or cunning,
> to love or hatred,
> to benevolence or envy,
> to generosity or avarice,
> O, what inconstancy!
> O, how many dangers!
> O, how sober and watchful we must be! (Serfes, 2001)

It might be pointed out here, that Jung's conclusion in *Answer to Job*, namely that the world is such because *the divinity is itself divided*, actually turns this mature Christian experience of good and evil *within the person* on its head, leaving a split God with the responsibility to come to know Himself through a whole, individuated man who resolves the conflict of the opposites, uniting them for Him. From an Orthodox perspective therefore, Jung has in fact grasped *man's* end of the process of spiritual growth,[9] but is in error with respect to God's operations.

Nevertheless, the psychoanalysis of human motivations, including the Jungian perspective on the value of human consciousness, probably can significantly contribute to the mature Christian appreciation of reality, at least in terms of the psychological insights it offers. Interestingly, Tournier (1982), a Swiss Reformed Christian physician and contemporary of Jung, shares the Orthodox Christian perspective on evil, but also suggests that Christian teaching and psychoanalysis actually coincide on their understanding:

> When we are young, good and evil seem quite distinct from each other. Parents and teachers do all they can to persuade the young of this. Legends and fairy tales too, always make a clear distinction between the virtuous folk and the wicked ogre who is the incarnation of all evil. Eventually we lose our illusions and discover that evil is everywhere, insinuating itself into our noblest actions. How often does the hidden selfishness of love turn into tyranny; how much pride there can be in 'good works'; how much hate in the most altruistic political and social campaigns; [...] Jesus was able to look into this unconscious region of men's minds. He sternly denounced the sin of the 'righteous', as Ricoeur points out—the sin which proceeds from the depths of the heart, despite outward appearances of virtue. At this point the gospel is in line with modern psychology. [...] I have seen people quite overwhelmed by this discovery, as their experience of life or psychological analysis brought them to maturity, so that they looked back with a certain nostalgia to the simplicity

[9] Cf. Thunberg (1985), ch. 4.

> of their childhood, when good and evil were clearly distinguishable from each other (pp. 26–27).

Tournier (*ibid*) uses Jesus' parable of the wheat and the tares (Matt. 13:28) to show how He tried to demonstrate that good and evil are mixed up together in this world, not to be separated until the harvest of the final judgment—a cosmic event initiated by God, not just an intrapsychic process within man. Scripture teaches clearly that good and evil do exist; our notions of 'right' and 'wrong' (words, actions, thoughts, feelings etc) are mostly based on this assumption of the 'objective' existence of good and evil—however, what good and evil really *are*, ontologically, and what we think or suppose they are by social convention, are two very different things. God really is, as Nietzsche and Jung imagined Him at times, 'beyond good and evil' in this sense, beyond any social definition of these qualities. Thus it is perfectly true that, as the stages of moral development outlined by Kohlberg (Crain, 1985; pp. 118–136) suggest, there is a stage of psychological growth which should take our individual morality beyond social conventions, mores and even norms, to universal principles, if we are to become mature persons. Whether we imagine this mature moral ability rises above, dives below, or journeys beyond social rules or collective moral codes is a matter of which metaphorical image we are using to conceptualise our morality as if it were a 'thing', an object, reifying it. Saints like the fool-for-Christ, figures like the *yurodivy*, also purposely defy social convention, but do so at their own expense, purposefully cauterizing social hypocrisy and pharisaism. As Evdokimov (1998) suggests:

> Asceticism has nothing to do with moralism. The opposite of sin is not virtue but the faith of the saints. Moralism exerts natural forces, and its fundamental voluntarism submits human behaviour to moral imperatives. We know how fragile every autonomous and immanent ethical system is, for it is not a source of life. [...] That is why in the tragic conflicts of existence, in the

> depths of some overwhelming sorrow or loneliness, moral and sociological principles are powerless (p. 163).

Thus, when investigating the link between suffering and creativity, Tournier reaches similar conclusions with De Beausobre:

> What then of the relationship that exists between deprivation and suffering, and creativity—apparently between evil and good? But relationship is not the same as cause. [...] The person matures, develops, becomes more creative, not because of the deprivation in itself, but through his own active response to the misfortune, through the struggle to come to terms with it and morally to overcome it—even if in spite of everything there is no cure (*ibid.*, p. 28).

De Beausobre, however, goes even further in suggesting that it is possible, though much more difficult, to find redemption even when experiencing the evil deed from the side of the perpetrator:

> You can, of course, participate in such an evil deed either as agent or patient, as causing or enduring the suffering that marks it. And so intimately are good and evil entwined that it is possible to gain your insight into God's composition for the deed from either side. [...] You may be on the side of evil and be fully aware of the good you are crucifying, fully aware of the real place of the event in God's composition and of your own holy place within it; or you may be a participant on the side of suffering good and, in this case, see its crucifixion so to speak from within. In either case though, you can only reach an understanding of the event through your own personality, yet this understanding remains impersonal (*ibid.*, pp. 22–23).

It is not immediately clear what is meant here by the suggestion that the perpetrator has a 'holy place' within the deed; one possibility is precisely that, should the rare occasion arise that a perpetrator of evil becomes fully aware of what they are doing, the 'holiness' of their place in the act is acquired through being granted an understanding of the way in which at a profound level, everything is indeed taking place by God's leave and even to the ulterior good, to the inevitable confounding of the purposes of evil. It is a participation in evil, but one which leads to repentant contrition, and to the realisation that the evil must cease, for which we have ultimate responsibility. Even so, De Beausobre is quite explicit that this is not the whole of her meaning, and therefore a part of what is meant here, must surely be accessible only through spiritual experience itself. What is remarkable, is her confidence in the total event as it transpires being *within* divine ordinance, thus potentially offering to each of the participants a special insight, one might say 'gnosis.'

It is interesting, too, to compare her insight to that of Nietzsche's mentor and one of Jung's major influences, Schopenhauer (1788–1860), whose esteem for asceticism led him to think highly of Buddhism and Vedanta Hinduism, as well as of some monastic Roman Catholic sects. For Schopenhauer, cases do exist of the over-affirmation of the will; that is, in cases where one individual exerts his will not only for their own fulfilment but for the improper domination of others, such a person is unaware that he is really identical with the person he is harming, so that the Will (in Schopenhauer's special sense) in fact constantly harms itself, and justice is done in the selfsame moment in which the crime is committed, since the same metaphysical individual is both the perpetrator and the victim. It is interesting that the monist assumptions of Schopenhauer and Jung's *unus mundus* may have similar ethical implications, but these are not due to epistemological similarities with the qualified and spiritually informed 'dualism' found in Christian ethics, where e.g. to strike another person is not wrong because 'we are one' in an ontological sense, but because the other is an image of God, and the perpetrator, himself also created in the Divine Image, thereby strikes at his soul's own expense. The advantage in the Christian conception is that ontological boundaries between persons are maintained, even while the profound significance of kindness is affirmed, and their *at*-one-ment as children of God and persons-in-relation is recognized.

Whether on the active side of the perpetrator however, or more frequently on that of the passive victim, De Beausobre's view perhaps concurs with Roman Catholic author J. P. De Caussade (1996), who suggests that, with divine aid, a perspective on events may be reached, eloquently defined as necessary for sanctity:

> Sanctity consists in willing what happens to us by God's order. If we understood how to see in each moment some manifestation of the will of God, we should find therein also all that our hearts could desire (p. 120).

The assertion is thus, that however gruesome a certain reality is, it is the task of the Christian, through prayer and ascetic practice, to come to a realisation of Divine Will in it. Christians claim that just as their true self, the core of their personality, is the image of God in which they have been created, so too their true will can only be reached when it is in harmony with God's will, whatever this may be at each moment (cf. Hopko, 2006; pp. 39–41). Crucially, De Beausobre goes on to suggest that such understanding and heightened awareness as she describes, can only be reached if one belongs to the Church:

> It is vital for you to feel and to know beyond all possible doubt that notwithstanding all the tormentor's devices, there is and always will be within you something that is built on rock. That is something that cannot be torn out of you or severed from the rock, because it is the core of your personality and one with the rock it is built on. [...] The tone of the fortitude shown by the tortured is very different when they think of themselves only as poor, or brave, lonely wretches, and when they think of themselves as members of the mystical body of Christ. Only the latter are likely to come through without succumbing to hatred (*ibid.*, p. 24).

Despite De Beausobre's above suggestion, it may nevertheless be possible to draw on her example for an understanding of the application of the concept of creative suffering in non-Christian (or even non-religious) contexts. Since the isolated event of suffering alone in Orthodoxy is considered incomplete, it is the way we respond to suffering which determines its overall meaning. This could also be one way of understanding Jesus' words in Mk. 7:14–15. Humanity has inherited a fallen world, and the effects of the fall (Ware, 1996) are both physical (a liability to fatigue and bodily pain, aging and finally bodily death) and moral—we have an inherited inclination to be sinful, and find it easier to do ill than good; and we are subject to boredom, depression, absent-mindedness, forgetting, inner conflict and lack of willpower; also, we often feel trapped in situations where no good choices seem available, and we often end up doing what we know is wrong when we sincerely want to do what we know is right (Rom. 7:18–19, 24). This is not what God intended for mankind, and hence, through Jesus' voluntary suffering and sacrifice on the cross (John 10:15, 18; Phil. 2:8), there has been a *cosmic, ontological change* in the very character of our human existence, and the meaning of our suffering. Through His free choice Christ has made it possible for us to be redeemed from the "body of death" (Rom. 7:24) which brings about the effects of the Fall, by being baptized and expressing our faith in Him within the Church, and by living "according to the Spirit" (Rom. 8:1). In this way, we can look forward to the restoration of our original prelapsarian glory, already in this life—as witnessed by the existence of numerous saints—and certainly also in the life to come. Therefore, the experience of suffering in this life is viewed by Orthodoxy as being permitted by God, not as a punishment or as a result of some 'divine savagery' (Jung, CW 11:746), but as an opportunity for learning and growth, spiritual maturation and a deepening of repentance (Monachos Moisis, 1990). Christ freely embraced his suffering and crucifixion, and we are thereby freed to do likewise. Ware (2004) writes that:

> If Christ is at that moment in agony [in the garden of Gethsemane], "sorrowful even to death," with His sweat falling to the

> ground "like great drops of blood," this is because He is free, because He is at that moment confronted by a choice. Humanly speaking He does not have to die; it is still possible for Him to withdraw and make His escape. Freely, deliberately and at incalculable cost, He brings His human will into conformity with the divine will: "Not as I will, but as Thou wilt" (Mt. 26:39) (p. 114).

In a Jungian sense, Christ in the garden of Gethsemane may be seen to be struggling to hold the tension of the opposites of His divine and human wills, until the 'third' transcendent function emerges through the alignment of the human to the divine will. Put this way of course, the process sounds much simpler than it is! Ware (2004) examines the experience of Iulia De Beausobre, asking the pertinent question:

> What is it that changes suffering from a destructive into a creative force, that transforms a violent death into an act of martyrdom, a miscarriage of justice into an atoning sacrifice? (p. 112).

He goes on to answer that

> Innocent suffering does not by itself make someone into a martyr. It is also required that we on our side should voluntarily *accept* that suffering, even though we may not have originally chosen it. [...] Suffering is made creative and death becomes sacrificial, if and only if they are willingly accepted by the one who has to suffer or die (*ibid.*, p. 113).

For the Christian, an added dimension which non-Christians cannot possess is the knowledge that, not only do we accept suffering in order to transfigure it, but

> Christ our God is Himself suffering with us, and that through this divine co-suffering we in turn are enabled to suffer with, in and for others (*ibid.*, p.13).

In summary then, the three main characteristics of creative suffering as a process of spiritual and psychological growth, may be said to consist in the following:

1. *Acceptance*: a voluntary acceptance of suffering, both in its voluntary and involuntary manifestations.
2. *Discernment*: The acquisition of a heightened state of awareness whereby the place of the event in the larger scheme of things is understood and appreciated (to Christians, this is an awareness or discernment of God's particular will for the event).
3. *Faith*: The profound sense of a power in which one's entire being is grounded, which suffers in solidarity[10] with us and offers us the strength to continue in our struggle (again, for Christians this power is none other than Christ; cf. Heb. 2:18).

It is argued here that these three characteristics of acceptance, discernment and faith, both in a Christian and non-Christian context, can and do characterize the creative use of suffering, as it occurs in the patient's and therapist's biographies, and later emerges in the intersubjective field of transference-countertransference dynamics in analytical psychology, spiritual direction and other helping practices. As described in the following chapter, both the Jungian analyst and the Orthodox priest-confessor can put these therapeutic attitudes and aspects of their personality and experience to use, calling on the resources available in the wounded healer archetype, so as to be of service to their clients even through their personal complexes.[11]

---

[10] Ware (2004) uses this term, which could be a less provocative one than 'faith', but paradoxically may not convey the active quality of trust in this compassionate 'higher power' which the term faith, even in its secular uses, arguably does.

[11] Note that De Beausobre above, emphasizes that the insight can only be reached *through one's personality*, even if itself it is ultimately impersonal.

CHAPTER NINE

Asceticism and the Imagination

> Why is every 'delectation,' every 'sweetness' a sin? Because the moment of delectation marks the strengthening of our personal sensations; the more intense the delectation, the greater is the break with the universal harmony around us. Delectation leads to self-love, self-love to the disintegration of harmony, and disintegration to death (Elchaninov, 1967, p. 26).

The above quotation from the diary of Fr. Alexander Elchaninov, suggests the need for ascesis is not due to sin being simply a moral trespass, an accrual of debt to the Creator (though it is these things, too); properly understood, sin is an ontological break with the harmony of the universe. This is also why there is little purpose in considering Orthodox anthropology separately from its cosmological dimensions.[1] Orthodox spirituality treats human faculties in

[1] Indeed, it might be said that from an Orthodox perspective every anthropology is grounded in an implicit cosmology (Nellas, 1987; 1997) and Jungian psychology probably forms no exception to this rule. It would be interesting to explore fully its cosmological implications, above and beyond Jung's own formulations of cosmological concepts such as *unus mundus*, the psychoid archetype, etc. Archbishop (then Bishop) Chrysostomos did seem to find common ground with Jungian analyst Dr. Thomas Brecht, who together with him "argued that, one touchstone of scientific validity being the universality of observations independently made, the common ground of the two divergent systems of Eastern Orthodox and Jungian mysticism suggests a universality and scientific validity

very particular ways, always based on its Christocentric world-view, but not merely in a scholastic manner, by syllogism or rational argument as Roman Catholic, and subsequently Protestant theology have done. This is where Orthodox theology and the empirical science of analytical psychology have their meeting place: in *experience itself.* It is in this sense tragic that Fr. Victor White was a neo-Thomist, for it may be argued that, had he been Orthodox, there may have been more avenues of discussion with Jung on certain points (while again perhaps fewer on others).

In discussing the relation of asceticism to subjective experience however, it is expedient to return briefly to a consideration of Paul Evdokimov's approach to psychoanalysis (see also ch. 1). The ascetic discipline of Orthodox spirituality is, as previously suggested, primarily experiential, and hence profoundly psychological; the external practices aim at a *condition of mind.* It is not inappropriate therefore, that Evdokimov gave so much attention to the science of psychology, since the mystical theology of the Eastern Church can be seen both as a psychological science, and as a therapeutic discipline, as several researchers have suggested (cf. Vlachos (1994), Chirban (2001), Chrysostomos (2007), etc.). Evdokimov suggests that

> The development of modern psychology and the rapid multiplication of its subfields have profoundly transformed our knowledge of the human psyche. Psychology, from being an abstract, functional and associative and descriptive science, has become more and more a science of the whole person (1994, p. 79).

While Evdokimov clearly values the contributions of general psychology to man's self-understanding, however, he is also quick to point out that as a science, it is at a loss in its search for a definition of mental health and pathology. Therefore, at the same time as he grants

---

in Jung's assumptions about the "great unknown." "(Chrysostomos & Brecht, 1990: p. 197).

validity, e.g. to Freud's observations, he also warns against the confusion and incompleteness which result from attempting to understand man without reference to the God-ordained laws which govern our inner psychic economy. Without this understanding, Evdokimov asserts that a trivialisation of evil[2] and a superficial grasp of human well-being are bound to result:

> Without God man lives in profound confusion, and is totally ignorant of the laws governing his inner "economy." Left to himself, he sinks into the neurotic [...] It is not surprising that Freud saw in mental illness a "stratagem," an escape from inner conflicts that had become unlivable. Ignorance of these deeper laws, often supported by occult doctrines, leads to simplifications in which evil is reduced to imperfection, and the ascetic struggle to a mere search for health. [...] The most perceptive psychiatrists detect spiritual disorder behind psychic illness; lack of a scale of values, inability to discern and make a decisive choice. [...] Whether he likes it or not, a man exists only in his relationship to the Absolute. If a man does not accept the transcendent, he either absolutizes the immanent or turns himself into the absolute. [...] Sooner or later, any analysis of the human soul comes upon a residue that is irreducible to empiricism, to the merely psychic (*ibid.*, pp. 79–80).

Evdokimov can be seen to share Jung's sense of the limits of empirical knowledge and of the importance of having a sense of the transcendent; but they differ significantly in their assessment of credal faith; Jung sees absolute dependence on God, alongside dependence on the State or the social collective, as being just another potential barrier to individuation, and suggests that the lack of discernment or diminished

[2] Evdokimov appears here to share the Jungian concern that evil is underestimated, but he does not attribute this to the existence of evil as an equal and opposite entity to divine goodness; instead he indicates the insufficiency of a hyperoptimistic understanding of human nature.

conscious choice observed in the mentally ill patient, can be as much a result of forfeiting personal judgment for credal belief, as it is more obviously perhaps in the case of 'mass-mindedness,' or a merely statistical appreciation of reality. It is astonishing however, to see how closely Evdokimov mirrors Jung's general concerns and vice versa:

> But it is possible to have an attitude to the external conditions of life only when there is a point of reference outside them. The religions give, or claim to give, such a standpoint, thereby enabling the individual to exercise his judgment and his power of decision. They build up a reserve, as it were, against the obvious and inevitable force of circumstances to which everyone is exposed who lives only in the outer world and has no other ground under his feet except the pavement. If statistical reality is the only reality, then it is the sole authority. There is then only one condition, and since no contrary condition exists, judgment and decision are not only superfluous but impossible. Then the individual is bound to be a function of statistics and hence a function of the State or whatever the abstract principle of order may be called (Jung, 1993, pp. 19–20).

Jung placed great emphasis on the religious instinct within us, and the search for meaning in our lives. He claimed that man has a natural urge to seek meaning; the psyche has a myth-making, or mythopoeic, function. If man is deprived of his faith in collective myths, the mythopoeic function turns in an inward and downward direction, appearing in dreams (which are private myths) and symptoms. Neurosis, for Jung, is an indirect consequence of the loss of collective myth—hence, every neurotic problem is fundamentally a result of repressed and unconscious spirituality. Similarly, the cure for neurosis is to be found in the recovery of a sense of awe, a contact with the meaningful numinosity of our existence.

Nevertheless, one may ask how a sense of the numinous can be recovered and experienced if our rational intellect persists in describing what we are experiencing as "myth"? How can a god be believed in, if at the same time he is thought to lack objective existence, if he is just a symbol for another reality, which remains forever unattainable? In fact, with one crucial difference, this is not entirely unlike what official Orthodox Christian doctrine teaches about God's unknowability.[3] Although it would certainly be heretical to describe the living God of Orthodox Christianity as merely symbolic—and the idea that Christ was a sort of apparition, less than real or embodied, was a feature of heretical docetism—it is nevertheless a teaching of the Orthodox Church that the ultimate essence, or nature of God is unknowable both in this life and in the life to come. We *can* fully know God experientially, but only through His energies, and subsequently in His Person as Christ, to Whom we nurture a reciprocated personal and communal relationship; His divine essence, however, is entirely unknowable, indeed far beyond human intellectual capacity.[4] Perhaps, therefore, there is an almost Christian modesty—albeit of a misguided, radical Protestant strain—in Jung's repeated post-Kantian assertions about the inaccessibility of metaphysics to investigation by the methods of science, in his constant circularity on matters concerning absolute truth. Credal differences aside therefore, it is not surprising that Evdokimov, as a Christian lay theologian, is keen keen to enlist psychology, and especially psychoanalytic thought, in the service of the Orthodox ascetic struggle, and has no difficulty in embracing what is useful to this struggle while pointing out whatever may be harmful or detrimental. Evdokimov quotes St. Paul (Rom. 7:15) as formulating "the law of irrational resistance" (*ibid*, p. 80) which psychoanalysis tries to counter and engage by acting indirectly on the human subconscious. Evdokimov explains that

[3] Cf. Meyendorff (1998) "The Unknowable makes itself known while remaining unknowable and its unknowability is deepest for the one who sees It" (p. 38).

[4] This does not negate the fact, however, that "The mind, purified and enlightened by divine truth, descends through a laborious effort of concentration into the heart, and there the unified and purified human person sees the unseeable" (Nellas, 1987; 1997, p. 191).

> In its [psychoanalytic] view, the psychic life is fed by images that convey a fundamental inclination, the *libido*. Such images have an effective side which can be detached and then linked to another series of representations: this is the classic method at the beginning of treatment. The subconscious cannot be influenced through commands: the human will resists any direct order. The most effective way of entering the subconscious is through the *imagination*; this fact reveals the great power of images. But the most delicate question upon which healing depends is precisely the recognition of the nature and the source of such power. [...] This brief survey already indicates the extent to which modern psychology parallels Christian asceticism in its preoccupation with spiritual health. Both bring into relief the intensity of the "invisible warfare" that will shed light upon the "underground" darkness of the subconscious, and lead to a "metamorphosis," a *metanoia* ("conversion") and transfiguration (1994, pp. 81–2).

It can be seen that Evdokimov has a deep understanding of the centrality of the imaginative faculty in psychoanalysis, and he links this with the Christian ascetic endeavour. Nevertheless, he points out that general psychiatry cannot substitute for the definite guidelines of religious spirituality, in this all-important endeavour to transform the images which make up our mental set. Thus he adds:

> By itself, psychiatry is only a technique, only a method. If an ethic is to be established, the need for a metaphysic is clear (*ibid.*, p. 82).

Evdokimov's thesis is the very opposite of that of post-Jungian thinkers like Hillman and Mogenson, in that Evdokimov is very clear about which images humans must aspire to; only a relationship of love with a personal God can truly satiate soul hunger, bypassing the post-lapsarian condition of the imagination altogether, and cleansing and fulfilling the mind through direct relation with and perception of the divine glory of the Beloved. In this way, Orthodox ascetics may be said to discover the Image through purification of the soul's images. Evdokimov explains:

> The extreme austerity of Eastern asceticism, including the prohibition against nourishing one's spiritual life with images ("Guarding the mind"), represents a very refined culture of the imagination. Indeed, it is above all a question of purifying the very power of the image through purity of heart. [...] This is the practice of well-directed intentionality: "Using your imagination, look into your heart" (*ibid.*, p. 84).

Therefore too, where Mogenson (2005) can write that

> The dramaturgy of the Passion can still upstage the soul's relationship to its own images and cause it to suffer against the wrong background. Ironically, a large part of the job of psychotherapy [...] is releasing the soul from the collective neurosis which in the guise of religion sanctifies estrangement of the soul from its own images and experiences (p. 18).

Evdokimov instead, suggests that

> Psychoanalysis attempts to track down and uproot from the soul images that are "ugly" and plant "beautiful" ones in it. Such an art requires a profound understanding of the imagination. Synesius, the Bishop of Ptolemaïs, placed the imagination and its images between time and eternity; it is thanks to such images, and to the memory that protects them, that we have knowledge. But, he adds, the demons also take advantage of this and feed upon our imagination. On his part, Jung observes in his *Psychological Types* that "complexes" are comparable to demons. [...] While psychiatrists look for the "beautiful image," the ascetics look for the restoration of the original form — the image of God (*imago*

> *Dei*) reaching toward God. But the most difficult problem for psychiatrists is knowing how to restore someone's confidence in life and in one's own destiny, and how to interpret the concrete meaning of a given life. This is the great evangelical mystery of the personal Cross (1994, pp. 82–3).

It may be suggested that Evdokimov errs when he writes that psychoanalysis aims to uproot "ugly" images, replacing them with "beautiful" ones. Indeed, this may be said more readily about asceticism itself, which urges the spiritual athlete to guard the senses and concentrate either on no images at all, or at least on Christian imagery. However, this would be an equally erroneous understanding of the actual function of the discipline of the imagination in Orthodox spirituality, which is much more complex than a conscious meditation on pious imagery, or even a zen-like cultivation of an 'empty mind.' Furthermore, if Evdokimov is incorrect regarding the aim of psychoanalysis with respect to changing internal representations, then what exactly is 'treatment' or 'mental health'? For all the fashionable relativism current in psychotherapy, Evdokimov may have an important point to make in suggesting that without a metaphysic, an ethic is not possible—even if that ethic is perceived as being the unfolding of the soul's own innate wisdom or realisation of itself, and even (as in the case of Hillman and the post-Jungians) if the diversity, multiplicity and differentiation of the soul and its many components are honored for their own sake.

The study of the imaginative faculty has a long philosophical history, dating back to Aristotle in its Western context. In Orthodox ascetic spirituality, the *φαντασία* ('phantasia'), as the image-producing faculty of the psyche is, as the glossary of the English edition of the *Philokalia* explains,

> [O]ne of the most important words in the hesychast vocabulary. As one begins to advance along the spiritual path one begins to 'perceive' images of things which have no direct point of refer-

> ence in the external world, and which emerge inexplicably from within oneself. This experience is a sign that one's consciousness is beginning to deepen: outer sensations and ordinary thoughts have to some extent been quietened, and the impulses, fears, hopes, passions hidden in the subconscious region are beginning to break through to the surface (Palmer *et al*, 1979, p. 360).

Thus far, the description of the activity of the image-making faculty is practically identical to an *abaissement du niveau mental*, followed by an active imagination process as found in the Jungian vocabulary. The definition then continues:

> One of the goals of the spiritual life is indeed the attainment of a spiritual knowledge [...] which transcends both the ordinary level of consciousness and the subconscious; and it is true that images, especially when the recipient is in an advanced spiritual state, may well be projections on the plane of the imagination of celestial archetypes, and that in this case they can be used creatively, to form sacred images of sacred art and iconography (*ibid.*, p. 360).

This is an important point to notice: Orthodox spirituality does not reject all imagery, just as it does not reject all dreams, which both Holy Scripture and the lives of the saints frequently refer to (cf. Karakovouni, 1996; Florensky, 2000). Indeed, it is recognised that some imagery may be divine in origin. For the spiritual novice, however (and this would include, in their humility, many spiritual elders), severe caution is advised when dealing with *any* imagery, 'good' or 'bad.' A rule of thumb is to ignore all imagery during prayer, when demonic activity is said to be at its height (e.g. Sophrony, 1973, p. 100). Hence the definition continues:

> But more often than not they [the images] will simply derive from a middle or lower sphere, and will have nothing spiritual

> or creative about them. Hence they correspond to the world of fantasy and not to the world of the imagination in the proper sense. It is on this account that the hesychastic masters on the whole take a negative attitude towards them. They emphasize the grave dangers involved in this kind of experience, especially as the very production of these images may be the consequence of demonic or diabolic activity; and they admonish those still in the early stages and not yet possessing spiritual discrimination [...] not to be enticed and led captive by these illusory appearances, whose tumult may well overwhelm the mind (Palmer *et al*, *ibid.*: pp. 300–1).

Hence too, every evening Orthodox Christians during the reading of the Little Compline pray

> And grant unto us, O God, a watchful mind, chaste thought, a sober heart, a sleep gentle *and free from every satanic illusion* [και πάσης σατανικής φαντασίας απηλλαγμένον] (Fr. Lawrence, 2008; italics mine).

It may be noted that Jung saw active imagination as an application of the transcendent function, which is a function of the psyche calling persons to inner growth and increased or 'higher' consciousness. Here Jung's idea may be compared to Teilhard de Chardin's 'Law of Complexity/Consciousness' concerning the natural development of matter towards greater complexity, and the evolution of humanity towards increased consciousness and absorption into the ultimate consciousness of the Omega Point, effectively God. This view of the phenomenology of spirit may also be likened to Rogers' (1980) formulation of a 'formative tendency,' which in humans is expressed as the 'actualising tendency,' very similar conceptually to Jungian individuation. Of course, only a superficial understanding of Orthodox deification would equate spiritual growth with Jungian individuation in a linear fashion, but the question of whether the transcendent function has anything to contribute to the understanding of theosis remains interesting, especially in the light of writings such as those of St. Maximus the Confessor (cf. Thunberg, 1985).

Returning to active imagination as a point of comparison with Orthodox prayer, Jung was certainly influenced by the Ignatian 'spiritual exercises' which apply the faculty of the imagination in a Christian context, through *lectio divina*, involving imaginary dialogue with Jesus and other scriptural personages. It is, therefore, also very interesting that St. Nicodemus, compiler of the Philokalia, also translated and adapted the Ignatian exercises for Orthodox readers,[5] although elsewhere he writes very clearly concerning the imagination, that

> The devil has a very close relationship and familiarity with the imagination, and of all the powers of the soul he has this one as the most appropriate organ to deceive man and to activate his passions and evils (Chamberas, 1989, p. 149).

Nevertheless, as Bishop Kallistos Ware writes,

> Despite his Orthodox traditionalism, [...] [w]hat Nicodemus seems to have found valuable in such volumes was their use of discursive meditation, allowing full scope to the imagination; this, he felt, helpfully supplemented the type of image-free, non-discursive prayer commended by Hesychasm (Ware, 2003).

It appears therefore, that St. Nicodemus did credit the human imagination with a possible spiritual function. As Wood (2003) writes, in Nicodemus a purified imagination is the gateway between sensory experience and a loving will:

[5] Gillet (1997) explains that "Nicodemus shared with Macarius [of Corinth] a sympathetic attitude towards certain notions prevailing in the Latin West. He translated into Greek (1796) the *Spiritual Combat* of the Theatine Lorenzo Scupoli, and in 1800 he even published *Spiritual Exercises* closely based on those of St. Ignatius, comprising thirty-four meditations, each in three points" (p. 66).

The internal sensory defence for the mind is the imagination, the mediator between the external senses and the mind. This world of thoughts also must be guarded and controlled and not permitted to envision and remember inappropriate sensory events and experiences. The imagination has greater authority than the senses themselves. Rational, spiritual imagination is developed through elevated meditation where the prayer of the heart unites the mind with God, actively loving God and loving others, and cleansing the heart (the will) by cleansing the senses and the powers of the body (Wood, 2003).

CHAPTER TEN

Microcosm and Macrocosm in the Healing of Suffering

It has been shown thus far, that Orthodox criteria for dealing with human suffering offer an approach to treatment, if not in fact quite definite treatment guidelines, and a specific perspective with respect to the anthropological and psychological ramifications of the art of helping. These ramifications moreover, can be seen to derive not from any rigidly didactic, dogmatic basis, but instead to be grounded in experience, as it is lived within the spirituality of the Orthodox Church.

In the concluding chapter, the function of the psychotherapist and the spiritual director will be explored under the rubric of the archetype of the Wounded Healer. It may be stated aforehead that there is a collective aspect to this archetype. Both psychotherapy and spiritual direction may, when observed externally, appear quite isolated professions, locked away in a consulting room or confessional, with only one's clients or spiritual children to be concerned about; the collective, and indeed macrocosmic, aspect of the wounded healer archetype however, suggests this is far from the case, since the wounding and suffering experienced and held in the psyche of the spiritual director and the engaged psychotherapist, is potentially a suffering-for-the-world. This pertains both to the biography of the therapist as it affects his relation to the client, and to the difficulties narrated by the client, inasmuch as they are seriously considered by the therapist.

Writing from a person-centred perspective, Rogers (1961) points to this dimension when he suggests that in his experience of counselling, he found his most private, personal and unique insights and emotions to be the 'very element' which spoke most deeply to other persons. He formulates the principle that "what is most personal is most general" (p. 26). Nouwen (1979; 1994) reinforces this principle in his own seminal study of the wounded healer concept within the experience of Christian ministry, eloquently illustrating it with examples from pastoral practice. He writes that "[…] when one has the courage to enter where life is experienced as most unique and most private, one touches the soul of the community" (p. 73).

Orthodox Christian spiritual directors have expressed this collective, macrocosmic aspect of healing, by writing of prayer that sheds tears for the world. Elder Sophrony (1996) for example, writes that

> It is precisely thus, through suffering, that we grow to cosmic and meta-cosmic self-consciousness. […] In wearying penitential prayer for the whole world, we merge ourselves spiritually with all mankind […] the same cosmic life that flows through us flows in the veins of everyone else (pp. 76–77).

Hence too, Fr. Justin Popovich (1922), for just one other example, enjoins the spiritual healer, who "walks around the grievously sick patient with prayer," to

> Expand and deepen your soul with prayer, and you will begin to cry over the mystery of the world […]. Make your heart prayerful, together with your soul and your mind, and they will become inexhaustible fountainheads of tears for all mankind (Popovich, 1922).

It is perhaps important to note, that both Fr. Popovich and Fr. Sophrony, in harmony with Orthodox spirituality and drawing on scriptural teachings such as Rom. 8:22 and Mk. 12:31, extend the benefits of such prayer not only to mankind, but to the whole of creation.

Jungian psychotherapy also senses and articulates the macrocosmic implications of healing work, both when together with one's patients, but also when the therapist is alone, in her own inner life; hence Stevens (2001) writes of one summer evening standing on the cliffs of North Cornwall, when the scene induced in him a sense of *phrike*, or awe, which he describes as being beyond subjective willpower, and moreover he was having this experience *for the whole of humanity* (p. 111).

One broader aim of this study is, therefore, to arrive at a schematic but informed response, among all the possible viable alternative responses, to a question for further research. The generality and enormity of this question will be immediately apparent: namely, *in what way is the psychotherapists' relationship to self and to the client paralleled in and influenced by the relation of the individuating human microcosm to the universe as macrocosm?* In other words, how can the way in which the therapist relates to himself and to the client during the therapeutic process, be itself related to, or be analogous to, or be perhaps an aspect of the way in which the therapist's growth/individuation process participates in the greater process of cosmic 'evolution'—whether this complex notion is understood literally or metaphorically; objectively or pragmatically; traditionally, as having its roots and destiny in the divine life, or through modernist eyes, as originating in matter?

It has been clarified at the outset, that the proposal of this, and any question as a topic for research involves making several assumptions. Those relevant to this study will hopefully have become clearer, though it may nonetheless be useful to highlight some of the more striking assumptions when these occur. What is being asked here, is in what way the psychotherapists' relationship to self and to the client is paralleled in and influenced by the relation of the individuating human microcosm to the universe as macrocosm; hence, an explicit assumption is being made that the 'dependent variable'—call it d—which will take on an 'experimental value' in this context, i.e. the relationship which the therapist has to self and client, *is definitely in some way*, whether by analogy ('paralleled in'), or by actual effect ('influenced by'), related to the 'independent variable,' call it i, i.e. the relation of the individuating human microcosm to the macrocosmic universe, as both analytical psychology and Orthodox Christianity suggest may be the case.[1] It is *not* being proposed here that either variable is meaningless or non-existent, or that there exists no relation between the two, although this is one possible view, which would of course preclude any further discussion of the issue.

Furthermore, the 'independent variable' *i* mentioned above, is itself filled with epistemological assumptions and terminology which will need to be further explored and clarified: there is an assumption that human beings *are* microcosms, an assumption that these human microcosms *do something* Jung called 'individuation,' and a further assumption that this process of microcosmic individuation is related in some way to a view *of the entire universe as a macrocosm which itself 'grows' and 'individuates' in some way.* The magnitude of these assumptions is consciously and modestly acknowledged, as are the numerous difficulties of enunciating any coherent 'scientific' statement based on them. Abstract and ill-defined though these notions sound to the sceptical mind, however, it may be recalled that even by strictly materialist accounts, humans are made of the same 'stuff' as the universe, and it is likely that some of the atoms in our own bodies first came into existence within the chemical laboratory of a distant star, where the heavy elements like carbon and oxygen which are vital to the complex chemistry of terrestrial life have developed. The 'anthropic principle' theories of scientific cosmology even suggest that the laws of physics themselves are "finely tuned to permit complex chemistry, which, in turn, permits the development of biology and ultimately of human life" (Coles, 2001, p. 126). The level of 'coincidence' involved in this happy marriage of cosmic elements and physical laws resulting in the emergence of life, is simply astonishing. Whatever personal conclusions one may draw from this scientific data, at least the assumptions underlying variable *i* seem less abstract and speculative from this perspective.

[1] Cf. Von Franz (1992); Sherrard (1992); Nellas (1987; 1997); Thunberg (1985), Gregorios (1988).

Concerning man as microcosm, Von Franz (1992) states that in the *Corpus Hermeticum* (lib 8.5) man is viewed as being formed in the image of the cosmos, and she goes on to cite Olympiodorus, who writes that

> Hermes calls man the small cosmos (μικρόν κόσμον) because he too is endowed with all that the cosmos possesses. The great cosmos has land and water animals. Man has fleas, lice and worms. The great cosmos has rivers, wells and oceans, so equally has man his intestines. The macrocosmos has dwellers in the air, man has mosquitoes. The macrocosmos has breath which ascends as wind, man has the same. The macrocosmos has the sun and moon, man has his two eyes [...] (*ibid*, p. 170).

In occult literature too, as Wilson (1971) explains,

> Magic shares another fundamental principle with mysticism: the notion 'As above, so below' [...]. In mysticism, this means that the soul and God are one and the same. [...] The occultists of the Middle Ages and the Reformation saw man and the universe connected by thousands of invisible bonds . [...] there are a thousand 'correspondences' between man and the macrocosm (pp. 299–300).

Von Franz (*ibid.*) also suggests that what for the alchemists was the "animating power in matter" (p. 169) is to modern psychology the unconscious. The contents of the total consciousness (consisting of both conscious and unconscious) of both the psychotherapist and the client have been shown by Jung to be interdependent (CW 16 para. 422). It follows from this observation that the psychotherapist has a special responsibility towards the client to become aware of the deepest layers of being within themselves; it is generally agreed by most psychodynamic schools, for example, that a conscientious psychotherapist will need to become aware, both during their training and later on in their career, of how their childhood past and their main complexes—though a different term may be used by different schools to describe those factors which seem to have autonomous influence on the personality—can act as a prism through which the reality of the client is distorted. Many would argue also, and would be probably correct, that this knowledge is sufficient for a therapist to be effective in their work with clients. It is evidenced repeatedly in almost every therapy, that the significance of childhood experience to individual and collective psychology cannot be overestimated.

However, the idea of microcosm and macrocosm as explored by Jungian analytical psychology, suggests that these are in fact not the deepest layers within us; persons are not only influenced by the way their individual past is brought to bear on the present; just as people are not born into a cultural or biological vacuum, behaviour cannot be predicted on the grounds of individual—or even family—history alone. Even taking biology and culture into account, there also seems to be a factor 'X' at work influencing human behaviour and confounding the attempts of social scientists to predict and control it—a factor which Hillman (1996), drawing on the work of Plato and Jung, calls our personal 'daimon.' Hillman explains:

> The soul of each of us is given a unique daimon before we are born, and it has selected an image or pattern that we live on earth. This soul-companion, the daimon, guides us here; in the process of arrival, however, we forget all that took place and believe we come empty into this world. The daimon remembers what is in your image and belongs to your pattern, and therefore your daimon is the carrier of your destiny (p. 8).

In this view, human persons may influence or be influenced, but not entirely determined by, biological, cultural, familial, or individual history. They are also teleological beings living towards a specific future, guided by a mysterious image or pattern towards their particular destiny. Regardless of whether or not the particular description offered by Hillman is correct, it would seem that if the view more generally associated with religion, that destiny plays a part in human life, is accepted also by psychotherapists, then they could benefit in their work by becoming familiar with the territory of what Ouspensky (1981; 1990), citing the psychiatrist Dr. R.M. Bucke's Boehme-influenced work, has called 'cosmic consciousness':

> The prime characteristic of cosmic consciousness is, as its name implies, a consciousness of the cosmos, that is, of the life and order of the universe [...]. Along with the consciousness of the cosmos there occurs an intellectual enlightenment or illumination which alone would place the individual on a new plane of existence — would make him almost a member of a new species (p. 265).

Arguably therefore, to be of help to the client, the conscientious psychotherapist needs to gain personal insight not only into their own and their client's past, family and social context, etc., but also into this radical vision of the 'life and order of the universe,' beginning with their own role in this life and order as a 'microcosm'; this is arguably precisely the nature of the universal religious quest, and hence just as true for the spiritual director as for psychotherapists. Since man is a part of the universe, it follows that by studying the universe in the manner of a natural scientist or otherwise, he will come to learn something about himself — and conversely too, that by studying himself, he will come to know something about the workings of the universe at large. Therefore, Origen urges the spiritual seeker to

> Understand that you have within yourself, upon a small scale, a second universe: within you there is a sun, there is a moon, and there are also stars (cf. Baehrens, 1920: p. 336).

Bishop Kallistos Ware (1998) further elucidates elsewhere, that seen from this perspective

> Man stands at the heart of God's creation. Participating as he does in both the noetic and the material realms, he is an image or mirror of the whole creation, imago mundi, a "little universe" or microcosm (p. 49).

Interestingly moreover, man may be viewed in Orthodoxy not only as the microcosm, but even as the macrocosm itself, as Nicodemus the Hagiorite suggests:

> He [God], therefore, has created man to be a cosmos, a world unto himself, but not a microcosmos within the greater one, as the philosopher Democritos declared and as other philosophers have upheld. Such philosophers considered man to be a microcosmos, minimizing and restricting his value and perfection within this visible world. God, on the contrary, has placed man to be a sort of macrocosmos — a "greater world" within the small one. He is indeed a greater world by virtue of the multitude of powers that he possesses, especially the powers of reason, of spirit, and of will, which this great and visible world does not have (Chamberas, 1989, p. 67).

In Christianity, the function of human consciousness ('reason,' 'spirit' and 'will' in Nicodemus' words) is, therefore, of universal, cosmic significance, and as Gregory of Nyssa suggested, those who compare man to a 'little world,' in fact perceive little difference between men and gnats or mice, since what makes man great is not the fact of being composed of the four elements, as other creatures are, but the fact of being created, using these very elements, into the image and likeness of God (*PG* 44:177D–180A).

The ancient idea of man as a microcosm,[2] and of the cosmic significance of human consciousness, also found its way, with some sig-

[2] McGinn et al. (1986) suggest the idea of man as microcosm has Oriental origins, subsequently entering Christian spirituality via Democritus, Plato and the Stoics. They point out significantly that in Christianity (via Philo) the micro-

nificant differences, into the work of Jung, particularly his writing on Paracelsus (e.g. 2001, Part 1). Jungian analyst Thomas Moore (1992) puts it this way:

> The Renaissance magus understood that our soul, the mystery we glimpse when we look deeply into ourselves, is part of a larger soul, the soul of the world, anima mundi. This world soul affects each individual thing, whether natural or human-made. You have a soul, the tree in front of your house has a soul, but so too does the car parked under that tree (pp. 267–8).

Anima mundi is the World Soul, a pure ethereal spirit, which was proclaimed by some ancient philosophers, and in particular Plato, the Neoplatonists and the Stoics to be diffused throughout all of nature. It was thought to animate all matter, in the same sense in which the soul was thought to animate the human body. In the 4th century BC, Plato wrote in one of his dialogues that

> [...] this world is indeed a living being endowed with a soul and intelligence. [...] a single visible living entity containing all other living entities, which by their nature are all related (Timaeus, 29/30).

The idea is sometimes said to have originated with Plato, but the concept has been discovered to be of more ancient origin, prevailing too in systems of eastern philosophy, such as the Brahman-Atman of Hinduism. The Stoic philosophers too, such as Cleanthes and Epictetus, believed it to be the only vital force in the universe, with which we must align ourselves; similar concepts were held by the hermetic

cosm is always such "because it is created in the image of God" (p. 296). Significant Church Fathers using the concept were the Cappadocians, especially Basil of Caesarea, Gregory Nazianzen, Gregory of Nyssa, and Maximus the Confessor, although it should be stated that the term *mikrokosmos* was not directly employed in all cases, and never outside the general context of the divine Logos.

philosophers like Paracelsus, and by others like Spinoza, Leibniz, and later, significantly for the intellectual tradition of German Idealism from Boehme to Schelling (1775–1854), Hegel (who saw in Napoleon an incarnation of the World Soul), on to Jung. The idea of *anima mundi* has also resurfaced in more recent times, elaborated since the 1960s by Gaia theorists such as James Lovelock. In alchemy, the 'Soul of the World' is the theory of the law that governs everything, and it encompasses a part of the philosophy of inner alchemy (Roob, 2005; p. 11). This is similar to the hermetic principle "all is one, one is all," from which Jung derived his notion of *unus mundus*. In this theory, it is believed that everything is part of one soul, and that everything is just a small part of a larger cycle, represented symbolically by the Ouroboros, in which the dragon or serpent eats its own tail, making a circle or flow.

A line of historical development may be traced from the idea of the *anima mundi* in the ancient Mediterranean, to Jung's collective unconscious. O'Neill (2007), writing on the history of the Tarot cards, in fact traces the concept of anima mundi from Plato's *Timaeus* to the Greek Neoplatonists like Plotinus (AD 204–270), who in trying to explain how a connection may exist between the infinite, immaterial and unchanging Source or God with the finite, material and changing world, posited a series of emanations which gradually bridge the gap between material and immaterial. This idea of emanations was also developed by the Stoics. The Neoplatonists made the World Soul an important emanation of God, his lowest aspect in fact, and referred to the *anima mundi* in the feminine. O'Neill (*ibid.*) suggests the 'World card' in the *Tarot de Marseille* derives from this Neoplatonic concept; but importantly, he also posits that it found its way via Roman authors like Cicero, Seneca and Virgil into the writings of the Renaissance humanists like Marcilio Ficino, who were immersed in Neoplatonism, and from there to Western ecclesiastical authors like Peter Abelard and Meister Eckhardt (who identified the anima mundi with the Holy Spirit), Hildegard of Bingen and others; O'Neill goes as far as to suggest that

> By the 13th century, the World Soul, a fundamental Neoplatonic concept, became a standard item in the vocabulary of orthodox [*sic*] Christian philosophers, theologians and mystics (*ibid*, p. 4).

This is, of course, a post-Schism development; similarities between Orthodox Christian theology and Neoplatonism however, are perhaps also not accidental. According to the same author, Neoplatonism influenced the Eastern Church through Origen, St. Basil, Gregory of Nyssa, and "became codified into Christianity" (p. 2) by St. Maximus the Confessor. Via Michael Psellus (1018–1079) and Gemistos Plethon (c. 1360–c. 1450); Neoplatonic ideas then travelled to Italy and virtually sparked off the Renaissance.

It is, therefore, also not surprising that Jungian notions borrow heavily on this history of ideas, both from Orthodox and non-Orthodox sources. The notion, for example, of 'archetype,' is derived simultaneously both from Hermeticism, and from its Christian usage in the works, for example, of the Orthodox saint, Dionysius the Areopagite. Jacobi (1962) explains that

> Jung took the term 'archetype' from the *Corpus Hermeticum* (Scott, *Hermetica*, Vol. I, 140, 12b) and from Chap. 2, Par. 6, of the *De Divinis nominibus* of Dionysius the pseudo-Areopagite, which reads: But someone may say that the seal is not the same and entire in all its impressions. The seal, however, is not the cause of this, for it imparts itself wholly and alike in each case, but the differences in the participants make the impressions unlike, although the archetype is one, whole, and the same (*της αυτής και μιάς αρχετυπίας*) (p. 39).

As suggested above, the *anima mundi* is closely linked in Jungian psychology to the idea of the collective unconscious, another term for which is the 'objective psyche.' It is this objective psyche which, for Jung, gives human existence the characteristic of 'psychic reality,' which Jung insists is not a metaphysical, but a psychological notion.

Avens (1980) explains that from a post-Jungian perspective, the universe may be recast

> ... within the archetypal, imaginal and polymorphous psyche thereby freeing it, on the one hand, from a merely humanistic orientation and, on the other, connecting it through psychic reality with the reality of the physical world: for when all is said and done it just may be that, as Jung has said, "'at bottom' the psyche is simply the 'world.' [...] Jung claims to have no metaphysical assumptions other than the reality of the psyche. His theory of archetypes is a means of dealing with his ideas about the universe not metaphysically but psychologically. But it is of utmost importance to recognize with Ira Progoff that: "archetypes are a psychological but not psychologizing concept. They are used not to explain away man's beliefs about reality, but to give a deeper insight into their symbolism as primordial intuitions of life." Archetypes are psychoïd, reflecting not only views of the world, but "man's elemental contact with the world": they "penetrate to the Adamic past and so ... recapture the intuitions contained in the first appearance of symbol formation (pp. 49–51).

It is perhaps clear from the above that, despite Jung's protests to the contrary, Jungian psychology does propose what could be understood as a meta-physical, transpersonal notion of the interaction between psyche and world, albeit one which espouses apperceptive, phenomenological criteria. The very stipulation that analytical psychology be *not* understood as 'psychologizing' implies that for Jung there is a fundamentally cosmological implication to the process of symbol formation. Hence in his autobiography he writes:

> The decisive question for man is: Is he related to something infinite or not? [...] Only if we know that the thing which truly matters is the infinite can we avoid fixing our interests upon

> futilities, and upon all kinds of goals which are not of real importance. [...] If we understand and feel that here in this life we already have a link with the infinite, desires and attitudes change. In the final analysis, we count for something only because of the essential we embody, and if we do not embody that life is wasted. In our relationships to other men, too, the crucial question is whether an element of boundlessness is expressed in the relationship (MDR, 1995, p. 357).

On a more abstract level, the idea of the *anima mundi* can obviously be tied in to the notion of the 'microcosm'/'macrocosm' and perhaps compared—as well as contrasted—to similar notions in Christian thought (e.g. in St. Maximus the Confessor, the idea of the reconciliation and renewal of all things in Christ) to indicate a 'mechanism' whereby Christian prayer and the Jungian alchemical imagination may coincide in 'acting' on God and the universe respectively, albeit from a vastly different set of underlying premises. Referring to one fictional example of what may be implied, there is a scene in Paulo Coelho's popular novel "The Alchemist" (2006, pp. 134–145) where the hero Santiago, under threat of death and to his own conscious denial of knowing how, nonetheless prays to turn himself into the wind—noting this is only a fictional example of course, it may be naturally objected that one cannot literally change into wind; but Santiago may nevertheless be viewed as having become conversant with the elements of an animated world,[3] through the joint use of prayer and his alchemical knowledge, gained in the novel through his alchemist mentor. It may be said that the fictional Santiago has found

[3] Coelho writes: "I have inside me the winds, the deserts, the oceans, the stars, and everything created in the universe. We were all made by the same hand, and we have the same soul. [...]" The boy reached through to the Soul of the World, and saw that it was a part of the Soul of God. And he saw that the soul of God was his own soul. And that he, a boy, could perform miracles" (pp. 140, 145). It is important here perhaps to mention that Coelho was involved in Crowleyan magic early in his writing career.

a way of entering perhaps, into the kind of 'cosmic consciousness' required of wounded healers, as suggested above.

Another example may be found in the famous 'Rainmaker' story which Jung was fond of quoting (Jung, CW14, pp. 419–420n), apparently from the real-life experience of Jung's associate Richard Wilhelm, whereby following unsuccessful petitions by Catholics and Protestants, as well as other local Chinese rituals, a 'rain-maker' is called to the despairing Chinese village suffering from drought, who simply requests a quiet house, where he remains for three days. When, on the fourth day, not only rain, but a snow-storm does arrive, unusually for the time of year, Wilhelm asks the old man how he made the snow, and receives the answer that the old man himself is not responsible for the snow—all he did was, coming from a part of the country which was in order according to the Tao, he waited three days until order returned within him in this disordered part of the country suffering from drought, and when it did, surely enough the snow came. The rainmaker story may also be positively contrasted with the scriptural passage from the epistle of James concerning Elijah (Js. 5:16–18).

Sedgwick (1994) connects this 'rainmaker idea' to working analytically with countertransference. Regarding his seminal book on the wounded healer, he writes that

> The goal [...] is to establish that there is a way of doing Jungian analysis that is based on monitoring and working with the analyst's countertransference. To this end I will show in more detail than usual the actual processing that takes place, the nuts and bolts of a countertransference-based way of working. This should shed light on the real implications of Jung's assertions that the patient and analyst are *both* in the analysis and that the analyst's getting right with himself - the "rainmaker" idea [...] — can have a crucial transformative effect on the patient (p. 7).

The phenomena of transference and countertransference have a hugely significant role in the history of psychotherapy (Carotenuto,

1991), going all the way back to Freud and the beginnings of psychoanalysis. It was Jung however, as discussed later, who used ideas from alchemy in his essay *The Psychology of the Transference* (CW16), and who first noted the transcendent aspect of the transference phenomenon, thereby suggesting the macrocosmic dimensions of the analyst's relation to self and client. Jung left it largely to other authors to explore the practical spiritual implications of his observation, always astutely avoiding the explicit integration of analytical psychology with any existing system of metaphysics or theology himself.

1 **Microcosm, Individuation and Psychotherapy.** The comprehensive question mentioned above, therefore, of how the relationship to self and client in psychotherapy is paralleled in and influenced by the relation of the individuating human microcosm to the macrocosm of the evolving universe as a whole, may serve to highlight some deeper spiritual implications of the processes of transference and countertransference observed in the consulting room. These processes may drive the 'undercurrents' of any relationship, not just the psychotherapeutic one—and therefore contain, or act as carriers, for the meaningful experience of suffering creatively in analysis and in life generally, since in "ordinary life creativity means making something for the soul out of every experience" (Moore, 1992, p. 198). If transference and countertransference are the wheels of the vehicle, the research question acts as its chassis—the cosmic, universal aspect of the process of individuation itself, the *magnum opus* which Jung made the overall aim of analysis. In Jung's own words, "[T]he realisation of the self also means a re-establishment of Man as the microcosm, i.e. man's cosmic relatedness" (CW18, par. 1573).

Many researchers have already been inspired to ponder the mystery of the human maturational process and self-realising capacity in its metaphysical aspect. Humanistic psychologists especially, have paralleled and, arguably, imitated Jung in providing their own psychological systems with their own equivalents to the individuation process, like the 'actualising tendency' (Rogers, 1961) and 'self-actualisation' (Maslow, 1967; 1993). Tudor & Merry (2002) for example, define Carl Rogers' neglected notion of a 'formative tendency' thus:

> [T]he directional tendency towards increased order and interrelated complexity found in nature from micro-organisms through crystals and in stellar space [...]. Syntropy rather than entropy [...], it supports the notion of an interconnectedness of all things and is reflected in the universality of the actualising tendency in humans. Rogers (1980) viewed this tendency as 'a base upon which we could begin to build a theory for humanistic psychology. It definitely forms a base for the person-centred approach' (p. 133). (pp. 57–58).

It can be seen that the 'formative tendency' as described by Rogers owes something to the notion of an *anima mundi*. Though the distinct and valuable tradition of humanistic and existential-phenomenological thought, and its contribution as a separate school to the discipline of psychotherapy, are indisputable as has been previously alluded to, it seems nonetheless fair of Papadopoulos and Saayman (1991) to point out in acknowledging the ancient history of this concept, that

> Humanistic psychology, the so-called third force in psychology... seems to have settled down after a frantic period of adolescent omniscience, and appears now to afford the acknowledgement that Jung spoke about 'self realisation' half a century earlier than the humanistic psychologists (p. 3).

Very briefly, the central project of 'self-realisation' in Jungian analysis may be defined as the enlargement of the ego as centre of consciousness, through the Self—the archetype of wholeness which represents the sum total of conscious and unconscious psychic processes, and acts as an ordering principle in the personality; the aim is to effect a shifting of the centre of consciousness on the ego-Self axis, away from the narrow field of the 'ego-complex,' in a direction deeper 'inwards' towards the Self (Edinger, 1972 & Edinger, 1992). In Edinger's own words, this is an ongoing process:

> The process of alternation between ego-Self union and ego-Self separation seems to occur repeatedly throughout the life of the individual both in childhood and in maturity. Indeed, this cyclic (or better, spiral) formula seems to express the basic process of psychological development from birth to death (p. 5).

Samuels, Shorter and Plaut (1986) define individuation as a "person's becoming himself, whole, indivisible and distinct from other people and collective psychology (though also in relation to these)" (p. 76). Moore (1992) relates this process to the 'path of the soul,' the often irrational and unpredictable journey leading to the marriage of soul and spirit, the *hieros gamos* between animus and anima, which is another way of expressing the necessity of incarnating the Self into the world:

> Another description of the soul's path can be found in Jung's concept of individuation. [...] individuation is not a goal or destination, it is a process. As the essence of individuation, I would emphasize the sense of being a unique individual, being actively involved in soul work. [...] The individual hard at work in the process of soul-making is becoming a microcosm, a "human world" (p. 261).

Jung formulated that "the aim of individuation is nothing less than to divest the self of the false wrappings of the persona on the one hand, and of the suggestive power of primordial images on the other" (CW6, par. 757). Such a demanding therapeutic aim must necessarily involve the whole patient and the whole therapist — "ars requirit totum hominem" (CW 16, p. 35) — in a common search for the patients' own truth, over against the context of their collective environment — a truth which is differentiated from, yet also contributive towards, the accepted wisdom of the society within which the journey of individuation takes place. It is evident therefore, that the Self, which is also according to Edinger (*ibid.*) and *pace* Jung, "most simply described as the inner empirical deity ... identical with the *imago Dei*" (p. 3), has a powerfully spiritual aspect in clinical practice. This suggests further, that just as individuation can be seen as a fundamentally spiritual process, so too the particular manifestation of profound, developmentally-linked emotional and cognitive phenomena is psychotherapy, such as transference and countertransference, must have spiritual aspects — indeed, perhaps psychotherapy itself, when understood as a spiritual discipline and engaged in ethically by the responsible clinician, can be seen to be nothing less than a form of mutual prayer. Here perhaps, what Archbishop Chrysostomos of Etna (2004) writes about psychotherapy and spiritual guidance needs to be taken into account:

> By way of a few concluding remarks, let me say that *a good psychologist uses therapeutic tools and techniques and approaches psychological and emotional problems much in the same way that a spiritual Father does.* By studying psychology we can learn something about the dynamics of spiritual guidance, avoiding dangers in the latter pursuit by understanding those implicit in the former. But *psychology is not spiritual guidance.* The Fathers of the Church, superb psychologists and students of human behaviour in their own right, bring to bear on psychology the Grace of the Christian life. In so doing, they transform mere psychology and add to it those expansive dimensions of spiritual guidance [...] that make it something quite different from psychotherapy and counselling *per se* (pp. 26–7, italics same).

Some of the practical issues highlighted by this complex relationship between psychotherapy and spiritual guidance, will therefore be explored in the next and final part.

PART THREE

Countertransference and the Wounded Healer Archetype

Introduction

Thus far, an examination of suffering in Jungian psychology and in Orthodox Christianity, has led to an exploration of several factors which influence the experience of and creative response to suffering, as articulated within these disciplines. In this final part, an application of the perspective offered by the notion of 'creative suffering' to the therapeutic process, will be attempted.

It may therefore be useful to begin with a consideration of *vocation*, or the discovery of one's calling in life, which is the ultimate aim perhaps of most psychotherapy and other forms of psychospiritual healing, but surely also the dominant framework of meaning surrounding the suffering experienced in any walk of life, in any culture or historical period. As Ulanov (2008) writes, when the call to vocation is answered,

> Our personal response plays out in the conditions of our culture, our time in history, and our community, and may be our particular contribution to shared existence with others. To consent often means more suffering; to consent always means more consciousness of how much suffering there is among all of us. [...] Moreover, to take up one's own vocation means exposing oneself to what governs the objective psyche at this time in history, in the community, in the group, and sometimes even in the world, and suffering the problem in one's own individual life and working it over and over for its transformation (p. 50).

Ulanov (*ibid.*) reaches this conclusion by considering vocation in Jung's sense of a call to becoming who we "are given to be" (p. 49), which Jung (see below) viewed as a call from the Self deserving religious attention. Ulanov gives the example of a daughter who, alone among family members, becomes conscious of generational complexes, enlightening and changing dysfunctional behaviour patterns for the whole family; also the example of an abused child who as an adult does not continue the cycle of abuse, but tries to understand the origins of destructive behaviour (p. 50). She thus explains that, since "we are all part of the people as a whole, and each of us receives the same call" (p. 49). Since vocation must be individually incarnated in the specific conditions of our environment, to follow one's true vocation is to respond creatively to our life's suffering, thus serving the collective soul.

While it can be of potentially redemptive value when creatively engaged, however, the question of who one is, and what one is meant to do with one's life, can nevertheless itself become a source of suffering and agony. Especially when nearing mid-life, the age at which Jung maintained introspection should normally begin, the sense of self-recrimination, existential guilt, and mounting debt to one's unrealised potential, often increases with the oppressing awareness of underachievement. Unfulfilment is, as Jacobs (1986) points out, frequently keener when previous life stages have not been successfully traversed, leaving behind 'unfinished business' (*ibid.*, p. 188). Life's otherwise 'necessary losses' (Viorst, 1986) — with personal death at their supreme pinnacle — may seem impossible to navigate under such conditions, leaving a frozen vacuum of trapped meaning in their wake.

Such feelings of the vanity of human existence are not unusual in an increasingly competitive social milieu and restrictive, inhuman job market. It is worth noting that Jung referred to the source of many of these feelings as 'the unlived life,' as Hollis (2001, p.120) reminds us, and linked them to the person's unconscious replication, compensation for, or individual attempt to heal their own parents' unresolved issues (the 'unlived life' of the parent). Theologically, too, it may be claimed that that parent's sins would be visited upon their children (Exodus 20:5), had Christ not atoned for human sin, sending the Comforter (John, 14:16) to those who respond creatively to suffering Thus, transgenerationally powerful dynamic forces, which in Jungian terms may be perceived as archetypal (cf. Stevens, 2006, p. 85), come to influence choices made across the life span, and these forces will especially menace those persons who are unreflective about their calling—even psychotherapists, whose work often directly involves counselling others on such matters.

CHAPTER ELEVEN

Vocation in Life and in Psychotherapy

1 **Psychotherapy as a Choice of Profession.** There are several reasons one may choose an 'odd' profession like psychotherapy. As previously suggested, life choices are usually motivated by forces from the external environment working in conjunction with inner needs and impulses, in other words by opportunity meeting disposition. Psychotherapy is probably no exception to this rule; no psychotherapist can afford to practice what Freud himself called the "impossible profession,"[1] however, without an in-depth knowledge of their own motivation for doing so, if this lack of self-knowledge is not to remain an unconscious hindrance in their work, leading to their eventual burn-out. Jung says of the therapist that

> Presumably he had good reasons for choosing the profession of psychiatrist and for being particularly interested in the treatment of the psychoneuroses; and he cannot very well do that without gaining some insight into his own unconscious processes. Nor can his concern with the unconscious be explained entirely by a free choice of interests, but rather by a fateful disposition which originally inclined him to the medical profession (1998, p. 13).

[1] Cf. Freud (1937), quoted in Malcolm (1997): "It almost looks as if analysis were the third of those "impossible" professions in which one can be sure beforehand of achieving unsatisfying results. The other two, which have been known much longer, are education and government."

Jung's last sentence above suggests that, in accordance with folk wisdom, psychotherapists do not tend to be 'normal' people[2] — they are in fact most often 'drawn' to psychotherapy for reasons of their own, a 'fateful disposition,' and not simply through intellectual interest. The history of psychotherapy demonstrates that therapists can be quite unstable (e.g. Goldwert, 1992), and given the happy circumstance when their oddness is in fact accompanied by an equally strong will to self-knowledge, their instability and maladaptation has generally proved a *good* thing for psychology, furnishing it with some of its strongest hypotheses concerning the origin of neuroses and psychoses! Writing from a psychoanalytic perspective, Coltart (1999) explains that the personal eccentricity of psychotherapists is actually common knowledge in their own circles:

> That a 'normal' person is unlikely to be a gifted therapist is almost an *idée reçue* in our strange world [of psychoanalysis] (p. 7).

The same author also reminds us that psychotherapy is a path of living without easy answers, on which uncertainty and insecurity paradoxically act as guides, linking the therapist to others:

> [W]e approach the paradox at the heart of the matter: psychotherapists are trained from their weaknesses; all other professions build on their strengths. (Coltart, *ibid.*, p. 39).

[2] In talking about the risk of 'unconscious infection' through contact with their patients' neuroses, Jung says the therapist has to be more experienced than the patient at making the constellated contents of the neurosis conscious; nevertheless, he adds the therapist "[...] might perhaps be so normal as not to need any unconscious standpoints to compensate his conscious situation. At least this is often how it looks, though whether it is so in a deeper sense is an open question" (Jung, 1998, pp 12–13). Jung is open to the possibility of madness or abnormality affecting the therapist at a profound level, even when he or she appear normal and well-balanced.

Hence too, in his seminal textbook on the art of psychotherapy, Storr (1990) confirms this observation through his personal experience of therapists, and further explains that

> Psychotherapists often have some personal knowledge of what it is like to feel insulted and injured, a kind of knowledge which they might rather be without, but which actually extends the range of their compassion. [...] The experience of being rejected by one's fellows... may leave the individual with a curious mixture of hostility and suspicion directed toward ordinary people combined with an especial compassion with those whom he feels have been rejected like himself. It is a mixture which I think I have often detected in the personalities of psychotherapists (p. 177).

The rich diversity of possible motivational factors leading to psychotherapy as a choice of profession, imply that the selection of trainee therapists is — or in the interests of future clients should be — a complex and important procedure, one which ideally continues throughout the training period, through regular reviews of the whole training and learning experience. Aveline (1996) writes regarding the selection procedure that

> Personality is all-important. [...] As a selector, I look for the functional motivators[3] listed by Guy (1987), and also the six qualities identified by Greben (1984): empathic concern, respectfulness, realistic hopefulness, self-awareness, reliability and strength of character. These are the qualities that are necessary if the therapist is to win the patient's trust; they give him the sense of being

[3] Aveline (1996) lists these 'functional motivators' elsewhere in his text as including a natural interest in people, the ability to listen and talk, psychological-mindedness [*sic*] and the ability to empathize, the capacity to tolerate and facilitate expression of feeling, emotional insight, introspection and the capacity for self-denial, tolerance of ambiguity and intimacy, warmth, caring and laughter.

> tended to and valued. Women often seem to have these qualities in greater abundance than men. It must be stressed that no one is perfect: what is required for this work is a sufficiency of these qualities. In addition, I look for two markers of maturity in life: that the trainee has struggled with some personal emotional conflict and achieved a degree of resolution, and that she has enjoyed and sustained over years a loving, intimate relationship. The first may bring in its wake humility and compassion, the second an active commitment to and capacity for good relationships [...]. (Aveline, 1996: p. 373; references in original).

Discovering the motivations behind our choice of profession can be enlightening and very therapeutic in itself; but like most therapeutic endeavours, it requires a good dose of humility, as Aveline (*ibid*) suggests. In focusing on countertransference issues, for example, a psychotherapist needs to be keenly aware of their personal shadow (cf. Page, 1999), and the way in which power struggles, unmet developmental needs, existential dilemmas and unresolved conflict — in brief, all the dynamics of their own psyche — affect both their choice of profession, and the way they come to conceptualise cases and offer treatment. When we do not become conscious of these dynamics, our work and our clients will suffer, as the hidden shadow of the powerful "Healer-Patient" archetype — the Charlatan, the Saviour or the Witch — will be constellated in the unconscious and overwhelm any effort at authentic and conscious mutuality (cf. Guggenbühl-Craig (1999)).

All this goes to suggest that psychotherapy cannot therefore be an ordinary 'nine-to-five' job when it is engaged in creatively; it is in fact best described as nothing less than a vocation for service to others. Coltart (*ibid.*) puts it thus:

> I believe that the strong sense of rightness for oneself of this particular path in life not only can justifiably be called a vocation, but also that it is that very vocational quality which is the source

> of the deepest and most sustained experience of survival-with-enjoyment. One will need to withstand a great deal of hardship in the pursuit of a vocation — indeed, the kind of patient endurance required is one of the recognized ways in which a vocation is tested (*ibid*, p. 8).

These feelings seem to be echoed and confirmed by Hollis (2001), who writes that the price of this sense of rightness is nothing less than a sacrifice, an issue returned to later in this chapter:

> We will be most nearly real when we serve our vocation. We will not be spared suffering, but we will be granted a deeply felt sense of what is right, even when suffering isolation and rejection. That deeply felt sense of what is right for us, which Marie-Louise von Franz calls "the instinct of truth," is how we can find what it is we are able to do with this precious and fragile gift of life and the transcendent reality we are summoned to serve. This sacrifice of the ego will constitute our greatest gift to the world (p. 111).

2 **The Spiritual Significance of Vocation.** Having focused a little on the particular calling of the psychotherapist, it may therefore be useful to look also at vocation in more general terms, as our "gift to the world," in Hollis' (*ibid*) words, which involves a sacrifice.

Despite a growing interest in spirituality, it has been suggested earlier that psychotherapists still frequently maintain an attitude of hostility to religion and traditional religious dogma. Ulanov (2004) laments this tendency, and suggests that while

> Spirituality is claimed; religion is eschewed as moralistic, coercive, dogmatistic, narrow-minded, with punitive superego rules that squelch emotion, sexuality, aggression. This split of spirituality from religion poses a problem, but one that invites inquiry. To include in our idea of psychic reality the freedom with which

> the divine approaches us opens for discussion both psychological and theological categories. (p.64)

Perhaps then, this very 'freedom with which the divine approaches us,' prevents the art and science of psychotherapy from being contained within any merely secular definition, even if such definitions may be practical and workable in relative terms. Hence it is perhaps, not difficult to see that religion may offer insight into the psychotherapeutic vocation, just as analysis may offer insight into our attitudes towards religion. In the particular case of the calling to heal others psychotherapeutically through intimate knowledge of our own wounds, Ulanov (*ibid.*) puts it beautifully where she suggests that

> The spirit often uses psychological complexes to speak its own purposes, using what is at hand. Hence it is difficult to separate psyche and spirit because in life they are intertwined. Sometimes pathology is the stable in which Christ is born, the only door the spirit can gain entrance (p. 64).

Scripture assures us that everyone at birth has a specific talent, and that we are not meant to bury that talent in the ground, but to multiply it, cultivate it and make it bear rich fruit (Mt. 25:14–30). Writing from a Russian Orthodox perspective, Father Thomas Hopko[4] (1997) stresses the importance of finding and keeping one's unique calling. He makes some rather astonishing, but nonetheless inspiring claims in this regard:

---

[4] Although the article by Fr. Hopko from which several quotations will be used here, is based on a talk, and therefore not strictly-speaking an academic paper, Fr. Hopko is himself an academic former Dean of St. Vladimir's Seminary in New York. The talk he gave on vocation has proven of such seminal importance to Orthodox ideas on work, that Bezzerides (2006) describes it as "a noteworthy exception" (p. 12) to the lack of Orthodox articles specifically addressing the issue of vocation, and may justify the extensive quoting which follows.

> Everyone, or in Biblical language, the "many" are called. But not all are chosen. Some are rejected not because they have no vocation from God, but because they refuse to accept their calling (*ibid.*, p. 1).

Orthodox Christian theology reassures us that everything created by God, both in the spiritual and in the material realm, from the holy angels at His throne, down to the last grain of inanimate matter, is good in its essential nature. Each being has its natural place and destiny allocated to it according to the divine wisdom within the created order (Matt. 10:30). Furthermore, all things are made holy and sustained in holiness by virtue of being continually suffused and penetrated by the divine energies, the Holy Spirit, of whom Orthodox Christians say daily in prayer that He is 'everywhere and fillest all things': the entire cosmos is suffused with Divine goodness. Indeed, modern Orthodox commentators on the environmental crisis have even detected a crucial difference between Western and Eastern Christian understandings of this issue, the West generally drawing on Aristotle, and the East on Plato for their respective world-views. Hence Chryssavgis (1996), discussing the work of Philip Sherrard writes:

> Accordingly, Sherrard examines the cosmologies of the pre-Renaissance world and of modern technology. His description of the fatal consequences of the world-view prevalent in the Renaissance and post-Renaissance periods is depressing indeed. [...] [H]e describes the extent of the resulting dehumanization of humanity and the desacralization of the natural world. Sherrard argues here, as elsewhere, that our ecological problems derive in large part from the Aristotelian philosophy espoused by Western Christian thought, since according to this philosophy the divine substance cannot interrelate with or interpenetrate the material universe. This ideology paved the way for our modern scientific predicament (p. 350).

Just as in Western theology there has perhaps been an increasing gulf between matter and spirit since Aquinas, there has also been an increasingly compartmentalized view of the human soul. In contrast to this view, and over against the notion of the Unconscious, Orthodox spirituality introduces the theological concept of the Uncreated, and of course the underlying divine non-analytic reality which this word signifies. Kantian philosophy proposes that the contents of consciousness are at one remove from 'things' themselves, and phenomena are thus opposed to noumena; Jung sensed moreover, via von Hartmann, and to some extent Freud, the existence of a 'hidden life of the mind,' behind ordinary consciousness. Between Kant and Jung therefore, consciousness is alienated both from the world and from itself. Orthodoxy instead, knows at first hand that material 'things' *themselves* are symbols of the underlying *logoi* by which their nature and destiny is established in the divine Kingdom 'behind' reality - to use a spatial metaphor, for a reality which, however, is ultimately 'not of this world.' As Rossi (2008) writes

> One of the basic principles of the patristic theology of creation as synthesized by Saint Maximos is the underlying integrity of the creation as created by God. Creation and all created being are held in being by the thought, word and will of God. Everything God creates and holds in being is a particular manifestation of God's will. Creation is God's will incarnated in each creature. Each created thing is itself a word, or logos, spoken by God, which finds its meaning, purpose, goal and end in and through the Divine Logos (Rossi, 2008).

Thus the symbol, in Orthodox understanding, *is* the sacrament, and participation in it means allowing symbol and sacrament to act upon us as the site of transferral of the divine energies. The Uncreated is not accessible to human consciousness — not in this life, nor even in the next; yet Orthodoxy teaches that the essence of God nevertheless communicates its presence by means of the divine energies which permeate the whole of creation and man's soul. The hesychastic experience of the Uncreated Light of Tabor, is in fact a direct refutation of the Aristotelian denial that divine energy can penetrate material creation,[5] at the same time as it is an affirmation of God's transcendent, ultimate mystery.

When something is holy, it is complete, whole, sound, integrated, incorruptible, functional and healthy; another word which has been used for this is 'chaste.'[6] The Greek word for 'good,' *καλόν*, is related to *κάλλος*, or beauty; Christianity perceives that truth, beauty and goodness coinhere, something can therefore only be truly described as 'holy,' when it is characterised by all three qualities. Seen from this perspective it becomes apparent that God, being love in His very nature, created a cosmos consisting not only of inanimate matter, but also reasoning beings that have free will—the angels and men. The first to fall from His grace, in other words the first being which freely chose to act against his own glorious nature, destiny and vocation and thereby become un-holy, was God's once brightest angel, Lucifer, who was so beautiful, that he fell in love with his own beauty and arrogantly chose to worship himself instead of praising his Creator,

[5] Cf. Rossi (2008): "The cosmos is a book of revelation and the Scripture is a revealed cosmos. Both consist of logoi, words, which reveal, when read with the Spirit, the will and mind of God. Both are transfigured through Christ. The disciples who witnessed the Transfiguration were also transfigured, not only in spirit and soul, but also in body. The uncreated light and grace of Christ, streaming from his transfigured face, body and garments, transfigured the very senses of the apostles, allowing them to behold his glory, as of the only begotten of the Father, "full of grace and truth." Since the human nature shared by Christ with all humanity, according to the Fathers, is a microcosm of the whole created order, the fact that the transfigured body of Christ reveals His divinity in a flood of uncreated light, and that this same transfiguring uncreated energy streams from his face, body and clothing and illumines and transfigures the bodies of the apostles, means without doubt that the whole of creation is lifted up, and is meant to be lifted up, transformed and transfigured by the irresistible power of the grace of the Logos."

[6] Evdokimov (1994), i.e., uses the Greek translation of 'chastity,' *sophrosyne*, to suggest that "a sophrosynic being is one who is chaste in the structure of the spirit, integrated" (p. 278).

thereby willingly rejecting his vocation as God's most splendid creation, wanting instead to be God the Creator himself. It was, therefore, according to Christian theology, the Devil, the Adversary, who first freely chose to pervert and undermine the perfection of the natural order of creation in this way. He begat spiritual suicide, and brought the phenomenon of death as a reality into existence through his act. Since his fall, everything which similarly rebels against its natural function, everything which is disintegrated, unsound, incomplete, unchaste, in some way participates in the Devil's nothingness, in his dark non-being *contra naturam*, παρά φύσιν. Lucifer then felt envious of man, because of God's great love for us, and was unable to tolerate our paradisal bliss. He, therefore, seduced humans into sin, and carries on seducing them to this day. God nonetheless allows him to continue to exist, even after Christ's permanent cosmic defeat of the devil through His Resurrection,[7] because He wants to make us stronger spiritual athletes; by strengthening our resolve against sin, and by purifying our thoughts, the will to love God and walk in the path of our natural destiny hence becomes stronger and clearer. In the Christian understanding, the spiritual seeker who keeps the divine commandments, is protected by God in this encounter with evil, whatever the circumstances: in the laconic words of St. John Chrysostom, "God did not only allow for the sober and attentive persons not to be hurt, but He made [sobriety and attentiveness] beneficial for them" (PG 49, 266).

Evil in Orthodox Christianity, is any incitement to move away from our natural condition, to a condition inferior to it. Since human nature and destiny are bound up with one another, Hopko (*ibid*)

[7] Writing from a Protestant Christian perspective, Embry (2005) explains that "Jesus conquered the world, not so that we could live in the world as if we have no pressure or suffering; but so that, through Him, we can also overcome the pressing burdens that will surely come" (p. 82). This perspective on salvation would find Orthodox Christians in complete agreement. She also writes, "we all need our pain; our pain helps to make us who we are. God uses our pain to help others who are hurting, to draw us closer to Him, and to form character in us. Our suffering conforms us to Jesus in His glory" (pp. 81–2).

makes it clear that each person not only has a vocation, but also a supreme responsibility to accept this calling in life, whatever is the price associated with it (and this may be compared with Jung's very similar attitude towards vocation, which is discussed below). Bezzerides (2006) therefore also suggests that vocation is a response to God's own initiative in creating and loving a person, and in offering His only-begotten Son for human salvation. Hence she offers the following as a working definition of 'vocation' for Orthodox Christians:

> Vocation is one's ongoing and unique way of being in the world that is a response to Christ's call to love God with heart, soul, mind and strength, and one's neighbour as oneself. (Bezzerides, *ibid.*, p. 10).

3 **The Psychological Significance of Vocation.** Scientific methodology, however, can at times be unable to help us get to know ourselves at the depth required to discover our true vocation, perhaps because our particular problems lie beyond its reach, or maybe because certain ultimate aspects of human experience in general, simply lie outside the domain of science as objects of study; or perhaps again, science and technology just have not evolved yet to that degree of sophistication. Perhaps for this same reason Steiner (1992), writing on Heidegger's distinction between the *fraglich* and the *fragwürdig*, states that

> There are no terminal answers, no last and formal decidabilities to the question of the meaning of human existence or of a Mozart sonata or of the conflict between individual conscience and social constraint. [...] "The wandering," says Heidegger, "the peregrination toward that which is worthy of being questioned, is not adventure but homecoming." Man, in his dignity, comes home to the unanswerable. And that, of course, which is most *fragwürdig* is "Being" (pp. 56–57).

Psychotherapists witness daily the mystery of human being: that both our own difficulties in life, and the problems of others, are as a general rule not simple, nor are they solved simply. It has already been suggested that for Orthodox Christianity, human nature and destiny are interlinked, and our being, which Heidegger deems most *fragwürdig*, is essentially good, but since the Fall has also been engaged in a struggle against evil even within itself—primarily within itself as a fallen tendency towards sin. It may not be coincidental, therefore, that an in-depth investigation of the *fragwürdig* spiritual issue of vocation is absent both from Freud's opus, and to a lesser extent from Jung's (cf. discussion below). Despite the fact that both these men were highly creative and prolific, they may, in their otherwise audible silence on the matter, have sensed the difficulty of accounting for the mystery of vocation in scientific language. Nonetheless, Freud was clearly dedicated and very deeply attached to his own work from an early age, obviously experiencing a strong sense of vocation in himself; Storr (1989) suggests that

> His intellectual precocity, and his dedication to work, which remained compulsive from boyhood onwards, are characteristic. He wrote to his friend, Fliess, that he needed a 'dominating passion.' He claimed that he could not contemplate a life without work, and that, for him, the creative imagination and work went together (p. 8).

It is interesting to note from the above comment, that in his own experience Freud observed a link between work and creative imagination—the creative imagination being so fundamental also to Jung, that

> Jung goes so far as to say that the creative imagination is "the only primordial phenomenon accessible to us, the real Ground of the psyche, the only immediate reality." It is the divine principle itself. And this symbol of the creative spon-

taneity of the unconscious ultimately stands behind the creation of any religion (Von Franz, 1993, pp. 219–220).

Von Franz here, would place creative imagination at the centre of both Jungian theory and religious history. Understandably, it seems Jung took a similar attitude to work and creativity, viewing both as natural and necessary to psychic well-being. Sharp (1991) states that for Jung, creativity was one of five prominent instinctive factors in the psyche (the other four being reflection,[8] activity,[9] sexuality and hunger). As already seen in the section on creative suffering, creativity can indeed prove to be very important to mental health, and Symington (2001, p. 45), echoing Berdyaev's personalism, argues elsewhere that madness is precisely a blockage of the ability to synthesize the constituents of our humanity into the free and personal, and to exercise therefore our ability to relate.

Perhaps then, the fact that for both Freud and Jung creative work was a necessary and natural function in their own lives, may account for their implicit classification of it within the domain of the 'instinctive' in the respective psychologies they formulated, but paradoxically (and also equally surprisingly) for their subsequent lack of theory concerning the phenomenon of vocation. Moraglia (1997), for example, points to this absence of any extensive treatment of vocation in analytical psychology, contrasting it with Jung's own dedication to his work.[10] He offers a definition of human work, and goes on to say that:

[8] Reflection includes the religious urge and the search for meaning, which for Jung are also instinctive, yet at the very least these introduce a 'cognitive' or mental dimension to the direction of instinctive drives, which seems absent from the Freudian model discussed above.

[9] Sharp links this to the urge to travel, love of change, restlessness and play. May it not also be associated with the restless need to work, reported by creative individuals such as writers, artists, etc.?

[10] Passages such as that from MDR (Fontana press edition, 1995, p. 130) in which Jung describes how his heart pounded as it became clear, "in a flash of illumination, that for me the only possible goal was psychiatry," show the extent to which a felt sense of vocation informed Jung's own professional career.

> The above definition underlines the pragmatic centrality of work in human life; the psychological precipitates of such an activity may well be fundamental. Jung's identification of the meaning of his life with his work [...], echoed by many creative individuals, bears witness to its importance. Yet, readers in search of an explicit psychology of the working life would vainly peruse his writings (p. 106).

As discussed later on, it would appear to be the case that, in the understanding of vocation, the central archetype of the Self comes into play, manifesting itself in a way which may prevent any over-specificity and formulaic psychological approaches. The emphasis placed by analytical psychology on the ego's establishment of a career and securing a social position in the first half of life, reminiscent of the Freudian (and subsequently the now-standard Eriksonian) relegation of vocational choice to the first two decades of life, has meant perhaps that depth psychology inherited a rather cavalier understanding of the complex place of ongoing work in a human life. It could be pointed out, that 'work' can mean a great many things, and 'vocation' perhaps even more;[11] hence it should not be considered too incongruent or inappropriate that, from the Orthodox Christian perspective, Fr. Hopko writes:

> [...] everyone is called to serve God and their fellow human beings in some form of life which God Himself wills. This "form of life" is not necessarily a job or profession. For example, some people may be called to suffer on this earth and to bear the re-

[11] Hence the humanistic psychologist A. Maslow (Maslow *et al*, 1998) writes that: "All human beings prefer meaningful work to meaningless work. This is much like stressing the high human need for a system of values, a system of understanding the world and of making sense out of it. This comes very close to the religious quest in the humanistic sense. If work is meaningless, then life comes close to being meaningless. Perhaps here is also the place to point out that no matter how menial the chores—the dishwashing and the test-tube cleaning, all become meaningful or meaningless by virtue of their participation or lack of participation in a meaningful or important or loved goal."

> sults of fallen humanity in the most violent manner; to be victimized by disease, retardation, affliction; to be the objects of other people's cares, or disdain. This is their vocation, and they are particularly blessed by God and loved by Christ in its acceptance and fulfilment (*ibid*, p. 1).

This may be compared with Ulanov's (Ulanov & Dueck, 2008) earlier comment that to take up one's vocation implies "exposing oneself to what governs the objective psyche at this time in history, in the community, in the group, and sometimes even in the world, and suffering the problem in one's own individual life and working it over and over for its transformation." Fr. Hopko is not speaking here through hardened insensitivity to these terrible human predicaments; what he writes makes sense, at least inasmuch as, if there is a transcendent God, then those people whom nature and society have assigned the role of being 'losers,' outcasts, and pariahs, are not in fact 'useless' *sub specie aeternitatis.*[12] Hence too, scripture and the Church Fathers reassure us repeatedly that the harder our life is in this world despite all our good efforts, the more loved we are by God:

> My son, despise not the chastening of the Lord; neither be weary of his correction: for whom the Lord loveth he correcteth; even as a father the son in whom he delighteth (Prov. 3:11–12).

This is a hard lesson, originating in the pre-Christian Hebrew Wisdom literature; but from a Christian perspective the message here lies, perhaps, in the enjoinder not to scorn or refuse one's appointed lot, however tough it seems. Christian teaching reminds us that we are called to embrace *who* we are, *where* we are, to 'blossom where we are planted'—in fact, it is sinful not to, as Fr. Hopko rather humorously goes on to explain:

[12] Questions of the absolute value of human life emerge very graphically when considering the practical bioethical dilemmas of abortion and euthanasia.

> One of the greatest obstacles to the discovery of one's vocation in life, which is a clear expression of our disobedience and self-will, is the desire to be someone else, someplace else, sometime else. We have all heard people say that if only they lived in another place, or in another time, or with other people... then they could be holy. Or, if only they were married. Or, if only they were not married. If only this, and if only that! We must come to see how sinful such an attitude is, how crazy and deluded. It is simply blasphemy. And it may well be the blasphemy against the Holy Spirit which Christ says cannot be forgiven, for it dares to tell God that our failures in life are His fault for making us the way we are (Mt. 12:31; Lk. 12:10) (*ibid.*, p. 6).

When considered in isolation from the Orthodox Christian teaching on the purpose of human existence, this can sound like fatalism, or even a guilt-inducing accusation; yet within the Orthodox framework, these words are paradoxically encouraging and hopeful, since they are based on a very different response to the Gnostic question on the origin of evil. Ironically perhaps, the atheist philosopher Nietzsche (1844–1900), refers to a somewhat similar—though not identical—kind of optimistic stoicism, which he calls *amor fati*, the 'love of one's fate,' an idea to be later taken up by Jung:

> My formula for greatness in a human being is *amor fati*: that one wants nothing to be other than it is, not in the future, not in the past, not in all eternity. Not merely to endure that which happens of necessity, still less to dissemble it—all idealism is untruthfulness in the face of necessity—but to *love* it (1968; 2004, p. 46).

Although 'fate' and 'destiny' are words with different semantic connotations (which Jungian analysts are well aware of), they may be treated as roughly equivalent in appreciating the meaning of *amor fati* as a concept for Jungian psychology. Whitmont (2007) offers a

Jungian interpretation of the concept of destiny as it applies in psychotherapeutic practice. He writes:

> In terms of what we know now of the objective psyche, destiny does not imply an absolute determinism. We encounter it, I would say, as an unfolding plan, as the prepersonal yet individual pattern of an intended wholeness. Arising from the Self, this plan needs the cooperation of consciousness for its realization in actual life, and its fulfilment within the limits of the ego's capacity. Thus, destiny, or fate, is the unfoldment of the Self-archetype in time and space. Destiny, in this sense, may be experienced merely as meaningless bondage and pointless suffering or it may be experienced as the fulfillment of one's own deepest, but as yet unknown, identity; that is, as creative freedom. This will depend largely upon the individual's capacity for awareness, his ability to experience symbolic significance, and to attempt a cooperative acceptance of the tragic as well as the joyful patterns of his life.[...] The prevailing attitude of "If only I, my parents, or society had been different, or had acted differently"—which necessarily carries guilt and blame in its wake[13]—can be transformed into a feeling for life as a creative experience, as a search for fulfillment and realization. A destined identity poses a potential which is always waiting, at any point in time and space, to be actualized by our efforts, our trials and errors, and our creative improvisations in personal situations. Such a viewpoint offers a challenge even in the face of despair. In its suffering, the soul can discover meaning (pp. 25, 35).

More specifically, Whitmont (*ibid.*) suggests that

> What we suffered as children or adults as the result of disturbed relationships with parents and other close associates may be

[13] This observation may be paralleled with Fr. Hopko's description of an "if only this, if only that" attitude described earlier. Obstacles to holiness, it appears, can be quite similar to the sort of obstacles that lie in the path of Jungian individuation.

> seen not just as accident or misfortune but as a destined emotional impasse essential for the actualization of our own particular pattern of wholeness (p. 26).

Indeed, due to the actual nature of synchronicity, and the psychoid psychophysical aspects of the archetypal reality underlying space-time, our life is lived not simply in a forward manner, but both 'proactively' and 'retroactively' so to speak, in that the future may be as much of an influence on the present, as the past is:

> [...] what must be experienced at the age of sixty-six could well necessitate and precipitate certain experiences at the age of three or four. [...] Destiny, as it is actualized for the individual in his parents, his circumstances, and society generally, constitutes a challenge to the unfoldment of the Self, which can achieve its full expression only when the ego is roused to conscious effort through an active polar opposition. [...] A further implication would be that the evolutional needs and intents of the Self are the prime factors in the constellation of child-parent relationships—that is, in the particular archetypal patterns which are set up in early life to provide, as it were, the staging for the play: it is as though we, or rather the Self, selected the parents needed for our particular life drama (*ibid.*, pp. 28, 31, 34).

Not only does the future impinge on the present, but we (as Self) even 'choose' our parents! Obviously this understanding of destiny as an 'unfoldment' of the Self archetype through conscious effort of the ego, calls into question any notions of a deterministic or reductionistic fatalism, while at the same time retaining the significance of meaningful connections between life events. This matches the Christian view that, while biography and history do occur in linear time, man nevertheless has free will, and *sub specie aeternitatis* destiny and predestination thus also do not equate with one another, since the causality which applies to linear time cannot be valid from the divine perspective of eternity – there is no past, present and future in the One whose name is 'I am,' Who views all events throughout our individual life-spans as though they were happening simultaneously, forming a tapestry of meaning. Perhaps even in Whitmont's Jungian phraseology concerning the recognition of a 'prepersonal' pattern present within the Self archetype as the blueprint of vocation, a trace of the operation of the Divine Logos through the expression of our personal, unique *logoi* may be found. And just as the Church Fathers unanimously point to humility as the key to Christian fulfillment, Whitmont (*ibid*) too advises us finally that

> *Amor fati*, then, includes an awareness of ourselves, of our inner and outer limitations, and the kind of acceptance and willingness to concern ourselves with them which makes the striving for adequate fulfillment within such limitations into a challenge to creative improvisation. Only by so accepting ourselves in the light of the overall pattern of our destiny can our sense of compulsive bondage be transformed into motivation. In no other way does the energy of the Self, its sustaining *pneuma*, become available to us for use as an inner freedom permitting us to exert some conscious choice (p. 36).

The Christian understanding of "loving one's fate" or 'bearing one's cross' (Lk. 14:27) however, is not the same as the Nietzschean or Jungian one (neither, of course, are these identical to one another, but for the purposes of this discussion they may perhaps be treated as roughly equivalent). Nietzsche's notion of amor fati is based on the idea of eternal recurrence, namely that time is cyclical, and therefore a supreme affirmation of life for him, would be the love of a fate we are destined to experience repeatedly.[14] Although the Book of Eccle-

[14] Jung addressed these Nietzschean ideas in his *Zarathustra* seminars. He did not wholly agree with the notion of eternal recurrence, as he wrote in a letter to Rvd. A. Rudolph: "The 'Untimely Meditations' were to me an eye-opener, less so the *Genealogy of Morals* or his idea of the "Eternal Return" of all things" (Jung, 1976, pp. 621–2).

siastes does support the notion of there being 'nothing new under the sun' (Eccl. 1:9), and some purport this to be a reference to eternal recurrence, Christianity does not subscribe to the ancient idea that time is cyclical, and hence would not advocate loving one's destiny as a response to a recurring Sisyphean predicament, to which mankind is condemned. Time is linear in the Christian understanding, and everything is leading towards a unique goal and realisation. Also, in scripture there is an implicit recognition throughout, that human suffering is linked to sinfulness and the circumstances of the Fall; it is not by any means our 'natural' condition, hence we are called neither to mere passive acceptance of our fate, nor to taking any masochistic or nihilistic pleasure in it.

Scripture is not idealist either — it does not maintain that the only things which can be directly known are our ideas, or that the external world is in some way a product of our mental existence. Yet again, the scriptural rejection of idealism is on different grounds to those put forward by the proto-existentialist, Nietzsche. Kantian transcendental idealism makes a distinction between things-in-themselves, or noumena, and our human perception of them, or phenomena; roughly speaking, idealists believe that the three-dimensional world of space, time and matter that we perceive around us is not 'real' in an absolute sense, and is furthermore, as Bishop Berkeley suggested, a construct of the human mind – not quite a 'figment of the imagination' as such, but an experience which is dependent on underlying a priori mental structures which shape both the way we perceive things, and the way we reason. To the post-Kantian idealist, actual reality is noumenal, and hence inaccessible to us as rational, sentient beings.

Christian epistemology, however, does not sail so dangerously close to solipsism as some streams of post-Kantian thought; the scriptural, Christian understanding of truth does not share this gnoseological basis, and thus traditional ways of understanding scripture, for example, were either historical — literal (as in the School of Antioch), or allegorical (School of Alexandria). In the Christian understanding, the world has always been a *real* place, even as we do perceive it and reason about it, with the faculties of our soul, and our senses and rational faculty are considered (usually) reliable indicators of reality. Therefore, while Christianity understands and appreciates God's ultimate unknowability and profound mystery, it has a higher opinion, and more connected view, of our human capacity to *know* than that which idealist philosophy permits, but also none of the logical pitfalls of radical empiricism. Contrary to popular gnosticized impressions of Christian thought, traditional Christianity actually does value the senses, and the information we glean from them, as it also values matter itself; but this doesn't mean that it perceives knowledge which is gained by the senses as being necessarily distortion-free or globally accurate, since our senses are subject to delusion (*plani* / *prelest*). Hence, for example, Theophilus of Antioch, writing ca. 185 AD, suggests that regarding the possibility of seeing God,

> [...] if you say, "Show me thy God," I would reply, "Show me yourself, and I will show you my God." Show, then, that the eyes of your soul are capable of seeing, and the ears of your heart able to hear; for as those who look with the eyes of the body perceive earthly objects and what concerns this life, and discriminate at the same time between things that differ, whether light or darkness, white or black, deformed or beautiful, well-proportioned and symmetrical or disproportioned and awkward, or monstrous or mutilated; and as in like manner also, by the sense of hearing, we discriminate either sharp, or deep, or sweet sounds; so the same holds good regarding the eyes of the soul and the ears of the heart, that it is by them we are able to behold God (cf. 1997).

There is, therefore, a distinction between things as perceived by the senses, and things perceived with 'the eyes of the soul.' In the same passage, Theophilus also introduces a crucial factor in the Christian anthropology of perception, that of the effects of sin on the senses:

> For God is seen by those who are enabled to see Him when they have the eyes of their soul opened: for all have eyes; but in some they are overspread, and do not see the light of the sun. Yet it does not follow, because the blind do not see, that the light of the sun does not shine; but let the blind blame themselves and their own eyes. So also thou, O man, hast the eyes of thy soul overspread by thy sins and evil deeds. As a burnished mirror, so ought man to have his soul pure. When there is rust on the mirror, it is not possible that a man's face be seen in the mirror; so also when there is sin in a man, such a man cannot behold God. [...] All these things [*sins*], then, involve you in darkness, as when a filmy defluxion on the eyes prevents one from beholding the light of the sun: thus also do iniquities [...] involve you in darkness, so that you cannot see God ((cf. 1997) On the Trinity, Bk 1 ch. 2, italics mine).

Christian gnoseology is thus neither idealist nor empiricist, nor yet romantic—though it would probably concur with William Blake's famous dictum that "If the doors of perception were cleansed, everything would appear to man as it is, infinite" (The Marriage of Heaven and Hell, 'A Memorable Fancy,' pl. 14)—the crucial difference being that, where Blake, influenced by Swedenborg, relied primarily on his imaginative faculty to gain entrance to his visionary worlds, Orthodox Christianity goes about the cleansing of the 'doors of perception' through asceticism and spiritual purgation, admitting at most only of the partial use of a purified imaginative faculty as suggested by St Nicodemus discussed earlier, and this not in the context of genuine *theoria*, which transcends imagination. In fact, both scripture and patristic counsel strongly and actively discourage us from falling prey to our own unreformed imaginations through the sin of pride. It is perhaps for this reason that in the famous words of the Magnificat, a prayer sung by the all-pure Theotokos following the Annunciation, which was also regularly said by expectant Jewish mothers for centuries prior to this event (Orthodox Study Bible, p. 138), the Mother of God quotes the book of psalms, saying:

> He has shown strength with His arm; He has scattered the proud *in the imagination of their hearts* (Lk. 1:51, italics mine).

It is thus prideful imagination, too, which makes us believe that we are the sole authors of our own destiny; Hollis (*ibid*) calls it "hubris" (p. 13). To Blake's dictum, therefore, Christianity might add "blessed are the pure at heart, for they shall see God" (Mt. 5:8).

God, therefore, is not just an unknowable transcendent; He is "everywhere and fillest all things" (Orthodox Prayer to the Holy Spirit), to be seen, felt, heard — if only we are suitably prepared for this. For Orthodox Christianity, God is Uncreated and 'wholly other' to everything mundane and created, but man's mental and spiritual faculties nevertheless equip him with the ability to perceive not only the visible, but also the invisible. This is the bold claim of Orthodox theology as it is expressed, i.e. in the writings of St. Gregory Palamas. It is for this very reason that St. Seraphim of Sarov so strongly declared that the sole aim of the Christian life is the acquisition of the Holy Spirit; this is what living in the Kingdom of God — even during our brief stay on earth — is about, and it is what all the saints, in the diversity of vocations lived out in Christ, attest to.

4 **Jung and Vocation.** It has been already suggested that an extensive treatment of the phenomenon of work is absent from analytical psychology. Nevertheless, Jung can be said to have been very taken with the idea of finding one's vocation in life, since, to all intents and purposes, he equated it with the process of individuation. Storr (1998) writes that Jung was interested in

> ...the exceptional individuals whose own nature compelled them to reject conventional ways and discover their own path. In Jung's view "Nature is aristocratic, and one person of value outweighs ten lesser ones" (CW 7, par. 236) (p. 192; reference in original).

Jung, therefore, linked the ability to individuate to one's innate nature, and he accordingly writes:

> What is it, in the end, that induces a man to go his own way and to rise out of unconscious identity with the mass as out of a swathing mist? Not necessity, for necessity comes to many, and they all take refuge in convention. Not moral decision, for nine times out of ten we decide for convention likewise. What is it then, that inexorably tips the scales in favour of the *extra-ordinary*? (quoted in Storr, *ibid.*, p. 199; original italics).

Jung it seems, did not think necessity is the mother of invention. Creative individuality, he suggests, must be driven by something else.[15] We have already seen that even Nietzsche suggests, instead of merely stoically putting up with our fate or—even worse—trying in some way to deny it, or pretend it isn't true, what bestows our character with greatness is our ability to love the very fate we have been assigned, even though its inexorable progress lies beyond our control. Jung similarly proposes that it is the *attitude* we take towards the necessity of fate which defines our destiny, and this destiny he identifies with our vocation. For Jung, this vocation is

> [...] an irrational factor that destines a man to emancipate himself from the herd and from its well-worn paths. True personality is always a vocation, and puts its trust in it as in God, despite its being, as the ordinary man would say, only a personal feeling. But vocation acts like a law of God, from which there is no escape... Anyone with a vocation hears the voice of the inner man: he is *called*. That is why the legends say that he possesses

[15] Neither, however, does Christian scripture see our lives as being driven relentlessly onwards by harsh necessity, as if at the mercy of the ancient Greek goddess *Ananke*—the fearsome mother of the *moirae* or fates, whose compelling power none can resist, and who spitefully avenges those who try to escape her by increasing their bonds.

> a private daemon who counsels him and whose mandates he must obey (quoted in Storr, 1998, pp. 199–200; original italics).

We see then that, for Jung, there is an inexorable, irrepressible quality to vocation, a personal 'law of one's being,' which is nothing less than a *principium individuationis.* Jung thus clearly shows his influence by the Romantic philosophers; if a man has a sense of vocation, then "there is no escape," "he must obey." It is what sets a 'chosen' man apart from others:

> The only thing that distinguishes him from all the others is his vocation. He has been called by that all-powerful, all-tyrannizing psychic necessity that is his own and his people's affliction. If he hearkens to the voice, he is at once set apart and isolated as he has resolved to obey the law that commands him from within. "His *own* law!" everybody will cry. But he knows better: it is *the* law, *the* vocation for which he is destined, no more "his own" than the lion that fells him, although it is undoubtedly this particular lion that kills him and not any other lion. Only in this sense is he entitled to speak of "his" vocation, "his" law (quoted in Storr, *ibid.*, p. 202; original italics).

Jung reaches here an almost religious appreciation of the might and power of one's calling. Thus,

> Fidelity to the law of one's being is [...] a loyal perseverance and confident hope; in short, an attitude such as a religious man should have towards God (CW 17, par. 296).

In fact, neurosis itself for Jung,

> ... is thus a defence against the objective, inner activity of the psyche, or an attempt, somewhat dearly paid for, to escape from the inner voice and hence from the vocation. For this "growth"

> is the objective activity of the psyche, which, independently of conscious volition, is trying to speak to the conscious mind through the inner voice and lead him toward wholeness. Behind the neurotic perversion is concealed his vocation, his destiny: the growth of personality, the full realisation of the life-will that is born with the individual. It is the man without *amor fati* who is the neurotic; he, truly, has missed his vocation, and never will he be able to say with Cromwell, "None climbeth so high as he who knoweth not wither his destiny leadeth him (Storr, 1998, pp. 207–7; original italics).

Frustration of the call to individuate leads to neurosis. Moraglia (*ibid*) points to the two different 'kinds' of individuation found in analytical psychology, the 'natural' and the 'analytically assisted.' While analytically assisted individuation concerns people in analysis, which is best left to the second half of life in Jung's opinion, Jung nevertheless acknowledges the 'natural' kind of individuation which will inevitably take place in a human life, even if it is not analysed. Moraglia (1997) writes that:

> [...] Jung also considered individuation as a natural and universal process, regarding 'the urge and compulsion to self-realisation' as a 'law of nature,' and as such 'of invincible power' (p. 107).

Moraglia goes on to quote Jung, who suggests in 'Answer to Job' that when the demands of individuation are not met

> [...] the process of individuation will nevertheless continue. The only difference is that we become its victims and are dragged along by fate towards that inescapable goal which we might have reached by walking upright if only we had taken the trouble and been patient enough to understand in time the meaning of the numina that cross our path (Jung 1954; 2002: par. 167).

For Jung, therefore, analysis, individuation and the realisation of our vocation are intimately and inextricably interconnected. It is noteworthy from a Christian perspective too, that "taking the trouble and being patient enough" to "understand in time the numina that cross our path" may be one way of describing the spiritual life. Furthermore, it is also interesting, from an Orthodox Christian perspective, that Jung refers to Cromwell,[16] the Protestant hero, in one of the above quotes on vocation. Jung's own religious background in the Swiss Reformed Church, which abides in the Protestant principle of *sola fide,* possibly failed to teach the young Carl while there was time and when he still sought this instruction, about the awesomely difficult and vigorous character of genuine ascetic Christian spiritual *praxis*, or about the meaning and purpose of seeking God actively. It is not surprising that Jung's mystical temperament as an adult was channelled into other paths, and led him to the affirmation that

> The Age of Enlightenment, which stripped nature and human institutions of gods, overlooked the God of Terror who dwells in the human soul. If anywhere, fear of God is justified in face of the overwhelming supremacy of the psychic (quoted in Storr, 1998, p. 201).

Indeed, modernity has been to some extent founded on the notion that we have escaped the myths through conscious repudiation of revealed religion, in favour of a purely rational natural science. If we consider contemporary theories of human origin, however, a different picture emerges. For example, cosmology offers the theory that in the beginning, there was a Big Bang, a cosmic explosion. This is an image from which reason may begin to work, but it is not itself a rational statement: it is a mythical construct. Similarly, we may

[16] It emerges that Cromwell was also something of a hero for Freud, who, as Black (1993) explains, "[...] approached psychoanalysis with the attitude, as he famously said, of a *conquistador.* In boyhood his heroes were subversive military commanders such as Cromwell and Hannibal [...]" (p. 8).

consider the theory of biological evolution. Man's ancestors emerged from the seas, and they in turn emerged from a cosmic soup of DNA. But the majority of creation myths also begin with the same image of man emerging from primordial oceans — take Genesis 1, or the Babylonian creation epic as examples — which is the myth, and which the science? Jung was perhaps correct in maintaining that our gods may be taken away, only to be replaced by others.

As Jung relates in his autobiography, his father, a minister with a personally brittle and fideistic nineteenth-century Protestant faith, feebly and impatiently told him to just believe, not stopping to clarify (and most importantly, to demonstrate) that we are *not* saved by faith alone, but by faith and works. Instead, Jung's boyhood mind seems to have been confused by distorted theological ideas which led him, as an intelligent young person, to some bizarre conclusions. For example, he concluded that an omniscient God "actually created human beings so that they would have to sin ... [but nevertheless] punishes them by eternal damnation in hell-fire" (1995, p. 63). This particular way of reasoning about God sounds heavily influenced by the doctrine of Calvinist predestination, which is harmful and fatalistic by Orthodox standards.

Nietzsche the German philosopher and Jung the Swiss analyst make a connection between love and greatness which is in fact almost straight out of the Christian *kerygma*. In scripture, however, there is no place for such fatalism or predestination as both Nietzsche and Jung seem to perceive at the heart of our existence; being created in the Image of the Uncreated, we are radically free beings, and we are free because God is free. Hence, for Jung, God is both unconscious and restricted by fate, and man is burdened with the task of bringing consciousness and freedom to God. As the following passage from *Answer to Job* suggests:

> We do not know whether he realises this, but we do know from the numerous commentaries on Job that all succeeding ages have overlooked the fact that a kind of Moira or Dike rules over

> Yahweh, causing him to give himself away so obviously. Anyone can see how he unwittingly raises Job by humiliating him in the dust. By so doing he pronounces judgement on himself and gives man the moral satisfaction whose absence we found so painful in the Book of Job (1954, 2002, p. 26).

This perspective on God makes the free, uncreated spirit that God is, subject to a set of laws outside Himself; and although it appears to raise man to a superior level to his Creator, it necessarily subjects humans to the same relentless laws of fate and justice. Evdokimov (2001) explains that

> We can define the relations between God and his creature in the categories of causality. In this case, God is the first cause who puts all things in motion, shows the way and returns all to this path. Human freedom is only the secondary instrumental cause drawing its origin from the primary, and determined by it. If the secondary cause sins, it is only because the primary tolerates it. Causal determinism is fatally situated in time, the primary movement finds itself inevitably there. That which establishes the primary cause is the universal pre-cause of all, and the prefix "pre" introduces time into the eternity of God. Humankind does not appear except inevitably, as the object of divine action. In such a causal scheme, the dubious Augustinian idea is led, through the iron logic of Calvin, to its conclusion: predestination to glory, condemnation to hell. The circle is buckled in upon itself without any possible exit: "Therefore according to the end for which humankind is created, we say that it is predestined to death or life"[17] (2001, p. 15).

Hillman (1996) develops the Jungian understanding of vocation further in his "acorn theory" of personal destiny. He maintains that

[17] Calvin, Institutions VIII, p. 62.

what the Greeks called the 'daimon,' the Romans 'genius,' and what Christians refer to as the Guardian Angel, is the same fundamental 'soul-image' which guides each particular life and calls it to a certain destiny. He intelligently critiques psychology for its deterministic emphasis on childhood trauma, and takes up Jung's lead in suggesting that there is a reason, a teleology to each individual existence, as

> The acorn theory proposes... that you and I and every single person is born with a defining image. Individuality resides in a formal cause—to use old philosophical language going back to Aristotle. We each embody our own idea, in the language of Plato and Plotinus. And this form, this idea, this image does not tolerate too much straying. The theory also attributes to this image an angelic or daimonic intention, as if it were a spark of consciousness; and, moreover, holds that it has our interest at heart because it chose us for its reasons (*ibid*, pp. 11–12).

Hillman's debt to Aristotle, Plato and Neoplatonism is a conscious one (and therefore open to the same criticism from an Orthodox perspective). In this much, Hillman does not seem to be departing from the Jungian perspective on vocation. Where Hillman is different perhaps, is in his understanding of neurosis as "[g]iven with the child, even given to the child, the clinical data are part of its gift... [The acorn theory] offers a way to regard [children] differently, to enter their imaginations, and to discover in their pathologies what their daimon might be indicating and what their destiny might want" (*ibid.*, p. 14).

Hillman also tries to offer a way out of the Jungian and Romantic leaning towards fate and fatalism, as opposed to creative participation in destiny. He says that

> When something doesn't fit, seems odd or strange, breaks the usual pattern, then more likely Necessity has a hand in it. Though she determines the lot you live, her ways of influencing are irra-

> tional. That is why it is so difficult to understand life, even one's own life. Your soul's lot comes from the irrational principle. The law it follows is Necessity, which wanders erratically. [...] Although Necessity's rule is absolute and irreversible, this determinism is indeterminate. Unpredictable (*ibid.*, pp. 208–209).

Despite the plea to indeterminacy, Hillman, like Jung, sets the *telos* of human life according to the rule and the unpredictable irrationality of an irreversible Necessity. It may be argued from an Orthodox perspective, that his post-Jungian Archetypal Psychology is burdened in this by the Gnostic dualism inherent in the classical Jungian heritage. Although Jung saw himself as a spokesperson for reminding Christian tradition of the importance of the body, the feminine, and of the reality of evil (something in which he may have been partially successful), he nevertheless ironically embraced, and self-consciously founded his analytical psychology on a spiritual tradition which Christianity—in part precisely *for* such reasons—had rejected early on in its historical development. This Gnostic tradition views the soul as trapped in material circumstances, in physical matter which is inherently evil. Traditional Christianity actually venerates matter through the Incarnation, the feminine in the person of the Theotokos, and radically acknowledges the reality of evil in human living via the actions and devices of the Devil; Jung could have rightly reminded Christianity of the dangers and consequences of its break with this tradition, and would have done service to the body, the feminine, and the reality of the experience of evil in doing so. By introducing Gnostic ideas into his psychology however, he effectively isolated himself from the tradition he so desperately wished to address and reform. Hence, behind Hillman's irrational goddess *Ananke* one may almost still hear the arbitrary whim of the evil Manichean Demiurge, *Yaldabaoth* tormenting the solitary human soul as a "spark of consciousness," in Hillman's words, trying to escape its unjust fetters in its fleshly tomb ("War," Heraclitus said, "is the father of everything," thus placing conflict at the epicentre of ontology). Despite Hillman's post-Jungian teleological belief in each life being informed by a particular, deep soul-image, through which the psyche converts events into meaningful experiences, his perspective on experience may ultimately concur with the famous words of the Bard from Macbeth, (Act 5, Scene 5):

> Out, out, brief candle!
> Life's but a walking shadow, a poor player
> That struts and frets his hour upon the stage
> And then is heard no more: it is a tale
> Told by an idiot, full of sound and fury,
> Signifying nothing.

5 **Towards a Resolution of the Issue.** Orthodox teaching reminds us instead, that whatever the limitations of our situation, we are always able to respond in a way which transforms and sanctifies it. Our choices, however, are not made arbitrarily and on our authority alone: man must cooperate for this in synergy with God, for whom "the very hairs of your head are all numbered" (Matt. 10:30). God, according to Christian tradition, is not bound by the laws of necessity, nor binds man according to them, and obedience to the divine will is similarly not an attitude of infantilizing submission born out of fear, but the supreme act of personal responsibility which a mature person is capable of. God's will for our lives is therefore also not arbitrary or irrational, but communicated through an act of personal communion between the human and divine persons. Hence, to the eloquent but troubled words of William Shakespeare quoted above, Orthodox Christianity may perhaps reply with the equally beautiful prayer of Metropolitan Philaret of Moscow (d. 1867):

> O Lord, I know not what to ask of thee. Thou alone knowest what are my true needs. Thou lovest me more than I myself know how to love. Help me to see my real needs which are concealed from me. I dare not ask either a cross or consolation. I

> can only wait on thee. My heart is open to thee. Visit and help me, for thy great mercy's sake. Strike me and heal me, cast me down and raise me up. I worship in silence thy holy will and thine inscrutable ways. I offer myself as a sacrifice to thee. I have no other desire than to fulfil thy will. Teach me how to pray. Pray thou thyself in me. Amen (MEOP, 1999, p. 24).

In this framework, God has a very specific destiny in mind for each and every one of us, a destiny it is possible to deny or refuse, but one which, when accepted, will lead to our ultimate salvation, our true happiness and fulfilment as persons freely obeying the divine call. Fr. Hopko continues:

> In a word, there is a divine plan and purpose for everyone. There is a "predestination," not in the sense that God programs His creatures or forces His will upon them against their will, but rather that God knows every person from before the foundation of the world and provides their unique life and the specific conditions of their earthly way which are literally the best possible conditions for them, however unacceptable this may seem to us creatures in our limited and fallen state. And God works together with each one of us so that, by suffering what we must on this earth, we may attain to life everlasting in the age to come (1997, p. 2).

In other words, not only is life assigned to persons by God in its specific parameters, but it is also the very life which He wisely judges to be the right one for each individual. This is not a mere platitude, but a great mystery, an indication that the Creator has something very specific in mind when He permits that persons may become frustrated in their chosen profession, their marriages, their friendships. God, for a very specific reason known to Him alone, does not want us to be happy and successful in this job, this marriage, this friendship at this time; more accurately perhaps, He does not want us to measure our happiness and success in the way we are now doing.

Hence the Prophet Job, far from teaching God anything about moral growth, in his trial prayed much like Metropolitan Philaret would in later millennia:

> The Lord gave, the Lord has taken away: as it seemed good to the Lord, so it has come to pass; blessed be the Name of the Lord (Job 1:21).

Reardon (2005) points out that the Book of Job addresses very similar questions regarding fate, as those one finds in Greek tragedy:

> More familiar to most readers, perhaps, are the possible parallels to Job from classical Greek literature, where fate (*moira*) causes men to suffer in order to preclude proud rebellion (*hybris*) from their hearts. The Greek tragedies come to mind in respect to Job [...] These examples are mentioned here, not because I think them historically related to the Book of Job, but because they do, in fact, touch on certain common themes. In respect to this point, however, it is important to observe that the God in the Book of Job is the LORD, the God of the Jews (*ibid.*, p. 14).

It is Reardon's final observation here, which makes all the difference to the significance of experiences, and which makes of suffering a vocation. Job suffers, but in the love and divine wisdom of the God of the Jews, not at the hands of an arbitrary and impersonal fate. It is worth noting here that, in the Christian understanding, individual destiny is not judged according to worldly criteria, but seen and understood in the light of a life to come, a next world, and a spiritual dimension — the world makes no sense on its own, and only becomes meaningful when viewed from a perspective outside it. Despite appearances, it may be that Jung thought something similar perhaps, when he wrote

> [R]eligion means dependence on and submission to the irrational facts of experience. These do not refer directly to social and

> physical conditions; they concern far more the individual's psychic attitude. But it is possible to have an attitude to the external conditions of life only when there is a point of reference outside them (Jung, 1993: p. 19).

Hence, Fr. Hopko goes on to assert that

> Some will be artists, scientists, business people, professionals. Others may have no particular job or profession. And some may be called simply to suffer, while others, in terms of this world, will hardly suffer at all. Some will have many temptations, and will bear heavy burdens because of the sins of the world and their particular inheritance of a fallen, broken, distorted humanity. And some may have to fight destructive memories, imaginations, and passions that seem at times impossible to bear. While others will be greatly blessed by receiving a highly purified humanity, for which they will especially have to answer before God. For, as Jesus taught, "to whom much is given, of him much will be required" (Lk. 12:48). But each person will have his or her own life to sanctify. And each will answer for what he or she has done. In the eyes of God none is better than the other. None is higher or more praiseworthy. But each must find his or her own way, and glorify God through it. This is all, ultimately, that matters. The rest is details (*ibid.*, p. 3).

It is worth noticing also, that although in the Christian understanding of vocation each person has a unique, individual destiny, at the same time all are also called to the same end: to sanctity, to become saints. This can be compared in some ways to Jung's suggestion, that although we each have an individual history and personal unconscious, our mind is rooted in the collective unconscious which is shared by all. The archetypes of the collective unconscious are those basic potentials for significance, the organs of the objective psyche which are not under our conscious control, and predispose us to those patterns for behaviour which render each of us a particular instance of collective humanity; they are like the roots of the tree which is our unique character and calling, our individual mind.

For Jung, especially in his later work, these archetypes are 'psychoid,' that is they shape both matter and mind. Everything we see, touch, hear, smell, taste, as well as think, dream, believe etc. is, in this neo-Kantian theoretical framework, the product of the archetypal organisation of our nonetheless uniquely individual, personal existence. If we have the courage to search for the source of these mythic, archetypal patterns which our lives enact, in other words the macrocosmic dimensions of our microcosmic being, we become more integrated and whole. Therefore it would not be perhaps amiss to also describe the Christian saint as the "Archetype of Orthodoxy" (Vasileios, 1999), just as Jesus Christ is the Archetype of the Original Man (Nellas, 1987; 1997). For Jung, in fact Christ Himself is the exemplar of the person who follows and realises his vocation:

> One of the most shining examples of the meaning of personality that history has preserved for us is the life of Christ. [...] Obeying the inner call of his vocation, Jesus voluntarily exposed himself to the assaults of the imperialistic madness that filled everyone [in the Roman Empire], conqueror and conquered alike. In this way he recognised the nature of the objective psyche which had plunged the whole world into misery and had begotten a yearning for salvation that found expression even in the pagan poets. Far from suppressing or allowing himself to be suppressed by this psychic onslaught, he let it act on him consciously, and assimilated it. [...] This apparently unique life became a sacred symbol because it is the psychological prototype of the only meaningful life, that is, of a life that strives for the individual realisation—absolute and unconditional—of its own particular law. Well we may exclaim with Tertullian: *anima naturaliter Christiana!* (Storr, 1998: pp. 204–5; original italics).

For Jung, Jesus fully realised the particular law of his vocation, thereby becoming a symbol of that process for others. This is not entirely incompatible with an Orthodox perspective; Rogich (1997) for example, writes that

> Christ is the fullest realization of the human self—originally made in God's image—as he represents a significant breakthrough in the slow growth of consciousness in humanity. His life, ministry, death and resurrection are interpreted [...] to mean that, by the light of grace, a human can be transfigured by one's original (archetypal [sic]) higher destiny. [...] In spiritual-theological terms, when the hesychast begins to leave behind the outer identifications of the human self—the senses and the rational mind—and begins to explore the inner world, consciousness becomes a journey which a person enters actively into in a free response to God. This means the sharp dichotomy of "nature" and "grace" is overcome and Christ and the human inner self are merged, where the Archetype and image within now co-constitute the human self, the "I-Thou" relationship no longer being presented as two autonomous and separate entities meeting, but as a new creation being formed – the emergence of the totally *deified person.* The experience of Jesus in prayer is then an empowerment enabling the believer to transcend all forces threatening to destroy the inner self, i.e., sin, the ego, and all negative passions, as well as allows one to hold together or to surmount the antinomies of uncreated and created reality (pp. 34–5, italics same).

It is clear, however, that to the Orthodox saint, Jesus is more than a symbol. Rogich (*ibid.*) quotes St. Gregory Palamas, who writes that:

> The original creation of the human, formed in the image of God, was for the sake of Christ, so that the human should be able one day to make room for the Archetype, and hence the law laid down

> by God in paradise was on His [Christ's] account, that is, to help the human being to be guided towards Christ (1997, p. 23).

"I no longer live," writes St. Paul, "but Christ in me." "Growth in God," Rogich (1997) explains, "equals growth in authentic humanity or personhood. [...] Christology fulfils anthropology, as Jesus Christ becomes the complete and fullest expression of the human self made in the image of God" (pp. 22, 24).

It is at once striking and paradoxical, therefore, when reading the lives of the saints, to see how different one saint is from another — no two saints are identical in character or life-events, yet all are equally glorified by Divine Grace.[18] All saints are images of Christ, yet the images are many; rational Christian sheep can therefore by no stretch of the imagination be compared to mindless, conformist cattle.

At the same time, it is equally true that while all saints are different, yet they each have a universality of being — "[T]he Orthodox saint has worth, not on account of his virtues, but because he is Christ Himself 'in another form'" (Vasileios, 1999: p. 20).[19]

[18] A brief search through categories of saints titles reveals the sheer diversity of their vocations: Confessor (one who has suffered for the faith but not martyred outright), Enlightener (the saint who first brought the faith to a people or region, or who did major work of evangelization there), Fool-for-Christ (a saint known for his apparent, yet holy insanity), Great-martyr (one who was martyred for the faith and suffered torture), Martyr (one who has died for the faith), Merciful (one known for charitable work, especially toward the poor), Passion-bearer (one who faced his death in a Christ-like manner), Right-believing (an epithet used for sainted secular rulers), Righteous (a holy person under the Old Covenant (Old Testament Israel) but also sometimes used for married saints), Wonderworker (a saint renowned for performing miracles), Unmercenary (a doctor who received no pay for healing), Stylite (a saint who lived on a pillar), and saints known by their professions, such as Soldier-Saints (St. George, St. Demetrius, St. Theodore Stratelates, Sts. Sergius and Bacchus) and St. Euphrosynos the Cook, St. Anastasia the Healer (Pharmakolytria). Obviously saints can come from all walks of life, be single or married, young or old, from among clergy or the laity.

[19] Mother Thekla of the Orthodox Monastery at Normanby, repeats in her own words the traditional spiritual understanding that in the saint, as in Christ, all

If we try, therefore, to understand and appraise the value of a life, or the meaning of a vocation, on the basis of natural or social criteria, we will inevitably be disappointed. In this world, some people seem to be 'born lucky,' the inheritors of what Fr. Hopko above calls "a highly purified humanity" — good health, social status, intelligence, beauty, a naturally optimistic disposition, education and breeding perhaps; but also a strong disposition to goodness, to self-control, to healthy thoughts and a pure imagination. Such people are often not only successful, but also popular, loved and genuinely lovable. These people are those to whom, in the Christian understanding, "much is given," and this gift is not free-of-charge: it comes with an added responsibility to be that much more well-liked by God, Who now expects a great deal from these lives, and will be that much more disappointed if these gifts are used to ill purpose, or to satisfy selfish lusts. Hence Elchaninov (1967) actually writes

> We must not think that there is only one kind of wealth — money. One can be rich in youth, possess the assets of talent, of natural endowments, the capital of health. These riches, too, are obstacles to salvation. [...] But what are we to do if God has granted us this or that earthly talent? Is it possible that we shall not be saved until we are divested of it? We may keep our riches (but not for ourselves) and still be saved; but we must be inwardly free of them; we must tear our heart away from them, and hold our treasures as if we did not hold them; possess them,

things are reconciled: "The holy bond which links together the far-flung souls of saints surely lies in the unification wherein so much that has fallen away is re-integrated, the nearest to wholeness that seems possible for a human being to achieve since the Fall. Sanctification comes step by step with the inner healing of the torn wrenching apart, the violent split of self-interest in the disintegration of disobedience. Such growth of healing unification manifests itself, strangely enough, in much the same manner from country to country and from generation to generation. [...] The lives of saints throughout the world and throughout generations are so alike, simply because one and all they proclaim that the laws of fallen man may yet be overcome by holiness" (Tavener & Thekla, 1994, pp. 3–4).

> but not let them possess us; lay them at Christ's feet and serve Him through them (pp. 69–70).

God has not singled certain people out for worldly success, because He favours them; He is "no respecter of persons" (Acts 10:34), and loves all His children more soberly and equally than any human parent is capable of—every human person paradoxically being God's unique, favourite child, for each of whom He is willing to create a new heaven and a new earth (Rev. 21:1). It is probably also significant to the issue of suffering and vocation, that the new heaven and earth spoken of here is swiftly followed by one of the most consoling verses in scripture, namely Rev. 21:4. God places persons in a particular context at the time of their birth, sending them into this fallen world apparently unequally provided for, not according to some passionate and subjective divine preference for some as opposed to others, but instead because human freedom requires an active participation in salvation, which begins here, but is only fulfilled in the next world.

God in the Orthodox understanding, also knows what bodily and psychological material and life circumstances He has assigned from the beginning of the world to each soul to work on, and in His infinite wisdom will judge progress according to its starting point, not according to where has been reached in worldly terms—how else could the parable of the workers who were paid the same wages, having started work at the end of the day, as those who started work at its beginning, be interpreted? In the parable of the talents also, the unequal starting points from the perspective of the worldly potential of each person are apparent: "To one He gave five talents of money, to another two talents, and to another one talent, each according to his ability" (Matt. 25:15). God does not expect the servant with one talent to make another five, but He also does not expect him to bury the single talent he has been given. Here one might agree with Hollis:

> How revolutionary to our childhoods it would be if Jung's identification of vocation were taught as our *raison d' être.* It would

> give us all a task, a sense of personal summons, a dignity, a lifelong mission. We would not be enjoined to pursue the delusory success which William James called the "bitch goddess." We might find our proper path even more along the trail of ruin, through the savannas of suffering. Certainly Jesus did [...] (*ibid.*, p. 110, original italics).

Fr. Hopko, however, through the basics of Orthodox theology, is saying even more than this. He is also saying that a vocation, a calling in life, may not appear on the outside to be a calling at all; yet it may be hugely important for the whole of humanity. Some are born with mental and bodily handicaps; others will contract or develop lethal and excruciating diseases; others will fail miserably and struggle with passions they are ultimately unable to overcome, like addiction and depression. All these people can give the opportunity to others to express their vocation for care. Some will live lives filled with regret, bitterness and frustration, will perceive themselves as rejected failures and perhaps die a lonely death, far from the comforting embrace of family or friends, misunderstood by all, defeated and unwanted. A person who has struggled with all this, and as Christ suggested to St. Silouan the Athonite, 'kept his mind in hell but not despaired,' has done so not for himself alone, but for all humanity, and will receive nothing less than a martyr's crown. Even if the struggle was ultimately unsuccessful from any conventional social or human perspective, the efforts will have proved fruitful to all, if only as an example and a spur to faith: pain and discomfort, deprivation borne with gratitude and transfigured through humility into joyful love, can be the most powerful lesson to others. It may be for this reason that God said to St. Paul "My grace is sufficient for thee: for my strength is made perfect in weakness" (2 Cor. 12:9). Archimandrite Vasileios of the Holy Mountain puts it in even stronger terms:

> Either we must feel disillusioned with ourselves, have the grace of complete failure, and be total "wrecks" (do not be

> shocked — this is a joyful event, not to be taken as something macabre); or else we must be tremendously sensitive, like a small child (1999, p. 37).

Those therefore, whom society and nature have dealt a "bad hand" are by no means failures, since God, as the reader and knower of men's hearts everywhere, will not judge anyone according to material achievements, but according to the way they have responded to His calling, which vocation essentially is. Christianity emphasizes the intention written on human hearts, and it is the intensity of the struggle to actualise that intention, not the glamour of the 'result' which will impress the Creator and earn His favour — which, incidentally, is also always granted as an unmerited gift. The alternative is to reject one's calling and in doing so, reject God's wisdom. Therefore, Fr. Hopko urges Christians to accept that

> God has made us who we are. He has put us where we are, even when it is our own self-will that has moved us. He has given us our time and our place. He has given us our specific destiny. We must come to the point when we do not merely resign ourselves to these realities, but when we love them, bless them, give thanks to God for them as the conditions for our self-fulfilment as persons, the means to our sanctity and salvation. Being faithful where we are is the basic sign that we will God's will for our lives. The struggle to "blossom where we are planted," as the saying goes, is the way to discern God's presence and power in our lives, to hear His voice, to accomplish His purposes, to share His holiness. Jesus said that only those who are "faithful in little" inherit much and get set over much. Those who are not faithful in the little things of life, and thereby fail to accept and to use what God provides, end up losing the little that they have, or — as Jesus says in St. Luke's gospel — the little that they think that they have, for even that "little" may exist only in their own deluded imaginations (Matt. 25:14–30; Lk. 19:11–27, 8:18). (1997, pp. 6–7).

Despite the frustration and disappointment then — or perhaps because of it — Orthodox spirituality suggests that God urges humans to continue to work out their salvation wherever they are placed, bringing only good will and readiness to obey Him at each moment; He will see to the rest. The purpose of having a vocation in life, be it a recognised profession or a call to suffering, seen by others or unseen by all, is that, through it, persons may come to carry out the Divine Will in and for their own being and that of others. The outcome of constantly being alert to hearing what this vocation demands, in this place, at this time, is nothing less perhaps than a personal vigil, leading to eternal joy in salvation. The ultimate Christian calling then, is to repentance, metanoia, and this means "the Kingdom of God is at hand" (Mk. 1:15) in a change of heart from frustration and envy to mourning for sins and feeling genuine gratitude for being exactly who one is, here and now. Vocation is not a once-for-all decision made on a single occasion and condemning us to a lifelong pursuit of worldly or even spiritual 'success'; it is also not a frantic search for material or psychological well-being. It is the continuing readiness to be transparent to receiving the Divine mercy at every moment, since as psychoanalyst Neville Symington writes, "[...] our human task is to allow the infinite, the absolute, to become that which permeates our nature" (2001, p. 31).

CHAPTER TWELVE

The Dynamics of Healing

1 THE HEALING VOCATION. It has been already suggested that those who offer help to others for a living may have a special vocation to do so. Obviously a broad range of occupations belong to the 'helping' category, and therefore the calling to be a teacher—for example—is likely to involve very different dispositional qualities and be informed by a substantially dissimilar set of biographical experiences than, say, the motivation to become a doctor. Nevertheless, it has also been indicated that although each person's unique life vocation is different, there are likely to be essential similarities between vocations; in an Eastern Orthodox context this has been expressed through the basic religious tenet that each of us is called to sanctity or sainthood, however diverse and colourful the 'cloud of witnesses' may actually be, as demonstrated by the many existing categories of saint. The martyr, the wonderworker, the unmercenary healer, the soldier-saint, the fool-for-Christ, the recluse, the socially engaged parish priest, the married and single pious layman; all are types possessing profoundly different characterological dispositions, yet each achieves holiness in their own particular, sometimes quite surprising way. Similarly in the context of analytical psychology, all persons can be said to share the common human potential and urge towards individuation, but again each individual will 'become who they are' by incarnating the Self in their own unique way.

In thinking about the nature of vocational calling and the ways in which the personal factor influences the professional, it may be fruitful to consider therefore the similarities and differences, the points of convergence and divergence in the experience of two very specific helping professions: those of the therapist and of the spiritual director. Jung already concerned himself with this theme, albeit with a different focus, in his essays "Psychotherapists or the Clergy" and "Psychoanalysis and the Cure of Souls," both of which may be found in Vol. 11 of his collected works. In these essays, Jung focuses mostly on the experience of the person seeking help *from* a priest or psychotherapist, or on a comparison between psychoanalysis as a medical method and the religious discipline of the 'cure of souls.' In this section of the book, some consideration will be offered instead to the experience of *the healers* themselves, shifting the focus of investigation to the way in which the ideas these professional helpers ascribe to, the theories the espouse, the feelings, sensations and intuitions they may have during their working hours and in their free time, the judgments they make, may all influence and be influenced by their particular professional experience with the people they are helping and the context or setting of their work. More specifically, the focus will be on the experience of the priest or other confessor/spiritual director offering pastoral care to Orthodox Christians on the one hand; on the other hand, the experience of the Jungian analyst in the consulting room will be reflected upon and contrasted with the former.

From the outset the above may seem a bold proposal, since it needs be stated that the author is neither a Jungian analyst, nor a member of the Orthodox clergy; he has, however, had the good fortune to benefit personally from the help offered by both such professionals, in Jungian analysis as well as in the sacrament of confession. Also, there is fortunately a sizeable body of literature written by both Jungian analysts (e.g. Sedgwick, 1994; Fordham, 1978) and Orthodox spiritual directors (e.g. Hausherr, 1990; Chryssavgis, 2000) which may be drawn on in looking for the appropriate terminology, the proper concepts and formulations which may adequately describe some of the profound states of awareness and (inter)subjectivity these healers enter into during the process of helping others. The writings of many other commentators from diverse psychological and spiritual backgrounds may also illuminate these experiences from other perspectives and novel points of view (e.g. Wosket, 1999; Kahn, 1991; Nouwen, 1979; 1994; Halifax, 1982).

As suggested above, the primary purpose of this exploration will be to determine to what extent concepts drawn from Jungian psychology, such as that of the 'Wounded Healer' or the 'Shadow' (e.g. Guggenbuhl-Craig, 1971; 1999) and from Orthodox Christian spirituality, such as creative suffering (e.g. De Beausobre, 1940; 1999) Godforsakenness (e.g. Sakharov, 2002) and spiritual fatherhood (e.g. Ware, 1998) may inform and cross-pollinate each other across their different disciplines.

While recognizing that points of contrast, disagreement and non-compatibility are both likely and inevitable when discussing two such diverse disciplines, the project is undertaken in a spirit of creative interdisciplinary dialogue, a practice of much value which possibly remains neglected due to current intellectual trends towards increasing professional specialization and workplace pragmatism. Knowledge in contemporary academic contexts can appear compartmentalized, with different university departments pursuing diverse scholarly endeavours in an isolated manner, as if the world were anything but the connected whole — the *holon* (Wilber, 1996; 2000) — it in fact is. In this sense, it is very likely that the numerous academic discourses representing perhaps differing domains of professional knowledge/power (Foucault, 1981), may frequently be using different words to say quite similar things. Hence Bouteneff (2006), in an important book on truth and dogma in Orthodox theology writes:

> If [there is] resonance across confessional lines, and if much is in agreement with philosophy, sociology, science, and people's empirical conclusions, that is a good thing. It should come as no surprise that human beings created in God's image read the world in which God reveals himself and come to similar conclusions (p. 15; words in square brackets mine).

Thus too, when writing on Christianity from a Jungian perspective and discussing the concept of the Kingdom of God in Jesus' teachings, Sanford (1987), himself both a Jungian analyst and an Episcopalian priest, seems to reach a very similar conclusion when he says that

> Those who have been given the opportunity to observe the universal nature of the structure of the inner world will have no trouble understanding why the kingdom is available to all. Just as there is a universality of form to the human body, so there is a universality to the inner person. The same typical (archetypal) structures are found in people everywhere and express themselves through their inner imagery. The Greek philosopher Plato would have ascribed this to the fact that all human beings are replicas of the Universal Man, the Idea of Man in the Mind of God. In the Old Testament each human being is created in the image of God. In Christian language it is the universality of Christ in all people. For Jesus it is the call of the kingdom to each person. To the psychologist it is the archetypal structure of the human mind and the universality of the urge to wholeness (p. 34).

Nevertheless, while giving due importance to commonalities and promoting the universality of experience, tentative conclusions may also be drawn regarding the specific implications of this kind of research for the applied practice of both professional domains. This needs to be done without encouraging confusion between their respective areas of activity, while simultaneously taking into account any possible areas of incommensurability, and even conflict, between the disciplines being discussed.

2 The Modalities of Therapeutic Relationship. The therapeutic relationship which is established between analyst and patient is characterized by several features. Writing from an integrative perspective, but basing her conclusions on the work of several other researchers, Clarkson (1990, 1995) suggests that there are in fact five possible modalities of client-psychotherapist relationship present in any effective psychotherapy. These are:

(a) the *working alliance*, a necessary cooperation between therapist and client which continues despite any emotional distortion which may otherwise characterize the relationship.

(b) The *transferential/countertransferential relationship* — a mode of relationship based on the unconscious dynamics taking place between therapist and client. The process of (Freudian) psychoanalysis may be said to consist in inviting the transference and then gradually dissolving it by means of interpretation (Greenson, 1967, quoted in Clarkson (1995)). This mode of relationship is in fact the most extensively written about in psychotherapy, and in keeping with psychoanalytic literature some basic concepts in this mode of client-therapist experience will be introduced below.

(c) The *reparative/developmentally-needed relationship* is defined by Clarkson (1995) as

> [T]he intentional provision by the psychotherapist of a corrective/reparative or replenishing parental relationship (or action) where the original parenting was deficient, abusive or over-protective (p. 11).

It goes beyond our current concern to comment further on this mode of relationship, which is both closer to a real parent-child form of bonding than any other in psychotherapy, and hence too, all the more ethically incumbent on the therapist. It involves therapeutic work which invites deep regression and is lengthy in terms of time demands. Hence it may be interesting to point to the explicit use of the term "Mother" and "Father" in Eastern Orthodox spiritual direction, where the spiritual director may be referred to as one's *spiritual father* or *spiritual mother*. This point will be developed further below.

(d) The *person-to-person relationship*. This is also known as the 'real relationship' between therapist and client, and it is a potent healing factor as it is based on the ordinary, real relationship which exists between the therapist and client as two people. The word 'ordinary' may be misleading here, as what is being addressed is not the stereotypical exchanges taking place on buses and in shops, but the actual, authentic fact of two real persons encountering one another without any special roles being performed by or attributed to either. This real relationship is eloquently described by the Jewish existential theologian Martin Buber in his book, *I and Thou* (Buber, 1996). It may be significant to point out that the real relationship precludes the modality of relation between objects, and is indeed "the opposite of an object relationship" (Clarkson, *ibid*, p. 14).

(e) The *transpersonal relationship*. This modality refers to the spiritual or inexplicable dimensions of relationship in psychotherapy, and will naturally be of direct relevance to the Jungian exploration of the therapeutic process being addressed here, as well as to the Eastern Orthodox relationship in spiritual direction. Clarkson (1995) significantly writes that, in the same way that the marital *coniunctio* is used to represent the alchemical process of transformation in Jungian theory,

> The transpersonal relationship is paradoxically also characterized both by a kind of intimacy and by an 'emptying of the ego' at the same time. It is rather as if the ego of even the personal unconscious of the psychotherapist is 'emptied out' of the psychotherapeutic space, leaving space for something numinous to be created in the 'between' of the relationship [...] Implied is a letting go of skills, of knowledge, even of the desire to heal, to be present. It is essentially allowing 'passivity' and receptiveness for which preparation is always inadequate. But paradoxically you have to be full in order to be empty. It cannot be made to happen, it can only be encouraged in the same way that the inspirational muse of creativity cannot be forced, but needs to have the ground prepared or seized in the serendipitous moment of readiness. What can be prepared are the conditions conducive to the spontaneous or spiritual act (pp. 19–20).

It can be seen from the brief discussion of these five modalities that the relationship between therapist and client may be fruitfully viewed from diverse perspectives, the five modalities summarized here being surely only an informed selection from a much broader range of possibilities. Before attempting to examine the specific interactions taking place in Jungian analysis and in Eastern Orthodox spiritual direction, however, it may be fruitful to focus first a little more fully on the cornerstone of analytic work, which is the transferential/countertransferential modality of relation.

3 Transference and Countertransference — History of the Concepts.

> The hallmark of psychoanalysis is the use of transference and countertransference as a guide to understanding the inner world (Bateman & Holmes, 1995, p. 95).

As the above quotation suggests, the concepts of transference and countertransference (T/CT[1]) as psychological processes taking place in the analyst and analysand have been fundamental to almost the entire body of analytic thought since Freud. No psychoanalytic theorist since Freud has failed to address T/CT in some way, nor can a psychoanalytically oriented clinician dispense with it as a cornerstone of therapeutic practice. Therefore, it is far beyond the scope or purpose of this study to provide an exhaustive summary of the lengthy history and development of these concepts from Freud onwards; instead, following a brief introduction relating to a general definition and history of these terms in their broadest use, specific themes relating to the use of T/CT by Jung and post-Jungians in analytical psychology will be explored.

[1] In fact, the two terms are often placed together and abbreviated to T/CT, a convention which will be used also here throughout when referring to both processes (Sedgwick, 1994, p. 3).

In his *Critical Dictionary of Psychoanalysis*, Rycroft (1968; 1995) defines transference as

> The process by which a patient displaces on to his analyst feelings, ideas etc., which derive from previous figures in his life (p. 185).

Significantly, Rycroft goes on to give several other variegated definitions of transference, each slightly different in its epistemological focus. The multiplicity of these definitions, as provided here and elsewhere, suggests that the concept varies substantially in its use by different theorists and across schools of psychoanalysis — indeed, it varies so much, that eventually Rycroft settles for the broadest possible definition:

> Loosely, the patient's emotional attitude towards his analyst (*ibid.*, p. 185).

Bateman & Holmes (1995) explain that, while there is general agreement among analysts regarding the existence of transference as a phenomenon, the debate concerning its *content*, i.e. what is actually 'transferred,' is ongoing, and seems to depend on the model of the mind, and the theory of development being espoused. As we will see, this is an important epistemological point in relation to the attempt to outline and describe a specifically Jungian model of the T/CT relationship.

As applies to transference, the related concept of countertransference has almost as frequently been a basic notion informing the work of most analysts in the last century, yet its definition has proved equally elusive and dependent on theoretical assumptions. Hence Rycroft (1968; 1995) defines countertransference as

> The analyst's transference on his patient (p. 28).

And he even goes on, rather dogmatically, to call his own preference for this use the "correct" one (*ibid.*, p.28). Yet he also has to acknowledge that countertransference is,

> By extension, the analyst's emotional attitude to his patient, including his response to specific items of the client's behaviour (*ibid.*, pp. 28–9).

When these terms are used therefore in their most general sense, as the patient's emotional attitude to their therapist and the therapist's emotional attitude to their patient, one can be perhaps forgiven for wondering what *else* the therapist-patient relationship could contain, other than T/CT.

Yet other levels or components of relationship do exist, as Gelso & Carter (1994) and others have shown elsewhere. In fact, entire schools of psychotherapy are arguably founded on interventions which are not based on T/CT. The person-centred approach to psychotherapy, for example, does not advocate a therapeutic focus on the T/CT relationship, not because these processes are considered unimportant,[2] or through any lack of therapeutic acumen, but because of an emphasis on the present, *here-and-now* 'real' relationship between therapist and client. Writing from this perspective, Shlien (1984) has even proposed a 'counter-theory of transference' on the logical premise that the *duplication* of a response and its *replication* are not the same thing — in other words, the therapist is not lovable because she resembles 'mother' in some way, but because she is genuinely a lovable person who elicits *for this reason alone* love from the client. Hence in person-centred work the feelings and attitudes of both therapist and client are perceived as being accurate reflections of the current emotional situation. It would be incorrect however, to assume therefore that the person-centred approach relies entirely on the conscious aspects of the interaction for its effectiveness; Rogers certainly recognised the existence and therapeutic value of forces which are outside the conscious control of the therapist, as the following quotation suggests:

[2] Carl Rogers was initially trained as a Freudian, and did consider that transferential attitudes existed in most cases, but rather similarly to Jung, he believed that they only occurred strongly in a small number of cases.

> I feel at times when I'm really being helpful to a client of mine, in those rare moments when there is something approximating an I-Thou relationship between us, and when I feel that something significant is happening, then I feel as though I am somehow in tune with thc forces in the universe or the forces that are operating through me in regard to this helping relationship that — well, I guess I feel somewhat the way the scientist does when he is able to bring about the splitting of the atom. He didn't create it with his own little hands, but he nevertheless put himself in line with the significant forces of the universe and thereby was able to trigger off a significant event, and I feel much the same way, I think, oftentimes, in dealing with a client when I really am being helpful (Kirschenbaum & Land-Henderson, 1989; p. 74).

Rogers' 'putting himself in line with the significant forces of the universe' calls to mind the 'Rainmaker' story told by Richard Wilhelm, as described above (ch. 2). Rogers may be seen to be commenting on a powerful level of relationship here, accessed through the I-Thou relation first introduced by Martin Buber, which lies firmly outside the boundaries of 'ordinary' consciousness, yet is also arguably not just a theoretical reconstruction of projective and unconscious dynamics in a primal warp-and-weft of mental contents as experienced within the T/CT relationship in the classical analytic situation; nor is it even a simple description of *participation mystique*, which Jung borrowed as a term from Levy-Bruhl and used as a concept in his own attempt to describe the complex events taking place in the therapeutic encounter. Hence it would be unfair to label Rogers' remarks as indicative of the wholesale acceptance of T/CT factors, but it may not be inaccurate or even contrary to Rogers' own phenomenological understanding, to claim nevertheless that a level of relationship between therapist and client which lies outside the range of ordinary consciousness is being acknowledged. Elsewhere Rogers also commented that "our organisms as a whole have a wisdom and a purposiveness which goes well beyond our conscious thought" (1980,

p. 106). The acceptance in person-centred theory of the operation of certain defence mechanisms (specifically denial and distortion) that prevent material which is inconsistent with the self-concept from entering awareness, as well as the postulation of a process of symbolisation as a way of making sense or deriving meaning from the contents of consciousness which is more or less representative of organismic 'reality,' indicate what may be seen as Rogers' *actual* position on the role of the unconscious in psychotherapy, a thesis which could almost be called post-Freudian in character, and can be summed up in the statement from a humanist post-Freudian thinker that

> [...] there is no such thing as "the conscious" and "the unconscious." There are degrees of consciousness — awareness and unconsciousness — awareness [sic] (Fromm, 1986; quoted in Tudor & Merry, 2002:30).

Hence, the integration of person-centred thought with psychoanalytic ideas may also not be epistemologically incongruent. Purton (1989) for example, suggests that the 'core conditions' of the person-centred approach can be extended in a Jungian direction, by the addition of a condition he calls "openness to the unconscious," through which the therapist is empathically in touch with both the unconscious material a client may bring to a session (such as dreams), and their own "subliminal" feelings, in an ethical effort to not interfere with the client's process.

Nevertheless, in psychoanalytic thought itself the T/CT level of the relationship between the doctor and his patient, the analyst and his analysand, or the therapist and his client is more explicit, integral to the therapeutic process, and crucial to the entire outcome of the analysis. Carotenuto (1991, p. 74) offers a beautiful metaphor in comparing the T/CT relationship in analysis, to the air which permits a dove to fly, by drawing on a speculation from Kant (1787, 1968), who suggested the dove may be excused in thinking it would fly better without the resistance of the air molecules, yet it is this very resistance which permits flight, which is otherwise impossible in a vacuum. Similarly psychotherapists may find T/CT phenomena initially disconcerting and troublesome, and be tempted to perceive these as hindrances to the work of helping the client, but ultimately they need to realise that it is often precisely these dynamic undercurrents which propel the relationship forward by adding significance, depth, and, to use a Jungian term, numinosity to the encounter.

Ever since Breuer fled his house 'in a cold sweat' (Jones, 1953), went on a second honeymoon with his wife, and generally started distancing himself from psychoanalysis in response to Anna O's erotic transference to him, the power of the phenomenon of T/CT to profoundly affect both analyst and patient became clear. Freud's natural initial response to transference was to consider it a 'contaminating influence' in the relationship, and he became concerned that, if it was a result of iatrogenic influence, psychoanalysis should avoid focusing on it in case the psychoanalytic method was seen as a form of modified suggestion, similar to the hypnosis he had abandoned as a method for treatment. Gradually however, it became clear to him that transference was not the product of iatrogenic suggestion, but he came to see it instead as the result of the formation of positive or negative affects and wishes which characterised the patient's infantile oedipal conflict, now being carried over into the relationship with the doctor as both a figure of authority and a nurturing influence in the analysand's life. Thus a *positive* or a *negative* transference could be formed, depending on the quality of the affects and wishes transferred.

Interestingly, it was another female patient who similarly gave rise to the concept of countertransference: this time a patient Jung became overinvolved with, Sabina Spielrein, became the 'Anna O.' of the countertransference. Carotenuto comments that

> There are strong similarities in the experiences of the two women. For instance, both of them came into contact with physicians experimenting with new procedures for the treatment of neurosis — Breuer with the method of catharsis and Jung through

> the practise of psychoanalysis. Each of the two women was the first clinical case of her therapist, and both of them — Anna O. who was twenty-one years old to Breuer's forty-eight and Sabina Spielrein who was nineteen to Jung's thirty — "fell in love" with her analyst, in keeping with the paternalistic approach in vogue prior to the differentiation of countertransference (1991, p. ix).

As a result of the intense growth of feelings between the young Swiss psychiatrist and the talented Burghölzli patient[3] in his care, the relationship between Jung and Spielrein became erotic, to the extent that Emma Jung had to intervene by talking to Sabina's mother. As a result, Jung himself — echoing Breuer — had to end the relationship abruptly, fearing a scandal. Jung wrote in a visibly defensive manner to his mentor in Vienna, saying

> The last and worst straw is that a complex is playing Old Harry with me: a woman patient, whom years ago I pulled out of a very sticky neurosis with greatest devotion, has violated my confidence and my friendship in the most mortifying way imaginable. She has kicked up a vile scandal solely because I denied myself the pleasure of giving her a child. I have always acted the gentleman towards her, but before the bar of my rather too sensitive conscience I nevertheless don't feel clean, and that is what hurts the most because my intentions were always honourable (McGuire, 1994, p. 99).

Even if Jung's claim to have had honourable intentions is accepted at face-value, his clarification for Freud in a later letter is perhaps quite incriminating:

[3] Spielrein went on to become an analyst herself, continuing her studies in the medical faculty at Zürich University and attending Jung's lectures, also collaborating with him as her dissertation advisor on the study of schizophrenia, which in turn influenced Jung's own thinking on the topic. She was also later the teaching analyst of Jean Piaget.

> Spielrein is the person I wrote you about. [...] She was, so to speak, my test case, for which reason I remembered her with gratitude and affection. Since I knew from experience that she would immediately relapse if I withdrew my support, I prolonged the relationship over the years and in the end found myself morally obliged, as it were, to devote a large measure of friendship to her, until I saw that an unintended wheel had started turning, whereupon I finally broke with her. She was, of course, systematically planning my seduction, which I considered inopportune. Now she is seeking revenge. [...] she is a case of fight-the-father, which in the name of all that's wonderful I was trying to cure *gratissime* (!) with untold tons of patience, even abusing our friendship for that purpose. [...] To none of my patients have I extended so much friendship and from none have I reaped so much sorrow (McGuire, 1994, pp. 110–1, italics same).

In a famous letter in response to Jung regarding this thorny and much-documented[4] story in the early history of psychoanalysis, Freud coined the term 'countertransference' for the first time:

> Such experiences, though painful, are necessary and hard to avoid. Without them we cannot really know life and what we are dealing with. I myself have never been taken in quite so badly, but I have come close to it a number of times and had a *narrow* escape. I believe that only grim necessities weighing on my work and the fact that I was ten years older than yourself when I came to [psychoanalysis] have saved me from similar experiences.

[4] The relationship between Jung and Spielrein has been the subject of a documentary, *Ich hieß Sabina Spielrein* (My Name was Sabina Spielrein, 2002) by Swedish director Elisabeth Marton. Spielrein also figures prominently in two contemporary British plays: *Sabina* (1998) by Snoo Wilson and *The Talking Cure* (2003) by Christopher Hampton. There is also a popular feature film biopic *Prendimi l'anima* (The Soul Keeper), directed by Roberto Faenza.

> But no lasting harm is done. They help us to develop the thick skin we need and to dominate 'counter-transference,' which is after all a permanent problem for us; they teach us to displace our own affects to best advantage. They are a '*blessing in disguise*' (McGuire, 1994, pp. 111–2, italics same).

One interesting similarity therefore, which is shared by the T/CT processes in their historical evolution as therapeutic concepts, is that both were initially formulated as *distortions* of the relationship between analyst and patient; but in the course of time, both have come to be seen as fundamental aids to analytic work. Transference was recognised as essential to analysis by Freud as early as 1912, when he wrote that 'finally every conflict has to be fought out in the sphere of transference' (quoted in Rycroft, 1968, p. 186). Countertransference was also recognised as an aid to analytic work, but much later, by researchers such as Heimann (1950), Little (1951) and Gitelson (1952).

4 T/CT IN ANALYTICAL PSYCHOLOGY. It has already been indicated that therapists who work psychodynamically generally accept the existence of the transference process as a basic tenet of their practice, although diverse epistemological premises allow considerable variation as to the definitions given to the particular contents of this process. This is understandable, since different theorists espouse different models of the human psyche, and therefore also of the structures and forces at work in human relationships. It is the author's opinion, in concert with Papadopoulos' (1997) encouragement of 'epistemological openness,' that the diversity of viewpoints and epistemological frameworks within psychoanalysis and analytical psychology, is reflective of the wealth, and not the poverty or even the confusion of analytic thought.

For Freud (1912b) the mechanism of transference was a sort of template of stored infantile images or representations in the unconscious. Freud differentiated between this mechanism as a structure, and the dynamics in the patient's current emotional relationship to the analyst, which are derived from this mechanism; hence, a patient may experience current feelings of love, hate, jealousy, sexual attraction, etc. towards the analyst (emotional dynamics), which are based on feelings they previously experienced in relation to a parent or sibling, which have been stored in the unconscious (mechanism). This initial distinction has resulted in the differing emphases on polarities of 'past conflict vs. present relationship,' and 'intrapsychic vs. interpersonal' in the numerous post-Freudian models of therapy. These various more modern approaches to T/CT — illustrations of which may be found in the formulations of Horney, Klein, the object-relations, ego psychology and interpersonal psychoanalytic schools — tend to broaden the concept of transference, to add emphasis to the nuances of meaning in the ongoing interplay between patient and analyst, in such a manner that transference becomes the medium through which the inner drama set up by the tension in patients' internally represented objects, is played out in the relationship to the therapist at various levels. In interesting similarity to Jungian thinking, these more modern schools of psychoanalysis generally do not view childhood neurosis as the only explanation for adult pathology, or view analysis of the 'transference-neurosis' as the sole method of cure (Bateman & Holmes, 1995, pp. 96-7).

However, as a result of political developments in the history of psychoanalysis which led to the marginalisation of Jungian thought, the unique approach to the T/CT relationship which developed within analytical psychology, has not been integrated into post-Freudian thinking on the issue. Nevertheless, as Samuels (1985) has indicated, pointing to the work of a host of post-Freudian thinkers such as Winnicott, Searles and Langs, Jungian thinking has preceded post-Freudian developments on such important issues as the appreciation of 'a creative, purposive, non-destructive aspect to the unconscious,' accompanied by 'a stress on the clinical *use* of countertransference' and 'the idea that analysis is a mutually transforming interaction, and hence the analysts' personality and his experience of the analysis are of central importance' (p. 10). It was Jung who gave Freud the stimulus and opportunity to coin and articulate his theory of countertransference; it seems appropriate therefore, that Jung was also the initiator of the concept of the training analysis, and one of the pioneers, together with Ferenczi, of mutuality in the analytical relationship. For Freud, each of us carries a personal unconscious which consists of various drives and instincts, mostly sexual and aggressive / self-preserving, which we seek to satisfy as individuals within the limits set by social norms, personal upbringing and the nature of our surrounding reality. Jung, on the other hand, goes beyond this atomized view of the individual, by extending the range of the personal unconscious into the collective unconscious, which may be conceived of as a repository of archetypal structures poised at the interface of spirit and instinct, and shared universally by all humans. Hence for Jung, in contradistinction to Freudian thought, the establishment of a conscious relation to the transcendent is not a regressive urge, but a healing factor, which puts us in touch with a deeper aspect of our nature, which Jung termed the Self.

A closer examination of Jung's thoughts on the T/CT relationship, as well as the elaboration of his insights by analytical psychologists after him, may, therefore, offer the opportunity of further articulating a Jungian and cross-disciplinary response to that part of the research question which deals with the crucial issues of the ways in which the therapist relates to him/herself while in relation to the client, and the associated teleological individuation goals which both analyst and analysand bring to the analysis, and which therefore influence and colour the therapeutic process.

5 THE PSYCHOLOGY OF THE TRANSFERENCE. Jung published his views on the transference in a long essay called *Die Psychologie der Uebertragung* in 1946, which first appeared in English eight years later in 1954, in Vol. 16 of his Collected Works with the above title. In this essay, Jung interprets the phenomenon of the transference within its archetypal context, by making reference to a set of alchemical pictures from the 16th-century text known as the *Rosarium Philosophorum.* Sedgwick (1994) writes of this essay that

> One can return repeatedly to "The Psychology of the Transference" to find value in Jung's alchemical symbols and perspective. He may not mention the word "countertransference" but he notes the centrality of the analyst's psyche. He comments on psychic infection, wounded healing and the analyst "literally taking over" the patient's sufferings. He speaks of mutual analyst — patient influence and transformation. Psychic contents flash back and forth mercurially between the participants (pp. 5–6).

In the above words can already be discerned the fact that Jung had a special and very particular approach to the T/CT phenomenon. The use of the apparently obscure source of alchemical images for describing the phenomenology of transference dynamics, is clarified when it is understood that Jung viewed the alchemical imagination as the historical link between Gnostic religious imagery and his own modern science of analytical psychology:

> As far as I could see, the tradition that might have connected Gnosis with the present seemed to have been severed, and for a long time it proved impossible to find any bridge that led from Gnosticism — or neo-Platonism — to the contemporary world. But when I began to understand alchemy I realised that it represented the historical link with Gnosticism, and that a continuity therefore existed between past and present. Grounded in the natural philosophy of the Middle Ages, alchemy formed the bridge on the one hand into the past, to Gnosticism, and on the other into the future, to the modern psychology of the unconscious (MDR, pp. 226–7).

Interestingly Jung characterises the sceptical Freud as a latter-day Gnostic (a view that would find critics of both Jung and Freud, like Eric Vögelin, in paradoxical agreement), since, in Jung's own words, Freud "had introduced along with [the modern psychology of the unconscious] the classical Gnostic motifs of sexuality and the wicked paternal authority" (*ibid.*, p. 227). The materialist tendency in philosophy (which the alchemists were forerunners of, but which for them was still only a latent theme in an otherwise spiritual world-view) had according to Jung become very powerful by the time psychoanalysis was outlined, and obscured Freud's ability to include in his theory "the primordial image of the spirit as another, higher god who gave to mankind the *krater*... the vessel of spiritual transformation," the *krater* being a "feminine principle which could find no place in Freud's patriarchal world" (*ibid.*, p. 227).

A brief digression may be worthwhile here, in order to further clarify something of Jung's specialized understanding of the term 'spirit.' For him

> [...] it is possible to interpret the fantasy-contents of the instincts either as *signs*, as self-portaits of the instincts, i.e. reductively; or as *symbols*, as the spiritual meaning of the natural instinct. In the former case the instinctive process is taken to be "real" and in the latter "unreal." In any particular case it is often almost impossible to say what is "spirit" and what is "instinct" [original italics] (TPOTT, p. 11).

As in so much of the rest of his thought, Jung is careful here to balance the apparent opposites of instinct and spirit; elsewhere he says more clearly that,

> The psyche is made up of processes whose energy springs from the equilibration of all kinds of opposites. The spirit/instinct antithesis is only one of the commonest formulations, but it has the advantage of reducing the greatest number of the most important and most complex psychic processes to a common denominator. So regarded, psychic processes seem to be balances of energy flowing between spirit and instinct, though the question of whether a process is to be described as spiritual or as instinctual remains shrouded in darkness. Such evaluation

> or interpretation depends entirely upon the standpoint or state of the conscious mind. A poorly developed consciousness, for instance, which because of massed projections is inordinately impressed by concrete or apparently concrete things and states, will naturally see in the instinctual drives the source of all reality. It remains blissfully unaware of the spirituality of such a philosophical surmise, and is convinced that with this opinion it has established the essential instinctuality of all psychic processes. Conversely, a consciousness that finds itself in opposition to the instincts can, in consequence of the enormous influence then exerted by the archetypes, so subordinate instinct to spirit that the most grotesque "spiritual" complications may arise out of what are undoubtedly biological happenings (CW 8, par. 407).

Jung does not ultimately settle on a materialistic or idealistic/'spiritual' interpretation of psychic reality, seeing the processes of the psyche, as he says, to be 'shrouded in darkness.' This may appear to be mystical or unscientific (two common criticisms regarding Jungian theory), but a closer reading reveals that Jung's way of talking about psyche is very purposive. Robinson (2005) says of Jung's position that

> The practical effect of this theoretical position is a portrayal of the psyche as being grounded in, and expressive of, humanity's instinctual nature. Yet, in contradistinction to Freud and the Freudians, for Jung this meant an expansion of the meaning of the term "instinct" to include not only the more purely physiological drives but also what one might call, loosely, the life of the spirit. Psychic structures, symbolic expressions, conscious articulations, and spiritual yearnings were all given an instinctual cast through the concepts and language of the archetypes. In short, the psyche was naturalized, but at the same time, nature was ensouled. Jung claimed this was not metaphysics, but science (p. 50).

Returning, therefore, to considering the reasons for Jung's choice of alchemical imagery to discuss the psychology of the transference, Jung can be seen not to view the alchemical imagery only as scientifically naïve medieval formulas for the transmutation of lead into gold, to be later superseded by the advance of scientific chemistry; instead, he sees alchemical symbols as the products of "creative fantasy" emerging from the unconscious of the "natural philosophers" as a result of their intense preoccupation with the opaque and secret nature of matter—in much the same way perhaps, as ancient cartographers and sailors imagined monsters residing in the bottom of the sea, or Athanasius Kircher produced definitions of Egyptian hieroglyphics which were internally consistent, but were understood by later Egyptologists as having been wholly idiosyncratic. The alchemists projected onto matter, as a patient projects onto a Rorschach ink-blot, the contents of their own unconscious. If this emphasis on the symbols produced by the unconscious should seem irrelevant or of marginal interest to applied psychology, it needs to be borne in mind that, as Jung clarifies

> Before the beginning of [the last] century, Freud and Josef Breuer had recognized that neurotic symptoms—hysteria, certain types of pain, and abnormal behaviour—are in fact symbolically meaningful. They are one way in which the unconscious mind expresses itself, just as it may in dreams; and they are equally symbolic. A patient, for instance, who is confronted with an intolerable situation may develop a spasm whenever he tries to swallow: "he can't swallow it" (Jung, 1964: p. 9).

Thus, the alchemical language and imagery Jung applies to examining the transference is symbolic, in as much as

> ...a word or an image is symbolic when it implies something more than its obvious and immediate meaning. It has a wider "unconscious" aspect that is never precisely defined or fully ex-

> plained. Nor can one hope to define or explain it. As the mind explores the symbol, it is led to ideas that lie beyond the grasp of reason. [...] Because there are innumerable things beyond the range of human understanding, we constantly use symbolic terms to represent concepts that we cannot define or fully comprehend (*ibid*, p. 4).

Moreover for Jung, the idea, or symbol, produced by the creative fantasy will not only be a substitute for the otherwise inaccessible underlying reality, but it will also be "an archaic though not inapposite *analogy*" (p. 4, italics mine). Hence the alchemical imagery as applied to the phenomenon of the transference does disclose something *real* regarding the nature of the dynamics involved: the chemical combination of bodies in the alchemical *vas*, as imagined and hence experienced by the alchemist, is both a representation and an analogy of the unconscious *coniunctio* taking place between the analyst and analysand during treatment.[5] The alchemical *vas* is the equivalent of the Gnostic *krater* previously referred to, and in the language of modern analytical psychology the transformation of the substances is parallel to "the inner transformation process known as individuation" (Jaffé, MDR, p.227n) which takes place in the hermetically-sealed, confidential, 'holding'[6] (Winnicott, 1986) environment of the therapeutic session.

---

[5] Hence, analyst and analysand are mutually changed by the process of T/CT. Von Franz (1992) explains this difficult notion, by suggesting that the "simple parallel [...] drawn between the structure of man and that of the universe [...]" in alchemical texts (i.e. the microcosm-macrocosm idea), "[...] is not only an idea, it is also a substance, indeed it is man who is the material to be worked on in the alchemical opus. [...] Man is an image (replica-μίμημα) of the cosmos, but this is not just an analogy, for *the parallel itself is something concrete*. It is, so to say, a substance, the earth of the Universe, which is also called the primal matter of the Cosmos. [...] This analogy, seen as matter, is latent as the "Divine Man" within every single human creature" (pp. 171–72, italics same). Jung drew on this alchemical tradition as the historical foundation of his own philosophically monistic view of the interaction between matter and spirit.

[6] "[...] I tend to think in terms of holding. This goes for the physical holding of

Jung's attitude to T/CT is a complex one. "The transference is far from being a simple phenomenon with only one meaning, and we can never make out beforehand what it is all about" (TPOTT, p. 11). Jung singles out the relationship to the parent of the opposite sex as one content which is projected very frequently onto the analyst during the process of transference. Depending partly—but again, not necessarily—on the genders present in the analytic dyad, the analyst comes to occupy the place in the analysand's psyche which is invested with the psychological significance of the father, mother, brother or sister, and the intensity of this transferential bond is such that it can be likened to a chemical combination, or coniunction of opposites, a procedure which significantly transforms both substances involved. According to Jung then, the "specific content" of the transference is "commonly called incest" (TPOTT, p.11). It is a projection which

> ...persists with all its original intensity [...] thus creating a bond that corresponds in every respect to the initial infantile relationship, with a tendency to recapitulate all the experiences of childhood onto the doctor (TPOTT, p. 6).

Jung, however, does not regard the intensity of the transference as aetiological in the way Freud did. He therefore also does not maintain that resolution of the "transference neurosis" will necessarily lead to a cure. It is pointless, according to Jungian theory, trying to elicit a transference from the patient in an attempt to divert the focus of the patient's problems onto the relationship with the analyst. For Jung in fact, the

---

the intra-uterine life, and gradually widens in scope to mean the whole of the adaptive care of the infant, including handling. In the end, the concept can be extended to include the function of the family, and it leads to the idea of the casework that is at the basis of social work. Holding can be done well by someone who has no intellectual knowledge of what is going on in the individual; what is needed is a capacity to identify, to know what the baby is feeling like" (1986, pp. 27–28).

> ... transference of a neurotic patient is equally neurotic, but this neurosis is neither new nor artificial nor created: it is the same old neurosis, and the only new thing about it is that the doctor is now drawn into the vortex, more as its victim than its creator (TPOTT, p. 7n).

Jung thus perceives the transference as a naturally occurring phenomenon, which acts as a hindrance or help in almost any intimate human relationship, citing the teacher, the clergyman, the general practitioner and "last but not least" the husband as examples. He contrasts, furthermore, the apotropaic Freudian attitudes of "warding off" the transference and keeping "the person of the doctor as far as possible beyond the reach of" the countertransference through the use of such techniques as asking the patient to lie on a couch, sitting behind them and avoiding eye-contact, with his own understanding that avoiding T/CT may not only "considerably impair the therapeutic effect" in certain cases, but also that

> It is inevitable that the doctor should be influenced to a certain extent and even that his nervous health should suffer. He quite literally "takes over" the sufferings of his patient and shares them with him. For this reason he runs a risk — and must run it in the nature of things (TPOTT, pp. 7–8).

For Jung, the doctor 'takes over' the suffering of the patient, and shares it. Even this brief flash of inspiration suggests that Jung's own presence as a healer would have been very powerful for those in treatment with him. It is not surprising therefore, that elsewhere Jung maintains too, that

> We could say, without too much exaggeration, that a good half of every treatment that probes at all deeply consists in the doctor's examining himself, for only what he can put right in himself can he hope to put right in the patient. It is no loss, either, if

> he feels that the patient is hitting him, or even scoring off him: it is his own hurt that gives the measure of his power to heal. This, and nothing else, is the meaning of the Greek myth of the wounded physician (CW 16, para 239).

In the above two quotations, the characteristically Jungian attitude to countertransference and the meaning of the analysts' suffering can be discerned, issues which will be addressed further below.

Although Jung does attach great importance to T/CT as psychological events however, it is also significant that he nevertheless does not consider either to be "absolutely indispensable for a cure" (TPOTT, p. 8), nor are they automatically present in every treatment in his estimation. He cites other important therapeutic factors, such as the patient's insight, their "good-will, the doctor's authority, suggestion, good advice, understanding, sympathy, encouragement, etc." (*ibid*, p. 9). Once again, these suggested factors imply Jung's humanity and presence in the consulting room. He also recognises, however, that such factors are of lesser importance where more serious cases are concerned, and perhaps indicates some of his own characteristic countertransferential responses, when he clearly states that

> I personally am always glad when there is only a mild transference or when it is practically unnoticeable. Far less claim is then made upon one as a person, and one can be satisfied with [the above] other therapeutic factors (*ibid.*, pp. 8–9).

Indeed, Jung himself suggests a possible deeper, more specific biographical reason for this discomfort he experiences with transference. Jung mentions in a letter to Freud, that as a child he was the victim of a sexual assault by an older man he had "once worshipped" (McGuire, 1974, p. 44). In this letter he explains to Freud that his apparent reluctance to write is not a result of his idleness, but partly in his intense admiration of Freud "both as a man and as a researcher," which results in Jung's "veneration" having "something of the character of a 'religious' crush." Jung even adds that this feeling provokes shame and disgust, due to its "undeniable erotic undertone":

> This abominable feeling comes from the fact that as a boy I was the victim of a sexual assault by a man I once worshipped. [...] This feeling, which I have still not quite got rid of, hampers me considerably. Another manifestation of it is that I find psychological insight *makes relations with colleagues who have a strong transference to me downright disgusting* (McGuire, 1974: p. 44, italics mine).

Jung was 32 years old when he wrote the above letter, and it may not be completely out of place to infer that the intense discomfort provoked in him as an adult by strong transference feelings from colleagues which Jung describes, would generalise out to a reluctance in handling the phenomenon of transference even with those possibly less threatening others, such as patients.

It is interesting too, from a theological perspective, that in the same context in which Jung speaks of his early sexual abuse, he also makes reference to religion, and the experiences of worship and veneration. Perhaps for Jung the feeling of surrender and submission which is so frequently involved in genuine spiritual communion with God, was made increasingly problematic by his experience of abuse as a child. This would also cast some light on the dream Jung recounts in MDR, where he enters a house with his father which has a large hall on the second floor, in which Jung's father turned to Jung and looking to a small door at the top of a flight of stairs said to him "now I will lead you into the highest presence"; upon which Jung's father knelt, touching his head to the floor, and Jung, though he "imitated him, likewise kneeling, with great emotion," nevertheless found that he could not bring his forehead down to the floor completely, leaving "a millimeter to spare" (Jung, 1995, p. 245). The Orthodox philosopher Philip Sherrard (1998) picks up on the inflation implied by the dream, and relates Jung's experience to the Iranian myth concerning the primeval king Yima, set over the world by

Ahura Mazda, who begins to see himself as the lord of creation; and thus Sherrard suggests that

> It is difficult to avoid the conclusion that Jung's own thought, culminating in the idea of the creature that surpasses its creator by a small but decisive factor, attains an identical point of self-assertion, with all the disastrous consequences this has for the integrity of human life (p. 157).

Indeed, it is difficult not to view the dream, in the light of Jung's childhood abuse experience, as deriving from early narcissistic wounding. Smith (1996), in his biography of Jung points to Jung's relationship with his weak and ineffectual pastor father, as a poor role-model for the male child's needs for identification and protection; and Jung's powerful but unreliable and uncanny mother as a major source of his later theoretical formulations, such as the anima and the Great Mother archetype. It is not perhaps surprising, given this parental background, and an isolated childhood characterised by schizoid[7] escape into a fantasy world, as well as an episode of sexual abuse (which itself is frequently cited as the cause of dissociation), that Jung should find as an adult the intense feelings provoked by the intersubjective field of transference and countertransference very hard to cope with. Equally however, this inner woundedness may have established Jung's predisposition to be particularly sensitive to the transpersonal overtones of the T/CT phenomena, urging him to look for the deeper healing factor within the transferential field of the therapeutic relationship, eventually leading to its conceptualisation as the alchemical vessel in which the union of opposites leads to the Self, finding incarnate expression in individual existence through the transcendent function.[8]

[7] Winnicott (1964) famously went as far as to suggest that "Jung in describing himself, gives us a picture of childhood schizophrenia, and at the same time his personality displays a strength of a kind which enabled him to heal himself" (p. 450).
[8] The implications of the transcendent function as expressed through and by

6 **T/CT and Orthodox Spiritual Direction.** Although writing on the subject is sparse, Jungian approaches to T/CT may lead into fruitful discussion with transference phenomena in Orthodox spiritual direction. Similarly to Jung, Archbishop Chrysostomos (2001) suggests that transference "demands [...] an ethical commitment on the part of the therapist" (p. 20), inasmuch as

(1) the process "lays that patient open to infection by the therapist" (*ibid.*, p. 20);
(2) positive transference can make the patient dependent on the therapist, so that he "becomes his psychological 'slave'" (*ibid.*, p. 20); and
(3) negative transference can be manipulated by the therapist to produce guilt, self-destructiveness and despair in the patient.

Archbishop Chrysostomos suggests further, that a spiritual guide must create a bond with a spiritual aspirant before any spiritual direction can be offered, and the ethical commitment which characterizes all such therapeutic bonds of trust needs to be present as much in spiritual direction as in any other professional relationship. Indeed, in the case of the spiritual father, the potential to abuse a paternal role towards the aspirant is in fact, increased by the paternal nature of spiritual fatherhood, making it especially important to base such fatherhood on "au-

T/CT dynamics, for the individuation processes of both therapist and client, become apparent through the application of the alchemical 'Axiom of Maria,' attributed to the 3rd century Jewish sage Maria Prophetissa, which states that 'One becomes Two, Two becomes Three, and out of the third comes the One as the Fourth.' Applied to the individuation process, this axiom suggests that out of an original unconscious wholeness (the One), a conflict of opposites emerges (the Two), which if held patiently and attended to without rushing to conclusions, eventually resolves through the transcendent function (the Third), thereby establishing a new, more conscious state of consciousness, which is characterised by relative inner calm and a sense of wholeness (the Fourth). Obviously this dialectical procedure may be used to describe the way in which both intrapsychic (consciousness/unconscious) and interpersonal (therapist / client) conflict or tension is creatively resolved.

thority and fatherly love *through* Christ, and not as a mere substitute for a parent" (*ibid.*, p. 22). Similar principles would apply with respect to the maternal nature of spiritual motherhood. Other ethical aspects of spiritual direction are brought out, according to Archbishop Chrysostomos, in the areas of sexual feelings and the temptation to break confidentiality, or gossip. Chrysostomos suggests that an area of spiritual direction which requires extra care not necessitated in ordinary psychotherapeutic encounters, is "*the added dimension of demonic forces*" (*ibid.*, p. 23), of which spiritual directors need to be aware.

Moran (1996) also suggests that Jung's particular approach to T/CT phenomena

> [...] can be developed in an Orthodox Christian way. Alchemy, like Platonism, Gnosticism and neo-Platonism—raises the authentic issue of the ultimate transfiguration of all human and indeed created nature as the 'secret' carried in the soul. A symbol read in this way is an anticipation of the final marriage of the psychic matter, or substance, of the creation with the transfiguring of the Holy Spirit (p. 144).

Moran points out, however, that Jung's error—as indicated by Buber—is in attempting to divinize the soul without sanctifying it first. It is therefore telling, and highly relevant to the discussion below on the wounded healer, that from an Orthodox perspective, far from achieving wholeness, the soul which is not wounded and broken by the divine love, as Moran explains, cannot achieve true contemplation, and cannot "be initiated by God into the Sacred Wisdom which operates by the mutual offering of love" (*ibid.*, p. 144). Jung, therefore, realised that only the wounded healer can heal, but as regarded from an Orthodox perspective, his approach essentially limited itself by excluding the process of sanctification.

7 T/CT **Dynamics and Healing.** In Jungian analysis and any therapeutic helping relationship founded on psychodynamic

principles, the quality of the interaction between the helper and the person being helped relies heavily on the analysts' ability to be in touch with the diverse contents and forces both within his own unconscious, and that of the patient. Indeed, both the Jung Lexicon (Sharp, 1991) and the Critical Dictionary of Jungian Analysis (Samuels, Shorter and Plaut, 1986) offer a diagram originally used in a slightly different way by Jung (cf. TPOTT, p. 59) which indicates the six main avenues of reciprocal communication along which dynamic information passes between the analyst and the patient. These six avenues are, briefly:

(1) Analyst's conscious — Patient's conscious
(2) Analyst's conscious — Patient's unconscious
(3) Analyst's unconscious — Patient's conscious
(4) Analyst's unconscious — Patient's unconscious
(5) Analyst's conscious — Analyst's unconscious
(6) Patient's conscious — Patient's unconscious

These are also described in greater detail by Samuels (2006) and numerous other Jungian authors elsewhere. Nevertheless, as these authors frequently acknowledge, despite its popularity, this relatively neat structure may be insufficient. Papadopoulos (2006) discusses Jung's epistemology and methodology, and indicates that this traditional way of analysing the interaction between therapist and client, while valid, is in fact constricting the understanding of the relationship by making the therapeutic dyad a closed system, and depriving it, therefore, of the wider collective parameters in which the conscious and unconscious of the therapist and client are embedded. Papadopoulos suggests that Jung himself in the investigations published in his study titled 'The Family Constellation' (1909) developed this epistemological insight by observing the fact that the differences between and among the response patterns of family members to an application of the word-association test were not random. Papadopoulos explains that

> In effect, this research indicated that within families there must be certain formations that are 'organising structures which are collectively shared.' [...] These 'shared unconscious structures' affect the ways that family members structure their perceptions, knowledge, relationships and overall psychological realities. These formations 'could be termed the Collective Structures of Meaning' (CSM). (p. 27).

From this it becomes clear that the sociocultural and collective context within which therapy—or indeed pastoral counselling, as will be seen—take place, will have a more than incidental influence on the nature, quality and content of communications taking place both on a conscious and an unconscious level. CSMs will effectively introduce, Papadopoulos continues,

> [T]wo more sources of potential knowledge: first, the interactional and relational patterns of experience; these include the family interactions and transactions as well as the network of inter-projections of unconscious material between members of the same family as well as with the wider sociocultural environment (including what Jung termed 'emotional environment'), and second, the 'shared unconscious structures'; these are structures that are not projected by one person onto another, but nevertheless are affecting certain subgroups within families. These must be structures of a 'collective' nature that contribute to one's creation of sense and the formation of knowledge (p. 28).

Although the above is specifically pertinent to family relations, the discovery of the sharing of unconscious structures did spur Jung on into formulating his theory of the collective unconscious, which of course is brought to bear in the consulting room (and probably in the confessional too) as much as anywhere else. What it means in practice is that the shared cultural and archetypal background of therapist and client, will surround the open system of the therapeutic encounter and inform it with imagery, shared perceptions and symbols and other contents. This may also be the reason why Jung entertained the idea of there being a racial or phyletic unconscious for different ethnic groups (which later proved controversial[9] due more perhaps to a lack of political tact and acumen on Jung's behalf in his own troubled historical times, than to the presence of any real racism in Jungian theory and practice — but see also Maidenbaum (2002)).

It can, therefore, be observed in practice that a 'communication breakdown,' or resistance/blockage in the analyst, a failure to become aware of material arising from any of these dynamic avenues of information, can result in projection of personal contents onto the patient, or neurotic countertransference which then sabotages the therapeutic process. Going by the simplified scheme suggested above, routes (5) and (6) in particular represent what is going on internally in the analyst and in the patient respectively, at the same time that the other routes represent what is going on in the intersubjective field between the two persons. More routes would have to be introduced to offer a complete map of family, society, and even cosmic dynamics, given the microcosmic/macrocosmic implications of the individuation process as suggested earlier. Fordham (1978) may be thus be unrealistically limiting when he discusses only two kinds of countertransference ('illusory' and 'syntonic'); Ulanov's model (1999; 2006) offers a threefold function for countertransference which may be closer to what is encountered in clinical practice. She writes that (a) 'normal' countertransference may refer to the therapists' 'natural' personal style, a rhythm for responding which is shaped both by their history with object relations, and — significantly — by their experience of the numinous; (b) 'abnormal' countertransference is

[9] This very discovery of shared unconscious structures, however, may also be part of the theoretical rationale prompting Hillman's timely enjoinder for therapists to move their practice out of the consulting room and into the culture at large, and for other post-Jungians like Samuels (e.g. 1993) to examine further the political ramifications of psychological being.

the result of patient material coming into conflict with the therapist's unanalysed complexes; and (c) 'objective' countertransference, where the patient's unconscious communicates (routes 2,4, and 6 above) the intentions of the Self to the psychotherapist, in such a way that the attuned therapist can articulate these back to the client so that growth can occur.

Countertransference in Jungian psychology is, therefore, both a potential source of distortion in the therapeutic relationship, and an invaluable instrument of empathic response. Nevertheless, it is apparent that the ramifications of the personal, cultural and collective aspects of the unconscious make it necessary that Jungian psychology should therefore naturally place a strong emphasis on the analyst's self-knowledge, and in particular his intimacy with his own areas of wounding, or woundedness. As Jung writes,

> "Ars requirit totum hominem," we read in an old treatise. This is the highest degree of psychotherapeutic work. A genuine participation, going right beyond professional routine, is absolutely imperative, unless of course the doctor prefers to jeopardise the whole proceeding by evading his own problems, which are becoming more and more insistent. [...] Arbitrary limits are no use, only real ones. It must be a genuine process of purification where "all superfluities are consumed in the fire" and the basic facts emerge (TPOTT, p. 35).

It is clear that Jung asserts the analyst's own unconscious contents are being activated by the therapeutic encounter with the patient's issues, and that furthermore, this is actually a *prerequisite* to therapy having a positive outcome. As quoted above, he writes, "It is no loss, either, if he feels that the patient is hitting him, or even scoring off him: *it is his own hurt that gives the measure of his power to heal*. This, and nothing else, is the meaning of the Greek myth of the wounded physician" (CW 16, para 239, emphasis mine). Samuels (2006) elaborates on this, saying that

> When referring to the idea of the 'wounded healer,' there is more involved than the ordinary idea that therapists are damaged persons who have become therapists for good unconscious reasons of their own. The idea of the wounded healer implies that the therapist must be wounded, recognise that, and do something constructive stemming from those wounds in relation to the client (p. 188).

It is, therefore, wounds which offer healers a window onto the patient's psyche. Indeed, people who are particularly sensitive to the areas of conflict or trauma in others, may experience a need to enact the drama of the other person's inner life, as they intuitively perceive it, even with their own bodies. McLaren (2000) calls the process by which this occurs "clairsentience," and refers to it as

> [...] the deepest form of empathy. It's a complete intuitive experience of another person's emotions in your own body (p. 19).

In those persons who have a highly developed receptivity to the psychic condition of others, clairsentience may be at work, triggering in them the shamanic expression of the wounded healer archetype. In analytical psychology, which consciously embraces the image of the shaman and the value of such ancient healing ritual (cf. Sandner & Wong, 1997), this phenomenon would for the most part be considered a particularly powerful instance of, or the result of, syntonic countertransference (Fordham, 1978). Ward & Zarate (2000, p. 24) ask whether psychoanalysis, too, may be akin to faith healing or shamanic ritual, and illustrate their proposition using an example from the work of Levi-Strauss, who in his book *Structural Anthropology* observed a shamanic ritual of the Cuna people in Panama, and drew parallels with psychoanalysis. In order to facilitate a difficult childbirth, the shaman of the Cuna enacted a myth in a ritual designed to restore the childbearing woman's soul by providing her with a symbolic language to give expression to psychic states which she could not previously express. Ward & Zarate explain that

> The shaman's words—his rendition and enactment of the myth—reintegrate the woman's suffering within a whole cosmology where everything is meaningful, and in doing so, real changes occur. Does psychoanalysis, too, anchor people's lives in a new kind of individual mythology—of good and bad objects, Oedipal struggles, internal worlds, trauma and repression, which the patient uses to put together a fragmented psyche? (*ibid.*, p. 25).

Writing as an anthropologist, Halifax (1982) refers to the shaman as the wounded healer, explaining that

> The opening of vision for the shaman unfolds in a transpersonal realization resulting from a crisis of death and rebirth, a transformation of the profane individual into one who is sacred. [...] The map of the hidden cosmos is revealed. The paths to and from the realm of death are repeatedly traversed. [...] The venerated images of the awakened psyche are communicated as living symbols in the process of inner spiritual transformations. [...] The shaman, however, is not afraid of the universe but feasts on its forces while allowing its forces to feast on him. [...] Through the experience of destruction comes instruction. Dismemberment by ravenous spirits allows for the reconstitution of the candidate [for shamanism] to a new and higher order of being. [...] The act of sacrifice and self-sacrifice prepares the shaman for the life of one who is specially chosen. [...] The shaman, unafraid, experiences death in order to gain control over the elements of the world of the untamed. The withdrawal into solitude through sickness opens the way for the inner initiation to take place. Myth in this case evolves from the ground of the diseased body-mind (pp. 17–20, words in square brackets mine).

Death and rebirth, dismemberment and reconstitution, sacrifice and initiation through sickness are references to the opposites experienced in the psychotherapeutic relationship, and constitute symbolic images which are as pertinent to contemporary spiritual direction as to the ancient tribal practices of the shaman. Indeed, Kirmeyer (2003) associates ancient shamanic practices to the ethos which characterises the vocation of healers, an ethos he links to the image of the wounded healer, and he argues this ethos remains relevant to contemporary medicine, psychology and psychotherapy.

Beyond referring to wounded and healthy parts of the personality, Jung's reference to 'the Greek myth of the wounded physician' is an indication that health and woundedness in the psyche are for Jungians therefore part of a much larger, universal archetypal dynamic, and they can in fact can be seen as the two main poles of the 'wounded healer' archetype. Put simply, during therapy the analyst projects the 'wounded' pole of the archetype onto the patient, and the patient projects the 'healer' pole onto the analyst. This may seem like an undesirable distortion of the reality of the status of both parties: no one is in fact completely healthy, and no one is completely ill. Yet, as Samuels (2006, p. 189) suggests, the polarisation of the archetype in this manner actually sets up the necessary dynamic which permits analyst and patient to recognise each other in their respective roles, and offers impetus for the healing process to be activated. This necessary dynamic is then gradually deconstructed, over the course of the treatment; as Samuels explains, this is because the patient "needs to get in touch, over time, with his or her healthy/healer parts, not only to be able to project them onto the therapist as part of an idealising transference" (*ibid.*, p. 190).

CHAPTER THIRTEEN

The Myth of the Wounded Physician

Given the importance of CSMs as suggested above by Papadopoulos (2006), the projections taking place between therapist and client cannot be limited to the personal level. With a view to the personal and clinical significance of collective imagery, it may be productive therefore to take a closer look at the Greek myth itself, as a cultural expression of the above archetypal dynamic.

In his study of Asclepius, the Greek god of healing, Kerenyi (1959) states that

> Wounding and being wounded are the dark premises of healing; it is they that make the medical profession possible and indeed a necessity for human existence. For this existence may — among many other possibilities — be conceived as that of a wounding and vulnerable being who can also heal, while the animal [existence] is merely wounding and vulnerable (pp. 76–7, words in square brackets mine).

For Kerenyi therefore, the phenomenon of wounding and being wounded is not only intimately tied to the very capacity to heal, but this same wounding — healing polarity is a characteristic feature of human existence, which distinguishes it from the rest of the animal kingdom. The "Greek myth of the wounded physician" which Jung refers to above is therefore significant as a collective fantasy about this distinctly human archetypal dynamic. The figure which Jung refers to in his quote is the divine physician Asclepius. Asclepius' teacher, the centaur Chiron, was himself also a 'wounded healer,' having taught the healing arts not only to Asclepius, but also to Achilles, Jason, Actaeon, and Asclepius' sons Machaon and Podalirius, but himself having suffered from an incurable wound. Both the myth of Chiron and that of Asclepius may therefore be worth considering briefly, as narratives founded on the Wounded Healer archetype.

1 **Chiron.** Chiron was a centaur, a mythical beast belonging to the pre-Greek Pelasgian pantheon, who was half-human and half-horse. Significantly however, several characteristics differentiated him from the other centaurs who lived with him on Mount Pelion in Thessally; where other centaurs were part of the retinue of Dionysus, drinking heavily and engaging in war with their neighbours, the Lapiths, Chiron was not unruly or lecherous. He is sometimes described as their ancestor, priest or ruler. Unlike other centaurs, he did not descend from Ixion and Nephele, or from Centaurus; his ancestors were Cronus (Saturn) and Philyra,[1] a goddess and daughter of Oceanus and Tethys. Graves (1961) says of Chiron that he was a great teacher:

> Now, the most famous school of Greek antiquity was kept by Cheiron [*alternative spelling of name*] the centaur, on the slopes of Mount Pelion in Magnesia. Among his pupils were Achilles the Myrmidon, son of Thetis the Sea-goddess, Jason the Argonaut, Hercules and all the other most distinguished heroes of the generation before the Trojan War. He was renowned for his skill in hunting, medicine, music, gymnastics, and divination, his instructors being Apollo and Artemis, and was accidentally killed by Hercules; after which he became the bowman of the Greek zodiac (p. 239).

[1] Her name means 'linden,' and she is associated with the wryneck, an ant-eating bird sacred to the Great Mother Goddess. Philyra may therefore also be seen as an aspect of Rhea, the Earth-Mother.

The Greek word for surgery, *χειρουργική*, gets its derivation from Chiron. The myth narrates that, when Hercules was invited to dinner by the Centaurs, a fight broke out during which one of his arrows struck Chiron in the leg,[2] causing a wound that would not heal, so Chiron had to suffer from it for the rest of his life, which since he was immortal would have been a very long time, had he not transferred his immortality to the bound Prometheus in a final gesture of self-sacrifice. A planetoid given the appellation 'Chiron' was discovered in 1977, the presence of which, within the context of personal horoscopes, is connected by astrologers to the archetypal pattern of the Wounded Healer (e.g. Reinhart, 1989).

2 **Asclepius.** Asclepius is said to have learned the art of healing from both Chiron and Apollo (Graves, 1955; 1960: 50.5, p. 177). He became skilled in surgery and the use of drugs, so that he was finally revered as the founder of the medical arts. Interestingly, in a characteristic split of the wounded healer archetype, Athene is said to have given Asclepius two phials of Medusa's gorgon blood, one of which could be used to raise the dead, and another for instant destruction. Asclepius brought the envy of the major gods onto himself, by raising so many from the dead, that Hades complained to Zeus that subjects were being stolen from him. Zeus at first killed Asclepius with a lightning-bolt, then raised him back to life. Like in the case of Prometheus, a bargaining over divine powers can be discerned,

[2] In another version of the myth, Chiron is accidentally scratched by the arrowhead while trying to care for the wounded centaur Elatus, who had taken refuge in his cave. The site of a wound has symbolic significance; for example, in the myth of how Achilles acquired his vulnerable heel, Graves (1961) narrates how "When Thetis picked up the child Achilles by the foot and plunged him into the cauldron of immortality, the part covered by her finger and thumb remained dry and therefore vulnerable. This was presumably the spot between the Achilles tendon and the ankle-bone where [...] the nail was driven in to pin the foot of the crucified man to the side of the cross, in the Roman ritual borrowed from the Canaanite Carthaginians; for the victim of crucifixion was originally the annual sacred king" (p. 318).

which is also relevant to the sacrifice required of the wounded healer, as will be observed below. Asclepius' associated animal was the serpent, and Meier (2003) describes the incubation rituals for the reception of healing dreams involving snakes or dogs (another associated animal) occurring to pilgrims visiting the ancient Greek Asclepeia, sanctuaries of the god such as the ones found at Kos and Epidaurus.

These myths may be viewed as collective cultural representations of underlying archetypal structures concerning the phenomena of healing. Meier (2003) concludes that

> [...] The experiences and methods of modern psychotherapy correspond to the methods and the conceptions underlying healing in classical times. [...] *Nomina mutantur, permanent numina*: time may effect changes of viewpoint, but, though the *nomina* change, the *numina* and their effects remain ever the same (p. 110).

Whether the healer is an attendant *therapeutes* at an Asclepian sanctuary, an Orthodox priest,[3] or a Jungian analyst, it may, therefore, not be exaggeration to suggest that the psychological dynamics of healing may be informed by similar phenomena in each case.

[3] Meier (2003, p.111) mentions that incubation in modified form still flourishes in Christian shrines today, a fact which may be borne out by Orthodox references to contemporary healings from saints. The shrine of Sts. Cyrus and John, unmercenary healers, was built on the site of a former sanctuary of Asclepius.

CHAPTER FOURTEEN

The Wounded Priest and the Wounded Psychotherapist

As stated above, the art of spiritual direction lies far outside the realm of expertise of the author of this book, hence by necessity what follows will be restricted to some general comments from the available literature. The author's experiences as an Orthodox Christian in confession with a number of priests and spiritual directors will also undoubtedly inform the quality of timbre, focus and content which is attended to in this section.

1 **The Wounded Priest.** While every ordained priest in the Orthodox tradition may hear confessions and give spiritual direction to the faithful, not every minister receives the special calling to do so. This special calling is recognised as a gift of the Holy Spirit, and is embodied in Orthodox Tradition in the figure of the elder (Greek:*geron*, Russian: *starets*; I will use this more familiar term from now on). It is important to note that the liberty of the Holy Spirit is such that a *starets* does not have to be advanced in years; he does not have to be a priest, and may be a monk or (more rarely) a nun, or even a lay man or woman. Ware (1998) explains:

> If the starets is a priest, usually his ministry of spiritual direction is closely linked with the sacrament of confession. [...] A starets in the full sense cannot be appointed such by any superior authority. What happens is simply that the Holy Spirit, speaking directly to the hearts of Christian people, makes it plain that this or

> that person has been blessed by God with the grace to guide and heal others. The true starets is in this sense a prophetic figure, not an institutional official. While most commonly a priest-monk, he may also be a married parish priest, or else a lay monk not ordained to the priesthood, or even — but this is less frequent — a nun, or a lay man or woman living in the outside world. If the starets is not himself a priest, after listening to people's problems and offering counsel, he will frequently send them to a priest for sacramental confession and absolution (p. 96).

It becomes clear therefore, that the Orthodox Church recognizes the calling to hear others' confessions and to offer counsel and guidance as a special vocation and gift of the Holy Spirit, which "bloweth where it listeth." This special gift or charisma is known as the grace of "fatherhood in the Spirit." Persons receiving the counsel of a spiritual father are therefore his spiritual children, whom he brings to spiritual birth, just as their biological father did on a physical level. The personal nature of this relationship between a spiritual father and their spiritual child is of paramount importance, and often matters which strictly speaking are liable to Church discipline are considered relative to this unique personal relationship in an act of theological "economy."[1] Ware (*ibid.*, pp. 95–8) describes the intense relationship between a starets and their spiritual children by referring to Fr. Zachariah in Dostoyevsky's novel, *The Brothers Karamazov*:

> What he [the starets] offers to his children is not primarily moral instructions or a rule of life, but a personal relationship. "A starets,"

[1] Evdokimov (1994) defines the phenomenon of economy (lit. "management of a household") as "the divine dispensation in creation and in the providential ordering of the world" (p. 273). It is a reality which prevents the Orthodox Church from slipping into pharisaic legalism in its appreciation of right and wrong, sin and virtue, even as Spirit-bearing fathers are nevertheless able to discern these clearly, as is each of the faithful according to their individual gift of discernment, the condition of their spiritual life and obedience to Christ's commandments.

> says Dostoyevsky, "is one who takes your soul, your will, into his soul and his will." Fr. Zachariah's disciples used to say about him, "It was as though he bore our hearts in his hands" (p. 95).

Already a central feature of the 'wounded healer' archetype can be discerned in this description of the quality of a *starets*' personal approach. The *starets* suffers vicariously for his children, taking their hearts, wills, soul into his own. This is a grave and serious responsibility, by which the *starets* takes on added culpability for his spiritual children's sins.

Yet there is also more to the woundedness of the *starets*. John Climacus points to it, when he writes:

> Those who have been humbled by their passions should take heart. Even if they tumble into every pit, even if they are trapped by every snare, even if they suffer every disease, still after their return to health they become a light to all, they prove to be doctors, beacons, pilots. They teach us the characteristics of every malady and out of their own experience they can rescue those about to lapse (Chamberas, 1982, p. 231).

It is clear that, in order to be able to 'take the souls' of others into one's own, a spiritual director must themselves know suffering and personal injury at first hand, and have emerged from it spiritually intact by God's grace. The passage from John Climacus above is not merely a recognition of the spiritual value of woundedness from the wisdom of a revered Church Father; it is a sound, scripturally-based teaching about the very nature of priesthood:

> For because he himself has suffered and been tempted, he is able to help those who are tempted... For we have not a high priest who is unable to sympathize with our weaknesses, but one who in every respect has been tempted as we are, yet without sinning... He can deal gently with the ignorant and wayward since he himself is beset with weakness (Hebrews 2:18; 4:15; 5:2).

The 'High Priest'—which in the letter to the Hebrews directly refers to Jesus—alone amongst men is tempted 'yet without sinning,' as a result of the perfected humanity and divinity inherent in His person. Human priests, however, are as liable to temptation and to sin as everyone else. What is different in the case of human priests, is that they are emphatically called to learn from their mistakes, to repent and to become sufficiently permeable to divine grace and open to suffering, so that their sins and passions may be overcome, and that they may then draw on this experience of healing to help others, for whom they also have special responsibility. Christ Himself, though as suggested above alone was tempted without sin, nevertheless grew in his humanity through the ultimate empathic/kenotic act of the Incarnation, as scripture attests: "For because he himself has suffered and been tempted, he is able to help those who are tempted" (Heb. 2:18). "What is not assumed is not healed," goes a patristic saying. Christ is like us in his human nature, except that His human nature is perfected, it is the best that human nature can be, it is our true nature; in such an ideal condition—were we ever able to achieve it—we, too, would be tempted without sinning, and saints do in fact frequently find themselves having this experience, as numerous stories from their lives attest. Nevertheless, Orthodoxy very explicitly teaches that none but God, regardless of their Church rank, is sin-free, and also very clearly instructs that the special grace of priesthood implies that the sacraments are effective when administered by a canonically ordained priest, regardless of their personal failings and flaws.

The acquisition of experience in spiritual warfare involves times of loss as well as victory, of weakness as well as strength. Indeed, writing from a Roman Catholic Jesuit perspective, Buckley (2008) asks the question:

> *Is this man weak enough to be a priest?* Is this man deficient enough so that he cannot ward off significant suffering from his life, so that he lives with a certain amount of failure, so that he feels what it is to be an average man? Is there any history of

> confusion, of self-doubt, of interior anguish? Has he had to deal with fear, come to terms with frustrations, or accept deflated expectations? These are critical questions and they probe for weakness. Why weakness? Because [...] it is in this deficiency, in this interior lack, in this weakness, that the efficacy of the ministry and priesthood of Christ lies (2008, italics same).

From the Orthodox perspective, Chryssavgis (2000) echoes the above words, and finds no obstacle in referring directly to the wounded healer archetype when discussing the work of the Orthodox spiritual director:

> This concept of woundedness or brokenness may, to some, sound negative or discouraging. Yet the idea of the priest as a "wounded healer," as a person who — before all else and beyond all else — is aware of his own personal weakness as being the occasion of divine strength through him, deepens and broadens the notion of the authority of ministry as service (*diakonia*) (p. 37, italics same).

A key characteristic of scriptural figures from Moses to Jeremiah, to Paul, is repentance, or metanoia, a change of heart which implies mourning for one's sin (Hausherr, 1982). This involves a conviction of one's own sinfulness, one's inadequacy in meeting the high standards God sets, one's culpability and sense of compunction in not having met them. Men who are simply confident, who can deal with all of life's demands in a practical and capable manner, cannot know what it is to be weak before the majesty of one's Creator, grateful for the superabundant mercy with which He forgives even the worst sins. To see God (theoria) is the supreme charism in Orthodox spiritual life, more important than any other gift of prophecy or wonderworking, and this cannot be granted to those who are unable to perceive their own sinfulness. Woundedness is breakability, and is the foundation of the very capacity to trust in God, not to be invulnerable. The inner strength of this kind of weakness is signified by Christ's body being broken and

His blood being shed as a healing sacrifice for all—"He is not weak in dealing with you, but powerful in you. For he was crucified in weakness; but lives by the power of God. (2 Corinthians 13:3, 4)." Seen from the scriptural perspective therefore, Christ died *for* humanity, which owed a debt to God, and out of love for us, God paid the price Him self, through the suffering, crucifixion[2] and death of His own incarnate Son, the Wounded Healer of humanity (cf. Isaiah 53:5; 1 Pet. 2:24). To Christians therefore, and preeminently perhaps to the Christian spiritual director, Christ paid the debt humans incurred for all time through His sacrifice on the cross, and only invites those wishing to participate in His ongoing salvation to refrain from further sin—since by sinning without repentance, new debts are incurred, and further spiritual growth is blocked. Thus, paradoxically, although Christ's sacrifice has already paid off the debt of sin for all time, humans who do not experience their woundedness in genuine *metanoia*, do not *allow themselves* to experience this, the constant Joy of His Kingdom (Ware, 1996).

The Christian spiritual director works on the ethical premise shared by the ancient Stoics, that only the truly good can be truly happy—but he knows this is achieved through genuine intimacy

[2] "The problem of crucifixion is the beginning of individuation; there is the secret meaning of the Christian symbolism, a path of blood and suffering-like any other step forward on the road of evolution of human consciousness. Can man stand a further increase in consciousness: ... Is it really worthwhile that man should progress morally and intellectually? Is that gain worth the candle: That's the question. I don't want to force my views on anybody else. But I confess that I submitted to the divine power of this apparently insurmountable problem and I consciously and intentionally made my life miserable, because I wanted God to be alive and free from the suffering man has put on him by loving his own reason more than God's secret intentions. There is a mystical fool in me that proved to be stronger than all my science. I think that God in his turn has bestowed life upon me and has saved me from petrification ... Thus I suffered and was miserable, but it seems that life was never wanting and in the blackest night even, and just there, by the grace of God, I could see a Great Light. Somewhere there seems to be great kindness in the abysmal darkness of the deity ... Try to apply seriously what I have told you, not that you might escape suffering-nobody can escape it-but that you may avoid the worst-blind suffering" (Jung, unpublished letter cited by Adler (1975)).

with their own woundedness. It will be seen below that the premises on which psychotherapists base their work, metaphysical premises aside, are not in fact radically different from those of spiritual directors, since as Chrysostomos of Etna (2004; see also ch. 8) writes:

> The psychotherapeutic bond between a patient and therapist is [...] not unlike the relationship between a spiritual guide and a spiritual aspirant [...] (p. 21).

2 **The Wounded Psychotherapist.** In a seminal article on 'The Archetypal Image of the Wounded Healer,' Groesbeck (1975) returns to this fundamental, primordial image underlying psychotherapy, pointing out simply that "every time a patient or an analysand comes to us he is most urgently seeking help to be healed from whatever he suffers." (p. 122). Groesbeck goes on to point out that there are two 'basic principles of healing,' these being (i) *allopathy*, or treatment which produces effects which differ from those produced by the disease, and (ii) *homeopathy*, or treatment which is based on the notion that 'like cures like,' as in the example of administering a drug which in a healthy person produces symptoms similar to those produced by the disease, e.g. the smallpox vaccine artificially inducing immunity by introducing a low dose of a variant of the pathogen itself into the sufferer's organism. Groesbeck suggests that

> [...] [D]epth psychology, beginning with Freud and psychoanalysis, developed mainly with reliance on a homeopathic approach, i.e. the reliving or re-experiencing in small doses of emotionally traumatic experiences whereby psychic integration or healing could take place, and 'blocks in development' could be removed (p. 123).

Jungian psychology is cited as emphasizing the homeopathic principle of 'like cures like' particularly strongly, since meaning and cure is sought within the symptom itself, conscious integration of rejected and unconscious aspects of personality being the method by which balance and wholeness are restored, and the process of individuation is activated. When this is then applied to the personality of the psychotherapist, it becomes clear why Jung emphasised that 'it is his own hurt that gives the measure of his power to heal' (*ibid*). Groesbeck (*ibid*) also draws attention to the importance assigned to the "totality of the patient's life" (p. 123) in homeopathy, and the destructive potential of treating parts of the patient in a specialized but isolated manner, as often experienced by patients treated in a conventional allopathic Western medical setting. The pertinence of this aspect of homeopathy to Jungian psychotherapy is also evident.

Groesbeck's intention is "to re-examine the intra-psychic aspects of the healing process, especially in the context of the transference between doctor (analyst) and patient" (*ibid*, p. 123). Although he accepts that "healing is, in the final analysis, a mystery" (*ibid*, p. 124), with his paper Groesbeck opens up a window into the homeopathic process whereby the wounded healer archetype influences both the analyst and the patient, by stimulating respectively the woundedness of the analyst and the inner healer of the patient. Psychotherapy is thereby recognised as a healing ritual informed by archetypal forces which therapists are called to harness, through assistance and participation in the therapeutic process, while carefully and studiously being involved in a process of reflection to avoid becoming inflated through identification with the 'healer' or 'saviour' (Sharp, 1991, p. 151) pole of the archetype, since as Whitmont (1993) suggests,

> The capacity, real or imagined, to bestow health, life and relief of suffering often serves as a defense for the healer against accepting and facing his own life's dilemmas, weaknesses, pains and fears of illness and death. In ministering to his need to maintain an image of himself as healthy and powerful, the healer projects and may induce upon the patient his own unaccepted and unredeemed weakness, illness or suffering. The need to ward off pain, disease and death from oneself in fact quite frequently provides the hidden motivation for seeking the healing profession (p. 207).

Thus, the psychotherapist who uses his art as a defence risks personal inflation and neglecting or even harming his patients; but the alternative requires even more courage, since in order to really empathise the psychotherapist risks actually becoming ill through a process of 'psychic infection,' whereby the patient's wounds either re-open his own past traumas, or through badly-managed countertransference actually deepen and augment the extent of personal neurosis and the dysfunctional behavioural repertoire associated with these old wounds. In fact, in the classical Jungian paradigm, the analyst risks even his own death, as witnessed in the case of Dr. H., Jung's personal physician, who in MDR (1961: pp. 322–324) dies after successfully treating Jung for a heart attack. Jung's dream of Dr. H. as a *basileus* of Kos (i.e. a healer from the temple of Asklepios at Kos) suggested to Jung that Dr. H. was himself in danger of losing his life, because he was in such over-zealous identification with the archetypal wounded healer, that he essentially exposed himself to the ultimate healer's act of sacrifice: dying in Jung's stead. Jung tried to warn Dr. H. after his own recovery from the heart attack, but interestingly Dr. H. was unwilling to discuss it, then went on to become ill, take to his bed and never recover. Groesbeck writes:

> The question of how deeply involved the analyst should become in taking upon himself the illness of the patient does not admit of an easy answer. While he must get close enough to be involved, activated and aware of his own wounds to catalyse the process [...] he must also be aware of the dangers of inflation as well as his limitations, including the possibility of his own death and demise. It is precisely the archetypal image of the wounded healer that can most help him here. If one 'leaves the healing to God,' he is much better off. In fact it was God who brought the illness, and hence knows the cure. Hence, though one must be involved deeply, paradoxically one must not be over-zealous in trying to cure (1975, p. 134).

At this point, a parameter of the wounded healer archetype is introduced which may be crucial to both the Jungian and the Christian paradigm of healing. The wounded healer is essentially one who lays himself open to 'psychic infection,' internalising and identifying with the patient's problems, taking the suffering into himself. It is not without significance that the myths of Chiron and Asklepios, as described above, suggest that these healers are "fatally smitten" (Groesbeck, p. 134). The archetype of sacrifice is everywhere to be found in the personal histories of healers, from doctors and nurses, to priests, teachers and psychologists. It is clear from this description, that the path of Christ as presented in scripture and Church Tradition, can also be viewed as being the story of a wounded healer, One who dies for the sins of others[3]. Of course, the significant difference between a Christian understanding and a Jungian one, is in whether it is believed that Christ's ultimate sacrifice is the 'once for all' metaphysical event underlying *all* sacrifices, both in ancient, pre-Christian times and in future ages up to the modern era.

It would appear therefore, that sacrifice is inherent to a therapists' development. The Jungian literature on the Wounded Healer concept is quite extensive in this regard, with Sedgwick's (1994) important study offering vivid clinical examples of a Jungian way of working with countertransference; this is well-documented elsewhere, and does not require further coverage for the purposes of this study. Both Jungians and others (e.g. Conti-O'Hare, 2002) have observed that a sacrifice is involved, whereby the healer must pay the price of getting in touch with inner trauma for the sake of becoming an effective helper. Patterson (1990), for example, suggests that there is a

[3] Contrary to established views on spiritual faith and practices in psychoanalytic circles, a Christian commitment with emphasis on humility, far from encouraging identification with the 'saviour' archetype, may actively prevent it in many cases. Of course, this does not mean that this type of inflation is uncharacteristic of many who do self-identify as Christians, and it stands to reason that the 'saviour complex' may commonly be found amongst members of the Church who perhaps ought to know better, just as professionals may fall prey to the 'helper syndrome.'

'Wounded Way,' as a therapeutic path along which healers typically journey. This journey consists of four stages, namely

1. *Technician stage*: acquisition of skills and techniques, within a learning context such as graduate school, seminary, convent etc. This is a stage of absorbing information, and anxiety is characteristically experienced about becoming a helper.
2. *Practitioner stage*: acquired skills are put into action in a professional setting, and anxiety often focuses on making one's presence felt. Burn-out may be experienced at this stage, which, if ignored leads to a spilling over of 'brokenness' (p. 79) into other areas of life, such as alcohol and drug abuse. The wounded healer is called at this stage to realise that deeper changes need to take place.
3. *Artist Phase*: beginning with a sense of brokenness, further growth may be experienced through immersion in the arts. The helper feels drawn to creative activity. Personal therapy with another helper can be instrumental for confronting inner woundedness at this stage.
4. *Wounded Healer stage*: the therapist comes to see his clients' sufferings as his own, and realises these clients are there also for the purpose of teaching him/her.

The link between countertransference, creative suffering and psychotherapeutic healing thus becomes apparent. Just as the Rainmaker had to first become infected by the people who "were all out of Tao and of themselves" (Spiegelman, 1996: p. 60), becoming himself disordered before he could withdraw to a secluded place and process his experience in order to return to the Tao for himself and the people, so the psychotherapist must open himself emotionally and spiritually, exposing his personal wounds to the danger of painful resonance with his patient's sufferings in the context of the countertransference, in order to be able to provide any real healing. The attitude which is necessary to the countertransference, is therefore Jung's 'religious attitude' (cf. CW11:9), which involves careful consideration and observation, patient reflection on inner experience in such a way, that we can reconnect (Lat. *religare*) with centredness, inner order, the Self. De Beausobre's concept of creative suffering discussed and elaborated earlier, could therefore be seen as one method of application of the Jungian religious attitude, deriving from Orthodox Christianity.

3 **Jung as Wounded Healer.** It is not uncommon for Jung himself to be perceived in Jungian circles and elsewhere (e.g. Goldwert, 1992; Dunne, 2000) as an incarnation of the image of the archetypal wounded healer. As Smith (1996) suggests at the beginning of his biography of Jung:

> This book presents Jung as a wounded healer who, because he confronted throughout his life the divided parts of his own psyche, was enabled to become a healer of others. [...] The central theme of this book, briefly stated, is that because of his "wounded" childhood, Jung was to embark, even as a child, on ways to integrate his life. [...] That is to say, over a span of years Jung was to confront creatively and to a significant degree overcome his personal pathology (p. 2).

And a little further on he reiterates,

> I will argue that Jung was a "wounded healer" whose explorations into the psyche were part of his creative effort to find wholeness and integration (p. 15).

Smith (*ibid.*) turns to a number of sources to identify the wounding in Jung's childhood, laying particular emphasis on Jung's relationship to his mother, whom he experienced as a divided personality, a woman who could unreliably turn from a conventional and amiable "innocuous and human" day-personality, into an "uncanny," "unexpected and frightening" night-time personality, an unconscious other who was moreover "a sombre, imposing figure possessed of unassailable authority" (Jung, MDR, pp. 65–6). Emilie Jung (nee Preiswerk), the daughter of a high-ranking Protestant pastor who held weekly conversations with the ghost of his first wife—for whom he also reserved a special chair in his study—used to sit behind her father Samuel, watching out for ghosts that might disturb him in his writing of sermons. Her husband to be, Johann Paul Achilles Jung, Jung's father, met Emilie at the home of his mentor in Hebrew grammar, Samuel Preiswerk. Like Samuel, Johann Achilles Paul wished to become an academic philologist, but lack of academic success led to a life (of failure?) as an unconvinced pastor in country parishes, and to subsequent tensions with Emilie, who became susceptible to bouts of depression for which she was hospitalized for weeks at a time. She crucially abandoned Carl, her young son, at the age of three for a three-month hospital stay; this traumatized the boy so much, that he later famously stated that

> From then on, I always felt mistrustful when the word "love" was spoken. The feeling I associated with "woman" was for a long time that of innate unreliability (MDR, p. 23).

Maternal depression has been observed to be quite common in the past history of psychotherapists (Storr, 1990, p. 178). Smith importantly suggests a missing piece of information not included in MDR, namely that Emilie Jung's depression only lifted following her husband's death, when Jung was 21 years old. In Smith's own words:

> In the first draft of *Memories*, with its pencilled and penned additions and deletions, Jung indicated some of the circumstances surrounding his mother's hospitalization in Basel. He explained that she was hysterical from disappointment with her husband, whose life took a turn for the worse after his final examinations at the University. [...] A crucial sentence that was omitted stated that his mother only recovered her health after his father passed away (*ibid.*, pp. 17–18).

With such underlying tension present between his parents, an unreliable mother, and a weak father lacking the conviction Jung probably needed him to have (see above, ch. 3), it is not perhaps amiss to describe Jung as having been a traumatized child, indeed, as noted earlier Winnicott thought of Jung as suffering from childhood schizophrenia. Whether or not this was the case, it cannot be denied that the founder of analytical psychology paid the price which his environment demanded in full, so that when his parents 'sacrificed' his opportunity to experience any genuinely happy and secure childhood, he nevertheless went on to become a powerful and profound personality like a clairsentient seer or a shaman, who meant—and continues to mean—a great deal to those who found a cure for their psychological difficulties, through consulting him or his works. To Marie-Louise von Franz (1998), for example, Jung was a healer for more than the individuals who came to see him; he was a healer for contemporary culture as a whole. As William H. Kennedy, her translator, notes

> [...] Jung lived a universal story, or myth; but he lived it individually, concretely, fully, and analytical psychology was born from this life, which was, of course, intimately bound up with the deeper spiritual problems of the age (p. ix).

Thus, if Jung suffered from inner trauma, the creative ways in which he resolved it seem to have contributed to the entire cultural heritage of the West. His contact with the primal dynamics of his own and his patients' unconscious psyches proved fruitful, confirming the potency of the wounded healer archetype in his own life. As Goldwert (1992) writes:

> Jung, the hero, had returned from the land of the dead[4] to lead others towards a new understanding of their psyches (p. 90).

[4] The underworld of the dead is for Jung a symbol of the unconscious.

CONCLUSION

Creative Suffering and the Wounded Healer

Following on from the above, it becomes increasingly apparent that, for priests and spiritual directors as much as for psychotherapists in general as instanced by Jung himself, the psychological 'wound,' or trauma, in analytical psychology is in fact—potentially—*the* richest source of buried psychological treasure in the personality (Rothenberg, 2001). Paradoxically, that part, or those aspects of a person, which were most abused by family, friends, and society, or violated by personal tragedy, can become the very place in the personality which has a 'crack' in it allowing in the light, so to speak—the 'basic fault,' to paraphrase a term from psychoanalysis, which permits a 'new beginning' (Balint, 1968). And it is precisely one's place of wounding and the area where the pain is coming from, that is one's point of entry into the psychological treasure of Selfhood, as envisaged by Jungian psychology, but also the place where a connection to spirit may be made through a religious discipline, whereby the 'original sin' may become a *felix culpa*. As Patterson (1990) suggests above, it is through this gap in the conscious ego, which is at first experienced as a shadowy 'blind spot' in a healer's identity and career, that the wounded healer will eventually be able, if they persevere, to reach down into their psychic depths, and it is also through this gap that the light of their deepest, truest archetypal Self will be able to manifest into the world and the consulting room, in a process of mutual benefit (Spiegelman, 1996).

For the sake of a final brief illustration, a clinical example of the potential within such a wound or trauma may involve an instance when a child has been systematically ridiculed by an insecure parent; that child carries within a deep sense of shame about himself (Jacoby, 1991). If later as an adolescent and adult he continues to live out his unconscious complexes, he will probably try to find relief by shaming others, ridiculing them just as he was ridiculed, or alternatively pretend to be nothing but an unnoticeable, victimized absence. But if he can rein both those temptations in, and introspect with creativity and psychological-mindedness, he will discover that he knows intimately how hurtful it is to disrespect someone. Suffering his wounds creatively, as suggested by De Beausobre (ch. 2), would imply this can be achieved through *acceptance* (of the past), *discernment* (of the greater teleological implications for his development as a personality) and *faith* (that things have happened like this for a reason; that ongoing survival is evidence of being in some way sustained).

Perhaps this person may acquire too, a special affinity with people who have been hurt in this most unjust way, but also with the psychological condition of their tormentors — and then his once angry, mocking, or self-negating personality may gradually be transformed through adopting a generally more compassionate, caring attitude. All this may contribute to him finding a vocation, as suggested earlier in this chapter: he now wants to work with disadvantaged children, or other members of society who are perceived as 'weak,' to help them learn to respect themselves even when others mock or disdain them for what they perceive to be their weaknesses. He may also be able to grasp the way in which any personality is not, in fact, 'real' without wounds, and — like Jung — be able to perceive the shapelessness, incompleteness and inauthenticity of those who feign a perfection for which they have, or have not suffered. In this way, he may be able to help them, too, by reminding them in appropriate ways that they *do* have a particular limited, non-omnipotent form, which is in fact a precious gift, valuable precisely for its particular unique, human shape — a part of the mosaic which makes a society of persons-in-relation, and an opening for the individual into discovering their own real destiny. It is not difficult to imagine, therefore, that this once traumatized child, might evolve into an able therapist or spiritual director.

The personal biographical process of maturity, then, can be meaningful also for others, precisely because of its archetypal, collective implications, as Nouwen (1979; 1994) writes:

> [...] The minister is called to recognize the sufferings of his time in his own heart and make that recognition the starting point of his service. Whether he tries to enter into a dislocated world, relate to a convulsive generation, or speak to a dying man, his service will not be perceived as authentic unless it comes from a heart wounded by the suffering about which he speaks (p. xvi).

Writing from a Jungian perspective, Neumann (1966) suggests that within the experience of personal suffering, there is also a profound impulse to convert personal wounds through creativity, into sources of collective healing. He writes that

> Because in his own suffering the creative man experiences the profound wounds of his collectivity and his time, he carries deep within him a regenerative force capable of bringing forth a cure not only for himself, but also for his community (p. 186).

Archimandrite Sophrony, who during WWII personally experienced such profound pain for the world as Nouwen and Neumann describe here, and prayed so fervently that his own health was affected,[1] confirms this experience, when he writes of the spiritual father that

> The sufferings of the whole world accumulate in his heart, and he prays with sorrowful tears for each and every man. [...] All

[1] Sakharov (2002) also suggests of the Athonite elder that, "Through such prayer he came to discover directly the interdependence of his own being and that of the whole of mankind, whose ontological unity became a central feature of his anthropology" (p. 28).

> of this he lives inside himself, as his own torment. But in reality he is not he himself—he merely takes on the burdens of other people (Sophrony, 1996, pp. 95, 109).

And echoing every wounded healer, including Freud and Jung, the starets further advises that

> According to the pastoral principle of the Fathers, one must not urge one's flock to try for what one has not achieved oneself. [...] One must either take into one's heart the difficulties and sorrow of those who turn to us, or, alternatively, enter into their hearts [...] unite with them. This exposes one to the danger of starting a conflict with them, of being infected [...]. I am of no account, but what is taking place inside me is not insignificant—not worthless in the eyes of Him Who created me (*ibid.*, pp. 99, 104, 115).

Whether or not such a conclusion is reached, it is hoped that the parallels with the countertransferential process in psychotherapy which have been discussed above, have now become more apparent. Ulanov (1999) reminds us that

> Countertransference covers vast areas. [...] Although other theorists [than Jung alone] notice something bigger going on in clinical treatment and even employ religious language to describe it, they deny its referent. Words like ontological (Laing), sacred (Winnicott), prayer (Bollas), faith (Bion), and resurrection of the body (Milner) are increasingly used to describe psyche while jettisoning the reality of God or of a transcendent realm of Isness, All, Source, and Goal to which the psyche belongs. [...] But in clinical terms, this means emphasis falls on the personal as the agent of change, to the exclusion of what Jungians call the archetypal and all that it mediates of reality beyond the psyche (pp. 6, 7; words in square brackets mine).

The archetypal image of the wounded healer has been associated in this study to the image of the Crucified and Wounded Christ. It is indubitably true that there are a number of other ways of discussing the immanent presence of the transcendent Other in the clinical encounter, ways which may be more suited to different spiritual and theoretical orientations; but it has at least been suggested here in a way which may merit further research, that the paradigm of creative suffering as it emerges out of a specifically Christian context, may be relevant to gaining a deeper understanding of the active role and deep significance of the therapist's particular and personal trauma within the therapeutic relationship. Furthermore, this paradigm suggests that personal trauma in the psychotherapist is potentially not only a source of pathology and an impediment to healing, but in fact a cornerstone acting as the psychological foundation by which any healing may take place. Thus, the main proposition set forth here, which perhaps applies equally to both therapists and spiritual directors, is that the work of healing involves a conscious recognition and acceptance of personal suffering and its moral and spiritual repercussions in the actual, lived biography of the therapist — suffering which not only needs to be 'worked through' (Rycroft, 1968; pp. 199–200) in personal training analysis or psychotherapy (or seminary training for priests), but which indeed later on comes to assume a pivotal role in the very nature, establishment, character and maintenance of the therapeutic relationship with clients throughout one's healing career.

Taking Jung as a prime example of a therapist who worked from within such a wounded healer perspective, it is maintained that Jung's own visions of a 'monstrous flood' and a 'sea turned to blood' just prior to WWI (cf. MDR, p. 199) may be cited as further instances of the intuitive attunement with the sufferings of his own times required of the wounded healer, an attunement which is both necessary and essentially inseparable from the help he offers people from within the walls of his consulting room, or even in the confessional.

Jung's original contributions to psychology are diverse and numerous. Perhaps, however, the implications of this central aspect of his approach to therapy, namely the significance of facilitating for the patient an encounter with the numinous, and the ensuing necessity for the psychotherapist to be engaged in an ongoing relationship with the numinous in their own lives, as well as in the current counter-transference to the client, is an aspect of psychotherapy that is currently neglected, or not explored to its fullest degree, in the pragmatic climate of professional regulation and evidence-based practice.

Here there may be lessons to be learned from traditional spiritual practices such as Eastern Orthodox spiritual direction, which rely on the living relation to, and experience of the numinous. The preoccupation with the universal applicability of the archetypal realm, perceived as an exclusively intra-psychic reality, and the fear of religious dogmatism, have perhaps led to the formation of a blind-spot for depth psychology, since as Ulanov (1999) claims, it may just be possible that "The Self makes a bridge to a reality that exists far outside our psyche and yet also deep within it" (pp. 5–6). It is certainly one area of Jungian depth psychology, but also perhaps of psychology in general, which can no longer afford to exclude the spiritual insights of theology and to pathologize the experiences of organised religion, without considerable cost to its own sincerity, intellectual integrity and therapeutic efficacy.

A further outcome of this research may be found in the suggestion that, in line with the collective and archetypal parameters of the phenomenon, the wounded healer needs to be closely in touch, not only with the personal sources of his/her trauma, but also the collective familial, social, cultural, historical, epistemological and indeed the spiritual conditions and crises of their times, the cultural *zeitgeist* as indicated by and discussed extensively in chs. 1 and 2. It has been suggested that, far from radicalism, this presupposes a patient tolerance of and creative dialogue with traditional dogma. Jung (e.g. CW 6, 1971 p. 119) and Jungian analysts following him (e.g. Von Franz, 1993), have been unanimous in declaring that individuation cannot take place in isolation, and that as a process it should in fact both presuppose and lead to improved social relations; analytical psychology may in fact be the psychology *par excellence* which looks beyond the personal, with its view of the psyche having phylogenetic roots in the collective unconscious, so it is all the more puzzling that the archetypes, and especially the Self, should be viewed as strictly intrapsychic by some analysts, leading to an *a priori* exclusion of the possibility of a dimension of being beyond the psyche, which nevertheless—just as the body and the physical universe do—also exists in constant communion and interaction with psychic reality. Here, too, it has been suggested that Eastern Orthodox theology and Jungian analytical psychology have a great deal to offer one another, both through areas of mutual practice and agreement, and where strong disagreement emerges. Ulanov's (2006) eloquent words may also apply here; she asks,

> But what is the theological enterprise, and what is the psychological project vis a vis religion? These two disciplines are like terrains on either side of a central river. When religion is dominant in culture, the two are one, what Christianity called the care of souls [...]. In the twentieth century, the one became two with depth psychology verging into a separate river from its original containment in theology. Now, in the twenty-first century, the two are converging to meet again, to send boats and bridges back and forth (p. 61).

From the outset, it has not been the aim of this study to resolve issues of the 'rightness' or 'wrongness' of either discipline, to impose one on the other, or to permanently settle any ongoing philosophical disputes concerning the confluent terrains of religious ontology and psychological being. Inasmuch as fairness and neutrality have not been maintained, the author takes responsibility, and hopes that where purely personal opinion is expressed, this is clear to readers. Perhaps, however, a small contribution has been made to a deeper comparative understanding of analytical psychology and Orthodox theology, as well as the potentially productive relationship between the two, in serving the needs of the human psyche.

Given their scholarly and respectful interaction, establishing constructive theoretical and practical bridges while not denying the existence of areas of irresolvable incompatibility or incommunicability, it may be possible for two philosophically quite divergent disciplines to cooperate. It is perhaps to just such creative interdisciplinary dialogue that wounded healers from all disciplines are invited into anyway, by the complex, multifactorial and urgent presenting concerns of their clients, which also render effectively meaningless any inflexible distinctions between the practical insights gained through ongoing resolution of personal trauma, and theoretical insights based on academic research.

References

Abbreviations Used

CW	*The Collected Works of C. G. Jung, Vols. 1–18*, ed. by Read, Sir H., Fordham, Dr. M. and Adler, Dr. G.; transl. R. F. C. Hull, Routledge and Kegan Paul Ltd., London.
MDR	Jung, C. G. (1995) *Memories, Dreams, Reflections*, Fontana Press, London.
MEOP	*A Manual of Eastern Orthodox Prayers* (1999) St. Vladimir's Seminary Press, Crestwood, New York.
OSB	*The Orthodox Study Bible* (2008) *Ancient Christianity Speaks to Today's World,* Thomas Nelson Publishers, Nashville, Tennessee. Note: Scripture quotations in the main text are from the OSB, or New King James Version.
PG	*Patrologiae Cursus Completus, Series Graeca*, edited by J.-P. Migne, Paris.
S. E.	Strachey, J., Freud, A. & Rothgeb, C. L. (eds.) (1953–1974) *The Standard Edition of the Complete Psychological Works of Sigmund Freud*, Vols. 1–24, Hogarth Press, London.
TPOTT	*The Psychology of the Transference*, Jung (1989; 1966) Routledge, London. Note: quotations from TPOTT/CW16 are from this edition, and hence given with page numbers, rather than original paragraph numbers.

Books, Articles, Websites

Abenheimer, K. M. (1956). "Notes on the Spirit as conceived by Dynamic Psychology," in *Journal of Analytical Psychology*, Vol. 1, No. 2, pp. 113–131.

Adler, G. (1975). "Aspects of Jung's Personality and Work," in *Psychological Perspectives*, Spring, Vol. 6, No. 1, pp. 10–18.

Aleksiev, Archim. S. (1994). *The Meaning of Suffering and Strife and Reconciliation*, transl. R. Dyonova, St. Xenia Skete, Wildwood, California.

Allen, D. (1984). "Acting Redemptively" [Online] Available from http://theologytoday.ptsem.edu/oct1984/v41-3-article2.htm, accessed 14/02/08.

Allen, P. M. (2008) *Vladimir Soloviev: Russian Mystic*, Lindisfarne Books, Rudolf Steiner Publications, Great Barrington, Massachusetts.

Anderson, Fr. D. (1997). "The Bible and Orthodox Tradition," in Allen, J., Sparks, J. N., Najim, M. & Stylianopoulos, T., Thomas (ed.) (1997). *The Orthodox Study Bible: New Testament and Psalms*, Nelson Publishers, Nashville, Tennessee, pp. iv–xii.

Andrew, Fr. (2005). "A Scandal in Greece" [Online] Available from: http://orthodoxengland.org.uk/scangree.htm, accessed 21/07/09.

Andrews, B. (2008). "NICE guidance," in *Therapy Today*, Vol. 19, No. 9, pp. 12–16.

Anthony, Metropolitan (of Sourozh) (1970). *School for Prayer*, Darton, Longman & Todd, London.

______ (2005). *Encounter*, Darton, Longman & Todd, London.

Antonopoulos, N. (Archimandrite) (2007). *Ypefthinoi gia Ola*, Akritas, Athens.

Arraj, J. (1988). "Jungian Spirituality: The Question of Victor White," in *Spirituality Today*, Vol. 40, No. 3, pp. 249–261.

Aveline, M. (1996). "The Training and Supervision of Individual Therapists," in Dryden, W. (ed.) (1996). *Handbook of Individual Therapy*, Sage, London, pp. 365–304.

AVENS, R. (1980) *Imagination is Reality: Western Nirvana in Jung, Hillman, Barfield and Cassirer*, Spring Publications Inc., Putnam, Connecticut.

AVGOUSTIDIS, FR. A. (1999). *I Anthropini Epithetikotita* (A Pastoral and Psychological Approach to the Ladder of St John the Sinaite), Ekdoseis Akritas, Athens.

______ (2004). *Psyxologia kai Pnevmatiki Zoi*, Ekdoseis "Tinos," Athens.

BAEHRENS, W. A. (ed.) (1920). *Origen: Homilies on Leviticus v, 2. Die Griechischen Christlichen Schriftsteller*, Vol. 29, Leipzig.

BAKOYIANNIS, V. ARCHIM. (1999). *Suffering and Salvation*, Tabor Press, Patras.

BALDWIN, A. (2004). "Psychotherapy: the New Religion?," in *Counselling and Psychotherapy Journal*, Vol. 15, No. 05, pp. 9–11.

BALINT, M. (1968). *The Basic Fault: Therapeutic Aspects of Regression*, Tavistock, London.

BATEMAN, A. & HOLMES, J. (1995). *Introduction to Psychoanalysis: Contemporary Theory and Practice*, Routledge, London.

BEEBE, J., CAMBRAY, J. & KIRSCH, T. B. (2001). "What Freudians Can Learn From Jung," in *Psychoanalytic Psychology*, Vol. 18, No. 2, pp. 213–242.

BERDYAEV, N. A. (1930). "Studies Concerning Jacob Boehme: Etude II. The Teaching about Sophia and the Androgyne. J. Boehme and the Russian Sophiological Current." [Online] Available from: http://www.berdyaev.com/berdiaev/berd_lib/1930_351.html, accessed 26/09/2007. (Original source: *Put,'* 1930, No. 21, pp. 34–62.)

______ (1937). *The Destiny of Man*, The Centenary Press, London.

______ (1977). "The Ethics of Creativity," in Schmemann, A. (ed.), *Ultimate Questions: An Anthology of Modern Russian Religious Thought*, St. Vladimir's Seminary Press, New York.

BEZZERIDES, A. M. (ed.) (2006). *Christ at Work: Orthodox Christian Perspectives on Vocation*, Holy Cross Orthodox Press, Brookline, Massachusetts.

BION, W. (1967). "Notes on Memory and Desire," in *The Psychoana-*

lytic Forum, Vol. 2, pp. 271–280.

BISHOP, P. (2002). *Jung's Answer to Job: A Commentary*, Routledge, London.

BLACK, D. (1993). "The Relation of Psychoanalysis to Religion," in Ward, I. (ed.) (1993) *Is Psychoanalysis Another Religion? Contemporary Essays on Spirit, Faith and Morality in Psychoanalysis*, Freud Museum Publications, London.

BLOOM, W. (ed.) (1991). *The New Age: An Anthology of Selected Writings*, Rider, London.

BODHAKARI (2008). "The Prison of the Self," in *Therapy Today*, Vol. 19, No. 6, pp. 30–33.

BOLLAS, C. (2002). *Free Association, Ideas in Psychoanalysis*, Icon Books, Cambridge.

BOUTENEFF, P. (2006). *Sweeter Than Honey: Orthodox Thinking on Dogma and Truth,* St. Vladimir's Seminary Press, Crestwood, New York.

BOUTENEFF, V. (1998). *Father Arseny, 1893–1973: Priest, Prisoner, Spiritual Father*, transl. V. Bouteneff, St. Vladimir's Seminary Press, New York.

BRAZIER, D. (1997). *The Feeling Buddha—A Buddhist Psychology of Character, Adversity and Passion*, Silkworm Books, Chiang Mai, Thailand.

BRECK, J. (2007). "On Keeping the Faith," in *Orthodox Church in America,* Sep. 2007, No. 1 [Online]. Available from: http://www.oca.org/CHRIST-life-print.asp?ID=138, accessed 4/10/08.

BREGMAN, L. (1975). "Fantasy: The Experiencer and The Interpreter," in *Journal of the American Academy of Religion*, Vol. 43, No. 4, pp. 723–740.

BRIANCHANINOV, I. (2006). *On the Prayer of Jesus*, New Seeds Books, Boston.

BROCK, S. (transl.) (1997). *The Wisdom of Saint Isaac the Syrian*, SLG Press, Fairacres, Oxford.

BROWNE, S. (2009). "Resisting Regulation," in *Therapy Today*, Vol. 20, No. 4, pp. 10–11.

Buber, M. (1996). *I and Thou*, 2nd Edition, T&T Clark, Edinburgh.

Bucke, R. M. (1905). *Cosmic Consciousness: A Study in the Evolution of the Human Mind* [Online]. Available from: http://djm.cc/library/Cosmic_Consciousness_edited02.pdf, accessed 20/04/07.

Buckley, M. J. (2008). "Because Beset by Weakness" [Online]. Available at: http://nysj.org/s/316/images/editor_documents/content/AscensionJesus%20is%20no%20longer%20limited%20by%20time%20and%20space.%20The%20A/Weak%20Enough.pdf, accessed 11/02/08.

Carotenuto, A. (1991). *Kant's Dove: The History of Transference in Psychoanalysis*, Chiron Publications, Wilmette, Illinois.

Carr, W. (1991). *Manifold Wisdom: Christians in the New Age*, SPCK, London.

Carter, W. R. (1990). *The Elements of Metaphysics*, McGraw-Hill Publishing Company, New York.

Chamberas, P. A. (1989). *St. Nicodemus of the Holy Mountain: A Handbook of Spiritual Counsel*, transl. P. A. Chamberas, Paulist Press, New York, Mahwah, New Jersey.

Chariton, Igumen of Valamo (1966). *The Art of Prayer—An Orthodox Anthology*, Faber and Faber, London.

Chirban, J. T. (ed.) (1996). *Personhood: Orthodox Christianity and the Connection between Body, Mind, and Soul*, Bergin & Garvey, London.

______ (ed.) (2001). *Sickness or Sin? Spiritual Discernment and Differential Diagnosis*, Holy Cross Orthodox Press, Brookline, Massachusetts.

Christensen, D. (1999). "Epilogue to the Fourth Edition: Signs of the Religion of the Future in the 1990's," in Rose, S. (1975; 1999) *Orthodoxy and the Religion of the Future*, St. Herman of Alaska Brotherhood, Platina, California, pp. 201–214.

Christodoulos, Priestmonk (1998). *Elder Paisios of the Holy Mountain*, Holy Mountain, Greece.

Chrysostomos, Bp. & Brecht, T. (1990). "Jung and the Mystical Theology of the Eastern Orthodox Church: Comments on Common Ground," in *Pastoral Psychology*, Vol. 38, No. 4, pp. 197–203.

CHRYSOSTOMOS, ARCHBISHOP OF ETNA (2004). *Orthodoxy and Psychology*, Center for Traditionalist Orthodox Studies, Etna, California.

______ (2007). *A Guide to Orthodox Psychotherapy: The Science, Theology and Spiritual Practice behind It and Its Clinical Applications*, University Press of America, Inc., Lanham, Maryland.

CHRYSSAVGIS, J. (1996). "Essay Review: A Tribute to Philip Sherrard (1922–1995)," in *Journal of Modern Greek Studies*, Vol. 14, No. 2, pp. 345–354.

______ (2000). *Soul Mending: The Art of Spiritual Direction*, Holy Cross Orthodox Press, Brookline, Massachusetts.

CLARKE, J. J. (1992). *In Search of Jung*, Routledge, London & New York.

CLARKSON, P. (1990). "A Multiplicity of Psychotherapeutic Relationships," in *British Journal of Psychotherapy*, Vol. 7, No. 2, pp. 148–163.

______ (1995). *The Therapeutic Relationship*, Whurr Publishers, London and Philadelphia.

CLEMENT, O. (1985). "Foreword," in Evdokimov, P. (1985). *The Sacrament of Love: The Nuptial Mystery in the Light of the Orthodox Tradition*, pp. 7–13, St. Vladimir's Seminary Press, Crestwood, New York.

______ (2000). *Three Prayers: The Lord's Prayer, O Heavenly King, Prayer of St. Ephrem*, St Vladimir's Seminary Press, Crestwood, New York.

CLIMACUS, ST. JOHN (1982). *The Ladder of Divine Ascent*, transl. C. Luibheid & N. Russell, Classics of Western Spirituality, Paulist Press, Mahwah, New Jersey.

COELHO, P. (2006). *The Alchemist*, HarperCollins, London.

COLES, P. (2001). *Cosmology: A Very Short Introduction*, Oxford University Press, Oxford.

COLLINS, J. & MAYBLIN, B. (1996). *Derrida for Beginners*, Icon Books, Cambridge.

COLTART, N. (1999). *How to Survive as a Psychotherapist*, Sheldon Press, London..

CONCILIAR PRESS (1988). *What Orthodox Christians Believe: A Concil-*

iar Press Compendium, Conciliar Press, Ben Lomond, California.

CONTI-O'HARE, M. (2002). *The Nurse as Wounded Healer: From Trauma to Transendence*, Jones & Bartlett Publishers, Inc., Sudbury, Massachusetts.

COOPER, D.E. (1990). *Existentialism*, Blackwell, Oxford and Cambridge.

COOPER, M. & MCLEOD, J. (2007). "A Pluralistic Framework for Counselling and Psychotherapy: Implications for Research," in *Counselling and Psychotherapy Research*, Vol. 7, No. 3, pp. 135–143.

CORBIN, H. (1972). "*Mundus Imaginalis*, or the Imaginary and the Imaginal," in *Spring*, 1972, pp. 1–19.

CRAIN, W.C. (1985). *Theories of Development*, Prentice-Hall, Upper Saddle River, New Jersey.

DAVISON, G.C. & NEALE, J.M. (2001). *Abnormal Psychology*, 8th Edition, John Wiley & Sons Inc., New York.

DAWKINS, R. (1976; 1989). *The Selfish Gene*, Oxford University Press, Oxford.

DE BEAUSOBRE, I. (1940; 1999). *Creative Suffering*, SLG Press, Oxford.

DE CAUSSADE, J.P. (1996). *Abandonment to Divine Providence*, Bantam Doubleday Dell Publishing Group Inc., New York.

DOURLEY, J.P. (2006). "The Foundational Elements of a Jungian Spirituality," [Online] Available from: http://www.jungianstudies.org/publications/papers/dourleyjp2.pdf, accessed 11.08.2008.

DUNLOP, J.B. (1988). *Staretz Amvrosy*, Büchervertriebsanstalt, Vaduz.

DUNNE, C. (2000). *Carl Jung: Wounded Healer of the Soul*, Continuum, London and New York.

EDINGER, E.F. (1972). *Ego and Archetype: Individuation and the Religious Function of the Psyche*, Shambhala, Boston and London.

______ (1987). *The Christian Archetype*, Inner City Books, Toronto.

______ (1992). *Transformation of the God-Image: An Elucidation of Jung's Answer to Job*, Inner City Books, Toronto.

EIGEN, M. (1998). *The Psychoanalytic Mystic*, Free Association Press, London.

ELCHANINOV, A. (1967). *The Diary of a Russian Priest*, Faber and Faber, London.

Elias, Rev. N. M. (1966; 1984). *The Divine Liturgy Explained*, 4th Edition, "Astir" Publishers, Athens.

Embry, B. E. (2005). *Creative Suffering*, Xulon Press, Longwood, Florida.

Euthymios, Metropolitan (2005). *I Sarx: Orthodoxi Theologiki Theorisi tou Somatos*, Ekdoseis Grigori, Athens.

Evdokimov, P. (1985). *The Sacrament of Love: The Nuptial Mystery in the Light of the Orthodox Tradition*, St Vladimir's Seminary Press, Crestwood, New York.

______ (1994) *Woman and the Salvation of the World*, St. Vladimir's Seminary Press, Crestwood, New York.

______ (1998). *Ages of the Spiritual Life*, St. Vladimir's Seminary Press, Crestwood, New York.

______ (2001). *In the World, Of the Church*, St. Vladimir's Seminary Press, Crestwood, New York.

Florensky, P. (1997). *The Pillar and Ground of the Truth: An Essay in Orthodox Theodicy in Twelve Letters*, transl. B. Jakim, Princeton University Press, Princeton, New Jersey.

______ (2000). *Iconostasis*, transl. D. Sheehan & O. Andejev, St. Vladimir's Seminary Press, Crestwood, New York.

Fontana, D. (1993, 2003). *The Language of Symbols: A Visual Key to Symbols and Their Meanings*, Duncan Baird Publishers, London.

Fordham, M. (1978). *Jungian Psychotherapy: A Study in Analytical Psychology*, Maresfield Library, London.

Foucault, M. (1981). *Power/Knowledge: Selected Interviews and Other Writings, 1972–77*; ed. Colin Gordon, Harvester, London.

______ (1990). *The History of Sexuality, Vol. 1: Introduction*, Penguin, London.

Frankl, V. (1959; 1984). *Man's Search for Meaning*, Washington Square Press, New York.

Freud, S. (1910). "The Future Prospects of Psychoanalysis," in S.E. 11, Hogarth Press, London, pp. 139–152.

______ (1912a). "Recommendations to Physicians Practising Psychoanalysis," in S.E. 13, Hogarth Press, London, pp. 109–120.

______ (1912b). "The Dynamics of Transference," in S.E. 12, Hogarth Press, London, pp. 97–106.

______ (1920). "Beyond the Pleasure Principle," in S.E. 18, Hogarth Press, London, pp. 7–64.

______ (1927). *The Future of an Illusion*, S.E. 21, Hogarth Press, London.

Fromm, E. (1962). *The Art of Loving*, Unwin Paperbacks, London.

Gaist, B. (1998). *In Search of Wholeness: Contemporary Psychotherapy and Eastern Orthodox Christian Spirituality*, MA dissertation, unpublished.

Gelso, C.J. & Carter, J.A. (1994). "Components of the Psychotherapy Relationship: Their Interaction and Unfolding During Treatment," in *Journal of Counselling Psychology*, Vol. 41, No. 3, pp. 296–306.

Giegerich, W. (2003). "The End of Meaning and the Birth of Man," *Guild Lecture No. 284*, The Guild of Pastoral Psychology, London.

Gillet, L. (A Monk of the Eastern Church) (1996). *Orthodox Spirituality—An Outline of the Orthodox Ascetical and Mystical Tradition*, 2nd Edition, St. Vladimir's Seminary Press, Crestwood, New York.

______ (A Monk of the Eastern Church) (1997). *The Jesus Prayer*, St. Vladimir's Seminary Press, Crestwood, New York.

Gitelson, M. (1952). "The Emotional Position of the Analyst in the Psycho-Analytic Situation," in *International Journal of Psychoanalysis*, Vol. 33, pp. 1–10.

Goldwert, M. (1992). *The Wounded Healers: Creative Illness in the Pioneers of Depth Psychology*, University Press of America, Lanham, Maryland.

Goleman, D. (1998). *Working with Emotional Intelligence*, Bloomsbury, London.

Grassi, J.A. (2000). *The Five Wounds of Jesus and Personal Transformation*, Alba House, New York.

Graves, R. (1961). *The White Goddess*, Faber, London.

______ (1955; 1960). *The Greek Myths*, Complete Edition, Penguin, London.

Gregorios, Mar P. (1987). *The Human Presence: Ecological Spiritu-*

ality and the Age of the Spirit, Amity House, Amity, New York.

______ (1988). *Cosmic Man: The Divine Presence*, Paragon House, New York.

Groesbeck, C. J. (1975). "The Archetypal Image of the Wounded Healer," in *Journal of Analytical Psychology*, Vol. 20, pp. 122–145.

Guggenbühl-Craig, A. (1999). *Power in the Helping Professions*, Spring Publications Inc, Putnam, Connecticut.

Halifax, J. (1982). *Shaman: The Wounded Healer*, Thames and Hudson, London.

Hall, C. S. (1982). *A Primer of Freudian Psychology*, Mentor Books, Penguin, New York.

Haule, J. R. (1996). *The Love Cure — Therapy Erotic and Sexual*, Spring Publications Inc., Woodstock, Connecticut.

______ (1999). *Perils of the Soul: Ancient Wisdom and the New Age*, Samuel Weiser Inc., New York.

Hausherr, I. (1982). *Penthos — The Doctrine of Compunction in the Christian East*, Cistercian Publications, Inc., Kalamazoo, Michigan.

______ (1990). *Spiritual Direction in the Early Christian East*, Cistercian Publications, Kalamazoo, Michigan.

Heelas, P. (1996). *The New Age Movement: The Celebration of the Self and the Sacralization of Modernity*, Blackwell Publishers, Oxford.

Heimann, P. (1950). "On Counter-Transference," in *International Journal of Psychoanalysis*, Vol. 31, pp. 81–84.

Hillman, J. (1996). *The Soul's Code: In Search of Character and Calling*, Bantam Books, Toronto.

Hinnells, J. R. (ed.) (1984; 1995). *Penguin Dictionary of Religions*, Penguin Books, London.

Hoeller, S. A. (1990). "Vladimir Soloviev: Russian Orthodox Apostle of Gnosis & Sophia," in *Gnosis: A Journal of the Western Inner Traditions*, No.16, pp. 29–33, The Lumen Foundation, San Francisco.

Hollis, J. (2001). *Creating a Life: Finding Your Individual Path*, Inner City Books, Toronto.

Hope, J. & Van Loon, B. (1994). *Buddha for Beginners*, Icon Books,

Cambridge.
HOPKO, T. (1997). "Finding One's Calling in Life" [Online] Available from: http://www.orthodoxytoday.org/articles/HopkoCalling.php, accessed 10/09/2009.

_______ (2006). *Christian Faith and Same-Sex Attraction: Eastern Orthodox Reflections*, Conciliar Press, Ben Lomond, California.

HORROCKS, C. & JEVTIC, Z. (1997). *Foucault for Beginners*, Icon Books, Cambridge.

HUGHES, A. (2005). "Ancestral Versus Original Sin: An Overview with Implications for Psychotherapy" [Online] Available from: http://www.antiochian.org/assets_manager/da42e6049df1d-08bff1865c1ac19e759.pdf, accessed 9/10/07.

HYDE, M. & MCGUINNESS, M. (1992). *Introducing Jung*, Icon Books, Thriplow, Royston.

JACOBI, J. (1962). *The Psychology of C. G. Jung*, Yale University Press, New Haven and London.

JACOBS, M. (1986). *The Presenting Past: An Introduction to Practical Psychodynamic Counselling*, Open University Press, Milton Keynes.

JACOBY, M. (1985). *Longing for Paradise: Psychological Perspectives on an Archetype*, Sigo Press, Boston.

_______ (1991). *Shame and the Origins of Self-Esteem: A Jungian Approach*, Brunner-Routledge, Hove and New York.

JAFFE, L. W. (1999). *Celebrating Soul: Preparing for the New Religion*, Inner City Books, Toronto.

JAMES, W. (1982). *The Varieties of Religious Experience*, Penguin, New York.

JOHN PAUL II (1984). *Apostolic Letter: Salvifici Doloris*, Libreria Editrice Vaticana [Online] Available from: http://www.vatican.va/holy_father/john_paul_ii/apost_letters/documentshf_jp-ii_apl_11021984_salvifici-doloris_en.html, accessed 3/08/07.

JUNG, C. G. (1954; 2002). *Answer to Job*, Routledge, London.

_______ (1964). *Man and his Symbols*, Aldous Books Ltd., London.

_______ (1971). *Dictionary of Analytical Psychology*, Ark Paperbacks,

Routledge & Kegan Paul, London.

______ (1976). *Letters*, Vols. 1 & 2, 1951–1961, selected and edited by G. Adler, Routledge & Kegan Paul, London.

______ (1988). *Psychology and Western Religion*, Ark Paperbacks, Routledge & Kegan Paul, London.

______ (1993). *The Undiscovered Self*, Routledge, London.

______ (1995). *Memories, Dreams, Reflections*, Fontana Press, London.

______ (1998). *The Psychology of the Transference*, Routledge, London.

______ (2001). *The Spirit in Man, Art and Literature*, Routledge, London and New York.

Kadloubovsky, E. & Palmer, G. E. H. (eds.) (1992). *Writings from the Philokalia on Prayer of the Heart*, Faber and Faber, New York.

Kahn, M. (1991). *Between Therapist and Client: The New Relationship*, Revised Edition, Owl Books, Henry Holt and Company, New York.

Kant, I. (1787, 1968). *Critique of Pure Reason*, St. Martin's Press, New York.

Karakovouni, E. G. (1996). *Ta Oneira*, Ekdosi B,' Apostoliki Diakonia, Athens.

Kelly, S. (1993). *Individuation and the Absolute—Hegel, Jung and the Path toward Wholeness*, Paulist Press, New York, Mahwah, New Jersey.

Kerenyi, C. (1959). *Asklepios: Archetypal Image of the Physician's Existence, Bollingen Series* LXV 3, Pantheon Books, New York.

Khele, S. (2008). "NICE Guidelines for Mental Health," in *Therapy Today*, Vol. 19, No. 10, pp. 40–41.

King, E. (1996). "The Use of the Self in Qualitative Research," in Richardson, J. T. E. (ed.) (1996). *Handbook of Qualitative Research Methods for Psychology and the Social Sciences*, BPS Books, Leicester, pp. 175–188.

Kirmeyer, L. J. (2003). "Asklepian Dreams: The Ethos of the Wounded-Healer in the Clinical Encounter," in *Transcultural Psychiatry*, Vol. 40, No. 2, pp. 248–277.

Kirschenbaum, H. & Land-Henderson, V. (ed.) (1989). *Carl Rog-*

ers: Dialogues, Constable, London.

KOKKINAKIS, A. (1975). *The Thyateira Confession*, The Faith Press, Leighton Buzzard, Beds.

KORNARAKIS, I. (1958; 2009). "I symvoli tis psychologias tou C.G. Jung en ti poimantiki psychologia," [Online] Available from: http://www.apostoliki-diakonia.gr/gr_main/catechism/theologia_zoi/themata.asp?cat=point&contents=contents.asp&main=katixisi&file=Dialogoi/page15.htm, accessed 9/7/2009.

KORNBLATT, J.D. & GUSTAFSON, R.F. (1996). *Russian Religious Thought*, University of Wisconsin Press, Madison, Wisconsin.

LACAN, J. (1994). *The Four Fundamental Concepts of Psychoanalysis*, Penguin, London.

LAMBERT, K. (1960). "Can Theologians and Analytical Psychologists Collaborate?," in *Journal of Analytical Psychology*, Vol. 5, No. 2, pp. 129–146.

LAMMERS, A.C. (1994). *In God's Shadow: The Collaboration of Victor White and C. G. Jung*, Paulist Press, New York.

LAURENCE OF JORDANVILLE, FR. (2008). "Small Compline for Use with a Priest" [Online] Available from: http://pages.prodigy.net/frjohnwhiteford/smallcompline.htm, accessed 13/08/08.

LEONARD, L.S. (1989; 2001). *Witness to the Fire: Creativity and the Veil of Addiction*, Shambhala, Boston and London.

LEWIS, C.S. (2001). *Mere Christianity*, Harper One, London.

LITTLE, M. (1951). "Counter-Transference and the Patient's Response to It," in *International Journal of Psychoanalysis*, Vol. 32, pp. 32–40.

LOSSKY, N. (2001). *In the Image and Likeness of God*, St. Vladimir's Seminary Press, Crestwood, New York.

______ (2002). *The Mystical Theology of the Eastern Church*, St. Vladimir's Seminary Press, Crestwood, New York.

LOUTH, A. (1976). *Theology and Spirituality*, SLG Press, Fairacres, Oxford.

______ (1983). *Discerning the Mystery: An Essay on the Nature of Theology*, Clarendon Press, Oxford.

______ (1997). *The Wisdom of the Greek Fathers*, Lion Books, Oxford.

Lyotard, J. F. (1984). *The Postmodern Condition: A Report on Knowledge*, transl. G. Bennington and B. Massumi, University of Minnesota Press, Minneapolis.

Mack, Fr. J. (1999). *Ascending the Heights: A Layman's Guide to the Ladder of Divine Ascent*, Conciliar Press, Ben Lomond, California.

Maidenbaum, A. (ed.) (2002). *Jung and the Shadow of Anti-Semitism: Collected Essays*, Nicolas-Hays, York Beach, Maine.

Main, R. (2006). "Religion," in Papadopoulos, R. K. (ed.) (2006). *The Handbook of Jungian Psychology*, Routledge, Hove, pp. 296–323.

Makrakis, M. K. (1993). *Psychologia tis Thriskeias*, Ekdoseis Armos, Athens.

Malcolm, J. (1997). *Psychoanalysis: The Impossible Profession*, Granta Books, London.

Maslow, A. H. (1967; 1993). *Self-actualisation and Beyond: In the Farther Reaches of Human Nature*, Arkana, London.

Maslow, A. H., Stevens, D. & Heil, G. (1998). *Maslow on Management*, John Wiley, Hoboken, New Jersey.

Mathers, D. (2001). *An Introduction to Meaning and Purpose in Analytical Psychology*, Brunner–Routledge, Hove, East Sussex.

Matthews, C. (2001). *Sophia: Goddess of Wisdom, Bride of God*, New Revised Edition, Quest Books, Theosophical Publishing House, Wheaton, Illinois.

McGinn, B., Leclerq, J. & Meyendorff, J. (1986). *Christian Spirituality: Origins to the Twelfth Century*, Routledge, London.

McGuire, W. (ed.) (1974). *The Freud/Jung Letters: The Correspondence between Sigmund Freud and C. G. Jung*, Bollingen series XCIV, Princeton Paperbacks, Princeton, New Jersey.

McLaren, K. (2000). *Becoming an Empath: How to Develop the Power of Your Emotional Intuition*, Study Guide, Sounds True Inc., Boulder, Colorado.

Meier, C. A. (2003). *Healing Dream and Ritual: Ancient Incubation and Modern Psychotherapy*, Daimon Verlag, Einsiedeln.

Melissaris, A. G. (1997). *Personhood Re-Examined: Current Per-*

spectives from Orthodox Anthropology and Archetypal Psychology, Epektasis Publications, Katerini.

MEYENDORFF, J. (1998). *St. Gregory Palamas and Orthodox Spirituality*, St. Vladimir's Seminary Press, Crestwood, New York.

MILTON, M., TAYLOR, M. & GAIST, B. (1998). "Professional Identities in the NHS: Existential Perspectives," in *Journal of The Society for Existential Analysis*, Vol. 9, No. 1, pp. 114–128.

MOGENSON, G. (1994). "The Collective Unconscious and the Leontocephalus: A Rejoinder to Noll," in *Spring*, Vol. 56, pp. 132–137.

______ (2005). *A Most Accursed Religion: When a Trauma Becomes God*, Spring Publications Inc., Putnam, Connecticut.

MONACHOS MOISIS (1990). *I Evlogia tou Ponou kai o Ponos tis Agapis*, Ekdoseis Tinos, Athens.

MOORE, T. (1992). *Care of the Soul: A Guide for Cultivating Depth and Sacredness in Everyday Life*, HarperCollins Publishers, New York.

MORAGLIA, G. (1997). "Work and Individuation," in *Harvest*, Vol. 43, No. 2, pp. 106–116.

MORAN, J. (1996). "Orthodoxy and Modern Depth Psychology," in Walker, A. & Carras, C. (1996). *Living Orthodoxy in the Modern World*, SPCK, London, pp. 131–158.

MÜLLER, F. M. (1882; 2000). *Lectures on the Origin and Growth of Religion: As Illustrated by the Religions of India*, Adamant Media Corporation, Boston.

MUSE, J. S. (2001). "Eros, Asceticism and Marriage: A Seamless Connection?," in Chirban, J. T. (ed.) (2001). *Sickness or Sin? Spiritual Discernment and Differential Diagnosis*, Holy Cross Orthodox Press, Brookline, Massachusetts, pp. 257–280.

NELLAS, P. (1987; 1997). *Deification in Christ: The Nature of the Human Person*, St. Vladimir's Seminary Press, Crestwood, New York.

NEUMANN, E. (1966). *Art and the Creative Unconscious*, transl. R. Manheim, Harper and Row, New York.

NICODEMUS THE HAGIORITE (2008). "Acceptance of God's Will" [Online] Available from: http://www.stjohnthebaptist.org.au/articles/acceptance.html, accessed 11/02/08.

Nietzsche, F. (1968; 2004). *Why I Am So Wise*, Penguin, London.

Noll, R. (1994). *The Jung Cult: Origins of a Charismatic Movement*, Princeton University Press, Princeton, New Jersey.

Nouwen, H. J. (1979; 1994). *The Wounded Healer*, Darton, Longman & Todd, London.

O' Neill, R. (2007). "Neoplatonism and the tarot" [Online] Available from: http://tarot.com/about-tarot/library/boneill/neoplatonism, accessed 10/04/07.

The Orthodox Study Bible (1993). 1st Edition, Conciliar Press, Thomas Nelson Publishers.

Otto, R. (1923; 1950) *The Idea of the Holy*, Oxford University Press, London.

Ouspensky, P. D. (1981; 1990). *Tertium Organum*, Arkana, Penguin, London.

Page, S. (1999). *The Shadow and the Counsellor*, Routledge, London and New York.

Palmer, G. E. H., Sherrard, P. & Ware, K. (eds.). (1979). *The Philokalia, Volume 1: The Complete Text; Compiled by St. Nikodimos of the Holy Mountain & St. Makarios of Corinth*, Faber and Faber, London.

______ (eds.) (1986). *The Philokalia, Volume 3: The Complete Text; Compiled by St. Nikodimos of the Holy Mountain & St. Makarios of Corinth*, Faber and Faber, London.

Papadopoulos, R. K. (1991). "Jung and the Concept of the Other," in Papadopoulos, R. K. & Saayman, G. (eds.) (1991). *Jung in Modern Perspective The Master and His Legacy*, Prism Press, Bridport, pp. 54–88.

______ (1997). "Is Teaching Jung within University Possible? A Response to David Tacey," in *Journal of Analytical Psychology*, Vol. 42, No. 2, pp. 297–301.

______ (ed.) (2006). *The Handbook of Jungian Psychology*, Routledge, Hove.

Papadopoulos, R. K. & Saayman, G. (eds.) (1991). *Jung in Modern*

Perspective: The Master and His Legacy, Prism Press, Bridport.

Papakostas, Archim. S. (1998). *For the Hours of Pain*, Zoe Publications, Athens.

Patterson, R. B. (1990) *In Search of the Wounded Healer: A Helping Professional's Guide to Inner Resources*, Dimension Books Inc., Denville, New Jersey.

Pennock, D. (1973). *Who Is God? Who Am I? Who Are You?* Greek Orthodox Archdiocese of America, Department of Religious Education, New York.

Plekon, M. (2001). "Introduction," in Evdokimov, P. (2001). *In The World, Of The Church: A Paul Evdokimov Reader*, St. Vladimir's Seminary Press, Crestwood, New York, pp. 1–9.

Popkin, R. H. & Stroll, A. (1986) *Philosophy Made Simple*, Heinemann, London.

Popovich, Fr. J. (1922). "Introduction" [Online] Available from: http://www.sv-luka.org/praylake/introduction.htm, accessed 26/12/08.

Porphyrios, Elder (2005). *Wounded by Love: The Life and Wisdom of Elder Porphyrios*, Denise Harvey, Limni, Evia, Greece.

Purton, C. (1989). "The Person-Centred Jungian," in *Person-Centered Review*, Vol. 4, pp. 403–419.

Ratzinger, J. (2002). *God and the World: A Conversation with Peter Seewald*, Ignatius Press, Ft. Collins, Colorado.

Reardon, P. H. (2005). *The Trial of Job: Orthodox Christian Reflections on the Book of Job*, Conciliar Press, Ben Lomond, California.

Reinhart, M. (1989). *Chiron and the Healing Journey*, Updated Edition, Arkana, Penguin, London.

Rhodes, M. C. (2005). "Logical Proof of Antinomy: A Trinitarian Interpretation of the Law of Identity," in *Theandros*, Vol. 2, No. 3 [Online] Available from: http://www.theandros.com/lawofident.html, accessed 15/12/08.

Richardson, J. T. E. (ed.) (1996). *Handbook of Qualitative Research Methods for Psychology and the Social Sciences*, BPS Books, Leicester.

Rieff, P. (1966). *The Triumph of the Therapeutic: Uses of Faith after Freud*, University of Chicago Press, Chicago.

Robinson, D. W. (2005). *Conscience and Jung's Moral Vision: From Id to Thou*, Paulist Press, New York, Mahwah, New Jersey.

Rogers, C. (1961). *On Becoming a Person: A Therapist's View of Psychotherapy*, Constable, London.

______ (1980). *A Way of Being*, Houghton Mifflin Company, Boston.

Rogich, D. M. (1997). *Becoming Uncreated: The Journey to Human Authenticity*, Light & Life Publishing, Minneapolis, Minnesota.

Romanyshyn, R. D. (2007). *The Wounded Researcher: Research with Soul in Mind*, Spring Journal Books, New Orleans, Louisiana.

Roob, A. (2005). *The Hermetic Cabinet: Alchemy and Mysticism*, Taschen, Köln.

Rose, S. (1994). *Nihilism: The Root of the Revolution of the Modern Age*, St. Herman of Alaska Brotherhood, Platina, California.

Rossi, V. (2008). "The Transfiguration of Creation" [Online] Available from: http://orth-transfiguration.org/library/orthodoxy/transfiguration/, accessed 18/11/08.

Rothenberg, R. (2001). *The Jewel in the Wound: How the Body Expresses the Needs of the Psyche and Offers a Path to Transformation*, Chiron Publications, Wilmette, Illinois.

Rowland, S. (2002). "Paul Bishop. Jung's *Answer to Job*: A Commentary" [Online] Available from: http://www.cgjungpage.org/index2.php?option=com_content&do_pdf=1&id=797, accessed 10/1/05.

Rycroft, C. (1968; 1995). *A Critical Dictionary of Psychoanalysis*, Second Edition, Penguin, London.

Sacks, O. (1985). *The Man Who Mistook His Wife for a Hat*, Picador, Pan Books, London.

Sakharov, N. V. (2002). *I Love Therefore I am: The Theological Legacy of Archimandrite Sophrony*, St. Vladimir's Seminary Press, Crestwood, New York.

Samuels, A. (1985). *Jung and the Post-Jungians*, Routledge, London.

______ (1989). *The Plural Psyche: Personality, Morality and the Father*, Tavistock/Routledge, London and New York.

______ (1993). *The Political Psyche*, Routledge, London.

______ (2005). "A New Anatomy of Spirituality: Clinical and Political Demands the Psychotherapist Cannot Ignore," Lecture Six, in Field, N., Harvey, T. & Sharp, B. (2005) *Ten Lectures on Psychotherapy and Spirituality*, Karnac Books, London, pp. 115–129.

______ (2006). "Transference/Countertransference," in Papadopoulos, R. (ed.) (2006). *The Handbook of Jungian Psychology: Theory, Practice and Applications*, Routledge, London and New York, pp. 177–195.

Samuels, A., Shorter, B. & Plaut, F. (1986). *A Critical Dictionary of Jungian Analysis*, Routledge, London and New York.

Sandler, J. (1992). "Reflections on Developments in the Theory of Psychoanalytic Technique," in *International Journal of Psychoanalysis*, Vol. 73, pp. 189–98.

Sanford, J. A. (1987). *The Kingdom Within — The Inner Meaning of Jesus' Sayings*, Harper, San Francisco.

Schaverien, J. (2007). "Countertransference as Active Imagination: Imaginative Experiences of the Analyst," in *Journal of Analytical Psychology*, Vol. 52, pp. 413–431.

Schopenhauer, A. (1818, 1958). *The World as Will and Representation*, Vols. 1 & 2, transl. E. F. J. Payne, Dover Publications, New York.

Schultz, J. (1997). "Thoughts on Evil" [Online] Available from: http://www.cgjungpage.org/index.php?option=com_content&task=view&id=799&Itemid=40, accessed 20/10/03.

Sedgwick, D. (1994). *The Wounded Healer — Countertransference from a Jungian Perspective*, Routledge, London and New York.

Serfes, Fr. D. (2001). "Orthodox Poetry by St John of Kronstadt" [Online] Available at: http://www.serfes.org/poetry/PoetrybyStJohn.htm, accessed 6/03/08.

Sergeev, M. (2003). "Liberal Orthodoxy: From Vladimir Solov'ev to Fr. Alexander Men," paper presented at the annual meeting of the Mid-Atlantic American Academy of Religion [Online] Available from: http://www.georgefox.edu/academics/undergrad/departments/soc-swk/ree/2003/sergeev03.doc, accessed 30/04/07.

Shamdasani, S. (1999). "Is Analytical Psychology a Religion? In

Statu Nascendi," in *Journal of Analytical Psychology*, Vol. 44, pp. 539–545.

______ (2003). *Jung and the Making of Modern Psychology: The Dream of a Science*, Cambridge University Press, Cambridge.

SHARP, D. (1991). *C. G. Jung Lexicon: A Primer of Terms & Concepts*, Inner City Books, Toronto.

SHERRARD, P. (1992). *Human Image: World Image*, Denise Harvey (Publisher), Limni, Evia, Greece.

______ (1995). *Christianity and Eros*, Denise Harvey (Publisher), Limni, Evia, Greece.

______ (1998). *Christianity: Lineaments of a Sacred Tradition*, Holy Cross Orthodox Press, Brookline, Massachusetts.

SHLIEN, J. (1984). "A countertheory of transference," in Levant, R. & Shlien, J. (ed.) (1984). *Client-Centred Theory and the Person-Centred Approach: New Directions in Theory, Research and Practice*, Praeger, New York, pp. 153–181.

SIMMONDS, J. G. (2004). "Heart and Spirit: Research with Psychoanalysts and Psychoanalytic psychotherapists about Spirituality," in *International Journal of Psychoanalysis*, Vol. 85, pp. 951–971.

SIMONOPETRITIS, ARCHIMANDRITE I. (2008). "A Synoptic View of the Orthodox Ascetical Tradition of Mount Sinai" [Online] Available at: www.aegeantimes.gr/pigizois/agglika/inegl_32.htm, accessed 6/03/08.

SINGH, K. (2000). *Guilt, Ideas in Psychoanalysis*, Icon Books, Cambridge.

SMITH, R. C. (1996). *The Wounded Jung—Effects of Jung's Relationships on His Life and Work*, Northwestern University Press, Evanston, Illinois.

SMITH, W. (1984). *Cosmos and Transcendence—Breaking through the Barrier of Scientistic Belief*, Sherwood Sugden & Co, Peru, Illinois.

SOARES DE AZEVETO, M. (ed.) (2005). *Ye Shall Know the Truth: Christianity and the Perennial Philosophy*, World Wisdom Inc., Bloomington, Indiana.

SOLOVYEV, V. (1996). *The Crisis of Western Philosophy (Against the Positivists)*, Lindisfarne Press, Hudson, New York.

SOLZHENITSYN, A. (1973; 2003). *The Gulag Archipelago*, The Harvill Press, London.

SOPHRONY, ARCHIMANDRITE (1973). *The Monk of Mount Athos*, St. Vladimir's Seminary Press, Crestwood, New York.

______ (1996). *On Prayer*, Stavropegic Monastery of St. John the Baptist, Essex.

SPIDLIK, T. (1986). *The Spirituality of the Christian East: A Systematic Handbook*, Cistercian Publications Inc., Kalamazoo, Michigan.

SPIEGELMAN, J. M. (1989). *Jungian Psychology and the Passions of the Soul*, Falcon Press, Las Vegas.

______ (1996). *Psychotherapy as a Mutual Process*, New Falcon Publications, Temple, Arizona.

SPINELLI, E. (1994). *Demystifying Therapy*, Constable, London.

STANILOAE, D. (1984). "Priest and King of the Creation," in Every, G., Harries, R. & Ware, K. (eds.) (1984). *The Time of the Spirit: Readings through the Christian Year*, St. Vladimir's Seminary Press, Crestwood, New York, p. 28.

STEIN, M. (1999). *Jung On Christianity, Encountering Jung Series*, Princeton University Press, Princeton, New Jersey.

STEINER, G. (1992). *Heidegger*, 2nd Edition, Fontana Press, London.

STEPHENSON, C. (2004). "Reading Jung's Equivocal Language," in *Harvest*, Vol. 50, No. 1, pp. 75–99.

STEVENS, A. (2001). "The Desire and Pursuit of the Whole (Analytical Psychology)," in Spinelli, E. & Marshall, S. (eds.) (2001). *Embodied Theories*, Continuum, London and New York, pp. 98–114.

______ (2006). "The Archetypes," in Papadopoulos, R. K. (ed.). *The Handbook of Jungian Psychology*, Routledge, Hove, East Sussex, pp. 74–93.

STODDART, W. (2005). "Foreword," in Soares de Azeveto, M. (ed.) (2005). *Ye Shall Know the Truth: Christianity and the Perennial Philosophy*, World Wisdom Inc., Bloomington, Indiana.

STORR, A. (1989). *Freud—A Very Short Introduction*, Oxford University Press, Oxford.

______ (1990). *The Art of Psychotherapy*, Arnold, London.

______ (1996). *Feet of Clay—A Study of Gurus*, HarperCollins, London.

______ (1996b). *Nietzsche and Jung*, J. R. Jones Lecture, University of Wales, Swansea.

______ (ed.) (1998). *The Essential Jung*, Fontana Press, London.

Sumner, Oswald Dom M. (1950). "St. John Climacus: The Psychology of the Desert Fathers," in *Guild Lecture No. 63*, The Guild of Pastoral Psychology, London.

Symington, N. (1993). "Is Psychoanalysis a Religion?," in Ward, I. (ed.) (1993). *Is Psychoanalysis Another Religion? Contemporary Essays on Spirit, Faith and Morality in Psychoanalysis*, Freud Museum Publications, pp. 49–56.

______ (2001). *The Spirit of Sanity*, Karnac, London.

Tacey, D. (2001). *Jung and the New Age*, Brunner-Routledge, Hove and New York.

Tavener, J. & M. Thekla (1994). *Ikons: Meditations in Words and Music*, Fount, Harper Collins.

Taylor, C. (1992). *Sources of the Self: The Making of the Modern Identity*, Harvard University Press, Cambridge, Massachusetts.

The Teaching of the Holy Fathers on Illness (1986). Nicodemus Orthodox Publication Society, Richfield Springs, New York.

Theophilus of Antioch (1997), *On the Trinity*, Book 1, [Online] available at: http://www.earlychristianwritings.com/text/theophilus-book1.html, accessed 17.09.07.

Thermos, Fr. V. (1996). *Homoiopatheis Anthropoi*, Apostoliki Diakonia, Athens.

Thorne, B. (2002). *The Mystical Power of Person-Centred Therapy: Hope beyond Despair*, Whurr Publishers, London and Philadelphia.

Thunberg, L. (1985). *Man and the Cosmos: The Vision of St. Maximus the Confessor*, St. Vladimir's Seminary Press, Crestwood, New York.

Tournier, P. (1982). *Creative Suffering*, SCM Press Ltd, London.

Tudor, K. & Merry, T. (2002). *Dictionary of Person-Centred Psychology*, Whurr Publishers, London and Philadelphia.

Ulanov, A.B. (1999). "Countertransference and the Self," in *The Journal of Jungian Theory and Practice*, Vol. 1, No. 1, pp. 5–26.

______ (2004). *Spiritual Aspects of Clinical Work*, Daimon Verlag, Einsiedeln.

______ (2006). "Theology after Jung," in *The Journal of Jungian Theory and Practice*, Vol. 8, No. 1, pp. 61–68.

Ulanov, A.B. & Dueck, A. (2008) *The Living God and Our Living Psyche — What Christians Can Learn from Carl Jung*, William B. Eerdmans Publishing Company, Grand Rapids, Michigan.

Vasileios, Archimandrite (1999). *The Saint: Archetype of Orthodoxy*, Alexander Press, Montreal.

Viorst, J. (1986). *Necessary Losses*, Fireside, Simon & Schuster, New York.

Vitz, P. C. (1977; 1994). *Psychology as Religion: The Cult of Self-Worship*, 2nd edition, Paternoster Press, Carlisle, Cumbria.

Vlachos, H. (1994). *Orthodox Psychotherapy: The Science of the Fathers*, Birth of the Theotokos Monastery, Livadia.

______ (1994a). *Orthodox Spirituality: a Brief Introduction*, Birth of the Theotokos Monastery, Livadia.

Von Franz, M. L. (1980). *Alchemy: An Introduction to the Symbolism and the Psychology*, Inner City Books, Toronto.

______ (1982). *Psyche and Matter*, Shambhala, Boston & London.

______ (1993). *Psychotherapy*, Shambhala, Boston & London.

______ (1998). *C. G. Jung: His Myth in Our Time*, Inner City Books, Toronto.

Ward, B. (1998). *The Wisdom of the Desert Fathers*, Lion Books, Oxford.

Ward, I. & Zarate, O. (2000). *Introducing Psychoanalysis*, Icon Books, Cambridge.

Ware, Bp K. (1982). "Introduction," in Climacus, St. John (1982). *The Ladder of Divine Ascent*, Classics of Western Spirituality, Paulist Press, Mahwah, New Jersey, pp. 1–70.

______ (1984). "Foreword," in Mantzaridis, G.I. (1984). *The Deification of Man: St. Gregory Palamas and the Orthodox Tradition*, transl. L. Sherrard, St. Vladimir's Seminary Press, Crestwood, New York, pp. 7–9.

______ (1988). *Praying with the Orthodox Tradition*, SPCK, London.

______ (1993) *The Orthodox Church—New Edition*, Penguin, London.

______ (1996) *How Are We Saved?: The Understanding of Salvation in the Orthodox Tradition*, Light and Life Publishing, Minneapolis, Minnesota.

______ (1998). *The Orthodox Way*, Revised Edition, St. Vladimir's Seminary Press, Crestwood, New York.

______ (2003). "The Hesychast Renaissance, 1750 - Present," [Online] Available from: http://ldysinger.stjohnsem.edu/@texts2/1980_kal-ware/07_hesyc-ren.htm, accessed on 30/10/08.

______ (2004). *The Inner Kingdom: Vol. 1 of the Collected Works*, St. Vladimir's Seminary Press, Crestwood, New York.

WHELTON, M. (2002). *False Gods: Counterfeit Spirituality in an Age of Anxiety*, Regina Orthodox Press, Salisbury, Massachusetts.

WHITMONT, E. C. (1993). *The Alchemy of Healing: Psyche and Soma*, North Atlantic Books, Berkeley, California.

______ (2007). "The Destiny Concept in Psychotherapy," in *Journal of Jungian Theory and Practice*, Vol. 9 No. 1, [Online] Available from: http://www.junginstitute.org/pdf_files/JungV9N1p25-38.pdf, accessed 20/12/08.

WILBER, K. (1996; 2000). *A Brief History of Everything*, Shambhala, Boston.

WILLIAMS, V. (2003). "Religion, counselling and psychotherapy: complementary or controversial?," in *Counselling and Psychotherapy Journal*, Vol. 14, No. 7, pp. 18–22.

WILSON, C. (1971). *The Occult*, Grafton Books, London.

______ (1984). *Religion and the Rebel*, Ashgrove Press, Bath.

______ (1990). *The Outsider*, Victor Gollancz Ltd, London.

WINNICOTT, D. W. (1964). "Review of *Memories, Dreams, Reflections*, by C. G. Jung," in *International Journal of Psychoanalysis*, Vol. 45, pp. 450–455.

______ (1965). *The Maturational Processes and the Facilitating Envi-*

ronment, Hogarth Press, London.

______ (1986) *Home Is Where We Start From*, Penguin, London.

Wood, K. (2003). "Practical Spiritual Counseling." (Featured Reviews) [Online] Available from: http://www.thefreelibrary.com/Practical+spiritual+counseling.+(Featured+Reviews)-a0100230880, accessed 30/10/08.

Wosket, V. (1999). *The Therapeutic Use of Self: Counselling Practice, Research and Supervision*, Routledge, London and New York.

Yannaras, C. (1996). *The Freedom of Morality*, St. Vladimir's Seminary Press, Crestwood, New York.

Young-Eisendrath, P. (1996). *The Gifts of Suffering: Finding Insight, Compassion, and Renewal*, Addison-Wesley Publishing Company Inc., Reading, Massachusetts.

Zernov, N. (1999). "Explanatory Notes," in *A Manual of Eastern Orthodox Prayers*, St. Vladimir's Seminary Press, Crestwood, New York, p. x.

Zohar, D. (1991). *The Quantum Self*, Flamingo, HarperCollins Publishers, London.

Zohar, D. & Marshall, I. (2001). *Spiritual Intelligence: The Ultimate Intelligence*, Bloomsbury Paperbacks, London.

Zweig, C. & Abrams, J. (eds.) (1991). *Meeting the Shadow: The Hidden Power of the Dark Side of Human Nature*, Tarcher Putnam, New York.

Index

F

G

N

About the Author

Byron J. Gaist is an Orthodox Christian psychotherapist based in Cyprus. He has worked individually and in groups with a diversity of clients in England, Germany, Cyprus and elsewhere, and has presented his work in seminars, conferences, trainings and other professional events relating to mental health and wellbeing. With an M.A. in Theology and Religious Studies from the University of Leeds, and a Ph.D. in Psychoanalytic Studies from the University of Essex, his major interest is in the interface between psychology and spirituality, and in particular the integration of psychology and Christian theology. Dr Gaist also takes an active interest in the arts, finding much recreation in looking at paintings, reading and playing the classical guitar.

CPSIA information can be obtained at www.ICGtesting.com
Printed in the USA
LVOW081901090413

328363LV00006B/689/P

9 781933 275406